August "Garry" Herrmann

August "Garry" Herrmann

A Baseball Biography

William A. Cook

McFarland & Company, Inc., Publishers
Jefferson, North Carolina, and London

LIBRARY OF CONGRESS CATALOGUING-IN-PUBLICATION DATA

Cook, William A.
August "Garry" Herrmann : a baseball biography / William A. Cook.
p.   cm.
Includes bibliographical references and index.

ISBN-13: 978-0-7864-3073-4
softcover : 50# alkaline paper ∞

1. Herrmann, August, 1859–1931.
2. Baseball team owners—Ohio—Biography.
3. Cincinnati Reds (Baseball team)—History. I. Title.
GV865.H47C66   2008   796.357092 — dc22 [B]   2007032040

British Library cataloguing data are available

On the cover: August Garry Herrmann
(George Grantham Bain Collection, Library of Congress)

Manufactured in the United States of America

*McFarland & Company, Inc., Publishers
Box 611, Jefferson, North Carolina 28640
www.mcfarlandpub.com*

Table of Contents

Introduction   1

For
Rhonda Brewer
I'm glad I met you

Introduction

To attempt to chronicle the life of August "Garry" Herrmann (1859–1931) as I have done on these pages was both a journey through the progressive era of American politics and the evolution of the modern game of major league baseball. In essence the story of August Herrmann is one that blends together the maturation of the American urban political landscape and the business of major league baseball in the early twentieth century. By 1912 no citizen of Cincinnati, with the exception of President William Howard Taft, was more widely known to the classes and the masses of the American people than August "Garry" Herrmann. Herrmann was a man who lived life large, a man of considerable notoriety in both politics and major league baseball, trusted, befriended and loved by multitudes. But today, nearly eight decades after his death, August Herrmann is on the outside of history looking in.

Just how did it come to pass that with all the accolades that were bestowed upon this extraordinary man during his lifetime, that in the end he fell into such a bottomless pit of historical isolation? Today most people in Herrmann's beloved birthplace of Cincinnati, both young and old, would be hard-pressed to recognize his name. In baseball circles, he has been overshadowed by his contemporaries in the national game, such as Ban Johnson, Charles Comiskey, Judge Kenesaw Mountain Landis, and Charles Ebbets.

August Herrmann was a remarkable man of many talents. A portly person with a silver mustache, Herrmann loved wearing tailor-made checkered silk suits with a flower in his lapel. His love of hearty Teutonic cuisine became legendary in baseball circles. One historian has referred to Herrmann as a walking delicatessen. He relished dining on such dishes as bratwurst, Thuringian blood pudding, potato salad and fried pigs feet. Herrmann is even credited with making fried pigs feet a regular item on the breakfast menu of the Waldorf-Astoria in New York City. Herrmann was a social person with a wide circle of friends. Throughout his life he remained forever loyal to his native Cincinnati and its people, especially those that had to labor hard for their livelihood. As a machine politician, he championed the little people of the city. Still, while Cincinnati and its people were his first love, he also dearly loved sports. He liked to bowl and eventually became head of the American Bowling Congress, but his first sporting love was always baseball.

Herrmann's story is one abundant with intrigue, compromise and irony. It has been suggested by more than a few historians that while August Herrmann was out at night stumping for political boss George B. Cox in various Over-the-Rhine saloons in the Cincinnati of the 1890s, perhaps sitting at a table in the same saloon were Ban Johnson (sportswriter for the *Cincinnati Commercial-Tribune*) and Charley Comiskey (manager of the Cincinnati Reds), plotting and planning to create the rival American League that would challenge the established National League's very existence. Such was the irony that in only a few more years, it would be Herrmann who would act as chief peacemaker in the effort to unite the two leagues and create the major leagues as they exist today.

In 1902, August Herrmann's dream to own a major league baseball team would be realized when he became part of a triumvirate of investors that included George B. Cox and the Fleischmann brothers, Julius and Max, of the yeast company fame, who bought the Cincinnati Reds from legendary baseball mogul John T. Brush. Herrmann then became the operating partner of the group for the Reds and continued to be part of the team's ownership until 1927. In 1903 the National Commission was formed, unifying the warring American and National Leagues and thus establishing the boundaries for the modern game. At the time, most of the credit for bringing the conflict to an end was attributed to the skillful administrative contributions of August Garry Herrmann. So it seemed only fitting that Herrmann was selected as the chairman of National Commission. He would serve as chairman from 1903 until early 1920. His demise as baseball's chief executive was a result of his enemies in the game forcing him to step down in order to establish a one-man commissioner's office that brought forth the reign of the legendary judge Kenesaw Mountain Landis. When Herrmann was forced to step down as chairman of the National Commission, his legacy in the national game was put on hold.

Maybe it was the infamous 1919 World Series that cast a spell on Herrmann's legacy. In the wake of the Black Sox scandal, most baseball historians have simplistically viewed Herrmann's Reds as illegitimate world champions. Or perhaps Herrmann's political associations have raised historians' eyebrows as well. Before August Herrmann became a big league baseball executive, he had been a big league politician, serving as a trusted lieutenant of George Barnsdale Cox, one of the most powerful political municipal machine bosses in American history. Consequently that close association with the controversial Cox is daunting upon Herrmann's legacy, although it may not be entirely fair to him or to Cox.

At the pinnacle of his power, George B. Cox controlled over 25,000 votes and 2,000 political jobs, enabling him to gain control of nearly every ward in the city of Cincinnati. While the Cox machine in Cincinnati was void of the overt corruption and the open association with the criminal influences that were so blatantly apparent in the politics of other big cities, the fact of the matter was that an entire spectrum of capitalism was tied to the workings of the Cox machine. Everyone got a piece of the pie, including August Herrmann. It is a fact that cannot be denied that the political success of George B. Cox was bolstered by his two able lieutenants, August Herrmann and Rudolf "Rud" Hynicka, who worked tirelessly to sustain his power base.

Herrmann, because of his charismatic personality and gift for public relations, did the front work for Cox as his ambassador of "Gemuetlichkeit" among Cincinnati's bulging German immigrant population of the 19th century, organizing the "bread and circuses" aspects of the machine. Herrmann also was a very skilled public administrator who worked tirelessly to protect the political interest of Cox while serving on the powerful city board of administration from 1891 to 1895. Later Herrmann chaired the commission that built the new waters works in the city. However, while Herrmann's activities were visible, the more reserved Rud Hynicka kept things moving for Cox from behind the scenes, functioning as the patronage manager.

In the aftermath of the 1919 World Series, major league baseball was forced to undergo administrative change or face extinction. In 1920 the National Commission was abolished and replaced with a one-man commissioner with absolute authority. National League president and August Herrmann nemesis John A. Heydler had been pressing for such governance for several years. Also by the early 1920s the drums of political reform could be heard clearly approaching Cincinnati city hall. It was now the order of the day, and a group of Eastern-educated, elitist men in Cincinnati waited in the wings for their opportunity to seize absolute power in the city government. By 1924, George B. Cox had been dead for eight years and August Herrmann had long since attempted to disassociate himself from the political arena. So it was to be that the voters of Cincinnati welcomed reform and approved a new charter plan for the city by a plurality of more than 2 to 1. Despite all the good that August Herrmann had done in his days as a public servant, his achievements would be swiftly swept away in a fervor of reform and suspicion by the victors.

To the governmental reformers, August "Garry" Herrmann was little more than a political crony of George B. Cox. It made no difference to them that it was Herrmann's tireless administrative efforts that had eliminated dangerous catastrophic disease by bringing clean drinking water into the homes of hundreds of thousands in citizens in Cincinnati. Homer Croy, an early twentieth century magazine writer, had once said of Herrmann, "Henry Chadwick may be the Father of Baseball, but Garry Herrmann is its Elder Brother." But to most baseball historians, August "Garry" Herrmann is considered as little more than having been a crony of American League president Ban Johnson during his tenure as chairman of the National Commission. It doesn't even seem to matter that Herrmann's skillful efforts played a large part in creating the modern World Series, an event that has now thrilled tens of millions each fall for more than a hundred years. In the end, it seems everyone was determined to prevent August Herrmann from assuming his rightful place in history. Perhaps it is not accidental, or not just an ordinary oversight, that Herrmann has yet to be elected to the National Baseball Hall of Fame. The negative connotations cast upon him over the years seem to have stuck. It seems as if today Herrmann is remembered more for his love of eating German sausages than his considerable life's work in municipal government and major league baseball.

The story of August Garry Herrmann has yet to be told, and this biography attempts to separate the facts from the myths that surround his life. Still, perhaps in the future there will be even more to add to the Herrmann story. From 1927 until 1960 the personal papers of Herrmann were stored in a closet in the upper grandstand of Redland Field (later Crosley Field). Then in the early 1960s, Herrmann's personal papers and letters, forty boxes in all, were donated to the National Baseball Hall of Fame in Cooperstown, New York, where they continued to sit nearly untouched and unarchived for over four decades.

Finally in early 2005, the National Baseball Hall of Fame announced that it was embarking on the task of archiving the Herrmann papers and anticipated that when the process was complete, the collection would encompass 100 linear feet of microfilm. Late in 2006, however, it was announced that the archiving process of the Herrmann papers had ceased after the discovery of mold. Consequently, many of the documents were sent to a conservation center for treatment. Those of us anticipating the release of the Herrmann papers were informed by the Hall of Fame that this unfortunate circumstance would necessitate a further delay in the restoration process, thereby delaying access to the microfilm until at least sometime in 2008.

When the Hall of Fame announced that it was going to archive the Herrmann papers, I had been writing the manuscript for this work for eight months and it was nearing completion. Still I looked forward to the opportunity to peruse the papers and was happy to delay completion of the project for over a year. But with a further delay announced by the National Baseball Hall of Fame, and after correspondence with Hall of Fame staff about the contents of the collection, I have decided to publish my work in advance of the release of the Herrmann papers. Based on my own extensive research and diligent preparation for this work, I am confident that I have produced here a thorough, competent and concise chronicle of the events involved in the life of August "Garry" Herrmann and invite the reader to be the judge.

I

Career Path to the Major Leagues

August Herrmann entered the world in Cincinnati, Ohio, on May 3, 1859, as the second-born son of Christian and Margaret (Meyer) Herrmann, both natives of Germany. His older brother, Charles, had been born a year earlier. Very early in his boyhood August Herrmann developed a love for baseball. On Sundays he would often walk eight miles and take a ferry across the Ohio River from his home in the Over-the-Rhine area to Ludlow, Kentucky, to see games being played. In 1869 the Cincinnati Red Stockings became the first professional team in the nation, consisting of a carefully selected roster of paid players that included such early stars as shortstop George Wright and outfielder Cal McVey. Under the leadership of manager Harry Wright, the Red Stockings would go undefeated in 1869, finishing with a record of 65–0–1. The Red Stockings played their home games on the city's west side in a ballpark with a wooden fence located on a flood plane of the Mill Creek Valley. It was there peering through a hole in the fence that young August Herrmann would see his first professional baseball games and develop the love of the game that would forever be etched into his psyche.

The innocence of youth, however, came to a quick and tragic end for August Herrmann. In 1870 his father died, leaving August, at the tender of age of eleven years old, and his brother, Charles, age twelve, to provide for the family's welfare. As a result of this untimely circumstance, his formal schooling ended after the fifth grade. Undaunted by the uncharted waters that lie ahead of him, a young, round-faced and bright-eyed boy, August Herrmann started out to seek his niche in the workaday world of the 1870s Ohio River metropolis of Cincinnati. Years later Herrmann was to remark that his education came from the "University of Hard Knocks."

He donned his father's overcoat, several sizes too large but the only coat he had, and began his quest for employment in the industrialized section of Cincinnati's West End, down near the river on West Second and Third Street. Walking down the cobblestone streets, he stopped momentarily at an open door. He walked through and began to ascend the stairs to the top floor of the building and found himself staring at a closed door. Inside he could hear the clatter of machinery. He knocked on the door, but got no response. So he knocked harder. Still without a response, he pushed the door open and found himself in a printing plant and type foundry. Upon making a cautious entrance, he encountered a young man working on a Washington hand-press and asked to see the foreman. The young printer pointed towards a man sitting on a stool. From that point Herrmann's "Dickensian" experience that morning is described in the May 1910 issue of *Human Life* magazine:

> The boy approached the man and managed to get out: "I want a job."
> The man unlimbered, smoothed out the skirts of his much-pocketed apron, and took out a plug and bit off a chew. Then as he surveyed the serious round-bound boy, he burst into a laugh. "Want to learn the trade?"
> "Yes sir."
> "Know anything about it?"

"No sir."

The foremen looked him over again. "I believe your face would smear up well, and that you would make a first-class devil. I guess I'll take you."[1]

Now the foreman of this printing establishment prided himself on assigning nicknames to all the boys he hired. So immediately he began to ponder what Herrmann's moniker should be. "I don't know whether to call you 'The Flying Dutchman,' or 'Sir Bolingbroke,' or 'Garibaldi.'"[2]

One of the printers suggested to the foreman that they call him "Bismarck." The foreman replied, "No, we can't call him Bismarck, we already have one Bismarck. We'll call him Garibaldi."[3] Standing there in his oversized coat with flowing tails and big brass buttons, Herrmann probably did resemble the Italian statesman in some way. However, his friends soon shortened "Garibaldi" to "Garry." The name would stick and Herrmann would proudly respond to it throughout the remaining years of his life. Garry, however, became more than just a nickname to Herrmann; it became an identity, and as the second-born son of Christian and Margaret (Meyer) Herrmann symbolized his right of passage from a naive boy seeking to sustain himself in hard times into a sophisticated young man of the world.

Garry's first day on the job was a turbulent one. He was sent out to retrieve a cartload of type. His employer didn't engage a team to bear the heavy load. While Herrmann was thankful for that, having virtually no experience with horses, he struggled attempting to haul the heavy load of lead. When he reached the top of a hill, he let the cart begin to roll down the street without his guiding it. Suddenly the cart picked up speed and he attempted to dash alongside to bring it under control. But the cart was too heavy and now moving too fast, and Garry watched helplessly as the load plunged into the Ohio River. The next day an account of the incident ran in the paper and his name was listed as Garry Herrmann. From there it was all uphill for Herrmann and he thrived on the challenge. Early on his burning ambition was to become the foreman and thereby be the one to assign names to the new boys employed with the shop. However, his solid work ethic took him much further than that.

While busy earning a living to help sustain his family, Herrmann still found time to excel in his favorite pastime, baseball. It has been said that Herrmann would rather play ball than eat. He became player-manager of a local team known as the Crescents. Probably inspired by his youthful remembrances of Cincinnati Red Stockings star player George Wright, Herrmann, although left-handed, was the team's shortstop. So sure was he of his team's capabilities that at least in one instance, he bet the team's entire carfare on the game. Legend has it that when Herrmann's nine played neighboring teams, if they won, they came home in carriages to a chicken dinner. However, if they lost, they walked home and dined on soup and sausages.

During one game Herrmann's nine was fighting hard, giving its all in a close game, when one of Herrmann's players made a bad throw, allowing the go-ahead run to score. Immediately Herrmann crossed onto the sidelines and fell in a heap. One of his players rushed to his side, thinking that he had been stricken with some sudden affliction. When asked what was wrong, Garry looked up with a dejected look on his face and said, "I wanted pie so much for supper. I've dreamed about it two nights now."[4] Garry also dreamed about managing or owning a big league team and signing his name on documents with a big rubber stamp, but at this point in his life he just wasn't sure how to achieve such a lofty goal. But he was determined to learn. Meanwhile, Herrmann kept his day job in the printing industry. He learned typesetting and proudly continued to carry his union card for the next forty years. As Herrmann became more mature, he began to show executive potential. Eventually his hard work paid off with Herrmann being named manager of the *Cincinnati Law Bulletin* when the publication was first started. This was an enlightening experience for Garry Herrmann, as it became his first exposure to the legislative and legal processes, and he made the most of the opportunity.

On May 30, 1881, Garry Herrmann became a family man when he married Annie Becker, daughter of Mathias and Catherine Becker of Cincinnati. The newlyweds moved in with Annie's parents, who lived on the third floor of a tenement house on Moore Street. It was there that the Herrmann's only daughter, Lena, was born. However, marital bliss was short-lived as soon tragedy would strike. One evening a fire broke out in the building and a desperate attempt ensued to save the family members. While Herrmann, his wife, their infant daughter and his father-in-law were all rescued, his mother-in-law died in the fire while being smothered with smoke. However, just as the tragedy of the death of his father had not deterred him, neither did the horrible death of his mother-in-law; August Garry Herrmann moved on with his life.

Yet before he would become a legend in major league baseball, August Garry Herrmann was destined to become a legend in Cincinnati politics. In 1882 he had his first taste of politics when he ran for a seat on the Cincinnati Board of Education from the 11th Ward. He was elected and continued to serve on the Board of Education until 1886. The period that Herrmann served on the Board of Education was one when there was considerable turbulence in the system. The system was poorly funded and under considerable public criticism. In the late 1870s, the Ohio Legislature repealed the law that had mandated racially segregated schools in the state. However, in Cincinnati, a majority of colored people mistrusted racially integrated schools. Subsequently, they petitioned Herrmann and the Board of Education and obtained several branch schools where the students would be taught by members of their own race. The large German population that had settled in the city also gained a mandate for the schools system-wide to teach at least part of every school day in German. In the end August Herrmann's tenure serving on the school board was a learning period. Although he oversaw the development of a special study outlining conditions in the city's school system, in reality Herrmann's four terms on the Board of Education were served without any notable distinction.

Then in the late 1880s, there was a conspicuous split in the solidarity of the Republican Party between its two most powerful members, former saloon keeper George B. Cox and beer baron George Moerlein. George B. Cox was already one of the most powerful political bosses in the country. It seemed as if Cox controlled one-half of the Republicans in the city and Moerlein the other half. In 1889, Cox and Moerlein had banned together to elect Civil War veteran and East Walnut Hills grocer John Mosby as mayor. The coalition had withstood a challenge by the reform-minded group "Committee of Five Hundred" to elect coal merchant Daniel Stone as mayor on the Citizens ticket, who had been supported by Charles P. Taft (half-brother of future United States president William Howard Taft) and publisher of the *Cincinnati Times-Star*. Mosby won the election, defeating his Democrat rival by just 544 votes, but rolled over Stone by 14,703 votes. However, soon after the election, the alliance between Cox and Moerlein split apart. When John Mosby moved into city hall, he began to yield to the considerable pressures from the local prohibition element and enforce the city's Sunday closing law that forbade the sale of beer and liquor on the Sabbath. As a brewer and connoisseur of Germanic culture and camaraderie, George Moerlein took Mosby's enforcement of the Sunday closing law personally.

The ordinance banning the sale of beer and whiskey in Cincinnati on Sundays had been problematic for many years. The Cincinnati Reds insisted on selling alcohol in their ballpark not only on Sunday, but everyday. Consequently, this was just cause for the pious owners in the National League to hold a special meeting on May 25, 1880, at the Cataract House in Niagara Falls, New York, and pass a resolution strictly forbidding the sale of beer and whiskey at any ballpark in the league. The Reds' owners voted against the resolution and continued to sell spirits in their park. As a result, in 1881 the Cincinnati franchise was expelled from the National League. Then in the fall of that year, a group of more liberal-minded baseball team owners from Cincinnati, Louisville, St. Louis, Baltimore, Philadelphia and Pittsburgh held a meeting at the Hotel Gibson in Cincinnati and formed the American Association. The new league was considered a major league and competed directly with the established National League while permitting the sale of spirits in their ballparks. Hence the circuit became known as the "beer and whiskey league."

But in 1890 with the big Sunday beer brouhaha looming, John Mosby would be running for re-election and Moerlein had split with Cox over the issue. Other bad blood had been brewing between Cox and Moerlein as well. It eventually spilled out following the election of 1890 when Hamilton County sheriff-elect Valentine Heim got into an argument with George B. Cox over patronage selections. Heim, who prior to the election had been an employee of the Moerlein Brewery, complained to George Moerlein, who told him to "tell Cox to go to hell and make your own appointments."[5] So Heim did just that, an act that the powerful Cox deeply resented.

As the city Republican convention of 1891 opened, the stage was set for a battle between the preferred candidates of Cox and Moerlein for city solicitor and police court judge. Prior to the convention, Moerlein, along with the assistance of city solicitor Theodore Hortsmann, had been attempting to push out the city's gas provider, General Andrew Hickenlooper and his company, and replace it with a company called the Queen City Natural Gas Company. To save his company from losing its city contract and suffering possible ruination, Hickenlooper turned to George B. Cox for help and opened his wallet wide. Therefore, Cox backed Frederick Hertenstein to run for city solicitor against Hortsmann, and thanks to the political generosity of Hickenlooper, he had plenty of cash to push the issue at the convention.

At the convention Cox spread his gas money around generously, but when the smoke cleared, Cox and Moerlein had split the nominations of candidates. Ellis Gregg, Cox's nominee for police court judge, was victorious over Amos Dye, and Moerlein's candidate for city solicitor, Theodore Hortsmann, won nomination over Hertenstein, Cox's candidate. However, the battle had left George Moerlein with mortal political wounds because he lacked the powerful outside alliances that Cox could muster. Also in the process, both August Garry Herrmann of the 11th Ward and Rudolph "Rud" Hynicka of the 9th Ward had abandoned Moerlein in order to back both of Cox's candidates. Moerline was effectively left with little influence in the wake of the convention and immediately began to slip into oblivion. Nonetheless, Cox was aware of the fact that, despite the Hickenlooper gas money, he had to buy votes, and if Herrmann and Hynicka had not backed Ellis Gregg for police court judge, he would have also been beaten by Moerlein's other candidate. Consequently, Cox was quick to embrace both Garry Herrmann and Rud Hynicka. The alliance of the three would become everlasting and would eventually serve as Herrmann's ticket to entering major league baseball.

Now in total control of the Hamilton County Republican Party, George B. Cox began working diligently during the day from his office, located over the Mecca Bar on Walnut Street, and in the evenings at a notorious big round table at Wielert's Garden, located at 1408 Vine Street. To maintain his power base, he began to appoint able lieutenants within the party. One such candidate that stood out from the others was August Garry Herrmann, the young, charismatic fellow from the 11th Ward in the Over-the-Rhine district that had helped him depose George Morelien. Herrmann had demonstrated that he was a prolific vote-getter in his ward by virtue of winning several terms to the Board of Education. Since 1887, Garry Herrmann had been serving the Republican Party loyally as an assistant clerk of the police court. However, by 1891, it was apparent to Cox that Herrmann was wasting his talent in such a mundane political position and decided it was time for him to serve on the front lines of the political battleground by sitting with him at the big round table at Wielert's Garden and making party policy.

Republican mayor John Mosby had just been re-elected, defeating Democrat candidate Gustav Tafel. On March 26, 1891, an act designated as the "New Charter," had been passed by the Ohio General Assembly establishing a board of administration for municipalities, with four members appointed by the mayor. The intent of the act was to consolidate administrative authority in municipalities by combining the decision-making authority of several departments, such as the Park Board, Board of Health, Board of Waterworks Trustees, Board of Infirmary Directors, etc., into a central committee with a broad base of legislative authority. George B. Cox had Mayor Mosby appoint Garry

August "Garry" Herrmann (circa 1890). Cincinnati Museum Center–Cincinnati Historical Society Library.

Herrmann to the Board of Administration for a two-year term. Herrmann would now serve as a front man for Cox while using his extraordinary public relations skills to hype the virtues of the machine. For his efforts, Herrmann would be paid a salary of $4,000 per year and be bonded for $50,000.

Another political over-achiever that Cox selected to keep tabs on his political affairs was Rudolph K. Hynicka. Known as "Rud," Hynicka was from Pennsylvania Dutch stock and had come to Cincinnati in the 1880s to take a position as a reporter for the *Cincinnati Enquirer*. He had joined the Republican Party and had been allied (as Herrmann had) with George Moerlein, Cox's most severe critic and adversary in the party. Now aligned with Cox, Hynicka took over the responsibility for maintaining Cox's infamous voter card file. The Cox file included information on voters in every ward, listing far-reaching specifics such as where they went to church, where they were employed, and whether there were any personal scandals in their backgrounds, ranging from divorces to bankruptcies to arrests. Hynicka became the real muscle behind Cox and maintained his political control by overseeing the city's Republican Central Committee that was comprised of ward and township captains. The Central Committee even eclipsed both the executive and advisory committees in party influence. It was the glue in solidifying the concept of cohesiveness in the machine that George B. Cox had deemed so necessary to win elections. The icing on the cake, of course, were the 2,000 political jobs that Hynicka had under his thumb by serving as patronage manager for Cox.

The likable, flamboyant Garry Herrmann, on the other hand, was the picture of sartorial elegance — smelling of perfume and dressed in silk underwear, silk plaid suits with a flower in the lapel, and silk stockings. He assumed his position on the board of administration with broad sweeping responsibilities and authority. Working out of his office, located in the middle corridor of city hall, he was soon acknowledged as the administrative brains behind the trio of Cox, Hynicka and Herrmann. It was said of Herrmann that he liked to handle people in bulk, and he used his keen business sense on a day-to-day basis. Herrmann had now advanced far beyond his youthful goal of assigning nicknames to newly hired printer's devils. Now he hired and fired people in the city government and framed the annual budgets for the municipality, schools and the University of Cincinnati. Later, a reporter for the *Cincinnati Times-Star* stated that during his tenure in city hall, Herrmann didn't reign, he ruled. When the Board of Public Service decided a particular matter should be reviewed by "the committee of the whole," documents were marked with the letters "C.O.W." Among bureaucrats in city hall, these documents were referred to as being routed to the cow. The cow was Garry Herrmann. In essence, Garry Herrmann had become a defacto city manager long before any such concept had been developed as a standard "modus operandi" in municipal government.

In 1931 *Cincinnati Times-Star* columnist Alfred Henderson wrote of Herrmann, "He knew practical municipal government, but he also knew more of the theory and literature on the subject than he generally was credited with knowing. He had one immense advantage in his day. He knew Cincinnati thoroughly — its mentality, its psychic, and political background. He was not as 'politically minded' as R. K. Hynicka, but in his time he realized that to get things done electoral considerations had to be estimated."[6]

Despite his considerable administrative responsibilities at city hall, Herrmann was also expected to deliver speeches and promote the "bread and circuses" aspects of the Cox machine. While Herrmann was to achieve some very notable career highlights in his political career, there still exists some ambiguity in his ethics. It seems Herrmann was somewhat removed from the ongoing controversy and criticism unleashed on Cox and Hynicka, although during his tenure it was not above him to occasionally accept a questionable honorarium from an entity seeking political access to city hall.

As the politically turbulent decade of the 1880s in Cincinnati faded into history and the Gay Nineties appeared on the horizon, the future of August Garry Herrmann never looked brighter, and his best work was yet to come. One story has it that a vaudevillian playing in one of the Cincinnati theatres at the time even made Herrmann part of his act. One of the char-

George B. Cox, political boss of Cincinnati (circa 1904). Cincinnati Museum Center–Cincinnati Historical Society Library.

acters on stage asked another where the city hospital was located. The other replied, "Just go down to the Eleventh Ward and yell, 'To hell with Garry Herrmann' and you'll hear an ambulance ring coming in your direction."[7]

As the 1890s began, George B. Cox handled party business from his office above the Mecca Saloon on Walnut Street, while Rud Hynicka took care of county business over at the courthouse. Garry Herrmann had been appointed to the Board of Administration for a term of two years and he worked tirelessly at city hall. It was during this period that Garry Herrmann became a nationally known figure in municipal affairs. Each day he dictated mounds of letters while directing scores of workers, hiring and firing city workers, receiving visitors, and keeping tabs on the budgets for the city, parks, schools and University of Cincinnati.

One of the unique characteristics of Herrmann's management style was he attempted to leave nothing to chance. When he finished the day's business, he would then anticipate what would be on the agenda for the next. He also handled the press with a touch of brilliance. In the course of each day's activities, he would take notes on a pad of what he thought might be of interest to reporters, taking care to include explanations of what he thought might be a complicated issue. In some way, he was introducing the modern concept of public relations in government. Alfred Henderson, a reporter for the *Cincinnati Times-Star*, described Herrmann as "a man of intense nature, but he had wonderful control of his emotions. He never got provoked except at crass ignorance. But he did not expect a $1,200 a year clerk to know so much as he. He believed in the 'spoils system,' yet among the higher officials he insisted on at least intelligence."[8]

It has been said that both George B. Cox and Rud Hynicka took their politics seriously. So did Garry Herrmann, but he decided to have some fun, too. Rud Hynicka wasn't much of a socializer and preferred to idle away hours in the solitude of his fishing camp on the Whitewater River. However, legend has it that nearly every day Garry Herrmann would drink beer or wine. Around four o'clock in the afternoon, Garry Herrmann would leave his city hall office and head over to Wielert's Garden on Vine Street. Usually standing at the door was the hulking figure of George B. Cox glad-handing patrons as well as movers and shakers of the machine as they entered the establishment. When Herrmann walked into Wielert's, he would momentarily stop to chat with persons at the bar, then immediately head for the big round table in the back that was reserved for the Cox inner-circle and their chosen guests. It was at the big round table where political deals where made. As the night progressed, Cox and Hynicka would take leave and head for home. Around midnight, as the crowd in Wielert's began to thin, Herrmann would assemble an entourage of selected individuals and adjourn to the exclusive Halvin Hotel, where he would sip wine with bankers and members of the city's elite class until 3:00 A.M. Regardless of how late Garry Herrmann stayed out the night before, he would arrive at his city hall office the next morning promptly at 9:00 A.M., perfumed and with a fresh flower in his lapel, ready for the day's work before him. The explanation that can be offered as to how Herrmann was able to keep up with this exhausting lifestyle year after year was that he simply enjoyed it.

It has been said that in his day, Garry Herrmann probably spent more money showing his friends a good time than anyone else in Cincinnati. On many weekends, Herrmann with an entourage of friends in tow would hurry out of the city to the Laughery Club. The Laughery Club was a country club that Herrmann had founded, located on the banks of the Ohio River about thirty miles downstream from Cincinnati, near Aurora, Indiana. The Laughery lie just across from an island named for the famous Indian fighter of the same name who was massacred there in the pioneer days of the Northwest Territory. Membership in the club was reserved for persons in select circles. High-level politicians, businessmen and entrepreneurs were among its members, and over the years, many notable dignitaries would be Herrmann's guests at the Laughery, including baseball executives, sportswriters and star players.

In fact, there was a baseball diamond at the Laughery and one of the most popular events of the year was the annual club game. August Herrmann would suit up and captain the club's Indians while playing shortstop. Herrmann spent a considerable sum of his own money in organizing the club, which had lavish grounds, a clubhouse and private cottages for members. The dining room and rathskeller were said to be the last word in appointment. While the club annually ran a deficit, Garry Herrmann would dig deep into his pockets and keep the enterprise afloat. Over the years he probably spent a small fortune entertaining friends there until Prohibition eventually closed the club in the 1920s. But Garry Herrmann regarded the Laughery Club as one of his playthings. It would become his retreat and he would find peace and solace in its tranquil environment following tumultuous political campaigns and, in future years, the turmoil of long summer battles in major league pennant races while serving as baseball's first chief executive. When Herrmann died in 1931, a reporter for a Cincinnati newspaper remarked in his obituary column on Herrmann, "Cox and Hynicka died richer, but Herrmann had the better time."[9]

In the 1890s Cincinnati was referred to as "the Paris of America." There was something for everyone in the city. Classical music flourished at Music Hall; nationally known actors and actresses were on the playbill at one of the many theatres such as Pike's Opera House; and there was horse racing and major league baseball. Cincinnati also had the reputation as the wettest city between New York and Chicago, which was probably an understatement. Downtown in one block between Twelfth and Thirteenth streets, there were 23 saloons. On Fifth Street between Main and Sycamore, there were no less than 20 bars. At the Bay Horse Cafe on Main Street, the bartender would shake a gin fizz for 30 minutes before serving it.

But the epicenter of frolicking took place on Vine Street, which had been referred to as the "spinal cord" of the city. In the area of Vine Street, beginning at the canal (Central Parkway today) and extending a mile and a half to McMillan Street, there were no less than 113 drinking establishments. The Over-the-Rhine district was at its zenith in the 1890s. Following every sunset German bands played and Teutonic cuisine and frothy mugs of beer were to be found in abundance in the saloons. In many of these establishments, a patron could get a free bratwurst with every beer or get twenty-one beers for a dollar. One lived for the moment in the Over-the-Rhine because most patrons truly believed that life didn't get any better.

Since being expelled from the National League in 1881 for selling beer and whiskey in their ballpark, the Cincinnati Reds had been competing in the American Association. In 1882 the Reds won the American Association pennant, led by pitcher Will White, who won 40 games with an ERA of 1.54. They also finished in second place in the 1885 and 1887 seasons. But in 1890, the Cincinnati Reds returned to the National League as part of an eight-team circuit. The 1890 season was a particularly turbulent one for major league baseball. Not only was the established National League facing competition from the American Association, but a new circuit, the Players' League, a.k.a. "the Brotherhood," had been organized by players dissatisfied with the reserve clause that allowed owners to control the destiny of the players by selling and trading them at will. The Brotherhood had attempted to acquire a franchise for Cincinnati, but to no avail. While the Players' League attempted to strengthen its rosters by raiding the established teams for players, after one season the league folded, mostly due to bad management practices. Following the 1891 season, the American Association also collapsed and its strongest clubs were merged into the National League, creating a lopsided twelve-team circuit.

Aaron S. Stern owned the Reds throughout the 1880s. However, following the 1890 season, Stern was tired of it all and sold the Reds franchise to Al Johnson and the Players' League for $40,000. Yet before the 1891 season began, the Players' League folded. The National League immediately tied up the sale of the Reds to Johnson in court. Eventually the National League was permitted to purchase the Reds and protect the territory in Cincinnati. To operate the club, the league appointed John T. Brush. Brush organized a stock company to purchase the club and in the years that followed, he profited enormously from an enterprise that had hardly cost him a dime to acquire. While Brush would keep his primary residence in Indianapolis while operating the Reds, his influence on the Cincinnati club's day-to-day operations was considerable.

John Tomlinson Brush was another self-made man. Born in Clintonville, New York, on June 16, 1845, Brush became an orphan at the age of four. Raised by his step-uncle on a farm in New York, as a teenager he started work in a country store in Utica. He saved part of his salary diligently and eventually saved the necessary capital to open a dry goods store in the city. As the business prospered, he opened branch stores in Troy and Lockport. It was at Troy that Brush saw his first baseball game and was mesmerized by the spectacle of it all. As his clothing business began to expand, Brush moved to Indianapolis, where he opened another store and also bought the Indianapolis baseball team. Then, in the early 1890s, fate dealt him the Cincinnati Reds for free.

While the lives of John T. Brush and August Garry Herrmann were on a collision course, two other men arrived in Cincinnati in the early 1890s who would eventually become contemporaries of Herrmann and ultimately have as much of a profound influence on shaping events in his later years as George B. Cox did on his earlier ones. Charles Albert Comiskey was born on August 15, 1859, in Chicago, Illinois. He was the third child in a family of eight. His father, John Comiskey, had emigrated from Crosserlough, County Cavan, Ireland, and become president of the Chicago City Council. As a boy, Comiskey began playing ball on lots in Chicago as a pitcher and first baseman. His skills at the game increased rapidly and his innovate style of play at first, where he played far off the bag and fielded grounders hit to the right side of the infield, before throwing the ball to the pitcher covering first base, was revolutionary for the times.

Comiskey eventually became a major league player-manager and led the St. Louis Browns to four consecutive American Association pennants (1885–1888). In 1890, he bolted the Browns for the Players' League, returning to St. Louis for the following season. After the American Association folded following the 1891 season, Comiskey through intermediary Ted Sullivan stated that he could be signed by a National League club if the terms included a three-year contract for $21,000. Sullivan relayed this information to George Howe, president of the Cleveland club, who was at that time meeting with other National League owners at the Fifth Avenue Hotel in New York City. At the meeting the following day, Howe announced the terms extended by Sullivan on behalf of Comiskey. John T. Brush rose from his chair and said to the other moguls, "I claim the man under those conditions."[10] Although the Boston club also wanted Comiskey, the league owners didn't want to fight Brush on the matter, so they awarded the player to Cincinnati. John T. Brush then offered Comiskey the job of managing the Cincinnati Reds. Although Comiskey privately detested the National League, with a three-year contract being offered, he accepted the job and thereafter remained eternally warm towards Brush.

Another person that would be closely associated with Garry Herrmann was Byron Bancroft (Ban) Johnson. Johnson was born in Norwalk, Ohio, on January 6, 1864, and later his family moved to Cincinnati and settled down in Avondale. His father was a school administrator, professor and minister who stressed upon him the virtues of getting a good education. Johnson first attended Oberlin College but was dissatisfied with the religious regimentation of the school. He told friends, "There's too much emphasis on chapel at Oberlin."[11] Eventually he graduated from Marietta College. Johnson was a large man who weighed close to 300 pounds and had played baseball at both schools as a catcher. The player that succeeded him as the catcher for the Oberlin team was Moses Fleetwood Walker, the first Negro to play in a major league game. Following his graduation from Marietta College, Ban Johnson still had higher career aspirations, and he enrolled in the University of Cincinnati Law School. When he left law school in 1887, he was offered a job by Murat Halsted as the sporting reporter for the *Cincinnati Commercial-Gazette* at the salary of $25 a week.

In his columns, Johnson gave expanded coverage in the paper to baseball. Ironically, Johnson intensely disliked Reds owner John T. Brush. He wrote negative comments about Brush in the paper because he felt that Brush was a penny-pincher who didn't make any attempt to spend money to improve the club. John T. Brush did have a reputation in baseball as a tight-fisted owner and that reputation preceded him to Cincinnati. As the owner of the Indianapolis team in 1888, Brush devised a salary plan adopted by the National League that classified salaries of players according to their skills. The Brush plan provided that each year the president of the National League, Nicholas E. Young, would arbitrarily put each league player in a salary classification based on his qualities of earnestness, habits and special qualifications. There were four classes in the matrix, ranging from A to E. If a player was deemed to be a Class A player, he could expect a yearly salary of $2,500, whereas at the bottom of the rung a player classified as a Class E player would receive a salary of only $1,500. While Brush's stupid rule didn't last long, it ultimately had as much to do with the formation of the Players' League in 1890 as the reserve clause.

In 1892, the Cincinnati Reds with Charles Comiskey as manager of the club finished in fifth place in a league of twelve teams. The only saving grace in the season was the work of Reds pitcher Charles "Bumpus" Jones, who in his first major league game on October 15, 1892, fired a no-hitter, beating Pittsburgh, 7–1. At that time the Reds played their games at League Park, a wooden park located on the site of an old brickyard at the corner of Western Avenue and Findlay Street. The *Cincinnati Enquirer* referred to the ballpark as a death trap. Home plate was laid out to face the west looking towards Price Hill, so in the late afternoon the setting sunlight beamed directly in the batter's eyes. The only major league game known to be cancelled because of sunlight happened at League Park in the 1892 season. This, of course, just added more grist to the mill of Ban Johnson to criticize Reds owner John T. Brush.

In the 1890s, ballplayers were huge celebrities, perhaps the equivalent of today's rock stars in that era. In order to attract crowds at the Reds' games, John T. Brush regularly paraded his players in wagons to League Park through the streets of the Over-the-Rhine district. Parades were nothing new to the residents and patrons of Over-the-Rhine, for they were always happening in the area. But the most spectacular parades where those that took place annually in early November on election night when the Blaine Club (a club founded by George B. Cox that honored 1884 Republican presidential candidate James G. Blaine) would march up Vine Street in a surreal ceremony. With bright, red fires burning in front of every Vine Street cafe, up the middle of the street behind the American flag would come a torch-light ensemble of the slightly rotund figure of Garry Herrmann in the middle, flanked by Rud Hynicka on his left, Squire Gass on his right and all the well-oiled Blaine Club members following. Outside of Wielert's Garden standing proudly would be the beaming, six-foot tall and bulky 200-pound figure of George B. Cox. All along the route people would cheer on the sidewalks and yell out to Garry Herrmann, "Hello Garry," "Way to go Garry!" It was political ballyhoo at its finest in the Over-the-Rhine, and Herrmann literally ate it up.

In the early 1890s, Ban Johnson, then 29 years old, and Charles Comiskey, 33 years old, became close companions and often spent evenings together bending elbows and each other's ear in the Over-the-Rhine area. While Johnson took every occasion to bash Brush in his newspaper column, Comiskey remained loyal to him; somehow the difference of opinion they had on John T. Brush did not get in the way of their friendship. Now Ban Johnson, like Garry Herrmann, was known to enjoy his highballs. It had been stated that on one occasion a friend had rebuked Johnson after seeing him come out of a saloon. Johnson replied, "What did you want me to do, stay in there indefinitely?"[12]

To allow for some privacy, Johnson and Comiskey did most of their quaffing in private clubs in the area. The Ten Minute Club was a private establishment on Vine Street often frequented by Johnson and Comiskey. There was no sign outside, and patrons were scrutinized by a doorman upon entering and then admitted after a polite bow. No German bands played in the establishment, and notwithstanding the sound of cocktail shakers and the occasional foamy swish of beer kegs being tapped, the place was rather quiet and cheerful. However, there was one non-negotiable rule in the club that stated at least one person at each table was required order a drink every ten minutes. Legend suggests that Johnson and Comiskey first discussed forming the rival American League over beers in the Ten Minute Club. The story has it that years later, after Ban Johnson became a good friend of Alfred H. Spink, a St. Louis sportswriter and uncle of J.G. Taylor Spink, who became publisher of the *Sporting News*, Johnson told Spink that one evening at the Ten Minute Club, he said to Comiskey, "There is room for two major leagues in this great country of ours." However, Comiskey is supposed to have stated in response, "You have to have a minor league before you can make it a major."[13]

In late March of 1893 as the season approached, the hot stove league was wrapping up its winter session in houses of hospitality throughout Cincinnati. Ban Johnson reported in the *Commercial Gazette* that nightly at the Grand Hotel, a small band of faithful were plotting ways and means for Captain Comiskey to win the pennant. The 1893 baseball season is regarded as the first season of the modern game. It was in that year that the distance of the pitching mound was moved from fifty-five feet to its present sixty feet, six inches. At the time most players thought the change would greatly favor hitters. A typical opinion of the rule change was stated by Reds center fielder Bug Holiday prior to the 1893 season. "Those people who are laboring under the impression that the lengthening of the pitcher's alley will not improve batting are greatly mistaken. It will make a decided change, and if anything, it will add too much to the batting of teams. Under the new rules it will be next to impossible for a pitcher to deceive a batter with an out curve, and I think the only chance for effectiveness will be in speed and a drop ball. The inshoot may bother batters, but to what extent I am unable to tell. I thought the rules good enough as they were for, as things are now arranged, there is no premium on good batting."[14]

However, over the course of the 1893 season, the change in rules had no effect on the lackluster play of the Reds. While the club finished second in fielding and led the loop in double plays, there really wasn't much for the fans to cheer about. The Cincinnati Reds finished in seventh place with a record of 65–63 in the 12-team National League, 20½ games behind pennant-winning Boston, led by pitcher Kid Nichols with 33 wins. Charles Comiskey split the playing time at first base with Frank Motz, hitting a paltry .220 for 259 at-bats. The 1893 season was such an uneventful one for the Reds that the most well-known event in the year had nothing to do with play on the field. On September 18, 1893, the largest Monday crowd of the season, 2,202, came to League Park. The crowd was not necessarily there for the game between the Reds and Baltimore, but rather for a wedding. Prior to the game, Reds assistant groundskeeper Louis Can was married to Rosie Smith. The marriage ceremony took place at home plate. The Reds collected $60 for the happy couple and the Baltimore players added another $40.

In the fall of 1893, John T. Brush sent Comiskey on a tour of the South to scout some potential players for the club. During his sojourn through the Southland, Comiskey came into contact with some investors who were interested in reviving the Western League, a minor league that had been struggling to exist since 1879, but had finally collapsed. Comiskey was not happy in the National League, as he still disliked the fact that it had smashed the Brotherhood, so he showed some interest in the venture. Furthermore, he recommended to the group that Ban Johnson, his friend back in Cincinnati, would make a great president for the league.

On November 20, 1893, a meeting was held at the Grand Hotel in Detroit to formally organize the Western League. Delegates representing teams from Grand Rapids, Sioux City, Minneapolis, Milwaukee, Kansas City, Toledo, Indianapolis and Detroit attended. John T. Brush just happened to own the league's Indianapolis franchise, which he used on occasion as a feeder club for the Reds. However, if the Indianapolis club was drawing better than the Cincinnati club, it was not uncommon for Brush to send some of his major league players to the minor league team to keep the turnstiles moving. When Brush learned that Comiskey had recommended Ban Johnson for the position of league president, he was annoyed. Unfortunately, Brush missed his train to Detroit and never made the meeting, so there is no way of knowing if he would have voted for Johnson. Charles Comiskey then approached Watkins, the manager at Indianapolis, whom he convinced to cast Brush's vote for Johnson. When John Brush learned that Watkins had cast his vote for Johnson, he began to rethink the situation and came to the realization that maybe it wasn't such a bad thing after all. At least it got Johnson out Cincinnati and would end the constant sniping and second-guessing he endured from him in the newspaper.

Even though Brush's vote was now in the affirmative, there was still minor opposition to Johnson at the meeting. Charles Comiskey made a passionate case endorsing Johnson for the job and, eventually, the owners bought it, electing him not only president of the Western League, but also secretary and treasurer. Ban Johnson accepted the job, but remained skeptical. He was well aware of the loop's inconsistent history and wondered just how long the job would last. In order to provide himself with an insurance policy, Johnson obtained permission from the *Cincinnati Commercial-Gazette* to take a year's leave of absence. However, for posterity, Ban Johnson was ready to advance into the annals of baseball history and never looked back. In less than a decade, events unfolding in the lives of John T. Brush, Charles Comiskey, Ban Johnson and Garry Herrmann would cause them to converge directly upon each other at the crossroads of the twentieth century.

In 1893, John Mosby was starting his third term as mayor and he appointed Garry Herrmann to a four-year term on the Board of Administration. On May 13, 1893, the new Romanesque, red granite Cincinnati City Hall was dedicated in a lavish ceremony. The huge building, located in the block bounded by Plum Street, Central Avenue, Eighth and Ninth streets, is still in use to this day. The building quickly became cramped and lacking in modern conveniences. However, the new building was equipped with electric lights and telephones, and in December 1893, Mayor Mosby, accompanied by twenty-two assembled dignitaries, made the first long-distance call from city hall to New York.

For the administration of Mayor Mosby, the year 1893 was in many ways a turbulent one at city hall. Both George B. Cox and Mayor Mosby had a penchant for preferring locally regulated monopolies to either municipal ownership or a wide-open competitive bidding process. This allowed the city to control the process by limiting the number of agencies that could

Opposite: Cincinnati City Hall. Photo by William A. Cook.

grant franchises while working out the details behind the scenes in negotiations between lawyers of various utilities and factions of the Cox wing of the Republican Party and his political ally, former Ohio governor and future U.S. Senator Joseph B. Foraker, who lived in the city.

A major flap involving the traction interest occurred in 1893, with Garry Herrmann's Board of Administration settling the matter as both Cox and Foraker worked as paid advisors in the background. At the time there were several independent transit companies working in the city. Early in 1893, the city's Board of Legislation had granted a 3-cent fare franchise to a company with heavy Cleveland interests to build a new electric line to Price Hill and be known as the Route 25 company. The new line had considerable support from the Republican-controlled *Cincinnati Commercial-Gazette* and the neighborhoods that it was going to serve. However, Mayor Mosby was quick to note that the city had been left out of the deal. Therefore, since the franchise did not call for a 5 percent cut of the company's gross earnings to be paid to the city, Mosby vetoed the deal. But when Mosby received a considerable amount of backlash from various politicians, newspapers, businessmen and building improvement associations, he rescinded his veto.

Nonetheless, Mosby continued to advance the belief that the Route 25 deal was a raid on the Cincinnati Street Railway Company. CSRC supported extending a traction line to the isolated western sections of the city by building a rapid transit line, but could not do it for its current 4-cent fare, much less a 3-cent fare proposed by the supporters of the new Route 25 company. However, in November 1893, the city reached a compromise solution worked out by the Board of Administration under August Herrmann. The details of the compromise had CSRC converting all of its existing service to electric, extending existing lines in the far-western parts of the city, and in return raising its fare from 4 cents to 5 cents on its horse-car lines. CSRC also would provide free transfers system-wide and pay 5 percent of its gross earnings to the city, along with a car license fee of $4.00 per lineal foot (inside measurement) to the city. Previously the transit company had been paying the city 2.5 percent of its gross earnings that according to Garry Herrmann amounted to $25,000 a year. With the new agreement and 5 percent payment on gross earnings to the city, it could now expect to realize about $500,000 in just ten years from the agreement.

Historical critics of Herrmann and the Board of Administration have maintained that by renewing all the franchises held by CSRC, they had eliminated competitive bidding in the process, which killed the attempt of the Cleveland interest to build the Route 25 line since the CSRC with the city's new agreement quickly extended one of its existing lines to Price Hill. Critics of the franchise structure also have stated that Herrmann and the Board of Administration actually granted CSRC franchise agreements for twenty-five years. This statement is simply incorrect.

It had been the goal of August Herrmann for the city to have a consolidated transit system for some time. In bringing about the compromise, Herrmann and the Board of Administration had actually derived a great benefit to the system's users and city's taxpayers by restructuring the franchise agreements of CSRC to expire at the same time. The franchise agreement with CSRC was structured to permit the company to change its horse-car operations in the territory to electric over a period of time and charge the same fare on the horse-car lines that they were receiving on their rapid transit lines (five cents), in order to provide capital for the conversion. The only actual increases in fares were for horse-car lines, namely the John, Seventh, Clark and Sixth Street lines, while on the Price Hill Line, there was actually a fare decrease. Also to expedite the process, Herrmann and the Board of Administration allowed CSRC to extend its existing rapid-transit lines over the horse-car lines mentioned above.

By forcing the conversion of horse-car lines to electricity, the Herrmann agreement permitted the extension of franchises on these lines (which currently ran from six to thirteen years) to twenty years. That represented the same length as the rapid transit lines, thus making all of the CSRC franchises expire at the same time. The facts are that Herrmann and the Board of Administration had done their homework. The agreement structure avoided the embarrassing circumstances of waiting for these agreements to expire one by one, and instead permitted the start of a conversion to a total electric transit system immediately. If the Herrmann agreement had not been implemented, the City of Cincinnati would have had the embarrassment of still having the ancient technology of several 1850-era horse-car lines operating over several principal routes in the city in 1905. Furthermore, the agreement stipulated that the CSRC was responsible for repairing the streets its system ran over during the entire length of the franchise, bringing a further savings to the taxpayers.

Two years after the new transit agreement was put into place, August Garry Herrmann addressed the Young Men's Business Club of Cincinnati at the Zoological Gardens on June 24, 1895. In his address he passionately commented on the successes of the Board of Administration in handling a wide range of the city's services, from the water works to the infirmary. However, at the end of his address he found it necessary to comment on the 1893 transit agreement crafted by the Board of Administration.

Herrmann said in part,

> In November 1893, the Board of Administration granted to the Cincinnati Street Railway Company permission to extend four of its existing rapid-transit lines over the territory occupied by what were then known as its John Street, Seventh Street, Sixth Street, Clark Street and Price-Hill horse-car divisions. This action was criticized at the time by not only the press, but the public in general. The question is often asked as to just what privileges the railroad company received under these grants, and what the city got in return. Our attention had recently been called to a contract of a similar character in the city of Toronto. It seems to me that the board is to be congratulated upon the fact that is was necessary to go out of this country to find a contract that would compare favorably with ours. Supposing in two or three places in the United States, or a half-dozen or dozen places in the world, there are better contracts of this kind; surely we need not be ashamed of ours under those circumstances. In referring to the Toronto contract, attention was called to the fact that there the fares are from three cents during certain hours to four and five cents, and that the city received eight percent and upwards on the gross receipts, according to their amount, and also eight hundred dollars per mile for mileage fees. All of this may be true; and yet, as in the operating of waterworks, all of the conditions should be taken into consideration. Everybody will admit that it is much more expensive to operate in Cincinnati over excessive grades than it is in Toronto on practically level streets. On this subject we have some information. As an illustration, to operate the Eighth-street Line on the Warsaw Pike, a distance of four thousand feet, less than four-fifths of a mile, requires 750 horsepower. In Toronto the company to which reference is made operates a system covering eighty miles, and only 3,000 horsepower is required for the whole of it. In Toronto the city makes all repairs caused by operating the roads, while here the company is required to do it. In Toronto double fare is charged after midnight, and at all times an additional fare outside of the corporate limits.
>
> Doubtless all of you have seen the character of the work the street-railroad company has and is now engaged in with respect to putting down the modern street construction required under our contract. On a few streets they did this work in connection with the improvement thereof. On all of the others, and I cite Fourth, Fifth, Sixth, Seventh, Eighth, Ninth, Central Avenue, Freeman Avenue, Baymiller, and a great number of others, they were required to take up the old construction and put down a new one. These streets are in better condition today than they ever were. All of this entire work under our contract is done at the expense of the company. Its cost is estimated at over a million dollars. In the Toronto contract, this kind of street construction is also provided for, the only difference being that there the city pays for the work of tearing up, excavating, repaving, etc. The company only furnishes the rails, for all of which they certainly should get a

large revenue. In Cincinnati our five percent is a clear gain, paid into the treasury; in Toronto, to use the language of one of their officials, "it takes the entire amount received for mileage and percentage to pay the interest on and to provide a sinking fund for the redemption of the bonds that the city has issued to do the work which the company does here at their own expense, and that Toronto will not derive any benefit from this income until after the redemption of these bonds." Considering these conditions, does not our contract compare favorably with theirs?[15]

Regardless of the criticism at that time of the transit franchise agreement, the whole affair became moot in 1896 when the Ohio State Legislature enacted the Rogers Law that authorized municipalities to grant a fifty-year transit franchise with a five-cent fare to be reviewed for revision after twenty years and each subsequent fifteen-year period thereafter. The act also allowed municipalities to consolidate their local transit lines into one company. Therefore, Garry Herrmann's dream of having a consolidated transit system in the city had been realized. If anyone profited from the deal, Senator Joseph B. Foraker would be the logical candidate rather than Cox and Herrmann. It was in fact Senator-elect Foraker who in 1896 had successfully lobbied the Ohio General Assembly into passing the Rogers Law that permitted the Cincinnati officials to grant a fifty-year franchise to the Cincinnati Street Railway Company. Senator Foraker also represented the transit company before Governor Asa S. Bushnell, who Foraker had assisted in getting elected in 1896, granted a $285,000 reduction in the company's tax valuation.

John T. Brush, president, New York Giants. National Baseball Hall of Fame Library, Cooperstown, N.Y.

As a result of his involvement with restructuring the transit agreement, Garry Herrmann became aware of just how disjointed the city's purchasing practices were. At the time, purchases were being made whenever anyone in city hall needed something. Various boards, department heads and subordinates simply bought whatever they needed. More often than not, preference was given to vendors who were friends or acquaintances. Articles of common use to the whole of the city government process were purchased by no less than a dozen persons at city hall in different quantities and at different prices. Herrmann had enough of such waste and created a centralized purchasing office, thereby inducing competition, inventory control and cost-effectiveness into the process. There were, of course, some disappointed employees in the city government that previously had special privileges in a decentralized purchasing system. Nonetheless, in the first year that Herrmann's centralized purchasing system was in place, the savings to the city was estimated at $25,000. Subsequently, the news of Herrmann's innovation traveled quickly. In the fall of 1894 in Buffalo at a meeting of city administrators representing boards similar to that of Cincinnati's Board of Administration, Herrmann presented a paper on the matter and his purchasing system was adopted in a number of other large cities.

Over the winter of 1893, Reds owner John T. Brush had spent $12,000 refurbishing League Park, located at Findlay and Western. A new iron and wood grandstand had been erected, increasing the seating and standing room capacity to about 8,000. Home plate had been moved from the southeast corner of the park to the southwest corner to keep the afternoon sun out of the batters' eyes. With dedication of the new facilities at League Park all set, the Reds opened the 1894 season on a wet April 20 against Cap Anson's Chicago Colts. However, the opening game was in jeopardy due to the rain that had poured down throughout the day. Groundskeeper John Schwab (father of Matty Schwab, Cincinnati groundskeeper for 60 years) worked feverishly to dry the field with sponges, buckets, large dippers and sawdust, while Bellstedt's Band played to the amusement of the crowd. The following morning, the *Commercial-Gazette* stated that President Brush was determined to have the opening yesterday, even if the players had to wear rubber boots and a mackintosh put on the ball.

At 2:30 P.M., the Chicago Colts arrived in carriages and began walking across the field. A steady applause rang down upon Cap Anson from the crowd of 6,283 on hand as he walked toward the bench carrying one side of the bat bag. The long row of boxes were filled with ladies and their escorts. James A. Hart, president of the Chicago club, shared a box with Mayor John Mosby, and droves of judges, city and county officials were in attendance with the overflow crowd in the bleachers. Mayor Mosby arrived late, causing all the speeches and other planned hoopla to be cancelled. At 3:05 P.M., Charles Comiskey, Cap Anson and umpire Ed Swartwood convened at home plate to go over the ground rules. The 1894 season began and the Reds defeated Chicago, 10–6. However, in the summer of 1894, those players that John T. Brush had sent manager Charles Comiskey south to sign the previous fall provided little help and the Reds had a miserable season.

Just about everything that could go wrong did. The team even experienced a horrific fire in the Chicago ballpark. On August 5, 1894, the game between the Chicago Colts and Cincinnati Reds was stopped in seventh inning when fire swept through the grandstand and bleachers, destroying the ballpark and causing panic among the 945 fans in attendance. The game was declared official, with the Colts leading the Reds, 8–1. When an investigation into the fire was launched, it was discovered that it had been ignited by a young boy lighting a cigarette. The Reds ultimately finished in tenth place in the National League in 1894 with a record of 55–75, 35 games behind pennant-winning Baltimore.

After three non-eventful seasons in Cincinnati, Charles Comiskey decided it was time to turn over the managerial helm of the Reds to Buck Ewing and move on. During his time in Cincinnati, Comiskey had come to respect John T. Brush. He felt that despite Brush's shortcomings at recognizing player talent, he was an honorable man and had learned how to compete within the political structure of the game with the other owners. Following the 1894 season, Brush offered Comiskey a new contract, but he declined the offer. The Western League had began operating in 1894 with Ban Johnson as its president, and Comiskey felt that destiny was calling him to be part of the new circuit while lending support to his old friend.

"Where will you go?" asked Brush.

"To St. Paul," Comiskey said. "I'm going to take over the Sioux City franchise and transfer it to St. Paul."

Brush could barely get the words out of his mouth. "St. Paul? Are you crazy? St. Paul is a graveyard."

"That's where I want to go," said Comiskey.

"All right. I see your mind is made up. Well, when you go broke, come on back. And mean-while, if you need help there, just let me know."[16]

When Ban Johnson packed up and left Cincinnati to head to Chicago to become the pres-ident of the Western League, it suddenly occurred to John T. Brush that he had Johnson just where he wanted him. So Brush showed his true colors. It was payback time and he began a negative campaign with other club owners to replace Johnson as league president. However, Johnson staved off the "coup de tat" and prevailed. As the combative nature of being a league executive strongly appealed to Johnson's personality, he made the decision to scrap his news-paper reporting ambitions and make baseball his lifework. The Western League had survived its first year under the administration of Ban Johnson, and so had he.

During the 1895 season, new manager Buck Ewing didn't fare any better than Charles Comiskey in turning around the hapless Reds. The club finished in eighth place in the National League with a record of 66–64, 21 games behind pennant-winning Baltimore. However, the Reds' season may have been jeopardized by owner John T. Brush. On March 16, before the start of the season, Brush sent six Reds to his minor league team in Indianapolis, thereby weakening the Cincinnati club. With the Indianapolis team making more money than the Reds, Brush wanted to make sure that he put the best possible team on the field to attract fans into the park.

Meanwhile, in St. Paul, the 1895 Western League season had been a struggle for Charles Comiskey, although he did make a profit. At one point his team lost 17 consecutive games, and it was prevented from playing games on Sunday due to an injunction. But Comiskey rolled with the punches and clearly demonstrated to everyone around him that he was in the Western League venture for the long haul. Furthermore, he and Ban Johnson began planning the future of the circuit.

At the end of the 1896 National League season, the Pittsburgh Pirates fired manager Con-nie Mack. Ban Johnson was well aware of Mack's abilities and offered him the opportunity to manage the Milwaukee team in the Western League. While Mack was offered the chance to return to Pittsburgh in 1897 as a catcher and pitching coach, he decided to travel to Chicago and meet with Johnson. The Milwaukee team was owned by attorney Matt Killilea, who remained behind the scenes while advising Johnson on various matters to move the league forward onto sound financial footing. Johnson told Mack that if he would take the Milwau-kee job, he would have total freedom in running the club. The offer fit the creative and inno-vate Mack like a glove and he immediately accepted. It was at that moment, without realizing it, Connie Mack assumed his destiny to become a legend in the history of major league base-ball.

By 1896, Garry Herrmann had shown remarkable leadership on the Board of Adminis-tration. Under Herrmann's guidance, the board had made deep cuts in administrative oper-ating costs in key municipal departments. Annual expenditures in the Street-Cleaning Department had been reduced from $198,347 in 1885 to $186,157 in 1894. In 1889 the Street-Repairing Department had repaired 232 miles of city streets at an expenditure of $104,924. By 1895, the cost for repairing 233 miles of streets was reduced to $95,000. The Park Depart-ment had spent $56,662 in 1893, but by 1895 was operating on an annual budget of $47,250. Costs were down in every department that Herrmann and the board exercised administra-tive oversight upon with the exception of the Electrical Department, which had been estab-lished to string wires in the city. As the work progressed, a cost increase had occurred due to the difference between the cost of lighting the city with electricity as opposed to gas.

However, the improvements made by the Board of Administration went much further than just reducing costs of city infrastructure. The board established four more fire companies and increased the surveillance by the Health Department of all markets in the city with regard to their sanitary condition and inspection of milk, meat, fruits and livestock, including the examination of cattle being shipped into the city. The Board of Administration also established a rule within the Health Department requiring all the district physicians to care for the poor who lived on the streets by furnishing direct access to medications instead of sending them to a local druggist, which caused delays in treatment of their various maladies and conditions. The board also pointed with pride to the fact that the average costs of treating a patient (referred to as inmates at that time) at its infirmary was 21½ cents per day, the lowest in the history of the institution. In 1888, the infirmary had a yearly census of 694 patients with an operating budget of $83,631. By 1894, under the board's control, 833 patients were treated with an annual budget of $79,972. Citizen advocacy committees such as the Board of County Visitors (appointed by the Court of Common Pleas to be a watchdog group over the operations of the infirmary) gave the institution considerable accolades during this period of the Board of Administration oversight.

Then in 1897, a funny thing happened to the Cox machine on its way to city hall: a Democrat was elected mayor. Since January of that year, the Democrat-controlled *Cincinnati Post* had been publishing a series of uncomplimentary columns on the inner-workings in city hall, dealing with patronage and how appointments to bipartisan committees occurred, all with the influence of George B. Cox from his office over the Mecca Bar. Then in the spring, the *Cincinnati Enquirer* jumped on the bandwagon and several coalitions of reform-minded voters banded together. The Democrat candidate for mayor, Gustav Tafel, fanned the flames of controversy by viciously attacking George B. Cox. He campaigned hard where the Republicans were most vulnerable. Throughout the neighborhoods on the hilltops, he "denounced the gangs which threatened prosperity, and promised to follow the example of Mayor Josiah Quincy of Boston in appointing an unofficial cabinet to help him make the city one of the most beautiful and prosperous in the United States."[17] On election day, Tafel was victorious as he received 35,868 votes, besting Republican candidate Levi C. Goodale's 28,433. Tafel's victory actually turned out to be a landslide for the Democrats as they swept every county office and nearly every state office on the ballot. George B. Cox issued a statement that he would be willing to step down as the so-called "boss" in Cincinnati. He had been wounded badly in the 1897 election, and in the aftermath of the Democrats' sweep of city hall, several scandals came to light. One such controversy involved the indictment of a secretary in the waterworks department who could not account for about $20,000 in missing collections. When it was discovered that George B. Cox had been the man's bondsman, it literally opened up a political Pandora's box for him.

Another scandal involved Sunday baseball in Cincinnati, which in the 1890s was still on the city books as an illegal activity. Rud Hynicka was still holding down the fort for the Cox machine as clerk of police court. Hynicka was always looking for a way to make a buck, honest or otherwise, and had developed a scheme whereby he would arrest ball players for playing games on Sunday. He would then have them freed on bail and not prosecute them because it was too difficult for the city to get a conviction. So following the election results that brought Democrat Gustav Tafel into the mayor's office, the *Cincinnati Enquirer* exposed Hynicka and stated that he had been making between $150–$200 a week on the scheme. Consequently, it became another damaging controversy for George B. Cox.

However, the Cox machine was far from smashed. Its core was left in tact with many familiar wards, such as the 18th, Cox's old ward now under the leadership of Lew Kraft, and the Hynicka-led 9th and the Herrmann-led 11th, all casting a majority of votes for the defeated

Goodale. As the future of George B. Cox was unclear, Senator Foraker asked Garry Herrmann to seek him out and determine what his future political plans were. Subsequently, Herrmann reported back to Senator Foraker that while George B. Cox was currently staying out of the limelight, he had no intentions of surrendering and was in fact quickly building a new coalition to mount a comeback.

Meanwhile, for several years August Herrmann and the Board of Administration had been advocating that the city build a new waterworks. The obsolete system that currently served the city included 264 miles of pipe and maintenance had become an intolerable task. The growing neighborhoods on the hilltops were increasing demand for water and the outdated pumping plant on Front Street could not deliver the necessary supply. In fact, in 1890 a crisis occurred when the demand for water exceeded the supply. Also, the water supply in Cincinnati had a reputation of not always being of the purest form. It was a rather common occurrence in some parts of the city for one to turn on a hydrant and experience slime emitting from it in the name of water. Furthermore, over the years there had been several incidents of typhoid in the city that many suspected was caused by the impurity in the water supply. A grand opportunity for improvement occurred in 1896 when the Ohio General Assembly appropriated $6,000,000 in bonds for the construction of a new water plant. To oversee the public works project, a five-man bi-partisan commission was appointed by Governor Asa B. Bushnell that included Maurice J. Freiberg, Charles M. Holloway, Leopold Markbreit, Dr. Thomas W. Graydon and Garry Herrmann.

At the first meeting of the commission on June 23, 1896, Garry Herrmann was elected Commissioner of Water Works, a.k.a. the chairman of the waterworks commission, by his fellow members. Immediately, Herrmann arranged to make the project his primary occupation. He set about the laborious task of selecting engineers and technical advisors, choosing the site, approving plans, letting contracts and supervising construction. He would endure costly litigation and force undesirable modifications of the original plans. In administering the behemoth task, Herrmann would serve as chairman during the construction of the works for twelve long, arduous and controversial years, and continue during its early days of operation.

By expediting the construction of the waterworks, Herrmann's supporters have historically referred to him as a one-man dynamo. On the other hand, his critics have maintained that he regularly ignored parliamentary procedure by rushing thousands of dollars of construction materials through the commission before anyone could comprehend the meaning of the motion before them. Perhaps the reality of Herrmann's operational methodology was that it was a little bit of both. But such was the managerial style of August Garry Herrmann; he was just too busy to stand on ceremony. In 1931, the *Cincinnati Enquirer* wrote in retrospect of Herrmann's administration and the construction of the waterworks, "Those trying circumstances were handled by him with tact and firmness, and with the intelligent and public-spirited cooperation of his fellow Commissioners, he was able to bring the enterprise to a final completion and deliver to the city a water system of which it has ever since been, justifiably proud."[18]

August Herrmann went to work diligently on the new waterworks project and quickly established himself with a national reputation as a knowledgeable source in the administration of municipal public works improvement projects, which led to his being elected president of the American Society of Municipal Improvements. Herrmann felt that it would be advantageous for the larger cities in the country to have a method of comparing tax rates to use as a gauge on efficiency in their application of fiscal management toward making decisions on public works improvements. To gather the required information for the report, Herrmann sent out a questionnaire seeking information on tax rates to twenty-nine cities with more than 80,000 population, excluding Syracuse, New York, and Worcester, Massachusetts, along with Greater New York. New York had merged with Brooklyn and three other boroughs and as a result could not provide the necessary information until the end of the year, too late to be of use in Herrmann's report. After receiving the responses and organizing the data, on October 26, 1898, Herrmann addressed the American Society of Municipal Improvements at its fifth annual convention in Washington, D.C., with the results announced in a speech titled "Rates of Taxation in the Larger Cities of the United States." In his report, August Herrmann said in part:

> Gentleman:
>
> In my annual address as the president of this society at its last annual meeting, I suggested that the Committee on Taxation and Assessment, to be appointed for the ensuing year, take up and submit a report at the next meeting of the society, showing the rates of taxation throughout the leading cities of the country — this report to show, among other things, the total assessable valuation of property for taxation (both real and personal), the percentage of value of real estate as returned for taxation in the various cities, the tax rate in each city, as well as a division thereof, showing separately the rate for municipal, county, state, educational, sinking fund and interest, special, and all other purposes that go to make up the grand total. Such a report, it seemed to me, would be of incalculable benefit to the members of the society, and would materially aid us at all times in making intelligent comparisons of the tax rates of our respective cities with those of other cities to be presented in a report of this kind.[19]

In the late 1890s, American cities were growing by leaps and bounds. The Industrial Revolution was in full throttle, and in the East, American cities such as Boston, Philadelphia and New York were being flooded with millions of European immigrants. The older cities of the East were finding that they had to improve antiquated public works systems. Consequently, work was beginning on replacing ferry systems with bridges, and old wooden water pipes were being dug up and replaced with iron pipes. August Herrmann's brilliant innovation of providing large cities with comparative tax rate data was a stroke of genius; it allowed for benchmarks and standards of performance relative to the return on tax ratables to be established. It was the first attempt by a national oversight body to bring some form of cohesion to the municipal management process. Furthermore, the data in Herrmann's report was accurate, concise, and did not demonstrate any bias. It did not show Cincinnati in anymore of a favorable light than any other city. Table A listed assessable valuation arranged on a uniform basis to determine the lowest and highest tax rate for 29 cities. St. Paul, Minnesota, was listed with the lowest tax rate and Jersey City, New Jersey, as the highest, while Cincinnati was ranked as the city with the 16th-lowest tax rate. The report was straightforward and hardly the work of propaganda forged by a machine politician.

Life continued to be on the upswing for Herrmann when, in 1898, he and his family moved into the new, large, red brick house that he had constructed at 47 Hollister Street in Mt. Auburn. It would become his home for the remaining 33 years of his life. At the time the house was constructed, it was abutted by an undeveloped rolling wooded hillside that laid between upper Vine Street, leading into Corryville, and Auburn Avenue in Mt. Auburn. In 1904, Herrmann used his political influence to turn the land behind his property into a magnificent public place, Inwood Park. Originally the land had been the summer home and deer lodge of George K. Schoenberger and for many years been called Schoenberger's Woods.

By 1898, George B. Cox, fueled with campaign money from the Cincinnati Gas and Electric Company, had built a new coalition, and that fall his candidates swept the Hamilton County offices by a large majority. Now George B. Cox was once again in a position to retake control of Cincinnati city hall, and the Democrats did all they could to help him. While

Democrat Mayor Gustav Tafel and his colleagues where abundant with spirit, they lacked experience and quickly discredited themselves through gross inefficiency. Both before and during the Cincinnati city Republican convention of 1900, Cox and Herrmann held a series of meetings, preparing to select their candidates. They were often joined in these meetings by General Andrew Hickenlooper and Norman G. Kenan. In the end, they endorsed Julius Fleischmann for mayor; it was a done deal at the convention, with the delegates simply rubber-stamping the endorsement of the four. The Democrats endorsed Alfred Cohen, a state senator, thereby setting up a campaign between two Jewish candidates for mayor.

Julius Fleischmann was yet another person who would have a profound influence in allowing Garry Herrmann to realize his ultimate dream of owning a major league team. Fleischmann had been born into a Jewish family in Hungary, but never really participated in formal religious services or activities. He came to America in 1866 and soon returned to Europe with a grand idea. Along with his brother Max, he returned to America in 1868 brought with him a test tube containing the first live yeast plants to enter the United States. It was from this rather unobtrusive start that the two brothers created the Fleischmann's Yeast Company that eventually would sell yeast products all over the world. Julius Fleischmann was an ideal candidate, as he had wide appeal among both the Cincinnati business community and labor organizations. Not only was he vice-president of the Blaine Club, but also had joined a wide range of fraternal organizations that included the Optimist Club, the Queen City Club, the German-Jewish–run Phoenix Club, and was even an honorary member of the Friendly Sons of St. Patrick. In addition, Fleischmann was considered his own man by the press and not regarded as a candidate controlled by the Cox machine.

By 1900, the Prohibition forces were beginning to turn up the pressure on the temperance issue. Carrie Nation was traveling from city to city brandishing an ax that she used to drive home the issue by smashing whiskey bottles in saloons. However, when she came to Cincinnati in 1901 and marched up Vine Street in the Over-the-Rhine district, she seemed overwhelmed by the number of drinking establishments she saw. Later, Nation was asked why she didn't wield her ax on her jaunt up Vine Street. "I would have dropped from exhaustion before I had gone a block," she replied.[2] In addition to his yeast factory, Julius Fleischmann also operated a distillery that produced gin. Being in the booze business, he had a liberal attitude about the Sunday closing laws that enhanced his attractiveness as a candidate for mayor, especially in the inner-city wards saturated with the large, thirsty German population. In the city elections of 1900, the Republicans were swept back into the mayor's office as Julius Fleischmann defeated Alfred Cohen by 5,500 votes. The Republicans also won twenty-two of thirty-one seats on the council.

Cox and Herrmann were jubilant. In August 1900 the two had also made a little political pin money at the expense of Andrew Hickenlooper, a long-time key political ally. General Andrew Hickenlooper was attempting to limit the business that the Edison Company was getting for providing private lighting and the laying of conduits. At the time, both Cox and Herrmann were actually on the payroll of Hickenlooper's gas and electric company. Still, that did not preclude Cox and Herrmann from covering both sides of the street. Senator James B. Foraker was the legal counsel for the Edison Company. Cox held a meeting with Foraker and then informed Hickenlooper that he intended to introduce two ordinances into the city board of legislation to extend the contract of the Edison Company to continue to providing private lighting and to laying conduits. The ordinances were adopted and, of course, the Edison Company gladly paid a fee of $12,000 to Cox, who in turn gave Garry Herrmann his cut of $3,000. Such were the political dealings of August Garry Herrmann in his days before major league baseball called him to lead the national game into the twentieth century.

II

The Rise of the American League

In 1899, Cincinnati Reds owner John T. Brush was buying shares of stock in the New York Giants. Brush, who was still at odds with Ban Johnson, also owned the Indianapolis franchise in the Western League. He had developed a scheme to make a profit on Western League players by drafting them under the presumption that he was going to have them play for the Reds. Instead, he would send them to his Indianapolis franchise. Then Brush would bring other players from Indianapolis to Cincinnati and sell them at a profit. Ban Johnson became disgusted with the practice and forced Brush to sell his stock in the Indianapolis franchise.

Meanwhile, Johnson continued to wait for the window of opportunity to open that would permit the Western League to compete against the National League. Under Johnson's administration, the Western League had gained a national reputation as a clean league with little controversy involving gamblers and one that was appropriate for family attendance at its games. Johnson stood behind his umpires and urged them to crack down on rowdy play and the use of profanity. Although overall attendance had been on the rise, there had been some franchise shifting in the Western League. The Grand Rapids team had moved to St. Joseph, Missouri, where it languished, then on to Omaha and finally back to Grand Rapids. Also, the Columbus club was replaced by Buffalo. For the most part, though, the league was fairly stable and Charles Comiskey had survived the graveyard of St. Paul. But interest in creating a new major league was building in other places.

In St. Louis, J.G. Taylor Spink, who at that time was the sports editor of the *St. Louis Post-Dispatch* was writing many letters criticizing the quality of play in the National League and urging the formation of a new major league by resurrecting the defunct American Association. He had allies in Christ Von Der Ahe, who had formerly owned a franchise in the American Association, and Cap Anson, who was harboring strong feelings of betrayal by the National League from his perceived treatment by Albert Spalding. Anson, who had played or managed in the National League from the beginning, had been forced out by Chicago owner Albert G. Spalding in a stock deal that prevented him from gaining control of the club. John J. McGraw of the Baltimore Orioles also was ready to join forces with Spink in hopes of getting a franchise for New York.

In 1899, J.G. Taylor Spink organized a secret meeting in a Chicago hotel to explore the possibility of forming a new league. When Ban Johnson learned of Spink's plans, he was confronted with the fact that he either had to act on his plans to form a league that would compete with the National League or join forces with Spink. In the end Johnson decided it was time to act on the plans he and Comiskey had chatted about while quaffing down highballs at the Ten Minute Club in Cincinnati earlier in the decade. As a result, on October 11, 1899, during a meeting at the Northwestern Hotel in Chicago, Johnson disbanded the Western League and formed the American League.

The National League treated Johnson's threat of a new league as a laughable event and sent him a communication requesting that his league send in its fee for minor league dues, as stated in the National Agreement. Spink's plans for a new league began to crumble when Cap Anson's backers in Chicago pulled out and John McGraw felt the league was destined for doom. The story goes that McGraw backed off when he was informed that the politicians in New York's Tammany Hall threatened to build streets through any ballpark built in the city that would compete with the Giants.

Then the National League shot itself in the foot. Prior to the 1900 season, at urging of the New York Giants' controversial owner Andrew Freedman, the National League reduced its number of teams from twelve to eight, tossing out the weaker franchises in Baltimore, Cleveland, Louisville and Washington. Not only did this ill-conceived downsizing create opportunity for the fledgling American League to expand into the East, it also caused some bad blood among National League owners, most notably Barney Dreyfuss, who owned the now-defunct Louisville club.

In essence, Dreyfuss had been robbed of his club by Freedman. In 1899, Dreyfuss had purchased controlling interest in the Louisville club for $50,000. Now as payment for the defunct franchise, the National League gave him the paltry sum of $10,000. However, as part of the agreement, Dreyfuss was permitted to buy interest in the Pittsburgh Pirates and sell his players. But Barney Dreyfuss saw the writing on the wall long before his club was contracted and was determined to rise again as a major league team owner. Rather than sell his best players, he began trading them to Pittsburgh. Such was the case with Honus Wagner. In January 1900, Dreyfuss traded Wagner to the Pittsburgh Pirates along with 13 other players on the Louisville team, including such notables as Fred Clarke, Deacon Phillippe and Tommy Leach.

Harry Clay Pulliam had been the president of the Louisville club before Dreyfuss bought controlling interest. He left baseball briefly in 1897 when he was elected to the Kentucky state legislature. However, he quickly realized that baseball was his true calling and returned to the Louisville club as its president in 1898. In 1900, Pulliam accompanied Dreyfuss to Pittsburgh and became secretary-treasurer and a stockholder in the club.

Ban Johnson recognized opportunity from the bone-headed action of Freedman. Johnson purchased the Cleveland franchise for the American League, then moved the Grand Rapids team there. The National League owners then left the back door open for the American League when it permitted Charles Comiskey to move his team from St. Paul to Chicago. In their infinite wisdom, the National League owners felt that by placing a minor league team in the city, it might be a deterrent to such ideas as the revival of the American Association. In St. Paul, the team's name had been the Orphans, but when Comiskey moved to Chicago, he renamed his team the White Stockings in honor of the city's original professional team. So the new American League, while not considered a major league in 1900, would begin play with teams in Buffalo, Kansas City, Indianapolis, Detroit, Minneapolis, Milwaukee, and now Chicago and Cleveland. As the new millennium loomed, the stage was set for a major battle, one so fierce that it would end with baseball nearly eating itself alive. And at this point in time, who would have thought that the future peace treaty to end the mess was going to be negotiated by a portly Cincinnati machine politician that loved eating sausage and sauerkraut, namely August Garry Herrmann?

As the Cincinnati Reds played through another lackluster season, early in the morning on May 28, 1900, fire destroyed the main grandstand at League Park. The only part of the park left unscathed by the raging flames were the bleachers alongside the left field line and right field side. John T. Brush had a roof constructed over the remaining stands, and in order to provide an acceptable view of the game, he moved home plate back in the right field corner, which meant that once more batters were facing the sun. The Reds would play in this ridiculous field configuration for the remainder of the 1900 season and all of 1901. With the seating capacity now greatly reduced, on days of big games some fans would choose to sit atop box cars in back of the outfield wall.

The fire also had destroyed the clubhouse and, as a result, bats and equipment were lost. At the time players were responsible for purchasing their own uniforms, all of which had been burnt in the fire. With so much disorder resulting from the fire, the Reds scheduled their next home games on the road while temporary repairs were being made at League Park. When the Reds got to New York, the replacement uniforms they had ordered were not yet available, so the Giants offered the team their road uniforms for the games. However, when John T. Brush suggested that the players should pay for their replacement equipment and uniforms when they arrived, the Giants withdrew the offer. Rather than have the club play the New York games in their street clothes, Brush backed down and agreed to pay the bill. Under these conditions the Reds did the best they could in the 1900 season and finished in seventh place in the new eight-team National League.

As the 1900 American League season began, Ban Johnson knew that if he were going to market the league as a major, he needed financing to promote it, build new ballparks and buy new players. Johnson went to Cleveland and met with Davis Hawley, a banker who had at one time been involved in the game. Hawley told Johnson that he was too old to get back in the game, but said that he had a couple of people that he wanted to introduce to him. Hawley introduced Johnson to a thirty-year-old coal magnate by the name of Charles W. Somers and a real estate operator by the name of John F. Kilfoyl. The two listened to Johnson's plan and agreed to help him. The agreement that the American League had been operating under was set to expire in October 1900. Johnson was tired of his league's players being subject to the National League draft and was ready to expand into the cities in the East the National League had abandoned.

The first shot in the baseball war that Johnson launched occurred when National League secretary Nick Young wired Johnson about the fact that he had not paid his annual fee registering the American League as a minor league. Johnson wrote back to Young, telling him that he desired to discuss the status of the American League in a personal meeting. Young never replied. Johnson, therefore, decided to take his case directly to the National League's annual meeting, scheduled to be held on December 10, 1900, in New York City. While the National League executives were in session, Johnson waited patiently in the corridor outside the room. When Johnson stepped outside the building for a brief moment, the National League owners adjourned their meeting, leaving Johnson with his hat in hand. The overt rudeness of the snub made Johnson more determined than ever to wage war on the National League.

Shortly thereafter, Johnson learned that it was more than just a snub. The National League owners had decided to start a minor league in the Midwest to compete directly with the American League. In response, Johnson decided it was time for him to make a pre-emptive strike and move into the cities of the East that the National League had abandoned the year before. As a result, for the 1901 American League season, Johnson abandoned the cities of Minneapolis, Kansas City, Indianapolis and Buffalo, and with money supplied by Charles W. Somers, moved those franchises to Philadelphia, Boston, Baltimore and Washington. Also, John McGraw agreed to help Johnson in Baltimore and Connie Mack was able to get backers for the Philadelphia team. Johnson was now sure that he had the geographical spread that he needed to launch a major league and was ready to sit down with National League owners and work out an agreement.

Another group that had also been given the cold shoulder by the owners at their meeting in New York was the Players Protective Association. The association had recently been formed as a type of union that provided protection against certain practices by owners such as John T. Brush and others that included farming them out during the season. After the players formed their association in June 1900 at a meeting at the Sturtevant House in New York, Samuel Gomphers invited them to join the American Federation of Labor, but the players declined. However, seeing their association wither away before it got a foothold, the group offered to help Ban Johnson, who kept his distance. The National League's freeze on the Players Protective Association worked and it soon disbanded. However, in the long run, the National League's decision may have been a huge mistake.

The players affiliated with the association were not ready to give up on the issues it had been founded upon. In fact, two National League players—Hugh Jennings, a star shortstop, and Chief Zimmer, a veteran catcher—sought out Ban Johnson and asked him if the American League would agree in its contracts to not farm, trade or sell players without the player's consent. Johnson told the press, "Of course I agreed to this. After expressing their friendliness to the American League, they took their departure."[1] It is also believed that in the meeting with Johnson, Jennings and Zimmer told him that at least half the players in the National League were ready to jump their contracts and join the American League. Upon hearing this, Johnson's confidence rose to an unprecedented level in his ability to wage war on the National League. He now knew that he could take the battle to the heart of the National League owners' interests, their gate receipts.

The American League met on January 28, 1901, at the Grand Pacific Hotel in Chicago to discuss its strategy for the coming season. Notable allies of Ban Johnson in attendance included Charles Comiskey, president of the Chicago White Stockings; Charles W. Somers, president of the Boston Invaders; John F. Kilfoyl, president of the Cleveland Blues; and Benjamin F. Shibe, president of the Philadelphia Athletics. At the meeting the league adopted a schedule calling for 140 games in the coming season, and set player limits on teams of 14, to be effective two weeks after the season started. Then the league formally recognized some of the principles established by the Players

Ban Johnson, founder of the American League and president, 1900–1927. National Baseball Hall of Fame Library, Cooperstown, N.Y.

Protective Association, which would immediately cause a flood of National League players to cross over the line and join Ban Johnson, thus establishing the American League as a major. Johnson even made an attempt to persuade the National League's biggest star, Pittsburgh's Honus Wagner, to jump leagues and sent Clark Griffith to Pittsburgh to try and persuade him to sign with the Chicago White Stockings. Wagner refused to meet with Griffith, later stating that he was afraid that if he did, he would have been unable to turn him down.

The most prominent player who jumped leagues for the 1901 season was Napoleon Lajoie. In the 1900 season, Nap Lajoie had batted .346 for the Philadelphia Phillies in the National League. In the 1901 season, Lajoie was joined in the American League by 111 players who had previous experience in the National League. In all, about 30 of the players that switched leagues had been regulars in the National League in 1900. The list of players included Roger Bresnahan, Jimmy Collins, Lou Criger, Mike Donlin, Hugh Duffy, Clark Griffith, Dummy Hoy, Ted Lewis, Joe McGinnity, John McGraw, Fred Parent, Wilbert Robinson, Cy Seymour and Cy Young.

The American League officially opened as a major league on April 24, 1901. While rain postponed three of the four games, the first contest took place in Chicago, where the White Stockings defeated the Cleveland Blues, 8–2. The White Stockings would win the first American League pennant and Nap Lajoie, playing at Philadelphia for Connie Mack, would win the triple crown by leading the league with a .422 batting average, home runs with 14 and RBIs with 125. The .422 batting average by Lajoie still stands as the American League record.

The National League actually attracted more fans through the turnstiles in the 1901 season (1,920,031) than the American League (1,683,584). However, the American League had most definitely established itself as a major league and a state of war did indeed exist between it and the National League. In two out of the three cities where Johnson's American League teams shared occupancy with a National League team, the American League team had the higher season attendance. So confident in the stability of his league was Johnson that he began planning for the 1902 season. He moved the Milwaukee franchise, which had the league's second-lowest attendance total in the 1901 season, to St. Louis, which at the time was the nation's fourth-largest city. He also continued his raid on the National League by attempting to sign its star players.

1901 Attendance Totals

National League	Total Attendance	American League	Total Attendance
Boston	146,502	Baltimore	141,952
Brooklyn	198,200	Boston	289,448
Chicago	205,071	Chicago	354,350
Cincinnati	205,728	Cleveland	131,380
New York	297,650	Detroit	259,430
Philadelphia	234,937	Milwaukee	139,034
Pittsburgh	251,955	Philadelphia	206,329
St. Louis	379,988	Washington	161,661
Total	**1,920,031**		**1,683,584**

The National League was far from laying down in confronting the American League issue. In 1901, the National League had outdrawn the upstart American League in attendance by 236,447 fans and produced an exciting pennant race between Pittsburgh and Philadelphia, with the Pirates finally pulling away in September to win by 7½ games. While the Cincinnati Reds finished in last place in the National League, one game behind the seventh-place New

York Giants, they had a larger gate for the season than four teams in the American League (Baltimore, Cleveland, Milwaukee and Washington).

The New York Mutuals, owned by Brooklyn businessman Bill Cammeyer, had been charter members of the National League in 1876, but the club folded after just one season. In 1883, New York returned to the National League as the Metropolitans, owned by two wealthy fans, Jim Mutrie and John B. Day. It was Mutrie and Day who first called the club's original home grounds on the upper east side of Manhattan the Polo Grounds. In 1885, it was Mutrie who changed the name of the club to the Giants and then managed the team to two National League pennants, in 1888 and 1889. Eventually, Mutrie and Day would sell the club to Andrew Freedman. Jim Mutrie's life would then slowly descend into a tragedy. Years later, when Mutrie had reached his eighties, John McGraw found him living destitute in a shack on the Staten Island waterfront. Mutrie's only source of income was derived from selling newspapers, so McGraw arranged for the New York Giants to pay him a pension.

Andrew Freedman, the owner of the Giants, was a former New York City politician who had served in the corrupt Democrat machine of Tammany Hall, where he had made millions of dollars during his days in public service through questionable deals in subway contracts. In 1895, he bought controlling interest in the New York Giants for $48,000. Immediately, he established himself as the most controversial and hated owner of a major league team. Freedman's management style resembled that of a Banana Republic dictator, and between 1896 and 1902, he hired and fired sixteen managers. He hated newspaper reporters, detested what they wrote about the Giants, and occasionally barred them from the Polo Grounds. But it was Freedman who was in the forefront of taking the battle to Ban Johnson and the American League, and it was he who was keeping the American League from expanding into New York by blocking ballpark sites in the city where a team might be located. In essence, Freedman saw the administrative structure of major league baseball in much the same way that he viewed politics: to control the process, he had to build a strong consensus and squash the opposition into submission.

To that end, one evening in August 1901, Freedman held a meeting at his plush estate in Red Bank, New Jersey, with representatives from the National League teams from Boston, Cincinnati and St. Louis, which he believed to be his supporters. During the meeting Freedman unveiled a plan that he asserted would allow him to control major league baseball. He wanted to establish a trust whereby National League teams would be pooled and owned through shares of common and preferred stock held by club owners. The league would then be governed by a board of regents, all managers would be paid the same salaries, and players could be blacklisted without any reason given. Of course, Freedman himself and a handpicked group of cronies who would actually govern the game. It was, in essence, machine politics morphing into machine baseball.

The practice of club owners having interest in more than one team was a rather common practice at the time. Cincinnati owner John T. Brush, who was supporting Freedman's plan, had been buying shares in the Giants while being the majority stockholder of the Cincinnati Reds. Over in Ban Johnson's new American League, coal, lumber and shipping magnate Charles W. Somers was bankrolling nearly half the league with interests in teams located in Boston, Cleveland, Chicago, and Philadelphia.

When the National League team owners in Brooklyn, Chicago and Philadelphia, along with the outspoken owner of the Pittsburgh Pirates, Barney Dreyfuss, learned of Freedman's proposal, they went ballistic. That winter at the National League meeting in New York, the league's team owners came to loggerheads on whom to elect as league president. The Freedman Trust supporters were behind the incumbent, Nicholas E. Young. However, the four owners opposed to the Freedman plan, holding the belief that Nick Young showed to much favoritism toward the agenda of Freedman, were in favor of electing the game's most respected elder statesman Albert Goodwill Spalding into the league presidency. As the two forces glared at each other across the table, the deadlock in the voting continued through 25 ballots. Finally, John T. Brush and a couple of the other Freedman Trust supporters became tired of it all and abruptly left the meeting. At that point, Albert G. Spalding realized that a quorum existed, decided to seize the moment, and quickly called for another ballot to be taken. With most of the dissidents out of the room, Spalding won. Spalding and a small band of supporters headed straight for the hotel where Nick Young was staying with his wife and seized possession of the league's books and records. The following morning, when Andrew Freedman learned of Spalding's election and the late-night raid on Nick Young's room, he was ready to contest the election results and filed an injunction that prevented Spalding from assuming the presidency of the National League. To avoid being served with the injunction, Spalding shrewdly stayed out of New York.

Meanwhile, Ban Johnson and his American League were preparing for the 1902 season. The National League, at the insistence of Andrew Freedman, had imposed a cap on player's salaries of $2,500 a year. Now with the metamorphous of the American League into a major league, a bidding war broke out to sign players, and the National League, with its traditional high-handed approach to labor relations, was ill-equipped to deal with the art of salary negotiations. Baseball's senior spokesman, Henry Chadwick, writing in the annual edition of *Spalding's Official Baseball Guide*, called the bidding war "a spirit of selfish greed."[2] The consequences were far-reaching, with the Milwaukee club moving into St. Louis. Several of the National League players in that city, such as Jesse Burkett, Bobby Wallace, Dick Padden, Snags Heidreck, Jack Harper and Jack Powell, signed with the St. Louis American League club. Several other National League star players jumped to the American League, including three members of the Philadelphia Phillies: Ed Delahanty, Elmer Flick and Red Donahue. This so weakened the Phillies that in the 1902 season, the club would fall to seventh place after finishing second in 1901 and being in contention for the pennant most of the season.

While Freedman's injunction allowed Nicholas Young to remain as National League president, Albert Spalding traveled around the country making dramatic speeches while winning much praise from the fans and press alike. The National League, however, was effectively left without any real leadership. The business of the league was at a standstill and there was hardly any empowerment in the office of its league president. Andrew Freedman had sealed his own doom, and now pressure was being applied to him by other National League owners to sell his controlling interest in the New York Giants to John T. Brush. On April 3, 1902, with the season fast approaching, the National League owners relieved Nick Young of his duties and appointed a three-man interim committee of John T. Brush, Arthur Soden and James Hart to run the league. However, the committee seldom met, and the actual business of the league was being conducted by Brush without consulting Soden and Hart.

In Cincinnati, John T. Brush was becoming concerned about his last-place franchise. During the 1901 season, the Reds had barely pushed enough fans through the turnstiles of dilapidated League Park (205,728) to out-distance Chicago by 657 fans for the fifth-highest attendance total in the National League. Now Brush wanted out. He had continued to buy stock in the New York Giants and was convinced that Andrew Freedman would have to sell the franchise to him. In fact, Brush had been convinced for several years that it was only a matter of time until Freedman would have to sell the Giants to him. The ongoing relationship between the two men had been absolutely nutty. On one occasion the short-tempered Freedman punched out Brush in the bar of the Fifth Avenue Hotel in New York. In retaliation,

Brush had an associate, Bert Dasher, beat up Freedman in public to send a message that he was not intimidated.

In 1900, a 19-year-old Christy Mathewson had been signed off the Bucknell College campus by the Norfolk club, and after posting a remarkable 20–2 record that season, was sought out by both the Philadelphia Athletics and the New York Giants. Both teams offered Norfolk $1,500 for Mathewson, and after careful deliberation, Mathewson chose the Giants over the Athletics because he believed that the Philadelphia club had a superior pitching staff and therefore he would have a better chance to prove himself in New York. Mathewson joined the New York Giants on July 17, 1900. He pitched mainly in relief and found major league hitters a bit superior to the ones he had faced in Norfolk, finishing the season with 0–3 record with a 4.76 ERA. As Mathewson's contract had been purchased by New York from Norfolk on a conditional basis, at the end of the 1900 season he was returned to that club so Andrew Freedman could recoup his $1,500 expenditure.

John T. Brush truly believed that he was destined, almost ordained, to own the New York Giants. One of the players that Brush coveted to be part of his forthcoming New York Giants club was Christy Mathewson. So when Andrew Freedman sent Mathewson back to Norfolk in the fall of 1900, Brush quickly purchased his contract from the Virginia club for $300, making him property of the Cincinnati Reds. Then on December 15, 1900, in order to have him in place for his eventual ownership, Brush traded Mathewson back to the New York Giants for pitcher Amos Rusie.

Veteran Amos Rusie was no slouch on the mound, and in nine seasons in the National League, he had posted a record of 243–159, even though he missed an entire year when he sat out the 1896 season in a salary dispute with Andrew Freedman over a pittance of $200. However, John T. Brush was aware of the fact that Rusie's glory days were behind him, and that he had arm problems, which would probably end his career very soon. John T. Brush's hunches on both pitchers turned out to be right on the money. In the 1901 season, Christy Mathewson would at one point win eight straight games and post a season record of 20–17 for the Giants. That began his brilliant Hall-of-Fame career in which he would win 30 games four times and 373 games in just 17 years. As for Amos Rusie, he would finish his career in Cincinnati in 1901, pitching in just three games while posting a record of 0–1.

Throughout the 1900 and 1901 seasons, the Cincinnati Reds continued to play their home games in the hideous temporary configuration put in place following the fire that burned most of League Park. Following the 1901 season, John T. Brush hired the architectural firm of Hake and Hake to replace the burned grandstand. The result was a new, elaborate 3,000-seat grandstand made with cement and sculptured iron that was renamed the Palace of the Fans. While the sections of the park that had survived the fire in 1900 were incorporated into the site plan, the new grandstand featured 19 new boxes along the front railing that could seat up to 15 fans with fat wallets. Beneath the grandstand was a section to accommodate 640 less affluent, standing-room fans. This area was near many of the strategically placed bars that sold copious amounts of whiskey and beer (12 glasses for a dollar) and became known as "Rooter's Row," where inebriated fans could stand behind chicken wire, view the game and offer slurred but nonetheless bodacious commentary.

On April 17, 1902, a midst much municipal hoopla and a packed house of 10,000, the Place of the Fans opened at the corner of Findlay Street and Western Avenue with the Chicago Cubs providing the opposition. The players proceeded to the ballpark from downtown in a trolley car parade dressed in their uniforms. Prior to the game, a band concert took place. With Mayor Julius Fleischmann out of town, the honor of addressing the crowd fell upon Judge William Lueders, a man with close associations in the Cox machine-controlled inner-city wards and a leading figure in the German charitable associations of the city. After delivering his lengthily address, a large roar of approval cascaded along the grandstand and across the field from the right field bleachers as Judge Lueders tossed a bright new ball into the waiting hands of Umpire Emslie, who called "play." From there it was all downhill for the Reds' faithful as the Chicago Cubs won the game, 6–1. The next day the *Cincinnati Commercial Tribune* summarized the game by stating, "The crowd came to cheer and root, and early in the game they did both, but no one left the grounds with a sore throat, unless it was inflicted in an effort to explain matters to friends or tell what should have been done to make the Reds a pennant aggregation."[3]

A month later, as Honus Wagner and the defending National League champion Pittsburgh Pirates threatened to run away with the pennant, on Saturday, May 17, 1902, in Cincinnati, the official dedication for the Place of the Fans took place. By this time the Reds, who had fallen to seventh place in the National League pennant race, were just barely keeping a 2½-game distance between themselves and the cellar-dwelling St. Louis club. Fan interest in the new park had already tanked and only 5,000 were on hand for the game with the New York Giants. However, the Cox machine was clearly visible in the ceremony. Seated in the box of John T. Brush were Mayor Julius Fleischmann and Garry Herrmann. In the dedication, Judge Howard Ferris spoke on behalf of the Reds ball club and Mayor Fleischmann accepted the honor on behalf of the fans. In his brief remarks, Fleischmann thanked John T. Brush for building the new grandstand and offered hope for him that in the future it would be filled to an overflowing capacity with fans.

Surely something had to be done with the sad state of baseball in Cincinnati. A fellow who managed the YMCA baseball team in Maysville, Kentucky, was so convinced that his club could beat the Reds that he was ready to bet the ranch on it and had been badgering the *Commercial Tribune* to arrange a game. By 1902, the Cincinnati fans had grown tired of John T. Brush and desired local ownership. The *Commercial Tribune* had been advocating local ownership back to the mid–1890s, when Ban Johnson was the sporting editor. The *Commercial Tribune* even referred to the club as being in foreign possession. The fans were also well aware of Brush's stock ownership in the New York Giants and felt that this conflict of interest prevented him from fielding a competitive team in the Queen City. There also was subtle dislike of Brush in Cincinnati since he had never really purchased the team, but had it laid in his lap when the league took possession of it in 1890 to protect it from the Players' League. However, Garry Herrmann and Mayor Fleischmann had taken notice of the state of Cincinnati baseball and within two months the fans and *Commercial Tribune* would get what they wanted, new ownership and, above all, local ownership.

On the day that the Palace of the Fans was officially dedicated, it was business as usual in Cincinnati baseball and the Reds once again took it on the chin from the Giants, 5–3, as the visitors scored all their runs in the ninth inning and the Reds' best player, clean-up hitter "Wahoo Sam" Crawford, went 0–4. The Reds players simply took another loss in stride. Furthermore, some of them seemed more interested in the superficial aspects of being on a major league team than playing hard. A case in point is what happened in the Reds' clubhouse prior to the dedication day game with the Giants. A few days before, first baseman Jeff Beckley had picked locker No. 1 as his own in the Reds' new clubhouse. All went well until the morning of the dedication game when Reds team captain Tom Corcoran reached the conclusion that his status on the club demanded that he should have locker No. 1. Corcoran attempted to evict Beckley from the space as the two players grappled and pummeled each other into near submission prior to the game. As other players separated the two combatants and the dust settled, Corcoran retreated and selected another locker.

As if the actions of Beckley and Corcoran weren't bad enough, another person who didn't seem too interested in the game was owner John T. Brush. Brush had invited St. Louis team president Frank de Haas Robison to be his guest at the dedication day game. That afternoon, Robinson's St. Louis team was playing Brooklyn. While the Giants' Dummy Taylor and the Reds' Noodles Hahn were locked in a scoreless pitching duel through the first seven innings, Brush had the scoreboard operators in the ballpark play a friendly joke on Robison. After the first inning, the scorekeeper put up five runs for Brooklyn and one for St. Louis. In the third inning, the scorekeeper on Brush's order put up nine runs for Brooklyn and none for St. Louis. The scorekeeper kept elevating the score with six more runs for Brooklyn in the fourth, and seven in the fifth. Eventually, the score escalated to 36 to 2 in favor of Brooklyn before Brush finally let Robison know that he had been duped. As Brush laughed himself silly, Robison remarked, "Well, John, for that I hope that this plaster of Paris shed of yours falls down before the day is out."[4] The actual score in the game had been Brooklyn 9, St. Louis 5.

Meanwhile, the American League season was moving right along, and attendance was good. In mid–May, the Detroit club (although they would soon go into a deep nosedive) was holding a slim lead in an exciting five-team pennant chase over St. Louis, Philadelphia, Boston and Chicago. The National League owners had gone to court in an attempt to reverse some of the contracts. One such owner was Colonel John I. Rogers, who owned the Philadelphia Phillies. Early in the 1902 season, the National League thought it had won a great victory over the American League when the Pennsylvania Supreme Court reversed a lower court decision and ordered Nap Lajoie, Bill Bernhard and Chick Fraser returned to the Philadelphia Phillies, the club that they had jumped from the previous year to join the Philadelphia Athletics. However, only Fraser returned to the Phillies as Ban Johnson quickly transferred Lajoie and Bernhard to Cleveland, thus returning payment to Charlie Somers for some of the financial assistance he had given in establishing the Philadelphia American League franchise. While Lajoie and Bernhard played out the 1902 schedule with Cleveland, they avoided playing in Philadelphia. When the Cleveland club played road games in Philly, the two players idled away the hours in Atlantic City before rejoining the club.

One of the hallmarks of Ban Johnson's operating policies for the American League was that he would hire credible umpires, back them up in disputes, and demand that they be respected by the players. Such an edict was difficult to enforce as professional players had been adversarial in their relationships with the game's umpires since its beginnings. During the early days of the 1902 season, Johnson found it particularly rough-going with players challenging his umpires' decisions. On May 20, Johnson suspended Hugh Duffy of Milwaukee for ten days after he had disputed a decision against his club. Later in the season, Johnson would suspend Baltimore pitcher Joe McGinnity for the rest of the season after he spit in the face of umpire Tommy Connolly, a future member of the Baseball Hall of Fame. But one constant source of trouble for Johnson was the on-field antics of Baltimore manager John McGraw. In June, Johnson suspended McGraw multiple times for run-ins with umpires. However, by early July, Johnson had enough of McGraw's constant harassment of the American League umpiring staff and suspended him indefinitely.

At that moment, John T. Brush saw a grand opportunity to land a haymaker on the American League, and he swung from the hip. On July 8, 1902, the National League scored a major victory in the war with the American League that smacked of collusion. With John McGraw, then 29 years old, having difficulties with Ban Johnson, John T. Brush persuaded him to resign as manager of the Baltimore club and sign with Andrew Freedman to manage the New York Giants. Johnson didn't see this coming and immediately accused McGraw of attempting to wreck the Baltimore franchise. A week later, John T. Brush purchased controlling interest in the Baltimore club and immediately began releasing the best players on the team. Dan McGann, Roger Bresnahan, Joe McGinnity and Jack Cronin signed with the Giants, thus being reunited with McGraw. Then Brush released Mike Donlin, Joe Kelley and Cy Seymour, who all signed with his Cincinnati team.

The purge of the Baltimore roster decimated the team and, on July 17, the Orioles couldn't field a team against St. Louis. There was serious concern that the franchise might not be able to finish its schedule of games and fold. But Ban Johnson fought back.

He invoked a league regulation that enabled him to take possession of the Baltimore franchise. He then pumped life back in the franchise by hiring Wilbert Robinson as manager and overseeing the hiring of replacement players to play out the schedule. In the end, the Baltimore franchise would finish dead last in the 1902 American League pennant race, but the franchise would be preserved and have a glorious future awaiting it.

III

The Machine Buys the Reds

For nearly a century, a romanticized rumor has been circulating in Cincinnati that George B. Cox had been strong-arming John T. Brush to sell him the Cincinnati Reds. The rumor even goes as far as to suggest that Cox threatened to build a new street-car line through the middle of League Park if Brush continued to resist his demands. No substantiation of such a rumor has ever been made, and many people have historically mistaken the antics of Andrew Freedman for those of George B. Cox. Furthermore, the notion of Cox attempting to threaten Brush with street-car tracks running through the center field wall of League Park becomes even more ridiculous when one considers that there were already sufficient street-car lines running outside of League Park. After the controversy with the Cincinnati Traction Company contracts of the late 1880s, it is a pretty safe assumption that George B. Cox didn't want to reopen that can of worms at any cost. The facts are that John T. Brush wanted out Cincinnati baseball and had methodically been putting all the pieces in place to make an exit as soon as possible to enable him to realize his life-long dream of owning major league baseball's most elite franchise of the day, the New York Giants.

Many observers considered Brush as the brains of the National League, and he was aware of the fact that if he was going to dispose of his interest in the Cincinnati Reds, then time was of the essence. Ban Johnson had been watching closely the faltering National League franchise in Cincinnati and had reached the conclusion that the time was right to move into the city. In fact, he had been tempting Garry Herrmann with the offer of a cost-free American League franchise if he entered the conflict and antagonized the National League owners. Herrmann, however, declined the offer. It should behoove the critics of August Garry Herrmann to take notice, that rather than accept an American League franchise for free, he preferred to enter into above-board negotiations for the National League Cincinnati Reds with John T. Brush by means of proper business protocol.

Knowing that the clock was ticking to get the deal done, on Monday, July 28, 1902, Brush traveled to Cincinnati and met with Garry Herrmann and Mayor Julius Fleischmann about disposing of his interest in the Reds as well as that of his minority partner, Ashley Lloyd, a prominent Cincinnati wholesale drug proprietor. As the war between the American and National leagues was nearing a showdown, an attempt to keep the meeting secret was made. But, in Cincinnati, the word of a possible sale of the ball club had been on the street for weeks and the local press was keeping a watchful eye on the movements of Brush and Herrmann.

That Monday evening in a local club, Brush, Herrmann and Fleischmann met privately for several hours, attempting to put the deal together. Late in the evening, John T. Brush named his price. "Mr. Herrmann, I will sell the Cincinnati Baseball Club for $150,000."[1] Although weary from the hours of negotiations, a huge smile appeared on the face of Garry Herrmann. He knew the price tag to purchase about 90 percent of the stock in the ballclub was in the range that his partners, Julius and Max Fleischmann and George B. Cox, could afford. "I will consider your offer, Mr. Brush, and give you an answer Tuesday at 10:30 o'clock."[2]

The next morning at 11:00 A.M., the press observed Garry Herrmann hurriedly entering the St. Nicholas Hotel (later the Sinton Hotel), where John T. Brush was staying. Brush and Herrmann met for a few hours, then emerged into a lobby filled with newspaper reporters anticipating a big news break. "I have nothing to say," said Herrmann. "I refuse to talk," said Brush. However, both men had wide grins in their physiognomies and it was apparent to everyone that the deal was done. Later in the day, reporters caught up with Garry Herrmann at his office in city hall. "I had another long conference with Mr. Brush Tuesday morning, and matters stand just as they did. Mr. Brush has gone to his home in Indianapolis, and will probably not return here for a week or more."[3] The deal was done, but it was a verbal agreement. Now Herrmann had to find a way to finance the purchase of the ball club.

Meanwhile, during the first week, Herrmann traveled to Indianapolis and continued to meet with Brush in an attempt to bring closure to the final outstanding issues on the table blocking the purchase of the Reds. Apparently, Brush, being the successful businessman that he was, still wanted to negotiate a few fine points. However, the paramount issue concerning Brush was that he was still hearing rumors that if he sold the ballclub to Herrmann and his associates, they were going to move the team to the American League. Brush wanted firm assurance from Herrmann that nothing of the kind would happen to the Reds. Herrmann took great strides to assure Brush that the team would remain in the National League and that his primary agenda was to put the ball club in the hands of local ownership.

On his way back from Indianapolis, Herrmann made a stop at the Laughery Club to attend the annual dinner for the club. News was beginning to circulate throughout Cincinnati that the acquisition of the Reds by Garry Herrmann and his partners had been approved by the necessary financial institutions. On the morning of August 9, J. Ed Grillo, a reporter for the *Cincinnati Commercial Tribune*, made a phone call to Herrmann at the Laughrey Club on the Ohio. Herrmann told Grillo that,

> Yes, the deal is closed, and I and my associates now own the Cincinnati club. The formal transfer of the stock has not yet been made, and in fact we do not take possession until next Saturday. The deal has been pending for some time. The reports spread around a week or so ago were decidedly premature, for at that time nothing had been closed and we had no assurance that Mr. Brush would sell to us. However, we have the club now, and we shall devote our attention to giving Cincinnati a great ball team. Everything depends on Manager Kelley in regard to strengthening the team. He is the manager not in name, but in every respect. He shall decide what the team needs and we shall be willing to pay for such material as he may desire. Money is not to be spared. We propose to make extensive improvements at the park. The wooden structures will come down and cement and concrete buildings will go up.
>
> We have our ideas, of course, as to what players we would like to have, but until Manager Kelley has made known his wishes, we shall do nothing. Cincinnati is a great baseball city. I have been a regular attendant at the games, and it struck me some time ago that the interest in the game here was falling off. This, of course, was due to the poor showing the team was making. I talked to my associates, and they agreed with me that Cincinnati should have a better ball team than it has. With that end in view, we bought out Mr. Brush. The game will boom here again. There is sure to be a revival of interest, for we will cater to the public and give the people what they want — a good team and good accommodations. Further than that I can say nothing at this time, but matters will soon so shape themselves. I hope that the public will have substantial proof that we are sincere in our effort to give Cincinnati a winning team."[4]

Most political scientists in their writings on early twentieth century political history in Cincinnati downplay the impact of George B. Cox and August Herrmann in the purchase of the Reds, delegate it to footnote status, or simply choose to ignore it as inconsequential. However, the media of that time had a more positive opinion of the Reds' new ownership. The popular sports paper of the time, the *Sporting Life*, referred to Herrmann, Cox and the Fleischmann brothers (Julius and Max) as the "Big Four." The Cincinnati press was highly in favor of the sale of the Reds to Garry Herrmann's syndicate, too. They regarded Herrmann, Cox and the Fleischmann brothers as able-minded sportsman who would spend the necessary money to bring quality players to the city that would once again make the Reds competitive while continuing the ongoing battle against Ban Johnson and the American League to undermine major league ball.

While it's true that the Reds' new ownership of Garry Herrmann, George B. Cox and Julius and Max Fleischmann were able-minded sportsman, it was also true that the quartet were able-minded politicians as well. The political advantages of the machine buying the Reds were substantial. The four men were well aware of the overwhelming public opinion in Cincinnati that the Reds should have local ownership and how deeply the community from the hilltops to the basin loathed the foreign ownership of John T. Brush. The Herrmann, Cox and Fleischmann brothers coalition recognized a good thing, and the purchase the Reds was as much about securing the political position of the machine with the voters as it was about winning pennants.

The sale of the Reds to the Herrmann, Cox and Fleischmann brothers was widely viewed as a positive commercial venture for Cincinnati in that it would bring many out-of-town visitors to the city, resulting in a boon to the merchants and tradesman in the community. Furthermore, the quartet turned the public perception of the Reds from being one that was occupied by foreign ownership into an inclusionary community enterprise. Almost as the ink was drying on the purchase agreement, Garry Herrmann announced that the new owners had no intention of retaining all the stock in the club and would make ample shares available for interested parties in Cincinnati to buy into, provided they retained controlling interest. It was the economic workings of the machine trickling down at its finest. It was patronage for the upper classes.

The following morning, on August 10, 1902, the purchase of the Cincinnati franchise by the Herrmann, Cox, and Fleischmann brothers coalition was officially announced. That evening the baseball faithful of Cincinnati, who had loathed the ownership of John T. Brush for so long, celebrated. When the sun went down, a long procession of cheering devotees of the Reds marched through the streets of downtown Cincinnati accompanied by red fires and music. The sale of the ball club seemed to mirror the celebration of a huge election victory.

In order to obtain the necessary funding for the purchase of the ball club, Herrmann had arranged for loans of $85,000, in addition to cash put up mainly by Cox and the Fleischmann brothers. However, Garry Herrmann, made perpetually cash-poor by his penchant for lavish entertaining, also scraped a few bucks together to buy into the deal. That morning a certified check for the amount of $150,000 was sent to John T. Brush via the Fletcher Bank in Indianapolis. About noon, Garry Herrmann received a long-distance call at the Laughery Club in Indiana from officials at the Lafayette Bank in Cincinnati, informing him that the stock for the Reds ballclub had been turned over to the bank and was being held for the coalition. In actuality, the coalition owned $11/12$ of the stock as a few minority owners who still owned $1/12$ refused to sell their interest in the ballclub.

The date for the official transfer of the stock to the new owners was set for August 16. The reorganization of a major league team in 1902 was much different than one that would take place today. At that time, the bare-bones organizational structure consisted of an owner who served as the president, a business manager or traveling secretary, a team manager, perhaps a few scouts and one stenographer, even though the use of typewriters was rare and most correspondence was scrawled in longhand. There were no modern farm systems, and bonuses paid to players were rare. Of course, in the formation of the new Cincinnati Reds' organization, it was a foregone conclusion that August Garry Herrmann would be chosen as the president. Also, Frank Bancroft was retained from the Brush ownership as business manager and Joe Kelley as the manager.

Joe Kelley, an outfielder and future member of the Baseball Hall of Fame, was an established major league star player who had played with John McGraw on the famous Baltimore teams that dominated the National League in the 1890s. Kelley was blessed with good looks. In fact, he was so vain that he carried a mirror in his pocket when playing the outfield to check for any hairs out of place. He was also a great hitter that finished a 19-year career with 2,224 hits and a .319 batting average. In 1893, Kelley had batted .393. On September 3, 1894, he went nine-for-nine at bat in a doubleheader. In the first game, Kelley had three singles and a triple and in the nightcap he had four doubles and a single. In 1899, he signed with Brooklyn and had three outstanding seasons. Then in February 1902, his father-in-law, John K. Mahon, purchased stock in Baltimore's American League franchise and offered some of the stock to Kelley. Kelley abandoned the Brooklyn club to sign with Baltimore and thus be reunited with John McGraw.

In May, John T. Brush traveled to Baltimore and checked in at the Stafford Hotel under an assumed name. He then spoke with Joe Kelley about becoming manager to replace embattled Reds skipper John A. McPhee, if not during the 1902 season, then possibly in the 1903 campaign. The Cincinnati press was saying that Kelley would come to Cincinnati and be given carte blanche to reorganize the club anyway he saw fit. However, Kelley was a stockholder in the Baltimore club and was quoted as saying that he wanted to stay put. When the Cincinnati press contacted Kelley in Baltimore, he stated, "There is no truth in the report that I will manage Cincinnati next season. I expect to end my baseball career in Baltimore. I own stock in the club and we are having a good season."[5] In July, when John McGraw left Baltimore for New York and the subsequent purge of players from the Orioles' roster began, Kelley was released from his contract with Baltimore and the process was put in motion for him to become manager of the Reds.

For several days prior to the official announcement of the sale of the Reds, Mayor Julius Fleischmann had been in New York. On August 9, Fleischmann left New York on his private yacht for Boston. The Reds were playing on a road trip in Boston, and when Fleischmann arrived there, he invited Joe Kelley to join him for a conference on his boat. The Reds' new ownership coveted retaining Kelley in the role of manager and were concerned that his loyalties might still be with John T. Brush. To that end, Julius Fleischmann decided that the best way to convince Kelley to remain with the Reds was to mimic the persuasion skills of Garry Herrmann. So, with Kelley aboard, Fleischmann's yacht was taken to sea and the Reds' manager was entertained royally. When they docked several hours later, Joe Kelley was committed to being the Reds' manager.

The 1902 Cincinnati Reds finished in fourth place in the National League with a record of 70–70, 33½ games behind the Pittsburgh Pirates. Under new manager Joe Kelley, the team had a record of 33–26. The Reds had slightly improved in the attendance department as they drew 217,300, an improvement of about 12,000 fans over the 1901 season. However, the Palace of the Fans lacked in seating, thereby depressing the total. But the Reds had a lot of potential on the field with a club featuring Noodles Hahn, who had finished with a record of 22–12, and five players who hit over .300 with Cy Seymour (.349), Jake Beckely (.331), Sam Crawford (.333), Heinie Peitz (.315) and Joe Kelley (.321), who inserted himself in the lineup as a utility player.

John T. Brush was glad to be out of Cincinnati. On September 9, 1902, Brush purchased controlling interest in the New York Giants from Andrew Freedman for $200,000. At the time, a rumor persisted that Brush was lacking the necessary funds to consummate the deal, so the other owners in the National League lent him the money to rid themselves of Andrew Freedman.

IV

The National Commission

As the 1902 season progressed, attendance in American League ballparks was strong and steady, and Ban Johnson turned up the heat on the National League. The Philadelphia Athletics scheduled ten games at home on days the Philadelphia Phillies were also playing at home. Despite the loss of Nap Lajoie, the Philadelphia Athletics under manager Connie Mack were still a formidable club, featuring six .300 hitters. The pitching on the Athletics was exciting, too, featuring two 20-game winners. The end result was the Athletics outdrew the Phillies at the gate on those dates by 59,367 to 6,928.

In the end, the American League won the quest for the fans in 1902, racking up a season total attendance of 2,200,457 compared to the National League total of 1,681,212. Furthermore, in the three cities where competing National and American League teams went head-to-head for fan support, the American League had the higher attendance in all three cities. In Philadelphia, where the year before, in 1901, the National League Phillies had outdrawn the American League Athletics by 28,608 fans, the tables were turned with the Athletics outdistancing the Phillies in attendance. There was no doubt in anyone's mind that Ban Johnson's American League was a major league. The National League knew it was in trouble, but at the moment didn't know what to do in order to bring peace.

But having such an astute politician as August Garry Herrmann enter the major league war on the side of the National League was not good news for Ban Johnson. Notwithstanding the ongoing war with the American League, Garry Herrmann was well suited to lead the Reds' day-to-day operations, too. Although he was mired down with his duties as the chairman of the waterworks commission and attempting to complete construction of the city's long-awaited and controversial new water plant, Herrmann dove head-first into his baseball duties. Being a politician, Herrmann knew the value of the press and immediately began to court them. Out-of-town baseball writers arriving in Cincinnati to cover Reds games may not have witnessed the best baseball in the National League, but they certainly were the best entertained baseball writers in the National League and perhaps in all of organized ball.

When writers were in town for a weekday series, in the evening they would be escorted by Garry Herrmann to the Peruvian Club. On Saturday nights, the visiting press was invited to join Garry out at the Laughry Club. Saturday nights at the Laughry with Herrmann became legendary as the fun and frolic extended nearly till dawn. Writers at the Laughry could expect a never-ending flow of bourbon and beer. Also, copious amounts of burgoo, a thick soup and a Herrmann favorite, were served up. At exactly midnight, a Laughry ritual would take place. A circus wagon was pulled in with the shade down. Then the assembled bleary-eyed mass would all join in a chorus, singing the old folk tune "Cousin Nellie." Suddenly, the shade on the wagon was pulled up to reveal the "Belle of the Ball." No one seems to recall just how the maiden was dressed, so one can only speculate. Eventually everyone retired to a private bungalow just in time to catch a few winks before heading back up the Ohio River to the Sunday doubleheader at the Palace of the Fans.

Garry Herrmann was already one of the most recognizable persons in the city of Cincinnati. Now he was about to step onto the national stage and would soon assume a reputation of considerable stature throughout the country. When one considers the ultimate impact that Garry Herrmann would have on the game of major league baseball, it is somewhat mind-boggling that so little has been written about his life. In 1962, sportswriter Dan Daniel stated,

> There never again will be another Herrmann, any more than there will be another Barney Dreyfuss, another Charley Ebbets or the likes of Steve and Ed McKeever, his feuding partners. There will never be another Chris Von der Ahe, who headed the St. Louis N.L. club from 1892–1897.
>
> Garry Herrmann was a figure out of feudal Germany of the Middle Ages. From 1903 to 1920 he was the chairman of the National Commission. But, about baseball intrigue and cloak-and-dagger, he knew little if anything. It is to be regretted that there is no expanded profile of Garry. His baseball writing companions in Cincinnati generally were too busy having a good time on their own to be bothered about setting down the details of the life and times of August Herrmann.[1]

Ban Johnson knew that it was only a matter of time before the National League would seek peace. However, the olive branch was extended by the National League even quicker than he anticipated. In December 1902, St. Louis Cardinals president Frank de Haas Robison was en route to New York City for the National League's annual meeting. When he discovered that American League owners Charles W. Somers of Boston and John F. Kilfoyl of Cleveland were also aboard the same train, he sat down with them and began to discuss the state of the current circumstances in major league baseball. As the three men got off the train in Manhattan, Robison promised that he would approach his National League colleagues with the suggestion of attempting to reach a peaceful solution in the war between the two leagues.

Charles W. Somers and John F. Kilfoyl were traveling to New York for a meeting with Ban Johnson to discuss moving the struggling Baltimore franchise to New York. Robison was aware of their mission, and when the National League owners met at the Victoria Hotel, he expressed his opinions explicitly on attempting to reach an accord with the American League. No one had suffered more than Robison in the war with the American League. His team was decimated by signing raids on his players and by having another franchise move into his city to compete for attendance dollars. Robison stood up before his National League brethren and stated, "I have made greater sacrifices and lost more money in the war than any of you, with the possible exception of Colonel Rogers (Philadelphia Phillies). I am tired of a fight that can only result in continued loss and ultimate ruin to all parties involved. I am in favor of opening negotiations with the American League, which I have reason to believe will be favorably received."[2]

A silence fell upon the meeting room. Prior to becoming the operating partner of the Reds, Garry Herrmann had observed the struggles of John T. Brush in Cincinnati as he tried to keep the Reds' franchise solvent. Herrmann had been approached by Ban Johnson with a lucrative offer of a no-cost American League franchise in Cincinnati if he would simply enter the war and attempt to crush the Reds' operations. But now as an owner of a National League club, he viewed a peace settlement as a rational course of action. Herrmann felt that there was sufficient population in the East to support two leagues as long as their schedules didn't conflict. He viewed the war as harmful to everyone in baseball and saw a peace settlement with the American League as a business opportunity for his franchise. He was also deeply moved by the passion for peace that was expressed by Robison and rose to address the meeting. "I see no sense in continuing the war for the sake of pride and stubbornness," said Herrmann. "What's the use of us fighting each other, when the crowd is on the bleachers yelling, 'Play Ball'?"[3]

Colonel John I. Rodgers of Philadelphia and James A. Hart of Chicago also agreed with Robison that the time to negotiate with the American League had arrived. The National League owners came to the conclusion that since Ban Johnson was in town at the same time, they should seek him out expeditiously and discuss his terms. Garry Herrmann was considered by his National League peers to be an old friend of Ban Johnson. Whether or not that was an entirely accurate assumption is irrelevant. The fact was Herrmann had known Johnson from his newspaper reporting days in Cincinnati and there was less bad blood existing between he and Johnson than most of the other National League owners. Therefore, Herrmann was chosen to lead the delegation that included Robison and Hart.

Ban Johnson was staying at the Criterion Hotel, and with quickness of dispatch, Herrmann, Robison and Hart jumped in a cab and headed over to speak with him. When they arrived, they found Johnson in the dining room with Kilfoyl. Johnson was astonished when he learned of the nature of the delegation's visit. He told Herrmann and his colleagues that he was in no position to give them any answers without consulting with the American League owners. Actually, Ban Johnson knew exactly what he wanted, for he had been fighting the war with the National League for several years and now had them right where he wanted them. He also was holding 51 percent of the stock for each American League club in a vault in his Chicago office to ensure no defections of clubs. He was in complete control of the matter and his allusion to seeking out the advice of the American League owners was unmitigated subterfuge. However, as a courtesy, Johnson assured the trio that he would get back to them within twenty-four hours. That being the situation, Garry Herrmann suggested that his delegation adjourn to the Criterion bar and make small talk over slow gin fizzes. The following morning, after calling Herrmann, Ban Johnson requested A. J. Fanner, an editor of the *Sporting News*, and Dick Mockler of the *St. Louis Globe-Democrat* to draft a peace treaty. A couple of weeks later when the proofs arrived, Johnson carefully perused them and determined that it wasn't necessary to change one single word. Immediately copies of the proposal were distributed to all involved parties and a peace conference was scheduled to take place at Cincinnati in early January 1903.

Meanwhile, the National League continued to meet in New York for five days. Rather than be proactive and decide how they were going to approach the impending meeting with Johnson and agree on vesting their delegation with the proper authority to negotiate a comprehensive peace settlement, the National League owners fell back on their blighted history and began considering ways to break up the American League or, at least, neutralize it. In a sense it was 1891 all over again. In fact, one of the members selected for the National League negotiating team was James A. Hart of Chicago, who along with John T. Brush and the late Charles Byrne of Brooklyn had represented the league in the 1891 fiasco held at Washington.

It had been Garry Herrmann's first official visit to New York as president of the Cincinnati Reds and he did it up big in grand "Herrmann style." He took a suite of rooms at the Waldorf Astoria and entertained lavishly. It would become a Herrmann tradition for the next two decades. When Herrmann entered the Waldorf's dining room in the morning and ordered his favorite Cincinnati Teutonic-style breakfast repast of fried pigs feet, the waiter was stunned and apologized for not having it available. But Herrmann was persistent, and after waiting for a time, the order was produced. The Waldorf then added fried pigs feet to its beefsteak menu.

As the date for the peace conference in Cincinnati drew near, Ban Johnson exploited the National League owners' inaction. He viewed their approach to the peace settlement as half-hearted by not providing the National League committee with a universal mandate to exercise final authority on all matters on the table. Johnson was of the mindset to take no prisoners in his final battle with the Nationals. However, Garry Herrmann knew how to play the game, too, and had been down this road many times in matters of Cincinnati politics and municipal dealings. Therefore, in an attempt to neutralize Johnson's attempts to cast a shadow of doubt on the pending conference, on January 4, 1903, Herrmann released the following statement to the Associated Press.

> It seems from the telegraphic dispatches from Chicago that an erroneous impression has been made relative to the National League committee. It has been intimated that the committee has not been delegated with authority to act. The contrary is the fact. Our committee has been given full power by the large majority of our clubs, and I so notified Mr. Johnson in my letter last Friday. The committee however prefers not fully and finally to exercise that power without reserving the right on their part to confer with their colleagues or business partners on the important matters that may present themselves during the conferences, with the understanding, however, that they will take such steps as will enable them at any time during the conferences to reach their colleagues without a moments delay.
>
> This action on our part has been taken for the reason that the club owners in our league have not been in consultation with reference to any of the important matters that undoubtedly would present themselves during the conferences, and we therefore, believe that it is only fair and reasonable that we should reserve the right to confer with those whose financial interests are at stake before coming to any final conclusion on important matters until they have had an opportunity to express their views, notwithstanding the fact that we have been given full power to act. By taking this action there will be no question but that the findings will be concurred in.
>
> If a reasonable reservation of this kind is to be a barrier to peace negotiations, then I cannot comprehend that the other side is anxious to secure it. The National League wants peace. In obtaining it there will be no objection on our part to have a fair, a frank and open discussion of all of the points about which there may be a difference of opinion.[4]

Despite attempts by Herrmann to counteract the propaganda and doubt being spread by Johnson on the forthcoming negotiations, in some cities the dye was already cast for suspicion. In Philadelphia during 1902, both the fans and press had experienced first-hand the superior quality of the ball played in the American League and were already climbing up on the battlements to defend Ban Johnson in the negotiations. The *Philadelphia Inquirer* was particularly stinging in its opinions leading up to the peace conference.

> It's the same old National League. It can no more change its tactics than the leopard can change its spots. The magnates never were noted for directness in their base ball dealings. They always preferred shooting around Robin Hood's barn, and invariably clothed their acts with an air of mystery which with some misguided persons, passes for business, penetration and wisdom. This has been demonstrated in the dealings looking to a peace conference which was set for today. When Mr. Herrmann, acting as chairman of the committee appointed by the National League to sue for peace with the American, he was courteously received by President Johnson, who assured him that his proposition would receive the attention that its importance demanded, but he also assured him that inasmuch as the American League, anticipating such a move on the part of the National, had already delegated him — Mr. Johnson — as a committee of one, with power to act, no conference would be held with a committee of the National League unless that committee was also clothed with power to act. Mr. Johnson made himself clear on that point to every one.
>
> Mr. Herrmann, who is a shrewd, hard-headed man of affairs, really believed that the National would grant to its committee full power to act. That he was mistaken is shown by the developments

of the past two or three days. It is the same old National League. It never has, and possibly never will learn anything by experience. It is trying to work the same old gag that it did in the Washington conference in 1891.[5]

Despite the rebukes and hype of the eastern press, as well as the constant threats, demands and excuses of Ban Johnson, Garry Herrmann held firm and went about the business of keeping the peace conference on track. With too many outstanding issues up in the air, the original date for the peace conference, set for Monday, January 5, came and passed. Subsequently, Herrmann set a firm date for negotiations to begin on Friday, January 9. All roads now led to Cincinnati, and Ban Johnson, knowing that it was time to put up or shut up, sent a telegram to Herrmann stating that the American League delegation would arrive in Cincinnati on Friday, January 9 and be staying at the Grand Hotel, where they would have a preliminary conference. He also informed Herrmann that the American League would be adding Charles Comiskey, the owner of the Chicago White Stockings, as a fourth member to the committee that already included Charles Somers, John F. Kilfoyl and himself. Herrmann then went about arranging for a suitable site for the conference at the St. Nicholas Hotel (later named the Sinton Hotel) that would accommodate the large number of newspaper correspondents expected to chronicle the proceedings and be a possible site for a big celebration should the two parties reach an agreement.

On Thursday, January 8, Pittsburgh owner Barney Dreyfuss arrived in Cincinnati and arranged a hurried meeting with Herrmann. It was a fact that no other National League owner had more at stake in the pending peace conference than Dreyfuss. Johnson was threatening to place an American League franchise in Pittsburgh, where the Pirates were dominating the National League in play and were a considerable draw at the gate. As Herrmann prepared to sit down and confer with Dreyfuss, he received a telegram from Robison advising him that he would arrive in Cincinnati that evening.

As Ban Johnson had added a fourth member to the American League negotiating committee, Herrmann also had to add another member. At the moment the National League committee consisted of Frank de Haas Robison of St. Louis, James A. Hart of Chicago and Herrmann. At the National League meeting that past fall in New York, the interim committee (Board of Control) that had administered the National League during the 1902 season had been dissolved on a motion by Chicago owner James A. Hart and the presidency restored. Harry Pulliam was then elected unanimously as president. At once Pulliam sold his stock in the Pittsburgh Pirates and assumed his new duties, leading to his appointment by Herrmann as the fourth member of the National League Committee.

Following a short morning conference between Garry Herrmann and Ban Johnson, on Friday afternoon at 2:00 P.M., January 9, 1903, the delegations from the National and American leagues finally sat down together in the St. Nicholas Hotel and began negotiations. Meanwhile, Barney Dreyfuss made himself comfortable in the hotel lobby while entertaining the press. Many prominent sportswriters of the time were in Cincinnati covering the peace conference, including Joe Jackson of the *Detroit Free Press*, Frank Hough of the *Philadelphia Inquirer*, Frank McQuisten of the *Pittsburgh Dispatch*, Gus Axelson of the *Chicago Record-Herald*, Ed Bernard of the *Columbus Dispatch* and A.J. Flanner of the *Sporting News*. To idle away the hours while the committees met, Dreyfuss held court with the reporters, amusing them with stories not only about himself, but also Harry Pulliam and other baseball notables.

As the first day of negotiations commenced, news began leaking out of the session that the suspicions of Ban Johnson and the Philadelphia press had been correct. The National League committee was being pressured by John T. Brush, representing three of the eight

Hotel Sinton, Cincinnati, Ohio.

National League club owners, to revert to the same old tactic the league had used in the negotiations of 1891 to neutralize the American Association by consolidating the two leagues into one twelve-team circuit. The amalgamation proposal put on the table by the National League was the following: In the East the new league would consist of the National League teams from Boston, New York and Brooklyn. From the American League would be the teams of Baltimore, Philadelphia and Washington. In the West the National League would keep its teams from Chicago, Cincinnati and Pittsburgh, while the American would send its teams from Cleveland, Detroit and St. Louis.

Immediately Ban Johnson let it be known to all present that he was adamantly opposed to league consolidation and demanded that the two leagues remain in tact or he would walk out. However, the issue was fast becoming moot as five of the National League club owners, including Garry Herrmann, had previously stated that they were in favor of keeping two leagues. With the amalgamation ploy off the table, Herrmann directed the discussion to the territory question. The National League was against any American League club being placed in either Pittsburgh or New York and was concerned about the American League's intended franchise shift from Baltimore to New York. For the moment, Johnson stalled on this matter, simply stating that he was against any territory restrictions and was not placing any restrictions on the National League to invade any city an American League club already occupied.

At 6:00 P.M. the committees adjourned for dinner in a private dinning room at the St. Nichols. The newspaper reporters surrounded Garry Herrmann and asked him for an update on the negotiations. Herrmann told the assembled mass, "We have just been talking the situation over. I hardly think that there will be anything to give out today, but I feel very much encouraged. The best of feeling seems to exist between the two committees, and that certainly is worth something. We are all on good terms and both sides are expressing candid opinions. In this way we expect to get at the right way to settle this war. It may be that we will be in session here for several days, for there are many things to be considered."[6]

More than just a peace settlement was being negotiated in the conference. The fact of the matter was that as the assembled parties from the two leagues sorted through their differences, a bonding was taking place, and friendships were being molded. Also, everyone was pleasantly surprised by the leadership ability demonstrated by Garry Herrmann. The American League delegation had the utmost confidence in Herrmann to pilot the peace negotiations through any turbulent waters that may lie ahead. Charles Comiskey, emerging from the conference room, exuded an air of confidence in the peace negotiations. "Well, of course, I don't know what will be done finally, but just now it looks to me as if there will be no trouble of finding a way of settling this thing. I like the way Mr. Herrmann talks in the meeting. He tells what he thinks and don't waste much time about it, either. Of course, we have only been talking matters over in a general way, but it is evident that the best of feeling exists between the two committees and that is what makes me feel encouraged. I don't see anything now to hamper our getting together on agreeable terms."[7]

Although Comiskey had previously lived in Cincinnati and managed the Reds in the early 1890s, he had never been formally introduced to August Garry Herrmann. The baseball peace conference in 1903 was the first opportunity for Comiskey to actually meet Herrmann, and he was immediately impressed with his demeanor. "This man Herrmann is so different from the other men who have been leaders in the National League that I am really surprised, and agreeably so," remarked Comiskey. "That fellow talks right. He has a way of getting at things

Opposite: The Hotel Sinton, Cincinnati. Author's collection.

in a jiffy, and he talks in a candid, straightforward way. If it is left to Mr. Herrmann, I think that there will never be another baseball war."[8]

At 8:30 P.M. the conference went back into session. During the evening session, the question was raised of how the disputed players' contracts would be settled. Several players had already signed two contracts. One such disputed player that was of great interest to the Cincinnati club and its fans was Sam Crawford. Following the 1902 season, Crawford, who had led the Reds in hitting with a (.333) average and led the league in triples (23) and total bases (256), signed a contract with Detroit in the American League. Garry Herrmann then enticed him to remain in Cincinnati and signed him to a National League contract for the 1903 season. There were many similar cases that would have to be negotiated between the two committees, including such star players as Ed Delahanty. Prior to the announcement of the peace conference, Delahanty had signed a two-year contract with John T. Brush to play for the New York Giants. However, Delahanty was already under a two-year contract with Washington, where he had led the American League in hitting in 1902 with a .376 average. In all, it was determined that sixteen players had disputed contracts between teams in the two leagues. Lastly, it was decided that all official statements to the press in regard to the proceedings would be made by Garry Herrmann. At 10:00 P.M., Herrmann called adjournment to the first day's sessions, with the parties agreeing to sit down again the following morning at 10:00 A.M.

By Friday evening, the lobby and bar of the St. Nicholas Hotel had become filled with baseball moguls, notables and reporters. John E. Bruce and C.J. McDiarmid, both attorneys from the American League St. Louis club, had arrived in town. The two were not only stockholders in the St. Louis club, but also the American League's legal advisors. At the peace conference, Bruce would play a pivotal role by assisting Ban Johnson in writing the National Agreement. Bruce also had Cincinnati connections. Although a native of Cleveland, the 35-year-old Bruce had moved to Cincinnati to practice law. Before becoming affiliated with the St. Louis club of the American League, Bruce had resided in the Cincinnati satellite community of College Hill where he served as mayor for several years. College Hill would be annexed into the city of Cincinnati piecemeal in 1911, 1915, and 1923. At the conclusion of the peace conference, Bruce would be appointed as secretary-treasurer of the National Commission.

Also staying at the St. Nicholas was Charles "Kid" Nichols, who between 1890 and 1901 had won 328 games pitching for Boston in the National League, including seven consecutive 30-win seasons. At that time Nichols was managing the Kansas City team and had been traveling throughout Indiana scouting players and decided to stop by to get the latest information of the peace negotiations first-hand. In 1904, Nichols would return to the mound for St. Louis of the National League and post a season record of 21–13. He continued to pitch through the 1906 season, finishing his big league career with a record of 360–203. In 1949, Nichols was elected to the National Baseball Hall of Fame.

Also roaming the lobby of the St. Nicholas Hotel was Billy Hart, the former mayor of the Cincinnati satellite community of Bond Hill. During 1903, under the administration of Mayor Julius Fleischmann, the communities of Bond Hill, Hyde Park, Evanston, Winton Place and a small strip of land near Avondale would be annexed into the city of Cincinnati. Out of a job in politics, Hart became manager of the Peoria team. Now he was seeking a new job in baseball while hanging out in the lobby of the St. Nicholas and rubbing shoulders with the major league magnates.

When the two committees came together the next morning, it was clear to everyone that in actuality there were only two issues separating the sides. One was the question of the Baltimore franchise shift to New York and the National League's determination to keep the American League out of both Pittsburgh and New York. The other was the issue of the disputed players' contracts. With the realization that the two parties were so close in reaching accord, the room was filled with an air of optimism. As the meeting reached a critical point, Garry Herrmann kept everyone's focus on the ultimate outcome and avoided a breakdown in negotiations when Ban Johnson offered a compromise stating that the American League would not attempt to place a franchise in Pittsburgh if the National League agreed to allow the transfer of the Baltimore franchise to New York. The matter was resolved, and Barney Dreyfuss had the "Steel City" all to himself. The two parties moved on to other matters and discussed the possibility of inter-league play and the pledge to honor players' contracts with a club as binding (the reserve clause). Hence, no player could jump from one league to the other. Also discussed was the agreement that each league would use the same rules and play a schedule created by a commission having oversight authority on the two leagues (the National Commission).

The matter of disputed players' contracts was resolved with both leagues making sacrifices. However, in the end it appeared that the American League got the better of the deal. Herrmann gave up his claim to Sam Crawford, and it was agreed that Ed Delahanty would have to honor his Washington contract. Brooklyn was hit hard by the agreement, losing both hitting star Willie Keeler to the New York American League club and pitcher Wild Bill Donovan to Detroit. In resolving the player contracts on a case by case basis, the American League wound up with nine of the players: Ed Delahanty, Sam Crawford, Alfonso Davis, Kid Elberfeld, Willie Keeler, Wid Conroy, Bill Donovan, Nap Lajoie, and Dave Fultz. The National League was awarded seven players: Vic Willis, Tommy Leach, Harry Smith, Rudy Hulswitt, Sandow Mertes, Frank Bowerman and Christy Mathewson. Also, the American League was still smarting over the actions of John T. Brush during the previous season when he arbitrarily weakened the Baltimore club by moving players to Cincinnati and New York. Therefore, to prevent further actions of this type, the American League demanded that a clause be included in the agreement that stated no club would be allowed to release any players for the intended purpose of weakening itself or the league.

By 4:00 P.M. the two committees were satisfied that an accord had been reached, and Garry Herrmann sent for two typists and typewriters to begin pecking out the agreement for signatures. The war between the National League and American League had ended. An expensive conflict that had lasted two years took just fifteen hours to end. In the negotiation process, a new star in major league baseball had risen, August Garry Herrmann. The following morning, the *Cincinnati Commercial Tribune* stated in its Sunday edition,

> Every man who emerged from the conference chambers tonight was loud in his praises of Herrmann. Every man gave him full credit for all that was accomplished. Both sides of the question praised him for the fairness, business judgment and integrity that he displayed. Herrmann was voted a most remarkable man by them. Modest to an extreme, Herrmann came out of the conference a great man in baseball. All other leaders of the National League were overshadowed by him. His manner of doing business was a revelation to the baseball world, and it is all the more remarkable when the fact is taken into consideration that Mr. Herrmann has only been identified with the game a very few months. Every question that arose was always left to Mr. Herrmann to settle. There were disputes, or discussions, as you please to call them, which were invariably left to Mr. Herrmann to decide, and he did it in a very few words and to the satisfaction of all concerned. Every man in that conference deserves credit for having done a noble turn for baseball, but above them all stands August Herrmann. It was he who made the conference possible, and it was he who settled in a very short time the questions which have kept the two leagues apart.[9]

In 1908, after working with Garry Herrmann for five years on the National Commission, John E. Bruce would remark, "I'd be willing to take every one of Mr. Herrmann's findings to the Supreme Court of the United States and I don't believe he'd be reversed in any case. He has been eminently fair, and from a judicial point of view his decisions rank as models."[10]

Harry Pulliam, the new National League president, called for a special meeting of the league's club owners in Cincinnati on January 19 to ratify the agreement and agree on the new schedule of 140 games. Likewise, Ban Johnson, the American League president, called for a special meeting of that circuit's owners to take place in New York later in the month. The National Agreement also called for the establishment of an oversight committee to administer the agreement and settle disputes between the two leagues and its players. Named in the agreement to carry out this responsibility were both league presidents, Pulliam and Johnson. After ratification, August Garry Herrmann would be added as the third member to the committee. It would have the responsibility of overseeing the National Agreement and thus be known as the National Commission, which the press immediately started to refer as baseball's supreme court. Herrmann was no doubt singled out for this job by the absolute commanding job he had performed in chairing the Cincinnati peace talks. The two league presidents and Herrmann then asked the editor of the *Sporting News*, Joe Flanner, to formally write the National Agreement. The document was then set in type by hand at the paper's composing room and a proof submitted to Harry Pulliam. Pulliam was totally satisfied with the document and made no changes. The peace agreement negotiated in Cincinnati on January 9–10, 1903, read as follows:

Cincinnati, O., Jan. 10.

At a prior date the National League and American Association of Professional Base Ball Clubs having appointed a committee, and the American League of Professional Base Clubs having appointed a committee, the object and purpose being for said committee to meet, discuss and agree upon a policy to end any and all differences now existing between the said two leagues; and said committee of the National League, consisting of Harry C. Pulliam, August Herrmann, James A. Hart and Frank de Haas Robison, and said committee of said American League, consisting of B. B. Johnson, Charles A. Comiskey, Charles W. Somers and H. J. Killilea, and said committees, having met at the St. Nicholas Hotel in the city of Cincinnati, on January 9, 1903, and continued in session until this 10th day of January, 1903, and after fairly and fully discussing all complaints and matters of grievances and abuses growing out of the present base ball conditions and having in mind the future welfare and preservation of the national game, have unanimously agreed as follows:

FIRST.— Each and every contract hereafter entered into by the clubs of either league with players, managers or umpires shall be considered as valid and binding.

SECOND.— A reserve rule shall be recognized, by which each and every club may reserve players under contract, and that a uniform contract for the use of each league shall be adopted.

THIRD.— After a full consideration of all contract claims by each and every club, it is agreed that the list hereto attached marked exhibits "A" and "B" is the correct list of the players legally awarded to each club. Exhibit "A" being the list of American League players and exhibit "B" being the list of National League players.

FOURTH.— It is agreed that any all sums of money received by any player from any club other than the club to which he is awarded by the exhibit hereto attached shall be returned forthwith to the club so advancing said sums and until all said sums of money so advanced are returned said player shall not be permitted to play with any club in either league.

FIFTH.— The circuits of each league shall consist of the following clubs: American League— Boston, New York, Philadelphia, Washington, Cleveland, Detroit, Chicago and St. Louis. National League— Boston, New York, Brooklyn, Philadelphia, Pittsburg, Chicago, St. Louis and Cincinnati. Neither circuit shall be changed without the consent of the majority of the clubs of each league. It is further provided that there shall be no consolidation in any city where two clubs exist; nor shall any club transfer or release it players for the purpose of injuring or weakening the league of which it is a member.

SIXTH.— On or before the first day of February of each year the president of each league shall appoint a Schedule Committee of three each, who shall be authorized to prepare a schedule of games to be played during the championship season by each in each league. This schedule shall be submitted by the committee within three weeks after their appointment to each league for their ratification and adoption. This committee shall be authorized — if they deem the same advisable — to provide for a series of championship games between all of the clubs of both leagues.

SEVENTH. — On or before the first day of February of each year the president of each league shall appoint a Committee on Rules of three each, who shall be authorized to prepare uniform playing rules. These shall be submitted by the committee within three weeks, after their appointment to each league for their ratification and adoption.

EIGHTH. — It is further agreed that said two leagues herein before mentioned shall enter into a national agreement embodying the conditions and agreements hereinbefore set forth; and it is further agreed that Presidents B. B. Johnson and Harry C. Pulliam be, and they are, hereby appointed each a committee of one from each league for the purpose of making, preparing and formulating such national agreement; and it is further agreed that they invite President P.T. Powers, of the National Association of Professional Base Ball Leagues to confer and advise with them to the formulating of said national agreement.

NINTH. — It is hereby agreed that each member hereby bind himself and his respective league by signing this agreement this 10th day of January, 1903.

(Signed)
HARRY C. PULLIAM
AUG. HERRMANN
JAMES A. HART
FRANK DE HASS ROBISON
B. B. JOHNSON
CHARLES COMISKEY
CHARLES W. SOMERS
H. J. KILLILEA[11]

The agreement document then concluded by listing the names of every player to be placed on the roster of every team in both leagues.

However, not everyone was happy with the agreement. In Indianapolis, a copy of the Associated Press dispatch detailing the agreement was shown to New York Giants owner John T. Brush. He was not impressed. "The report seems incomplete. There surely must be more of it than I have read. There should be some account of the National League members losing their pocketbooks to the committee from the American League, and I don't care to discuss the report until I have it all before me," said Brush.[12] Brush also was not happy about having an American League club coming into New York, thus providing competition for his Giants. He called upon Andrew Freedman to use his political influence to block attempts by the American League to find a suitable site for the team to play. Freedman did what he could, but Ban Johnson was persistent and found a site located on Manhattan between 168th Street and 165th Street, near 11th Avenue.

The site, previously owned by the New York Institute for the Blind, wasn't much to get excited about. It sat on swamp land, the terrain was pretty rough, and it was dotted by small boulders and dead trees. With the help of sportswriter Joe Vila, Ban Johnson found backers in Frank Farrell, a former bartender who then owned a gambling house, and Bill Devery, a retired New York police chief who was rolling in dough. Both were willing to invest $18,000, purchase the Baltimore franchise and move it to New York.

Joseph Gordon, a former New York State assemblyman with very good Tammany Hall connections, was named president, and the team was named the New York Highlanders. Immediately work began on filling in the swamp, blasting the boulders to clear the land, and constructing a 6,000-seat wooden grandstand. From these humble beginnings would rise major league baseball's most successful franchise. In 1913, the Highlanders would officially change their team name to the Yankees (although in the press they had often been referred to as the Yankees almost from the day they arrived in New York) and go on to win 39 American League pennants and 26 World Series titles through the 2006 season.

V

Fleischmann Re-elected and
a World Series Begins

Julius Fleischmann was now the majority owner of the Cincinnati Reds and he was still mayor of Cincinnati. In the spring of 1903, Fleischmann was determined to run for re-election. Despite the fact that he was an intrinsic part of the Cox machine, Fleischmann saw himself as a reformer and viewed his administration as one that was progressive. After all, his administration had undertaken the licensing and physical examination of prostitutes, advocated free public baths and free kindergartens in the public schools. In addition, the Fleischmann administration had improved the city's parks and infrastructure with extensive street resurfacing programs financed with bond issues, while starting the construction of viaducts and the elimination of ominous railroad grade crossings.

But by 1903 as the Progressive movement was building, there were those who wanted Cincinnati to enter into the twentieth century without the nineteenth century boss system of municipal government. Therefore, various Democrats and independent Republicans banned together in an attempt to attract a broader base of voters and break the Cox machine's stranglehold on city hall. They formed a nonpartisan coalition called the Citizens Municipal Party, more commonly referred to as the Citizens Ticket. The spirit of the Citizens Ticket platform was that every voter could keep their national affiliation, whether it be Democrat or Republican, but in this election they would form a common bond as concerned citizens who would elect candidates accountable to the voters and not to a select group of customers at Wielert's Garden. In essence, the Citizens Ticket was to be a voter referendum against the influence in the city's governance of George B. Cox and his gang, including Garry Herrmann. On March 7, 1903, the Citizens Ticket coalition held a huge rally at the Auditorium. With a band playing "America" and a thousand supporters cheering wildly, they denounced "bossism" in the city and nominated for mayor Melville E. Ingalls, a transplanted New England native and railroad magnate.

As Ingalls campaigned, he promised cleaner streets and attacked the Republican platform on several issues, including the issue of keeping the police department out of politics by enforcing a new municipal code that required all new appointments (such as the chief) come from the ranks and be performance based. Also, Ingalls attacked the Fleischmann administration for not managing the street-car company for the benefit of the people. In an attempt to counter propaganda being spread by the Republicans and reassure the large number of German and Irish voters in the city, Ingalls stated that he had no intentions of interfering with citizen's personal liberties and was not going to implement measures to control the management of saloons. However, he warned that his liberal attitude towards saloon operations did not preclude his cracking down on gambling dens in the city.

With Ingalls relentlessly bashing Julius Fleischmann on a daily basis, the latter's re-election efforts for a second term as mayor had gotten off to a rocky start. Then the unwitting participation of George B. Cox and August Herrmann in a controversial social event added to Fleischmann's troubles. Millionaire Moses Goldsmith of Walnut Hills had an undisputed reputation in the city for the most lavish entertainment of his guests. On March 23, Goldsmith invited the Republican Party elite to his home for a wedding reception and midnight dinner to honor his son, Leon, and his bride, a young lady from Montreal. Among those representing the Republican Party at the Goldsmith affair where both Mr. & Mrs. George B. Cox and Mr. & Mrs. August Herrmann.

That evening as guests arrived at the door the Goldsmith home, located on Beecher Avenue, the distinguished couples, including the Coxes and Herrmanns, were greeted by what appeared to be two members of the religious order Sisters of Charity. The guests were then seated in the palm room and served cordials by women dressed as pages and dancers. Suddenly the supposed nuns reappeared and in an instant removed their habits to reveal flesh-colored tights as they went into a jazzy ballet routine accompanied by a troupe of minstrel performers. Mrs. Goldsmith had created a grand musical program and provided the guests with extravagant souvenirs that included fine lace handkerchiefs imported from France. Card games took place in the upstairs rooms until midnight, when everyone descended the stairs and re-entered the palm room for dinner. Following the first course that consisted of oyster cocktail, halibut, small potatoes, cucumbers, tenderloin of beef and mushrooms. A toast entitled "The Father of Our Social Fraternity" was presented by George B. Cox.

The same night that Cox and Herrmann were indulging themselves in the gaudy opulence of the Goldsmith's hospitality, Melville Ingalls was stumping feverishly in the eastern section of the Over-the-Rhine at a rally held in the Eureka Hall, located just north of Liberty Street, at Hunt and Woodward streets. The meeting had not been advertised other than by the distribution of a few handbills. But the Citizens Ticket campaign seemed to be gaining huge momentum as every one of the 486 seats in the hall had been taken while scores of others stood in the aisles and in the rear. The following morning, the ruse involving the imposters assuming the dress of nuns during the gala at the Goldsmith's home was reported in the *Cincinnati Enquirer*, setting off a firestorm of negative backlash. The *Catholic Telegraph* scorned the episode as debauchery and the Knights of Columbus demanded the resignation of all Republican leaders that had been present at the Goldsmith home. Melville E. Ingalls immediately jumped on the bandwagon, and on March 25, held a huge rally at the Central Turner Hall at 1407 Walnut Street denouncing the Republicans and the event at the Goldsmith home as further proof of deep-rooted corruption in the party and city government.

With the election only one week away, Mayor Fleischmann suddenly became aware of the fact that Melville Ingalls could win. Therefore, Fleischmann, along with Judge William Lueders, who was running for re-election to the bench on the police court, began to campaign with conviction. Meanwhile, the Cox machine went into high gear organizing the hard-working, hard-drinking populace of the Over-the-Rhine wards, circulating rumors that alleged Melville Ingalls, the railroad tycoon who had 15,000 employees on his payroll, had once stated that $1.12 a day was a fair wage for a working man. They also suggested that he was obligated to the ministers and would close the saloons if elected.

With 83,872 registered to vote (including women who could vote in Cincinnati municipal elections), the Cox machine began to devout their efforts into a get-out-the-vote effort in the wards for the re-election of Fleischmann. Garry Herrmann did his part for the machine by making the obligatory speeches. Herrmann also took advantage of his position of being president of the Cincinnati Baseball Club to get some positive public relations going for Fleischmann. He held a meeting at the Palace Hotel with the local Knights of Pythias clubs represented in the Fraternal Baseball League and offered them the use of the Palace of the Fans on Sunday mornings during the 1903 season. It was agreed that all proceeds from the games would go to the Knights of Pythias Orphans' Home. By the first week in April, most of the controversy from the Goldsmith incident had subsided and only a few areas of the city, such as the heavily Irish-Catholic populated 20th ward of Price Hill, remained unforgiving.

On election day at the Blaine Club, Rud Hynicka, who served as chairman of the Republican Advisory Committee, arranged a system with different classes of accommodation by issuing red, white and blue tickets for the party faithful wanting to participate in the vote count. The lower floors at the club, accessible by the front entrance, were reserved for members who had been issued white tickets. Others who had been issued red and blue tickets would be permitted to gather in the upstairs rooms. Two policeman stood at the bottom of the stairs taking tickets. The red tickets were for distinguished guests and the blue for persons designated as clerks of the count. There seemed to be a considerable number of clerks that included Mayor Fleischmann, Ohio Lieutenant Governor Gordon, Judge Lueders, Congressman Nicholas Longworth, Gus Kirbert, Harry Hoffheimer, C. J. Christie, Max Burgheim and, of course, Cox, Herrmann and Hynicka.

Around 4:00 P.M., Cox, Herrmann and other key Republicans began to arrive at the Blaine Club to keep tabs on the returns. Cox sat downstairs in the library until the upstairs rooms were opened at 5:00 P.M. He then proceeded to a room on the second floor where he sat at a table with a big tally sheet in front of him keeping count of the returns coming in, with Herrmann, Hynicka and Judge Lueders close at hand. Somehow election results always seemed to reach the Blaine Club sooner than they reached the Board of Elections. By 5:30 P.M., the first returns began to arrive from various precincts in the 10th, 11th and 15th Wards that showed Fleischmann off to a commanding lead. There was no doubt where the election results were headed and immediately corks from champagne bottles began to pop.

At that point Ed Anthony came into the room and announced that Irwin Krohn wanted to bet 2-to-1 that Democrat Edward J. Dempsey would win election as superior court judge, and even money that he would get more votes in the election than Mayor Fleischmann. Rud Hynicka quickly advised Anthony, "Go out and bet him until he's blue in the face." About 7:30 P.M., everyone was losing interest in the count as the results were now certain. George B. Cox stood up and announced, "What's the use of counting? It's going to be nearer 20,000 than 10,000 majority for Fleischmann."[1] So immediately a lunch and drinks were served.

The fact was that everyone in the city seemed to already know the outcome of the election and spontaneous celebrations were taking place all over town. Red fires blazed, and there seemed to be more people out on the streets than during a presidential election year. Outside the Blaine Club, several thousand people who didn't qualify for any of the white, red or blue tickets had assembled and the First Regiment Band was performing a concert, playing "America," "The Star Spangled Banner" and "(Won't You Come Home) Bill Bailey." In between tunes the crowd began calling for Fleischmann. Fleischmann soon appeared at a window and made a brief statement of thanks. The band then struck up the tune "Then You'll Remember Me" and the crowd cheered loudly. Fleischmann exited the Blaine Club and threaded his way through the adoring crowd to the hospital next door, where his wife's brother-in-law, Dr. Christian Holmes, was holding court in his office with Mrs. Fleishmann and several other ladies. Judge Lueders bolted out the Blaine Club and began to lead the band on a parade down Sixth Street.

Julius Fleischmann won re-election to a second term as mayor over Citizens Party candidate Melville E. Ingalls in a landslide by 15,000 votes. A total of 61 percent of the voters had marked their ballots for Fleischmann, including 80 percent of the Negro vote. Riding to victory on Fleischmann's coattails, the Republicans also captured the majority vote in 21 of the 24 wards, winning all but four of the city council seats. In the race for judge of superior court, Republican Lewis M. Hoses defeated Edward J. Dempsey by 8,000 votes. However, Dempsey would be heard from in the future.

As the evening's celebration continued, the police detail at the Blaine Club went next door and cut a swath through the crowd to permit Mayor Fleischmann and his party that included Congressman Nicholas Longworth, Lieutenant Governor Gordon and Dr. Holmes to leave the hospital for a reception at the Queen City Club. As Fleischmann was leaving the Queen City Club, in the hallway he ran directly into the path of Melville Ingalls. The two men looked directly at each other momentarily, then quickly turned away to avoid any further eye contact or offer any congratulations or condolences. There was clearly bad blood between them.

At 10:00 P.M., Mayor Fleischmann and his entourage arrived at the Stage restaurant, where a dinner with George B. Cox, August "Garry" Herrmann and all the other Republican big-wigs took place. The booze flowed in abundance and every minute there seemed to be a toast to some winning candidate. As Fleischmann entered the Stag, Congressman Longworth and others broke into song and serenaded the mayor. At that point reporters caught up with Garry Herrmann and asked him for his view on the election results. "The victory means that the people of Cincinnati realize that they have had a good government and that the Republican Party stands ready always to redeem every promise it makes."[2] The celebrating continued until midnight, when the city, exhausted from the jubilation of the day, suddenly became still.

There was an atmosphere of national excitement about the coming baseball season of 1903. Garry Herrmann and the Cincinnati Reds had come out of the peace negotiations unscathed. The club did lose Sam Crawford, a popular player with the fans and a future member of the National Baseball Hall of Fame. However, the fact that peace was achieved, allowing Herrmann the opportunity to concentrate on increasing attendance and rebuilding the club for the future, was paramount to the long-range goals. In the coming season, Cy Seymour was expected to fill the void in the batting order left by Crawford's departure, and there was now more playing time available for manager Joe Kelley.

The long-anticipated season of peace in the major leagues was set to begin on April 16. Garry Herrmann had made some minor administrative changes for the coming season. Tickets for the Reds' opening game with Pittsburgh had been placed on sale downtown at Henry Straus' tobacco shop at 415 Vine Street. In accordance with league rules, he had issued season tickets to all the Reds players' wives. However, Herrmann decided to eliminate the use of side gates for VIPs in the 1903 season and instead installed a turnstile for exclusive use of the wives, employees and VIPs. As they entered, they would drop a coupon in a box so the Reds could get an accurate count of how many free admissions were in the park. Also, Herrmann had reached the conclusion that the traditional trolley parade on opening day was really a waste of time. He theorized that what fans wanted was a concert at the ballpark and a suitable pre-game ceremony. Garry Herrmann usually entered the gates of the Palace of the Fans about an hour before the game and cut a swath through the grandstand glad-handing friends and fans alike. It was the perfect showcase for his extraordinary political demeanor to be put on display, and Julius Fleischmann couldn't have asked for a better public relations gimmick.

However, the 1903 season was another disappointment for the fans as the Reds, despite leading the league in hitting with a .288 average, finished in fourth place, 16½ games behind the Pittsburgh Pirates. The Pirates were led by National League batting champion Honus Wagner (.355), who narrowly outdistanced manager and teammate Fred Clarke (.351) and the Reds' Mike Donlin (.351) for the title. Still, with the new ownership and executive management of Garry Herrmann, the Reds drew a whopping 351,680 fans through the turnstiles of the wobbly Palace of the Fans, an increase of 134,380 (38 percent) over the 1902 totals.

In the American League, major league baseball had arrived in New York. For days prior to the opening of the Highlanders' new ballpark in Washington Heights, blasting of rock and filling in and leveling the grounds had been going on. In fact, the right field portion of the park was still so unlevel that special ground rules were put in place for the first games. Ropes were stretched along the right field portion and any ball hit over them was ruled a double, rather than a home run. Undaunted, the American League showcased its new entry in major league baseball on April 29 before 16,233 fans. The famed New York 69th Regiment Band played the "Washington Post March" and "The Star-Spangled Banner," as all hats in the park were raised. Then league president Ban Johnson threw out the first ball and the Washington Nationals were defeated by the hometown New York Highlanders, 6–2.

The Boston Pilgrims won the 1903 American League pennant, outdistancing the Philadelphia Athletics by 14⅓ games, led by a trio of 20-game winners in Cy Young (28–9), Tom Hughes (20–7) and Bill Dinneen (21–13). In August, as the two teams were sprinting towards their league championships, Pirates owner Barney Dreyfuss and Pilgrims owner Henry Killilea agreed to face each other in the fall in a nine-game series for the world's championship. Killilea consulted with Ban Johnson on whether or not his club should accept the challenge. Johnson simply told Killilea that if he thought the Pilgrims could beat the Pirates, then he should play them. Hence, the first modern World Series was at hand. It would be the first post-season inter-league games since the 1880s, when the National League would on occasion meet a team from the old American Association.

The first modern World Series game took place on October 1, 1903, as 16,242 fans packed Boston's Huntington Grounds to witness Pittsburgh's Deacon Phillippe duel Boston's Cy Young. While Pittsburgh was victorious in game one, 7–3, scoring four runs off Young in the first inning, they would ultimately lose the series to the Pilgrims, 5 games to 3. However, the Pirates' players came out of top financially as Barney Dreyfuss allowed them to keep the club's share, thereby giving each Pittsburgh player $1,316.25 as opposed to the Boston players' winning share of $1,182.00 each.

The loss of the World Series to Boston was a huge embarrassment for the National League. However, it was only the tip of the post-season iceberg as three other post-season matchups took place. In Philadelphia, the Athletics beat the Phillies, 4 games to 3. Cleveland beat Cincinnati, 5 games to 2, and in Chicago, the Cubs and White Stockings split a 14-game series, 7 games each. To eliminate such post-season embarrassments, later in the fall at the National League meeting in New York, the league voted to extend the National League season from 140 games to 154 games. Likewise, the American League followed suit at its meeting in Chicago.

In the summer of 1904, the city of Cincinnati experienced the event-organizing skills of August Garry Herrmann at his absolute finest. Although he was knee-deep in the affairs of the fledgling National Commission while serving as president of the Cincinnati Reds and as chairman of the waterworks commission, Herrmann somehow found time to organize the Elks' national convention in the city that took place on July 17–23, 1904. At the time, Herrmann was the Exalted Ruler of Cincinnati Lodge No. 5 and served as chairman of the General

First modern World Series game, Huntington Grounds, Boston, October 1, 1903. Author's collection.

Reunion Committee. The Grand Portfolio for the event proclaimed it to be "the Greatest Reunion in the History of the B.P.O.E."

The wine-sipping, beer-guzzling and Thuringian sausage-munching social habits of August Garry Herrmann are more often than not the focal point of most articles written about him today. But this is a rather shallow profile of the man. One of the personal qualities inherent in August Herrmann, either ignored or forgotten, is that he was a person who strove to become literate. He possessed an extraordinary memory and cultivated his knowledge of the liberal arts with self-teaching methods, such as reading the classics and all that was considered to be the finest in literature of that time. His command of such literature was never more apparent than in his welcoming remarks to his brothers in his fraternity at the national convention of 1904.

As Exalted Ruler of Cincinnati Lodge, No. 5, and Chairman of the Reunion Committee, I have been chosen to extend to you a welcome and greeting in behalf of Cincinnati Lodge. To me this is an honor indeed — an honor, because the welcome and greeting is especially extended to the members of an order whose greatest object is the practice of charity — not unfortunate as we often see it practiced, but to practice it without ostentation. To my mind, this is one of the greatest principles known throughout the entire world. When practiced in this manner, I care not whether by an individual or by an organized body of men, such as the Benevolent and Protective Order of Elks, no result can follow but sunshine and happiness to the receiver and contentment and satisfaction to the giver. To the Elks assembled here this week, no injunction on my part is necessary. They well know the mottoes and principles of our organization — charity, justice, brotherly love and fidelity.

Not one has forgotten his obligation. Keep these mottoes and principles constantly before you and the obligation always in your minds, and all will be well. To the wives, families, relatives and sweethearts of all Elks, and to the visitors in general, it is my great honor and privilege to extend a most cordial welcome — a welcome to our city, to our home and to our hearts. May your stay with us be a pleasant one and may it leave impressions on your minds that will be lasting, to the end that the Benevolent and Protective Order of Elks may always stand out to you in bold relief, as an order devoted to the practice of grand principles, leading in pleasure, disseminating, happiness and brightness to others, yet at the same time lending a generous and helping hand to those in sorrow, sadness and distress.[3]

In downtown Cincinnati, the Mabely & Carew department store building was decked out in flags and bunting for the Elks convention and the people of Cincinnati experienced a grand parade. The Elks national convention in Cincinnati, organized by Herrmann, would set the standard for the conventions of the fraternity for years to come. A retrospective of Herrmann, written in 1912, stated, "It is not to baseball alone that Mr. Herrmann owes his national reputation. In 1904 the Elks held their annual reunion in Cincinnati, and it was the executive ability and broad good-fellowship of Mr. Herrmann, as head of the chief committees having charge of the entertainment of visitors, that still causes this union to be looked upon as the greatest in the history of Elkdom so far as hospitality is concerned."[4]

In the 1904 National League pennant race, Garry Herrmann's Cincinnati Reds did their best to put up a good scrap. However, in the end the Reds came up 18 games short, in third place, as John McGraw won his first pennant with the New York Giants. The Reds played their final game of the season in New York and experienced one of the strangest circumstances in the managerial career of John McGraw. The Giants already had the pennant wrapped up. McGraw had heard that a 52-year-old local attorney and former professional ballplayer by the name of Jim O'Rourke wanted to play just one more time in the major leagues. O'Rourke had played in the National League from its inaugural year in 1876 through 1893, with the exception of the 1890 season, when he had played in the Players' League. In fact, some historians credit O'Rourke, an outfielder with the Boston Red Stockings in 1876, with getting the first hit in National League history. McGraw told the graying O'Rourke to suit up, and on September 22, 1904, he caught nine innings while going 1-for-4 at the plate and scoring a run as the Giants defeated the Reds, 7–5. In 1945 Jim O'Rourke was voted into the National Baseball Hall of Fame.

In 1904 Boston had repeated as champions in the American League, and the New York Giants fans were excited about the possibility of meeting them in a World Series. But Giants owner John T. Brush and Giants manager John McGraw were against legitimizing the American League in a post-season series. Brush still believed the American League was an inferior circuit and not worth of playing his Giants in a post-season series. John McGraw was just as adamant in his opinion of the American League; he detested Ban Johnson and disliked the fact that Johnson was still angry with him for deserting the Baltimore club. Also, McGraw intensely disliked the fact that the American League had invaded New York.

McGraw's worst fear almost became a reality when it looked like the New York Highlanders could win the 1904 American League pennant. All summer the American League pennant race had been a five-team dog fight, and going into September, the outcome was unsure. Due to the uncertainty of the pennant winner in the American League, there was no way that Brush and McGraw were going to set themselves up for a possible post-season series with the Johnny-come-lately Highlanders. The New York Highlanders, led by spitball-tossing "Happy Jack" Chesboro, who won 41 games (a modern era record that still stands) battled the Boston

Pilgrims right down to the wire for the 1904 American League pennant. The pennant race was still unsettled on the final weekend of the season, with Boston and New York going head-to-head for all the marbles. On October 7, the Highlanders took a ½-game lead over the Pilgrims. However, the next day Boston swept a doubleheader to go back in the lead by 1½ games.

The final showdown was set for a season-ending doubleheader on October 10 at Hilltop Park in New York (near the present-day site of Columbia-Presbyterian Hospital). New York needed to sweep the doubleheader and the first game was a matchup of 41-game winner Chesboro against Boston's Bill Dinneen, who had won 22 games. Notwithstanding John T. Brush and John McGraw, there was a huge air of excitement about the doubleheader in New York. In the first game, the score was tied 2–2 in the ninth inning. Lou Criger, the Boston catcher not known for having any speed on the basepaths, led off with a single off Chesboro. Then following a groundout and a sacrifice, Criger advanced to third. Chesboro then lost control of a spitter that sailed over the catcher's head, allowing Criger to scamper home with the eventual winning run and clinch the pennant for Boston. In the second game, the Highlanders won 1–0 in ten innings.

Boston president John I. Taylor was still hopeful that Brush and McGraw would change their minds. Taylor even sent a message to the New York manager asking him to reconsider, but McGraw did not have the courtesy to respond. John T. Brush stated, "We are content when our season is ended to rest upon our laurels. The club that wins from the clubs that represent the cities of Boston, Brooklyn, New York, Philadelphia, Pittsburgh, Cincinnati, Chicago, and St. Louis, the eight largest and most important cities in America, in a series of 154 games, is entitled to the honor of champions of the United States without being called upon to contend with or recognize clubs from minor leagues. Neither the players nor the manager of the Giants nor myself desires any greater glory than to win the pennant in the National League. That is the greatest honor that can be obtained in baseball."[5]

There was little that Garry Herrmann as head of the National Commission could do about the circumstances. The 1903 World Series had been a voluntary arrangement between Dreyfuss and Taylor. Furthermore, there had never been any obligatory agreement between the two leagues to meet in post-season play. National League president Harry Pulliam, of course, supported John T. Brush. The real losers in the 1904 post-season flap were the fans, who had bought tickets in record numbers supporting their teams. The Boston fans took out their disappointment by branding Brush and McGraw as dirty cowards.

Major League Attendance

National League	Year	American League
1,681,212	1902	2,200,457
2,390,363	1903	2,345,888
2,774,301	1904	3,094,559

However, Pittsburgh owner Barney Dreyfuss disagreed with the opinion of Pulliam that the 1903 World Series had been a private arrangement. Dreyfuss contended that a regular post-season series agreement had been made between the leagues, with teams in the two leagues meeting each other in the corresponding manner in which they finished in the pennant races. Therefore, as the Pirates had finished in fourth place in the National League, Dreyfuss scheduled a series with the Cleveland Naps, who had finished in fourth place in the American League. John T. Brush was quick to point out that no such agreement had ever been made. Still, to the New York Highlanders, who had finished in second place in the American League, this all seemed like a good idea and they quickly issued a challenge to the Chicago Cubs, who had finished second in the National League. However, Cubs president James A. Hart agreed with Brush and would have none of it. Hart was of the opinion that such a series would become a wide-open affair and impossible to control. He stated that a player could even throw a game and get off without any discipline at all.

Over the winter of 1904–1905, there was an outpouring of considerable backlash expressed by both the press and public alike at the failure of major league baseball to hold a World Series in the fall of 1904. Garry Herrmann was a master at ascertaining which way the political winds were blowing. It was Herrmann who had for years on every election eve in Cincinnati provided George B. Cox with a rather uncanny forecast of the expected results at the polls, even when the Republicans were in jeopardy of losing. Therefore, Herrmann began to advance the opinion that perhaps a post-season series between the league champions just might be a great idea for major league baseball after all. Likewise, John T. Brush was far from deaf to the public storm of protest swirling about from his reluctance to play Boston in a post-season series. Brush also was hearing of Herrmann's proposal to make the World Series a permanent affair. Possibly sensing an opportunity at immortality while at the same time seeking to protect his gate receipts from the fan backlash, Brush suddenly announced that he had a change of heart and now felt that a post-season series between the two leagues' pennant winners would be a fitting climax to the season.

On February 16, 1905, the following resolution was adopted by major league baseball.

> The pennant-winning club of the National League and the pennant-winning club of the American League shall meet annually in a series of games for the Professional Base Ball Championship of the World. The control and direction of these games were delegated to the National Commission. The standard of play and sportsmanship in the four series contested under the auspices of the Commission has met with approval of public and press and in future events we will, through our representatives, take charge of the sale of tickets and thereby assume sole responsibility for the conduct of the business as well as the playing end of these games. Under this arrangement, the public will be protected from manipulation of tickets and the club-owner will be relieved of the importunities for favors from politicians and others with influence. The rate of general admission will be reduced so that regular patrons whose means are not commensurate with their love of and loyalty to base ball, may at a trifling cost, enjoy these annual events between champions. The interests of patrons and players are preeminent with the Commission.[6]

On October 2, 1905, the New York Giants split a doubleheader with the Reds at the Palace of the Fans, 5–4 and 4–3. The split clinched the National League pennant for the Giants. While a World Series had been adopted in theory by the major leagues, the actual operational plan for playing it had not yet been drafted. The next day, October 3, Garry Herrmann and Ban Johnson, American League president, sat down together and began working on a plan to hold the World Series. One of the first tasks for the National Commission was to establish a set of rules and financial administration for a World Series. Under the plan put together by Herrmann and Johnson, 10 percent of all revenues from the World Series would be set aside to finance ongoing activities of the National Commission.

There was, however, one small detail that Herrmann and Johnson were overlooking as they were ironing out the details for the 1905 World Series. The two were making the assumption that the teams to be playing in the series would be the New York Giants, who had already clinched the pennant by leading the Pittsburgh Pirates by six games with five to go, and the Philadelphia Athletics, who had not. The Chicago White Sox had been in the thick of the American League pennant race all summer, first with Cleveland until Nap Lajoie contracted blood poisoning, then with Philadelphia, which grabbed the lead on August 2, only to see the White Sox rebound and come within three percentage points of the lead on September 28.

Now, on October 3, Chicago was in second place, four games behind Philadelphia with four games left in the season. Charles Comiskey considered the actions of Herrmann and Johnson in planning a New York-Philadelphia World Series a snub. It both angered and hurt Comiskey, who stated that just in case the Chicago White Sox did pull out the pennant over the Philadelphia Athletics, he had no intention of playing the New York Giants in a World Series. Instead, Comiskey stated that he would play an inter-city series with the Chicago Cubs.

In New York, while John T. Brush liked the event planning skills of Herrmann and Johnson, he still wanted to recommend playing rules for the World Series. Subsequently, Herrmann and Johnson adopted the changes that became known as the "Brush Rules." It is the "Brush Rules" that are in use in the World Series even in the present day. Next, Herrmann and Johnson named Hank O'Day and John Sheridan, both of the National League, to umpire the 1905 World Series. As to who has the legitimate claim to the title of "Father of the World Series" is debatable. While Garry Herrmann has been vested with the title for over a hundred years, some consideration has to be given to Barney Dreyfuss for his proposal to play the first modern series in 1903 and also to John T. Brush, who codified the rules for the series. Garry Herrmann's participation is best recognized by his efforts in negotiating the World Series of 1905 rather than creating it as an annual event.

Still, there were some baseball executives who gave Herrmann full credit for creating the World Series. One such advocate for the "Father of the World Series" title belonging to August Garry Herrmann was Colonel Tillinghast L'Hommedieu Huston, co-owner of the New York Yankees in the late teens and early twenties. According to Huston, speaking in 1923 after the National Commission had been dissolved,

> Had it not been for the foresight and keen business sense of Garry Herrmann, there would be no such thing as the world's series as we know it to-day. Mr. Herrmann conceived the idea of an annual world's series between the champion teams of the leagues, which would make it compulsory for both clubs to play. He drew up the rules and regulations to govern the series and had them adopted by both leagues. So carefully and intelligently did he do this work that there have been no important changes in the rules as promulgated by him in the 18 years the series has been played. Under his guidance the event came the great the classic of the baseball year. For many years Mr. Herrmann, as Chairman of the commission, was in full charge of the series, and he handled it so well that there has never been any trouble or dispute about any of its workings.[7]

When Colonel Huston states that Garry Herrmann was in full charge of the series, that is almost an understatement. The fact is that each year the World Series became Garry Herrmann's private election night, New Year's Eve, 4th of July and Mardi Gras wrapped into one event. He traveled to the series in a private railroad car and took a large entourage with him that numbered a score or more. Of course, the car was stocked with only the finest of Cincinnati delicacies for his friends to feast upon. There was a seemingly never-ending supply of Cincinnati wine and beer of all the finest brands, including Gambrinus, Hudephol, Lackman, and Moreline. Tables were stacked almost to eye level with roasted chickens, boiled hams, liver sausage, sauerkraut, baked beans, coleslaw, blood pudding and other delicacies straight from Over-the-Rhine delicatessens. Garry spared no expense to please the palates of his guests.

Of course, Garry Herrmann's love of eating artery-hardening fare was legendary. Herrmann often stated that the only place you could get good food was in Cincinnati. The late National Baseball Hall of Fame historian Lee Allen called Garry Herrmann "a walking delicatessen." The stories of his love affair with food are numerous. One spring when the Reds were playing an exhibition game in Florida, Herrmann was introduced to the crowd. As the announcer went through the exhausting list of titles held by Herrmann, such as chairman of the National Commission, president of the Cincinnati Reds, etc., "Herrmann cupped his hands together and shouted to the crowd, 'Yes, and I'm the champion beer drinker and sausage eater too!'"[8]

In regard to Herrmann's love affair with food, legendary sports columnist Damon Runyon wrote, "His face reflected his manner of living. His nose was bulbous, his complexion at all times as red as the sunset. He loved to eat, and he loved to drink." Herrmann's weakness was sausage. "He simply had to have his sausage. I have tasted Garry's sausage, and while I never fell a complete victim to its appeal, I could understand why Garry liked it. It was okay." There was an occasion when Cincinnati mayor Julius Fleischmann, Herrmann's business partner, invited him to sail on his private yacht up Long Island Sound. Runyon states that, "Garry knew the trip was to last several days and sent a consignment of his favorite sausage to the dock to be placed aboard the yacht. Through some error the sausage was left behind. Garry stood the yachting trip just about 24 hours, and then requested Mr. Fleischmann to unload him at the first convenient port. 'I got to get back to where I can have my sausage,' he explained."[9]

On October 5, with the 1905 season about to conclude and the World Series set to start in Philadelphia on October 9, Garry Herrmann decided to invite the Reds team out to the Laughery Club for a day of frolicking in a stag event. Lunch was served picnic-style and a speech in regard to the coming election was delivered by Lee Crenshaw, proprietor of the Silver Moon, a flophouse located in the 8th Ward at 318 East Front Street and notorious for delivering a large number of fraudulent votes for the machine's candidates on election day. There was a well-kept baseball diamond at the Laughery and the occasion called for an intra-squad game made up of Reds players intermingled with visiting club members. One squad was captained by Reds center fielder Cy Seymour and the other by Tommy Corcoran the Reds' shortstop. Along the sidelines over 200 club members were spectators to the game, which was umpired by Mayor Fleischmann. Under a boiling early October sun, Seymour's club beat Corcoran's, 5 to 3. Fred Odwell, Reds right fielder, played his regular position and kept the "Seymours" in the game with two spectacular catches. Twice he had to vault a wire fence between the field and a corn patch and chase down long fly balls. It was Odwell's home run that drove in Reds utility player Al Bridwell with the winning run. However, in the bottom of the ninth, the Corcorans rallied and two men reached base. At that point, Captain Corcoran sent Garry Herrmann up to bat against "Rip" Vowinkel. Herrmann took a huge cut at a Vowinkel curveball and missed. Herrmann then summoned Reds groundskeeper Matty Schwab to pinch-hit for him and Schwab completed the strikeout.

Following the game, the majority of club members and Reds players rode in a procession of wagons that resembled pioneers slugging across the Oregon Trail to Aurora, Indiana, and caught the evening train for Cincinnati. However, for others the evening was young. The Laughery bar was opened by John Regan, a member of the Blaine Club who was often referred in the Cincinnati press as the "official saloonist of city hall," and drinks were on the house. As the evening wore on and other guests left, the participants dwindled to the hard core. Tommy Corcoran and Reds third baseman Harry Steinfeldt had been drinking heavily and becoming more agitated with each other by each glassful. Their emotions reached a boiling point and a fight broke out. Corcoran landed all the punches, and in an instant, Steinfeldt's bloody face looked like a pound of raw ground beef. Corcoran, then humble in victory, helped put Steinfeldt on the train before heading back to the Laughery to drink some more. John Regan opened a high-stakes crap game and was about $200 ahead when a tipsy Garry Herrmann entered the barroom and kicked over the table.

With 1905 being an election year, it took only a few days for the Cincinnati press to get wind of the post-game activities at the Laughery. Just as the press had made the affair at the Goldsmith mansion in 1903 seem symptomatic of corrupt political leadership in the city, the *Cincinnati Post* on October 9 ran a tell-all article of the event, headlining its column, "Laugh-ery Club Orgy Ends In Blows— Baseball Players Mixed Up — Garry Kicked Over Table, and Occasion was Most Enjoyable —for System."[10]

In the 1905 World Series, McGraw's Giants were ready and eager for their date with des-tiny against Connie Mack's Philadelphia Athletics. The Athletics, bolstered by a superb pitch-ing rotation of Eddie Plank (25–12), Rube Waddell (26–11), Andy Coakley (20–7) and Chief Bender (16–10), were considered the favorites to win the series. However, the Giants had a few pitchers of their own who were not too shabby in the presence of Christy Mathewson (31–8), "Iron Man" Joe McGinnity (21–15), Red Ames (22–8) and Dummy Taylor (15–9). The Giants beat the Athletics four games to one in a series that saw five shutouts pitched, three by Mathewson and one each by McGinnity and Bender. Christy Mathewson's performance in the 1905 World Series was without a doubt the finest in his storied career and arguably the finest in World Series history. In the span of six days, Mathewson pitched 27 scoreless innings, gave up 14 hits, walked one and struck out 18. His ERA for the series was an impeccable 0.00.

One of the more obscure facts about the series is that following Mathewson's 3–0 shutout of the Athletics in game one at Philadelphia, Connie Mack received a telegram that stated if he could get the Giants' band to play the tune "Tessie," there was no way that the Athletics could lose game two at New York's Polo Grounds. Just how Mack got the job done remains a mystery. But on October 10, 1905, as 25,000 fans in the Polo Grounds cheered the home-town team as they walked on the field, the strains of the New York Giants' band playing "Tessie" could be heard above the roar. Chief Bender then proceeded to beat the Giants, throwing a 3–0 shutout. The inclusion of the song "Tessie" as a sort of oral rabbit's foot was not a new innovation in the series. In fact, in the 1903 World Series, the Boston fans were particularly annoying to the Pittsburgh players and fans with their endless singing of "Tessie." Following the series it is was revealed by the *New York Times* that John McGraw had bet $400 on his club to win the series. However, at the time gambling was still viewed by major league baseball as an occupational hazard and the revelation of McGraw's wager didn't warrant even a yawn from Garry Herrmann and the National Commission.

VI

The Machine Crashes

By 1905 the Progressive movement was in full swing and reform crusades were starting to spread across the country, fueled in part by the radical writings of Lincoln Steffens in several books and magazines. In Cincinnati, Julius Fleischmann decided not to seek another term as mayor, and the Republicans nominated Harry L. Gordon. The administration of Julius Fleischmann had created some loose ends in the Republican Party, based on his conceptual philosophy of being a reformer. During Fleischmann's second term as mayor, George B. Cox had been attempting a political juggling act in order to keep his national and state alliances together. On one hand, he was attempting to remain loyal to his long-time ally, U.S. Senator Joseph B. Foraker, while on the other he was being leaned on by President Theodore Roosevelt and Charles P. Taft, publisher of the *Cincinnati Times-Star*, to limit Foraker's influence in party policy-making. Throughout the fall of 1905, George B. Cox found himself attempting to walk on Senator Foraker's shoes without messing up the shine.

If the disjointed agenda that Cox found himself coordinating wasn't bad enough, he was also getting a political cold shoulder from fellow Cincinnatian William Howard Taft, who had risen to a position of prominence in the Roosevelt administration. Sensing a run at the presidency, Taft wanted to project a squeaky-clean image and adopted an anti–George B. Cox stance. Taft realized that in many cities across the country, public opinion was changing towards machine government and that any run he might make for the White House in 1908 could be severally damaged by an insinuation that he had a close relationship with alleged political corruption advanced by the Cox machine in his hometown of Cincinnati.

In the 1905 Ohio state election race, Republican governor Myron T. Herrick was running for re-election. There was, however, some concern among the Ohio Republican Party power brokers that Herrick could not win second a term and that the party should nominate lieutenant governor Warren G. Harding. Still, the fact remained that Herrick was an incumbent, and party protocol dictated that he be re-nominated. To make sure that he had all his political ducks in a row in squelching the Harding nomination bid, Herrick contacted George B. Cox in Cincinnati and quickly obtained his support. In the fall of 1905, Governor Herrick's re-election campaign became a nasty affair. His Democrat rival, John M. Pattison of Cincinnati, the president of the Union Central Life Insurance Company, a Methodist and a temperance advocate, was alleging that Herrick not only had close ties with George B. Cox, but was subservient to him. Pattison was even stating that when Cox wanted a person appointed by Herrick, it was a done deal. Also, the *Cincinnati Post* was dedicated to the defeat of Myron T. Herrick. The *Post* referred to Cox as an ex-divekeeper who dictated Herrick's re-nomination.

With the Cox connotation looming over the legitimacy of his candidacy at a time when the popularity of bossism was in a national downturn, Herrick was in danger of losing the election. To counteract the Pattison strategy of linking him to Cox, Herrick requested that William Howard Taft come to Ohio and make a speech on his behalf. Taft was a supporter of Herrick and truly believed that he was independent of Cox's influence. Taft agreed and on Saturday, October 21, 1905, Taft spoke in Akron, Ohio.

The majority of Taft's speech was devoted to the Roosevelt administration's attempts to bring reform to the railroads in America through the implementation of new regulations, which were being opposed by Senator Foraker. Taft also addressed the allegations of Governor Herrick being a pawn of George B. Cox and the Republican machine in Cincinnati and Hamilton County. As Taft proceeded, he cast Herrick in the light of being his own man and an independent thinker, while calling his alleged subservience to Cox a grave charge. Taft then went on to describe the political environment that existed under the influence of Cox in Cincinnati. Taft stated that if he had thought that by speaking and supporting Governor Herrick he would be doing anything for the perpetuation of the power of the Cox machine in Cincinnati, or thought that Governor Herrick had entered into a corrupt bargain with Cox, he wouldn't be speaking in Akron. Taft stated that if the machine was to be broken up, then it must be broken up by the voters of Cincinnati and Hamilton County themselves. Taft concluded by stating that because his duties called him elsewhere, he would be unable to cast his vote in the coming election. But if he were able, he would vote against the municipal ticket nominated by the Republican organization in Cincinnati and for the state ticket.

The text of Taft's speech reached Cincinnati quickly and fell upon the Republican bosses like a missile launched from Akron. Upon hearing of Taft's statements, George B. Cox, Garry Herrmann and Rud Hynicka were stunned and beat a path to Weilert's cafe to hold an emergency meeting. Reporters soon arrived at Weilert's, forcing the trio to move the meeting to an undisclosed private location. While mum was the word with Cox, Herrmann and Hynicka, reporters caught up with Lew Kraft, who had joined the Cox inner-circle meeting. Kraft stated that Cox, Herrmann and Hynicka had decided to make no statement in regard to the allegations of Taft. However, Republican workers were already firing innuendoes at William Howard Taft, which obviously was an approved strategy of Cox, Herrmann and Hynicka. One such allegation was that Taft harbored a deep-seeded, almost pathological hatred of Cox. Most Cincinnatians, though, were interpreting Taft's remarks as an attempt by the Roosevelt administration to include the Cincinnati system in its national agenda to break up graft in business and politics. On Monday morning, reporters converged on Cox at his office over the Mecca saloon on Walnut Street. Cox, puffing on a big, black cigar, was still not commenting on the Taft speech. "I haven't got a thing to say. You fellows ought to know that I won't talk. Good-bye!"[1]

In actuality, Saturday, October 21 had been a horrific day for the Cox machine in Cincinnati. As Taft was delivering his manifesto in Akron, right in their own backyard the machine was being lambasted by Wisconsin governor Robert M. LaFollette, a champion of the progressive reform government movement and a politician who was at the very least dripping of liberalism. "Battling Bob" (as LaFollette was known) was running for the U.S. Senate from Wisconsin and had come to Cincinnati to deliver an address to the Cincinnati Association of Life Underwriters at the St. Nicholas Hotel.

While LaFollette had been advised in advance that any tirade against bossism would be considered off-base, it had absolutely no effect on him. For three solid hours, Governor LaFollette went right for the jugular of the machine, never easing up for a moment as the assembled association members literally ate it up, cheering wildly for the entire 180 minutes of his highly charged rhetoric. When LaFollette seemed to be slowing down, they yelled for more. In part, LaFollette told the association,

> I'll die fighting. I believe as firmly as I believe in God that the greatest question we ever faced is before us now and by the grace of the Almighty, I'll fight the conditions till I die. Fight, fight, fight! Don't show the white flag. It is the duty of every American citizen to inquire into the records of every official, city or state. If they are found to be good — retain them. If bad, throw them out! I do not know how it is in Cincinnati — but if you have a public servant, be he mayor, alderman, common councilman or whatever his office, if he fails to represent the people to the best of his ability, or if he become hostile in any way to the interest of the people whom he is supposed to represent, then I hold him as guilty of treason as Benedict Arnold.[2]

The crowd screamed for more at the top of their lungs.

The local Democrats in Cincinnati had nominated Edward J. Dempsey as their candidate for mayor to run against Harry L. Gordon. Dempsey, an Irish-Catholic and a former judge resided in Price Hill. In the spring elections of 1903, he had been defeated for a seat on the bench of superior court. The *Cincinnati Post* was making much of the fact that forty years prior to the 1905 election, Edward J. Dempsey and George B. Cox had been boyhood friends. The Dempsey and Cox families had lived in the same neighborhood, the boys attended public school together at 5th and Mound streets and played together in the area around the Sixth Street Market. The *Cincinnati Post*, leading the attack on George B. Cox and his associates, used the Dempsey-Cox common background story to set up the election as a voter referendum on political morality, based on the juxtaposition of their separate adolescent developments. The *Post* portrayed Dempsey as having been a hard-working student who ultimately made his life work of seeking justice for all men by using his own convictions as a scale on which to weigh conviction. As for Cox, the *Post* asserted that he chose politics as a profession, became an autocrat, and sought great power and wealth. For the most part, the voters of Cincinnati viewed it all as hyperbole and much to do about nothing. Nonetheless, aided by strong editorial backing from the *Cincinnati Post* and an anti–Cox campaign aimed directly at Hynicka and to a lesser degree Herrmann, Dempsey made some real political hay coming down the stretch towards election day by hammering away at charges of corruption in the city government.

The Cincinnati waterworks had been designed and built by Albert Von Stein, one of the preeminent civil engineers of the nineteenth century, and was the first in the United States to be worked by pumps. Van Stein had built the Appomattox Canal as well as the waterworks in Richmond, Lynchburg, Petersburg, New Orleans, Nashville and Mobile. By the early 1900s, the waterworks system being used in Cincinnati was obsolete, and political corruption had little to do with the quality of water that was being distributed throughout the city. Although a new water system was being constructed under the direction of a state-appointed commission and chaired by August Garry Herrmann, water was still a sensitive subject in Cincinnati. Physicians in Cincinnati were outraged by the condition of water being drunk by school children in the city. The *Cincinnati Post* did what it could to exploit the problem for political gain of the Dempsey campaign by publishing negative articles on the quality of water and pictures of school children drinking water directly from fire hydrants at their schools. The etiology of the problem with the city's water, according to Dr. Will C. Herman, was that the water intake for the Cincinnati system was below the point where sewage emptied in the Ohio River. Therefore, heavy rains that occurred in the fall, winter and spring caused an increase in the rate of typhoid because the drain washed all the filth and slime in the direction of the filtration plant. Dr. John Griewe, who had an office on Eighth Street, urged that hotels, restaurants and schools, both boil and filter water. He warned that typhoid bacilli were probably more active in November then at any time of the year, which, ironically, was election time.

As for Mayor Fleischmann's position on the water issue, the *Cincinnati Post* stated that,

> Mayor Fleischmann's indifference to the crusade for good water and his assertion that the move is "foolish" has been explained. The mayor's official interest in the welfare of the city has not been manifested, but his personal interest in his own children has caused him to keep his little ones free from the possibility of typhoid or other contagion carried into the schools by the impure river water by sending them to private schools. The danger at the public schools causes no anxiety to the mayor. Professional educators are employed to see that the little Fleischmanns are healthy.[3]

In addition to exploiting the purity of the water, the *Cincinnati Post* also attacked the water department as politically corrupt. In its edition of October 24, the *Post* stated that the Cleveland waterworks pumped 75 percent more water than the Cincinnati waterworks. However, the Cleveland waterworks had operating expenses of only $300,000 a year as compared with operating expenses of the Cincinnati waterworks that totaled $700,000 annually. Furthermore, the *Post* stated that total payroll expense of Cleveland waterworks was $145,000 a year as opposed to $416,000 a year in the Cincinnati department. Of course, it was alleged that the difference in the payroll expense was that the Cincinnati water department was rife with politically appointed workers who did nothing to earn their pay. The *Post* also alleged that when the Democrat administration of Gustav Tafel left the mayor's office in 1900, there was a surplus balance of operating funds in the waterworks of $169,770. However, under Mayor Fleischmann's control, expenses had been increased and by 1901 the waterworks had a deficit of $8,866. By 1902, the newspaper alleged that as a result of kickbacks to friends of the Fleischmann administration, the deficit in operating funds had increased to $25,618. Throughout that time, water rates in the city were rising. In 1900 water department receipts were $800,000. In 1901 they were $832,000, and by 1904, receipts had climbed to $919,000, all while deficits were created. According to the *Post*, the deficits were not made up and therefore in the years 1901, 1902, 1903 and 1904, the Board of Public Service spent $110,336.46 more than it took in from receipts.

It was also alleged that in order to accomplish the higher rates while still running a deficit, that surveyors (or as we call them today, meter readers) were sent all over the city to adjust rates. In buildings where there were no meters, surveyors charged water rates according to the number of rooms in the house, including a separate charge for every faucet, wash stand (wash bowl) and bathroom. To accomplish their mandated task of providing the Fleischmann administration with more water receipts, the surveyors developed methods to double-charge customers. Owners of six-room houses learned that they were being billed for a seven- or eight-room house. Any construction configuration with plaster on it was considered a room, including any storage rooms or attics.

While the Edward Dempsey campaign was a huge benefactor from the unsubstantiated corruption charges being leveled against the Cox-managed water department, Garry Herrmann did the issue a huge disservice by not responding to the charges of the *Post*. Two years later when the new water system was completed, Herrmann, as chairman of the Board of Trustees of the commissioners of the waterworks, would state in the commission's official report that most of delays in the construction had occurred as a result of litigation. Furthermore, since the passage of the original act by the state legislature in 1896 authorizing the construction of the new waterworks, there had been no increase in water rates and all fixed charges for interest and sinking fund to the present time had been paid out of revenues of the water department. Of course, this would cause operating expenses to rise, and for Herrmann to wait until 1907 to respond to the serious charges of the *Post* did little to help Republican mayoral candidate Harry L. Gordon in 1905. In many ways, it would seem as if August Garry

Herrmann was losing a step or two as a consummate politician. Nonetheless, Herrmann believed in the importance of the work being done by the Board of Trustees of the commissioners of the waterworks and what the building of the new water system meant to the future of Cincinnati. In some way, Herrmann envisioned the new waterworks as his legacy, and therefore refused to politicize the commission's work, even at the expense of electing a Democrat mayor.

As various entities began to sense that the Cox machine was vulnerable in the election, Edward Dempsey started to receive support form several of the city's clerics. A coalition of religious and business leaders in the city had been formed, called the Honest Elections Committee. The committee was chaired by soap manufacturing magnate James N. Gamble, with S. F. Dana serving as vice chairman, working along with Catholic Archbishop Henry Moeller, Episcopal Bishop Boyd Vincent, and Rabbi David Phillipson. The Honest Elections Committee set up its headquarters on the 6th floor of the First National Bank Building, began to solicit donations, and claimed that it had information gathered from credible sources of widespread election frauds, including false registration, illegal voting, and tampering with count and the returns.

The appearance of Archbishop Moeller publicly speaking out against George B. Cox was much more that than a phenomenal break with the constitutional concept of separation of church and state. The open participation of Moeller in the Cincinnati municipal race of 1905 was a giant leap forward in the expression of social consciousness by the growing Catholic population in the city and the formation of new political alliances. The Catholic press was encouraging its church members to take action on a wide variety of community issues, such as limiting the hours of operation for taverns, closing houses of prostitution, and speaking out against sensationalistic journalism. All of this civic reactionary support added enormous momentum to the campaign of Edward J. Dempsey, and he used it to fuel the fires of discontent in the city with a great display of political skill. Despite his strong temperance stance, he campaigned in the heavily German-populated wards that had traditionally been bastions of support for the Republicans' laissez faire policy on booze. Dempsey was even being aided by Germans, who were recruited by the Democrats to deliver his speeches in German.

As the political campaigns progressed through the fall, things began to look grim for mayoral candidate Harry L. Gordon, George B. Cox and the Republicans in Cincinnati and Hamilton County. Rud Hynicka, running for re-election as the Hamilton County treasurer, was also feeling the heat. During the campaign, a former bridge contractor by the name of John J. Dunn had been making accusations in forced depositions taken in upstate Sandusky County that the pool of highway and bridge contractors bidding on all the infrastructure work being done in the Ohio's 88 counties (including Hamilton) were made with the assistance of elected officials looting the taxpayers.

According to Dunn, it was well known throughout the state that no one except the Brackett Bridge Company would be awarded a contract in Hamilton County under the influence of George B. Cox and Rud Hynicka. Dunn contended that on July 27, 1898, Hamilton County had awarded a contract for a new bridge to Brackett for the cost of $36,000. The cost of the bridge was figured at $18,000. The remaining $18,000 was supposed to be profit for Brackett and its subcontractors. However, Dunn alleged that Brackett was going to keep $12,000 of the profits and divide the other $6,000 among contractors in its pool. When Dunn protested that the $12,000 amount being kept by Brackett was unusually large, the Brackett people told him that their expenses in getting the contract were quite large and that they were obligated to pay a large sum to a relative of a Hamilton County official, who would then distribute the money among various political leaders.

Dunn was skeptical about this, sensing that there were either irregularities in the bidding process by Brackett or that the relative of this county official was pocketing the money. So Dunn decided to investigate the matter and went to see George B. Cox. He told Cox what the Brackett people had told him. Dunn stated that Cox seemed surprised. Cox told Dunn that he should go and tell this to Rud Hynicka. Dunn went to see Hynicka, who also seemed surprised. However, Dunn stated that he would prove his allegations about the Brackett Bridge Company to Hynicka at the next bid opening.

The county was about to construct a bridge over the Great Miami River and bids were being received. The day of the opening, about ten minutes before closing time, the county officials responsible for opening the bids seemed to know what Dunn was up to and quickly pulled him off to the side and allegedly offered him a $1,000 to withhold submitting his bid. Suddenly, all the other bidders in the pool that were present attempted to find a reason to get him tossed out of the room. Dunn alleges that he observed the presiding official of the board shift his bid under a big book on the table, and when the appointed time came to read the bids, all were with the exception of his.

When the presiding official stated that all bids had been received and read, Dunn leaped over the railing and demanded that his bid be read. The presiding official stated that Dunn could not have possibly put in a bid because it wasn't there. When Dunn demanded that the presiding official look under the book, the official declared it had been an accident. The cost of the bridge had been estimated at $29,000 and Dunn's bid was for $30,000. According to Dunn, the Brackett Bridge Company's bid was for $40,000. After some additional haggling, Krug, the county engineer, interceded and stated that Dunn's bid did not meet the specifications for the kind of bridge being built. Furthermore, the plans and specifications that Krug had provided to Dunn contained a mistake. Dunn stated that while he sought the advice of a couple of attorneys, they bowed out; he suspected they were bought off.

About the same time, the waterworks commission was letting a bid for a railroad bridge for a waterworks switch. Dunn went back to Hynicka and said he believed that Dunn should have the contract based on what Dunn had done exposing graft in the county bridge contracts. Hynicka told him to go see the waterworks commissioner, meaning August Herrmann. Subsequently, Dunn got the contract. However, Dunn stated, when his company, the Ft. Pitt Bridge Company, completed the contract, they solemnly swore they did not want any further contracts with Cincinnati. The fact was that Herrmann and the waterworks

Rudolph "Rud" K. Hynicka, political leader. Cincinnati Museum Center–Cincinnati Historical Society Library.

commission had awarded the contract to the Ft. Pitt Bridge Company for $16,000, although a competing bid from the Union Bridge Company had been for $1,110 less to do the project. Dunn said in his deposition that when he first started attending bridge contract lettings, hardly anyone would notice him. But when he told them that Hynicka sent him, he had no trouble being heard. During the 18 months Dunn was in the bridge construction business, he estimated that a Hamilton County official made either for himself or others $150,000 on bridge contracts.

With bad news breaking on all fronts, Charles P. Taft did what he could with the *Cincinnati Times-Star* to build support for the Republican ticket, both at the state and municipal level. Still, the outlook for the election of Gordon was seemingly hopeless. The Akron speech of William Howard Taft urging Cincinnati Republicans to vote against the Cox machine candidates had caused havoc among the local party ranks, including defections. Then August Garry Herrmann committed the worst political faux pas in his career, which all but assured the election of Edward J. Dempsey. In the fall of 1905, August Garry Herrmann was wearing many hats with the waterworks commission, the Cincinnati Reds and the National Commission. To separate his baseball interests from his political interests, he had moved his primary office out of city hall to the Wiggins Block building at Fifth and Vine streets. However, over at city hall he was still the de facto city manager for the Fleischmann administration. He was also chairman of the waterworks commission and participating in the Gordon campaign. Perhaps Garry was a little too busy or for the first time in his political career feeling a great deal of pressure. He had been watching the polls closely, knew the score, and the level of his frustration was highly visible in his already reddened face. Then it boiled over.

During the late summer and fall of 1905, a capital improvement project was in progress that involved rehabilitating a city viaduct. As a result, street-car service on the Liberty Street viaduct had been suspended for a couple of months and people were getting tired of walking. The public had grown accustomed to taking their gripes to the political bosses when things got tough. But when a delegation of citizens converged on Herrmann at city hall with complaints about the Liberty Street viaduct's protracted closing, they must have caught him on a particularly bad day, because he shot the messenger. Frustrated with the reeling Gordon campaign and the negative publicity over the viaduct project, Herrmann blurted out in front of the delegation, "Let 'em walk!"[4] The Liberty Street viaduct rehabilitation project just happened to curtail street-car service to Price Hill — Democrat mayoral candidate Edward J. Dempsey's neighborhood. Consequently, Herrmann's unintentional mimic of Marie Antoinette's French Revolution era blurb "Let them eat cake" immediately became a battle cry for the Democrats. Edward J. Dempsey and his supporters used it in nearly every one of their speeches and anti–Republican signs were plastered all over Cincinnati, emblazoned with the phrase "Let 'em walk!"

It didn't take long for the anti–Republican forces at the *Cincinnati Post* to get into the street-car fray. The *Post* stated that while Garry Herrmann was telling the Cincinnati workingman "Let 'em walk," under his watch the city had bought 60,720 street-car tickets in one year for employees, which was as much as the total taxes paid by the Traction Company on all its car bodies. The *Post* reported that in the past year, street-car tickets distributed to city employees with tender feet included 23,000 tickets to the waterworks department, 11,000 tickets to the engineer's department, 9,000 to the city council, and 200 tickets by the city treasure. For years following the 1905 municipal elections, some political analysts and members of the press in Cincinnati held the opinion that Garry Herrmann's angry retort to those citizens seeking relief on the viaduct project had been the "coup de grace" to the campaign of Harry L. Gordon and the Republicans.

The credibility of Garry Herrmann was coming under fire from another angle as well. The *Cincinnati Post* was alleging that $7 million had been added in tax valuation to property in the past year. This was revealed in the 1906 budget for city expenses, submitted by Herrmann to the city council. According to the *Post*, the added valuation was an attempt at deception on the part of Herrmann to collect more taxes through a lower rate of taxation. The *Post* alleged that over a million dollars had been added to the valuation of property in Hyde Park alone. According to the *Post*, "Last year the tax rate was based on a valuation of $223,000,000. This year it is based on $280,000,000. Last year the city rate, including interest and sinking fund, was 12.24 mills on the dollar. To raise the same amount next year on the increased valuation would require a tax levy of only 11.84 mills. The rate, however, was only reduced to 11.997, making an increase in the amount raised by taxation of $50,000. The mayor's budget shows that he made very few changes in it after it had been prepared by Herrmann."[5]

With the election only two weeks away, Edward J. Dempsey took his campaign back to the old neighborhood of his youth, speaking at Yonofsky's Hall on West 6th Street. Rather than address the issues surrounding his opponent, Harry L. Gordon, in the mayoral election, Dempsey kept his campaign riding high on the anti–Cox bandwagon. To bang the drum louder, he pulled a page out of one of the editions of the *Cincinnati Post* to rekindle the magic issue of his adolescent association with Cox. Dempsey told the partisan crowd:

> I had then for a playmate George B. Cox, and I never dreamed that I should be called upon to ask your support in wrestling from him, for the people, their heritage, which he has stolen from them. The question before the people in this election is one of plain American citizenship. It is shall the people be the boss? The right to rule comes from the people, and in a properly managed government, the public officials are the agents of the people. There was a time when if you wanted an improvement made, you went to your Councilman. You do not do that now, for your Councilman is a dummy. You must see the Boss, who moves the members of public boards like pawns on a chessboard.[6]

Although the Republicans were starting to run for cover in the wake of relentless attacks coming from the Democrats and the *Cincinnati Post*, everyone knew that George B. Cox would not go down without a fight. To that end, the Citizen's Honest Elections Committee, headed by James N. Gamble and Archbishop Moeller, began to alert voters to the possibility of a massive strategy of voter fraud to be engineered by Cox on election day. The committee was predicting that in the city's 8th Ward Precinct I, more than 50 percent of the votes cast would be fraudulent. Precinct I ran from Front Street, between Sycamore and Broadway. Located within Precinct I was the notorious Silver Moon lodging house on Front Street along with several other similar dives.

Cox could pack these lodging houses with 200 to 500 men who would register and then on election day vote from these locations. As the election neared, if one ventured into the Silver Moon at midnight, he would encounter about 400 men lounging on double-deck iron cots on the building's four floors or slumbering on the floor of the so-called "floproom" at the rear of the first floor. There were similar low-brow lodging houses in other wards, such as the Indiana Hotel in the 18th Ward and the Oxford Hotel in the 8th Ward, Precinct E. According to a report in the *Cincinnati Post*, a detective hanging out at 518 Plum Street was told by a precinct worker, "I've got a lot boys cooped down at 141 Broadway."[7]

It was even alleged by the *Post* that lunatics voted. An article in the *Post* stated that, "on the first day of registration in October 1904, William Robinson registered from 230 Post-square. On October 22, 1904, he was committed to Longview Asylum and remained there until May 10, 1905, on which date he died. Yet at the November election of 1904, William Robinson voted from 230 Post-square. Robinson was a well-known character. He had killed a man and had spent one year in the penitentiary. After his release, the deed so preyed on his mind that he became insane. He had only been out of Longview seven days before the date that he was taken to the booth and registered."[8] Nonetheless, the *Cincinnati Post* had obtained the assurance of the Board of Elections that they would assist the paper in every way possible to identify voter fraud in the coming election, and the board even appointed a deputy clerk with the task of rooting out voter fraud. As election day approached, Rabbi David Philipson of the Citizens Honest Elections Committee wrote an open letter published in the *Post* to the voters of Cincinnati, drawing heavily on William Howard Taft's speech in Akron to describe the alleged corruption in Cincinnati municipal government. It crippled the machine.

On election day, November 7, 1905, it was clear by early afternoon that the Republicans were facing a disaster in the returns in every office, from governor to justice of the peace. As was the election day custom, around five o'clock Cox, Herrmann, Hynicka and other Republican leaders began to assemble at the Blaine Club to count the votes. While they were hoping for a miracle, it didn't take long to confirm the impending gloom and doom. By 5:30 P.M., well before the polls were closed, it was clear to all assembled at the Blaine Club that it was over; the Democrats were winning by a landslide. Pattison was winning election for governor and carrying on his coattails a large Democrat majority in both houses of the state legislature. Locally, Republican mayoral hopeful Harry L. Gordon was losing, and so was Rud Hynicka at the county level.

The city council elections in Cincinnati at that time were divided into election years for even- and odd-numbered wards. Twelve of the Republican council seats in odd-numbered wards were not up for re-election in the fall of 1905 and, consequently, the GOP would still retain control on the city council. However, the Republicans had been defeated for the three at-large seats that were up for election and lost six other seats in various even-numbered ward contests. Prior to this election, the Democrats had held just one seat on council.

At 6:00 P.M., George B. Cox quietly arose from his seat and approached a reporter. He told the reporter that he had decided to retire from politics. Cox then gave him a written, signed statement and asked that it be delivered to the Associated Press and carried in their newspapers across America.

> Now that the election is over and the people have signified their preference for city, county and state officials, and I sincerely trust they have selected wisely, I wish to announce to the public that from this day after 25 years of active service in the ranks of the Republican Party, my personal activity in politics shall cease. I will continue to vote the Republican ticket, but others must bear the burden of future campaigns. To the local Republican organization and the many friends that have stood with us in the past, I tender most grateful thanks for their unswerving loyalty and support. I hope for their future goodwill. Respectfully yours,
>
> George B. Cox[9]

The reporter then asked Cox what he thought had attributed to the landslide. Cox replied,

> "I am out of politics and simply a private citizen and do not care to discuss the matter."
> "Who will be the next leader of the Republican Party in Hamilton County, now that you have retired?"
> "I do not know."
> "Who will choose the leader?"
> "That will be a matter for the party to decide. I have nothing at all to do with it."
> "You are still a member of the Blaine Club, are you not?"
> "Yes, and I will continue to vote as usual."[10]

With Cox declaring himself retired and Hynicka defeated for re-election as county treasurer, the press turned to Garry Herrmann for answers regarding the future of the Republican Party. However, the last man standing in George B. Cox's triumvirate of party leader-ship was clueless. Herrmann refused to make any comments. He stated that he wanted a few days to analyze the returns before he could speak on the results. So it seems that Garry Herr-mann cut and ran that night. At the moment, Herrmann was unsure if he would be permit-ted to remain as chairman of the waterworks commission as such appointees were the domain of the state legislature. Anyway, he was busy; just over the horizon loomed the 1906 baseball season, and for the moment he just wanted to retreat to the tranquility of the Laughery Club for a few days and sort out all his options.

On January 1, 1906, Edward J. Dempsey was sworn in as the 29th mayor of Cincinnati. The broom was about to come out in city hall and immediately many Republicans started packing up. About 2,000 Republicans had been employed in the Fleischmann administration, staffing every possible position, including secretary, clerk, stenographer, messenger, city treas-urer, assistant city treasurer, superintendent of track elevation and subways, rod men, smoke inspector, police court prosecutor, title examiner and many more, not counting the mayor's direct patronage appointees. They all were about to become unemployed.

VII

The Ed Phelps Decision

In late May 1906, Garry Herrmann would face his first crises as chairman of the National Commission. However, the irony in the matter is that it was a crises that Herrmann himself had created. Pittsburgh owner Barney Dreyfuss kept a notebook on players in almost every league and he liked the dope he had accumulated on catcher Ed Phelps. In 1902, Dreyfuss purchased Phelps' contract from Rochester and signed him to play for the Pirates. Most baseball historians classify Phelps as an obscure ballplayer, but the facts are that Ed Phelps was a good catcher who could hit, throw and run the bases with speed. In 1903, Phelps did a credible job for the pennant-winning Pirates, playing in 81 games and hitting .282. In addition, he was the National League's first catcher in a World Series, playing in all eight games against Boston in 1903.

In the 1905 season, Ed Phelps had been the backup catcher on the Cincinnati Reds, playing in 44 games and hitting .231. In mid–May 1906, Garry Herrmann asked waivers on Phelps. However, before the 10-day waiver period had expired, Herrmann sold Phelps to the Boston Pilgrims of the American League. Then, on the 10th day of the waiver period, Phelps signed a contract with Barney Dreyfuss and the Pittsburgh Pirates. While the Pirates already had two catchers in George Gibson and Heinie Peitz, the fact that Phelps was a good hitter and fast on the bases made him desirable in a pinch-hitting role.

Under the existing rules of the National Commission, the rightful contractual claim to Phelps was to be decided by the chairman, who had absolute power in the resolution of such matters. At once a conflict of interest existed and Herrmann found himself on the hot seat. Furthermore, for Herrmann the circumstances surrounding the Phelps matter involved one of his most severe critics in Barney Dreyfuss. From the start, following the Cincinnati peace accord between the leagues in 1903, Dreyfuss had been against having a fellow club owner serve as chairman of the National Commission; his descent would only become more intense over the coming years. The popular magazine, the *Sporting Life*, began to run articles about the riff that had been opened over Phelps. Also, both National League president Harry Pulliam and American League president Ban Johnson began to publicly express their positions. Of course, Ban Johnson was out to protect the interests of the American League club owners at all costs. Harry Pulliam's position on the matter was and still can be subjected to scrutiny. Pulliam had been employed by Barney Dreyfuss in Louisville and remained fiercely loyal to him.

During the 1905 season, New York Giants manager John McGraw had made quite a fuss by accusing Pulliam of being blinded by his lingering loyalty to Dreyfuss. In May 1905,

McGraw was suspended after brawling with Pittsburgh manager Fred Clarke and shouting insults at Barney Dreyfuss from the field. McGraw then charged that Dreyfuss controlled the National League umpires through Pulliam. There was other bad blood between McGraw and Dreyfuss, over his alleged refusal to pay a gambling debt of $10,000 with the Pirates magnate. The matter became commonly known as the "Hey Barney" case in reference to a remark made by McGraw to Dreyfuss while standing on the balcony of the Giants' clubhouse. As the New York press began to vigorously defend McGraw, Harry Pulliam decided the case was too volatile for him alone to handle. So on June 1, it went before the National League Board of Directors, which included Charles Murphy of Chicago, Barney Dreyfuss of Pittsburgh, Charles H. Ebbets of Brooklyn, Garry Herrmann of Cincinnati and Harry Pulliam. The directors fined McGraw $150 and suspended him for 15 days. However, John T. Brush reversed the fine and suspension by seeking an injunction in Superior Court and forcing further hearings on the matter that ultimately exonerated McGraw. For years after, every time Barney Dreyfuss entered a major league ballpark other than his own, he was greeted with loud choruses of fans shouting "Hey Barney."

In the Ed Phelps matter, Garry Herrmann asserted that he received permission from the catcher to sell his contract to the Pilgrims as long as the Reds paid half the amount due in the transaction. But Ed Phelps was adamant in his position that he had never given Herrmann permission to sell his contract. Herrmann held firm, and for the moment, the award of Phelps' contract remained with Boston. A week later, Barney Dreyfuss learned through an independent source that Herrmann had bet $6,000 that the Pirates would not win the 1906 National League pennant. Herrmann did not deny the allegation of having made the wager. However, he attempted to soften the impact by stating that it had occurred after a great deal of jesting. Jesting was interpreted as meaning the wager had been made during a serious drinking episode. Caught between a rock and a hard place, Herrmann reversed his decision and awarded Phelps' contract to Dreyfuss and the Pirates.

The Phelps matter compromised the credibility of Garry Herrmann's chairmanship of the National Commission, and from this point

Barney Dreyfuss, president, Pittsburgh Pirates. National Baseball Hall of Fame Library, Cooperstown, N.Y.

forward, every inter-league matter that he adjudicated would be construed by his critics, paramount among them Barney Dreyfuss, as being weak and subservient to Ban Johnson. Although Herrmann had received numerous accolades for his skillful coordination of the 1903 peace accord between the leagues and for his work to make the World Series an annual event by including John T. Brush in the process, he was entering a learning curve. It seemed that Herrmann was failing to understand that the actions he was now taking as chairman of the National Commission and the decisions he had to render were subject to scrutiny on a national stage with far-reaching ramifications. His decisions were no longer being made solely for the edification and continued power of the local Republican Party in his closed-door office in Cincinnati's city hall.

At the moment, if there was any solace in the matter for Herrmann, it came in the form of a letter he received from a lady in Wisconsin that Herrmann in turn requested to be published in the *Sporting Life* in August 1906.

Mosinee, Wis.   July 27,

Mr. August Herrmann,

Dear Sir:

I know that it is very presumptuous of me to write you, but I simply cannot help it. I've been taking the *Sporting Life* for the last six months and could not help seeing all the fuss about the Phelps case.

Now I don't pretend to know a great amount about base ball, because it's only for the past two years that I have taken any interest in the major leagues. Just the same, let Mr. Pulliam or Mr. Johnson say what they may, and Mr. Pulliam certainly says enough to make one feel rather blue, just console yourself that you are right, and that even way up here in the backwoods you have some sincere admirers. Ever since I first heard of you you've taken the right stand in base ball matters, and I'm sure this last isn't an exception. If I was a great big stick in base ball matters I'd tell Mr. Pulliam a thing or two. As it is, I know I am doing an almost unprecedented thing, but please consider that I am nearly base ball crazy and that I could not see the only member of the National Commission that I have any sympathy with abused and not say a little something on the subject.

Very truly yours,
Amelia Roberts[1]

Tinker to Evers to Chance and a Little Help from Herrmann

During the offseason Christy Mathewson was employed as an insurance broker in New York. Over the winter of 1905–06, Mathewson recommended a $250,000 disaster insurance policy to Garry Herrmann that would exclude coverage for the players on the field, but cover most accidents off the field, including train wrecks. However, the real disaster regarding the Reds had been taking place on the field. Despite the fact that Cy Seymour, the Reds' center fielder, had won the National League batting crown in the 1905 season with a .377 average, there really wasn't a lot for fans to cheer about, and attendance had declined.

For the 1906 season, Herrmann was determined to induce more attendance at the Palace of the Fans. He reasoned that the seating capacity was inadequate and constructed a double-deck stands of concrete and iron down the left and right field lines. After three unsuccessful seasons and a fifth-place finish in 1905, Jack Kelley was fired as manager and replaced with Ned Hanlon, who had been piloting the Brooklyn club since 1899. While Kelley remained on the team as the club's starting left fielder, it would ultimately be another long, hot summer for the Reds. With Hanlon at the helm, the Reds finished in sixth place, 51½ games behind the Cubs. Garry Herrmann had promised the Reds' fans some big-name players for the 1906 club, but none materialized. In fact, on July 6, Herrmann sold Cy Seymour, the team's only legitimate star, to the New York Giants when John T. Brush forked over $12,000 for the center fielder. In the end, the team's quality of play remained marginal, and the enlarged seating capacity at the Palace of the Fans had only a minimal effect on increasing fan interest, resulting in an attendance of 330,056, which was an increase of only 16,129 over the previous season.

Despite the popularity of the New York Giants, overall the National League was still losing to the American League at the gate. In the 1906 season, the American League once again dominated the National League in attendance with a season total of 2,938,076 to 2,781,213. After an early-season challenge from the Giants, the Cubs ran away with the National League pennant, outdistancing the second-place New Yorkers by 20 games while posting 116 wins, which still stands as the major league record. However, Garry Herrmann was to play a pivotal role in helping the Chicago Cubs dominate the National League in 1906 through a couple of trades he engineered with them.

Harry Steinfeldt, a former traveling minstrel, had been the Reds' regular third baseman since 1898. At the time, the Chicago Cubs had without question the best infield in the National League if not the majors with Joe Tinker at shortstop, Johnny Evers at second base and Frank

Chance, their player-manager, at first base. However, the Cubs needed help at the hot corner and felt the best man for the job was Reds veteran third sacker Harry Steinfeldt. In March 1906, the Cubs offered Herrmann southpaw pitcher Jake Weiner and utility infielder Hans Lobart in exchange for Steinfeldt. Herrmann closed the deal without hesitation.

Both Harry Steinfeldt and shortstop Tommy Corcoran had been in Garry Herrmann's doghouse since their well-publicized donnybrook at the Laughery Club the past October, which had caused the Reds' president considerable political embarrassment as the Democrats were making mincemeat out of the Republican mayoral campaign of Harry L. Gordon. So it was certain that one or the other, Steinfeldt or Corcoran, would pay the price and be shipped out of Cincinnati. In the deal, the Cubs were throwing in Jake Weiner, a pretty good pitcher. In 1903, Weiner had a record of 21–9, in 1904 he had gone 20–14, and in the 1905 season he posted a record of 18–12.

To fill the void left by Steinfeldt's departure, Herrmann arranged a trade with the Boston Pilgrims that brought Jim Delhanty to the Reds to play third. Jim Delhanty was from the famous Delhanty family of Cleveland that had sent five brothers to the majors. The most famous of the Delhanty brothers, Ed, had mysteriously died at Niagara Falls during the 1903 season, but brothers Jim, Frank, Joe and Tom also played in the major leagues. The trade for Jim Delhanty also brought the Reds Chick Fraser, a pitcher who had posted a record of 14–21 for Boston in 1905. However, Fraser had won 21 games for Philadelphia of the National League in 1899 and 22 games for Philadelphia of the American League in 1901.

Harry Steinfeldt went on to play in four World Series with the Chicago Cubs (1906, 1907, 1908, 1910) and overall played in the major leagues for 14 years. In the 1906 season, he would lead the Cubs in hitting with a .327 batting average, finishing second behind National League batting champion Honus Wager with a .339 average. Also in the 1906 season, Steinfeldt would finish first in the National League in hits (176), second in total bases (232), and fourth in slugging average (.430) and tie for first in RBIs (83) with Pittsburgh's Jim Nealon. Unfortunately for Steinfeldt, Franklin P. Adams of the *New York Evening Mail* was unable to work his name into the well-known verse he wrote on the Cubs' infield of Tinker, Evers and Chance in 1906, so he never achieved the baseball immortality of his teammates. The verse was called "Baseball's Sad Lexicon" and went as follows:

> These are the saddest of possible words—
> Tinker to Evers to Chance.
> Trio of bearcubs and fleeter than birds,
> Tinker to Evers to Chance.
> Thoughtlessly pricking our gonfalon bubble,
> Making a Giant hit into a double.
> Words that are weighty with nothing but trouble —
> Tinker to Evers to Chance.[1]

While the Cubs were a good hitting team in 1906, leading the National League in both batting average (.262) and slugging average (.329), as well as a solid fielding club by leading the league with a .969 average, they were particularly pitching rich. The Cubs' pitching staff was led by Mordecai "Three Finger" Brown with a record of 26–6 and league-leading ERA of 1.04. The other starters in the rotation included Jack Pfiester (20–8, 1.56), Ed Reulbach (19–4, 1.65) and Carl Lundren (17–6, 2.21). For some reason, Garry Herrmann gave the Cubs' pitching staff an added shot in the arm. On June 2, 1906, Herrmann traded pitcher Orval Overall to the Cubs for pitcher Bob Wicker and $2,000. Wicker finished the season in Cincinnati with an undistinguished record of 6–14 after going 3–5 for the Cubs, while Orval Overall, after compiling a lackluster 3–5 record for the Reds, was brilliant for the Cubs, finishing with

The 1907 Chicago Cubs infield. From the left: Harry Steinfeldt, Joe Tinker, Johnny Evers, Frank Chance. Author's collection.

a record of 12–3 in Chicago. Overall would eventually have two twenty-win seasons for the Cubs and pitch in four World Series, compiling a post-season record of 3–1 with an ERA of 1.58 while appearing in eight games. Bob Wicker would be a bust in Cincinnati. He would pitch in 20 games, finish with a record of 6–14, and at the end of the season be released and never pitch in the major leagues again.

The Chicago White Sox won the American League pennant in 1906, setting the stage for major league baseball's first intra-city World Series. The 1906 Chicago White Sox, also known as "the Hitless Wonders," won the American League pennant despite having the lowest team batting average in the league (.230). On the other hand, the White Sox had a pretty solid pitching staff. The White Sox mound corps had compiled a league-leading 32 shutouts, led by Frank Owen (22–13), Nick Altrock (20–13), future Hall of Fame member "Big" Ed Walsh (17–13) and Doc White (18–6), who had the lowest ERA (1.52) in the league. With superb pitching, the White Sox won 19 consecutive games in August, during which they held the opposition to just 28 runs. During that span, the White Sox pitchers threw eight shutouts, four of them by Ed Walsh.

With the proud pictures of Garry Herrmann, Harry Pulliam and Ban Johnson, whose weight had ballooned to nearly 300 pounds, featured on the cover of the souvenir scorebook, the 1906 World Series began on October 9 and was played in some bitterly cold weather in Chicago that included snow flurries. Despite the fact that the Cubs' Ed Reulbach pitched a one-hitter to defeat the White Sox in game two and that they only had only one more hit in the series than the Cubs, the White Sox won the series in six games by virtue of their pitching staff achieving a 1.67 ERA.

In 1906, the Cubs played their games in a ballpark located on the west side of Chicago. One of the fans who had been feverishly following the rampaging Cubs all season was judge Kenesaw Mountain Landis. In the not-too-distant future, the careers of Judge Landis and August Garry Herrmann were destined to windup on a collision course. Becoming a federal judge did nothing to diminish the love Landis had for the Chicago Cubs and his favorite players— Joe Tinker, Johnny Evers, Frank Chance and Mordecai Brown. He attended several of the 1906 World Series games, was loud in his support for the Cubs, and is reported to have gotten into some heated arguments with White Sox fans.

By 1907, August Garry Herrmann was looking forward to the completion of the Cincinnati waterworks project. He was fully aware of what the success of the project would mean to his legacy and, at the same time, he was genuine in his desire to provide the residents of the city with a clean, safe water supply. To that end, the Board of Trustees in their report explicitly stated, "that they are ready to furnish any additional information that may be required; that its books and records are open for the inspection of the public, and to reiterate that it is their desire in presenting this matter at this time, to provide means to complete the new works at as early a period as possible, and turn it over to the proper authorities, to the end that the public will be the benefit of that which the new water works acts contemplate, — viz.: an abundant supply of pure and wholesome water.[2]

The good people of Cincinnati had long anticipated the opening of the new waterworks. Finally, on January 2, 1907, the new waterworks began partial continuous pumping of 10 million gallons of water per day to high-service districts of the city. Furthermore, it was anticipated that by February 1, all the water needed in the high-service districts could be pumped by the new facility, and that by August 1, the new waterworks would be fully functional and capable of providing all the water that was needed throughout the city. Then the only work left to be completed would be some minor work on reservoir number 2, some cleaning in old water mains, and a beautification plan for the grounds.

Herrmann was still serving as chairman of the commissioners of waterworks and on February 16, 1907, the Board of Trustees issued a detailed report on the progress of the public works project. Herrmann realized the mistake he had made by not defending the waterworks project in the municipal campaign of 1905 and the strong attacks upon the progress of the construction of the new system made by Edward Dempsey and his campaign's cohort, the *Cincinnati Post*. But now in 1907, Herrmann was taking the high ground. In his report he remarked that there would be a need for additional funds to complete the project, however that funding could not be obtained as the state legislature would not meet again until 1908. He also pointed out that the additional funds were not immediately required and that sufficient funds were available to complete all necessary work throughout the current year. So Herrmann recommended that all the work be completed and the additional funding worked out later.

The total amount authorized for the new waterworks by the state legislature had been $10 million. In early 1907, the total expenditures anticipated for the new waterworks were $10,504,651.62, with $8,390,941.95 spent to date. Herrmann and the board had arranged to operate the new waterworks until it was completely functional and then turn it over to the city. The anticipated cost of operation for the year was $145,000, of which any savings could then be applied by the Board of Public Service to the sinking fund, interest charges or whatever expense they deemed necessary. Also, by using an incremental implementation plan to bring the new pumping station on line, Herrmann and the board had developed a very sensible type of capital project analysis to compare the cost of operating the old system against the new. To this effect, Herrmann stated in his report, "This temporary operation of the pumping machinery by the Board of Trustees, 'Commissioners of Water Works,' during the present year, will also fully demonstrate not only the capacity of the machinery and its stability, but the cost of operation as well, thus serving as a guide for its future costs of operation and maintenance by the Board having charge of the water supply of the city, and will also enable a proper comparison to be made between the cost of running the old and the new system, and the saving effected by the latter."[3]

The protracted length of time required to complete the new waterworks project had bogged Herrmann down with pressing responsibilities and political fallout. Consequently, it limited his energy being expended in other areas of his considerable interests. Therefore, by 1907 Herrmann wanted to bring closure to the project, and in his report called for a joint meeting to be held as soon as possible with all parties having any standing in the matter of completion of the waterworks. On Friday, August 2, 1907, city engineers Kisinger and Benzenberg of the old and new Cincinnati Water Works conducted a second examination and test of all the valves, gates and mains that would be operational in the water system. Everything went well and they notified city controller-assessor Fussinger that they were ready to recommend to the Board of Public Service the immediate and permanent closing of the old Front Street pumping station, which would terminate the operation of the old waterworks. Although it would still be a few weeks before the new waterworks would be connected to the Third Street reservoir, the two engineers developed an interim plan to bleed water from the Eden Park reservoir to supply low-service areas with water until the connection was completed.

On Friday, August 9, 1907, the Front Street pumping station was shut down and the new waterworks began supplying water to the entire city. On Saturday, August 10, 1907, the Cincinnati Board of Public Service met in a closed-door session and closed the Front Street station, leaving 45 waterworks men unemployed. While there had previously been 126 men working on three shifts at the Front Street pumping station, only some of the machinists from the station, and a few men to assist with valves and gauges at the Third Street reservoir were retained and a few others were reassigned in the new waterworks. The opening of a new water plant had been kept secret from workers, so it was predictable that the usual charges of political graft would follow. The new waterworks had been constructed at a cost of just under $11 million. However, a few years after the completion of the works, a group of engineers from the East Coast appraised the system at $20 million. Much of the infrastructure of the 1907 system, with necessary technological upgrades added over the years, still serves the city of Cincinnati to this very day. August Garry Herrmann had served 12 years as chairman on the waterworks commission and done a remarkable job marshaling the completion of the project.

However, all through the summer of 1907 while Garry Herrmann was completing the new waterworks, the Cincinnati Reds were experiencing another dismal season. There was a slight decline in attendance, drawing 317,500 fans into the park as the Reds finished in sixth place, 41½ games behind the Cubs, who won the National League pennant for the second straight season. With the exception of Cincinnati native and local favorite Miller Huggins playing second base, the starting lineup of the 1907 Reds was different at every other position compared to the starting lineup of the previous year's team. Despite the large turnover in starting players, there was almost no attempt made by Herrmann and manager Ned Hanlon to acquire quality players as replacements.

With another losing season for the Reds on the books and the waterworks completed,

Garry Herrmann had other fish to fry. At the moment he was serving as president of the American Bowling Congress and making plans to hold the 1908 national tournament in Cincinnati at the Freeman Avenue Armory. While Herrmann had done nearly nothing to improve his ballclub, he conveniently passed the buck for its failure in the 1907 season to Ned Hanlon. Hanlon decided he had had enough, and after managing in the major leagues for 19 years, retired. For the 1908 season, Herrmann's response to fixing the managerial dilemma on the Reds was to hire John Ganzel. Ganzel had played in the major leagues for seven years with four clubs, beginning in 1898 with Pittsburgh, but had no managerial experience.

The 1907 World Series saw the Chicago Cubs defeat the Detroit Tigers in four straight games. Actually, there had been a fifth game in the series as the first game played in Chicago was called because of darkness after twelve innings with the score tied 3–3. The 1907 campaign had been Ty Cobb's third season in the major leagues and he won the first of his eventual 12 American League batting titles with a .350 average. Cincinnati Reds fans were keenly aware that the 1907 World Series was sprinkled with star players who had been Reds at one time, only to be sacrificed by Garry Herrmann. Harry Steinfeldt led all hitters in the series with a .471 average, and Orval Overall pitched 18 innings (including the called game) and finished with an ERA of 1.00. Also playing for Detroit was Sam Crawford, who despite having a lackluster World Series had the second-highest batting average, .323, behind Ty Cobb in the American League during the 1907 season.

IX

Accolades for Herrmann
and Merkle's Boner

The Cincinnati Republicans knew that if they were to recapture city hall in the 1907 mayoral election, they would need a squeaky-clean candidate. They nominated Colonel Leopold Markbreit, a Civil War hero and the editor of the *Volksblatt*, a German language newspaper published in Cincinnati. The coalition of Republicans and Democrats that had been forged for the purpose of defeating the Cox ticket in the 1905 mayoral election was now at odds over the re-nomination of Edward Dempsey. When Edward Dempsey won nomination over Frank Pfaff by a wide margin at the Cincinnati Democrat municipal convention of 1907, the coalition imploded. The Republican faction in the coalition, including some Democrats, supported Pfaff and were determined to run him as an independent candidate against both Markbreit and Dempsey. The result was a disaster for the Democrats. In the general election of 1907, the Republicans recaptured the mayor's office in a landslide, with Leopold Markbreit receiving 43,841 votes compared to Edward Dempsey's 23,566 and Frank Pfaff's 10,508. George B. Cox was back in the driver's seat.

In 1908, the popular magazine the *Sporting Life* celebrated its 25th anniversary. The magazine had been chronicling baseball since 1883 and was highly respected by all. In its 25th anniversary edition, published on March 14, 1908, it paid high tribute to the evolution of the game of baseball, debunking the silly notion that baseball had evolved from the English games of rounders and cricket. The edition editorialized that the game was purely American in its origin and design, and had evolved from a nineteenth century boy's game and played in American colleges as far back as 1825. The publication also paid glaring tribute to the three men it felt had guided the game into becoming a modern enterprise of high respectability: August Herrmann, Ban Johnson and Harry C. Pulliam.

The *Sporting Life* said of Herrmann:

> August Herrmann has written his name upon the pages of base ball history in letters that Time will not efface. A native born Cincinnatian, he had risen to a position of power in his own city through the force of ability and perseverance. In his youth he loved base ball, but as shortstop of the Crescents he did not gain half the prominence that he has won as Captain of the Indians at the Laughery Club. The Club game on the grounds of that organization just across the Indiana line on the Ohio River is an event of annual occurrence. Mr. Herrmann is a man of affairs. In addition to his position as President of the Water Works Commission, which is about completing for Cincinnati one of the greatest water-plants in the world, he as Chairman of the National Commission, is really Chief Justice of Balldom's Supreme Court. He is President of the Cincinnati Club and is the presiding officer of the American Bowling Congress, bringing to the bowling

From the left: Harry C. Pulliam, August Herrman, John T. Brush, Ban Johnson, Chicago, 1905. Chicago History Museum.

game the same enthusiasm which has marked his every effort for the good of base ball. Mr. Herrmann was one of the "Big Four" which acquired the Cincinnati Club by purchase from John T. Brush, Ashley Lloyd and associates in the early Fall of 1902. At that time, the National and American Leagues were in the thick of a fight to the death — a losing fight for both Leagues as Mr. Herrmann quickly discovered. He brought into play the leaven of peace and was largely responsible for opening the way to negotiations which led to an honorable peace. He was the one man who held the fullest confidence of the American League. He had refused to accept a free franchise from the American League in Cincinnati, preferring to acquire the National's Cincinnati Club in a strictly above-board businesslike way. The work that August Herrmann has done for base ball has all been along the line for its betterment and perpetuation. Although the Cincinnati Club has failed to recruit a pennant-winner during the Herrmann regime, efforts to round up a Class A team have been so persistent that the Club has not known a losing year — from the financial end — since he took hold of affairs.[1]

The *Sporting Life* article elevated August Garry Herrmann to the status of an American icon and brushed aside, in an instance, all those years of brokering back-room deals for the Cox machine. "Good Time Garry" was now chief justice of baseball's supreme court. Quickly, Herrmann seized the opportunity to write a letter to the editor, which was published in the anniversary edition along with similar letters from Johnson and Pulliam. Herrmann stated the following in his letter:

Cincinnati, O, March 10, — Editor *Sporting Life*.
It is not only with great pleasure, but with a due sense of the solemnity of the occasion, that I indict this tribute to *Sporting Life* and its distinguished editor, upon the completion of twenty-five years of unremitting and successful work in behalf of what has become firmly established as our national game. *Sporting Life* has not only been the chronicler of, but a might force in, all the great movements of the past quarter century whose cumulative effect is what to-day is the grand, solid, and I am sure enduring system of "organized ball," the like of which the world has never seen since its creation. Of your share of the Herculean labor necessary to bring the national game from it chrysalis state to the present scintillate condition we of the later base ball generation can have only a faint conception — yet my comparatively limited term in base ball gives me at least an inkling of how hard you must have worked and fought under all sorts of adverse conditions, for the great sport for twenty-five long years. And so I say that you deserve the approbation and the

thanks of every man connected in any way with base ball; and I am glad to be able to add my mite to the flood of congratulations sure to roll in upon you, although can but feebly express in words my statements upon such a significant occasion as your quarter-century anniversary celebration. So, I can only say from my heart that I desire, doubtless in common with many thousands of other admirers throughout the country, to extend my hearty greetings, my best wishes, and good cheer for the continued success of *Sporting Life* and its editor; and trust that the future course of the great paper will be even more beneficial to the sport in general than it has been in the past.[2]

The reality of the National Commission was, however, that throughout its first five years of operation, it had been a rather innocuous body in the administration of the game, issuing routine, nuts-and-bolts decisions on garden-variety issues between players and owners in accordance with the articles contained within the mundane National Agreement. Most highly controversial disputes were resolved by the two league presidents and affirmed by the respective board of directors. Typical of the National Commission's agenda were its actions taken on April 19, 1908, when it fined Jake Stahl and Mike Donlin $100 each for playing in 1907 with teams outside jurisdiction of the National Agreement. Rule 47 stated that no National Agreement player is permitted at any time, regular season or otherwise, to play in any games or against players, clubs, owners, and managers that are ineligible.

In March 1907, Jake Stahl had been sold by the Washington Nationals to the Chicago White Sox. Stahl refused to report and was then sold by Chicago to New York. After accepting the fine, Jake Stahl signed to play the 1908 season for the New York Highlanders in the American League. He played 74 games for the Highlanders before being sold to the Boston Pilgrims. He became manager of Boston in 1912 and won the American League pennant that year.

Mike Donlin, the other player who had been fined by the National Commission in its decision of April 19, 1908, would play in 155 games for the New York Giants in 1908, hitting .334, the second-highest batting average in the National League behind Honus Wagner with an average of .354. Donlin had fallen in love and married Mable Hite, a nightclub and vaudeville star with a national following. Following the 1908 season, Donlin took a leave from playing baseball and formed a vaudeville act with his beautiful wife. However, Mabel would soon die from cancer. Donlin went to California, attempted to convert his acting career into the movies, and appeared in several films with Buster Keaton. In 1911, he returned to the major leagues. He would sit out again in 1913, returning to play one more season with the Giants in 1914. Playing 12 years in the major leagues, Donlin finished with 1,287 hits and had a career batting average of .333.

The lion's share of actions taken by the National Commission was adjudication in disputes between players and owners in the minor leagues that were covered in the National Agreement. For the moment, the actions of the National Commission seemed to be more of service to the owners in clearing potentially libelous matters than actually exerting any ruling authority over baseball. However, in a few years hence, when more robust and controversial matters would find their way into the jurisdiction of the National Commission, the owners would begin to pull their wagons into a circle. For now, they were pleased with August Herrmann as chairman and with the cumbersome functioning of the body.

In 1908 under John Ganzel, the Cincinnati Reds finished in fifth place with a record of 73–81, only slightly better than under Ned Hanlon's guidance the year before. Although Herrmann had not made any significant changes in players from the previous season's club, attendance had actually soared as the Reds set a new season attendance record, drawing 399,200 through the turnstiles of the Palace of the Fans. But, as usual, before the conclusion of the

1908 season there was widespread speculation that John Ganzel would not return to manage the Reds for another year.

Although year after year Herrmann failed to field a competitive team, he was constantly looking for innovative ways to increase the Reds' bottom line as well as advance the popularity of the game of baseball. In fact, Herrmann had been mulling over the possibility of playing night games. A Massachusetts inventor by the name of George Cahill had developed a system for field lighting that held promise. As Garry Herrmann was chairman of the National Commission, Cahill approached him with the idea of playing an experimental night game. Herrmann found the idea intriguing, and to expedite the process, in August 1908, he recruited investors and formed Night Baseball Development Company to raise the necessary $50,000 capital to install experimental lights in the Palace of the Fans. If all went as planned, he would schedule an exhibition night game during the 1909 season.

The 1908 National League season concluded with one of the most famous and complicated events in major league history, one that would ultimately involve Garry Herrmann in the process of sorting it all out. A prelude to the coming controversy occurred on September 4, 1908, in Pittsburgh. The world champion Chicago Cubs had been fighting an uphill battle all year while looking to win the National League pennant for the third year in a row. On that day, the Cubs were in third place in the National League, behind the league-leading New York Giants and second-place Pittsburgh Pirates. Only three games separated the three teams in the standings, and the Cubs were facing the Pirates. The game entered the bottom of the tenth inning with the score tied at 0–0. The Pirates were at bat, there were two outs, and two men were on base. The Pirates' Warren Gill was on first base when the next batter produced a hit, driving in the winning run. However, as soon as the run scored, Gill immediately veered off the basepath before reaching second base and headed to the clubhouse. The Cubs' alert second baseman, Johnny Evers, immediately called for the ball and stepped on second, appealing to umpire Hank O'Day to rule a force-out and thereby end the inning and negate the run. But O'Day claimed that he had not seen Gill divert off the basepath before reaching second and refused to make the call. The Cubs protested to the National League office and president Harry Pulliam upheld O'Day's call. Later, O'Day realized that he had in fact made the incorrect call. However, all he could do was to mentally file the incident and wait for another opportunity to make the correct call in the future. That didn't take long to happen.

On September 23, 1908, the defending world champion Chicago Cubs had moved into second place, only six percentage points behind the New York Giants. The two teams were scheduled to meet that afternoon in a game at the Polo Grounds. That morning Giants first baseman Fred Tenney woke up suffering from a lumbago attack. The intense pain would prevent Tenney from playing that day, and he would be replaced in the Giants' lineup by nineteen-year-old Fred Merkle. Irony exists in Merkle being available for service, as he had been seriously ill only a couple of months earlier. In July, Merkle had been hospitalized at Good Samaritan Hospital in Cincinnati with a case of blood poisoning in his foot and the doctors were seriously considering amputating his foot to save his life.

When the game began on September 23, the stands were packed with 25,000 screaming fans as the Giants' Christy Mathewson dueled with the Cubs' Jack Pfiester, who was so prolific in beating the Giants that he was nicknamed "Jack the Giant Killer." Going into the bottom of ninth inning, the score was tied at 1–1. There was one out when the Giants began to rally. Art Devlin singled and then was forced at second by Moose McCormick for the second out. Fred Merkle was up next and lined a single to center, sending McCormick to third. Then Al Bidwell followed with a single to center, sending McCormick home with the winning run.

However, young Fred Merkle, on his way to second, for some reason suddenly turned the other way and headed for the clubhouse in center field.

What followed seems more like an episode of the *Keystone Kops* than a conclusion to a major league game. As the fans started to pour onto the field, it was déjà vu for Johnny Evers, and he called for the ball from center fielder Solly Hoffman. Because of the crowd spilling onto the field, Hoffman was unable to see Evers, so he tossed the ball towards first base, where Cubs shortstop Joe Tinker was standing. Giants' pitcher "Iron Man" Joe McGinnity, who was coaching third base, realized what was happening and wrestled Tinker to the ground, extracted the ball from his grip, and threw it into the stands. At that point Cubs pitcher Rube Kroh, who was not in the game, saw a fan catch the ball and demanded it from him. When the fan resisted turning over the ball, Kroh decked him, retrieved the ball and tossed it to Evers. A crowd had already assembled around Evers, who stepped on second base while standing on his toes, waving the ball and appealing to umpire Bob Emslie. Emslie in turn requested assistance from home plate umpire Hank O'Day, who ruled Merkle out at second base.

At this point, the eleventh inning should have begun with the score tied 1–1. However, the Giants were already in the clubhouse, darkness was setting in, and O'Day was between a rock and a hard place. He reasoned that if he forced the game to continue, it might cause a riot among the fans milling about the field. Likewise, if he ruled a forfeit, chaos was likely to result. Therefore, in the spirit of the public's safety and perhaps that of the umpires, too, O'Day ruled the game a 1–1 tie and to be replayed in the event that it might be necessary to determine the National League pennant winner. When John McGraw realized that Merkle had been called out, he flew into a rage and began yelling at O'Day. McGinnity joined in, telling O'Day that he threw the ball into the stands and the one that Evers had was tossed to him by someone on the Cubs' bench. By now the crowd began to sense something was up and was beginning to move towards the arguing trio of McGraw, McGinnity and O'Day. At once the police and ushers noticed the crowd moving in for the kill, intercepted them, and began escorting them off the field, thus avoiding a potentially ugly incident.

The next day, on September 24, both the Cubs and Giants demanded a forfeit of the game because the crowd couldn't be controlled. In fact, Chicago manager Frank Chance arrived at the Polo Grounds with his team and lined them up in their positions on the field. He then ordered pitcher Andy Coakley to throw three balls to catcher Johnny Kling, whereupon Chance declared a forfeit under Rule 55, which stated that clubs must play a tied or postponed game on the visiting team's next visit. However, National League president Harry Pulliam upheld Hank O'Day's decision. Pulliam's official decision read as follows: "In the matter of the New York-Chicago game of September 23, 1908, at New York, I have received the written reports of the umpires in charge of the game, Messers, O'Day and Emslie. The report that the game resulted in a tie score —1 to 1— and that it was impossible to continue the game after the ninth inning. Without entering at this time into the merits of the controversy that has arisen over the game or passing upon the legality of the decision, the game will be recorded as reported, namely a tie score. That is the official standing of the case at this time."[3]

Both the Cubs and Giants then appealed to the National League Board of Directors, comprised of August Herrmann, Barney Dreyfuss, George Dovey, Charles Ebbets and Charles W. Murphy. The *Sporting News* felt comfortable with the decision being left to the board of directors and stated, "Everybody knows Garry Herrmann who is one of the squarest, fairest-minded and most honorable men ever connected with the game. He decides all cases on their merit and the weight of evidence presented."[4]

Following the game of September 23, the Giants went into a tailspin, beginning with losing a doubleheader to the second-division Cincinnati Reds on September 25 and then losing three games to the Philadelphia Phillies in the last week of the season. Meanwhile, the Cubs won eight out of ten games. The Pittsburgh Pirates were in the race until the end and could have clinched the pennant on October 4, but lost a head-to-head battle with Cubs, 5–2. While the Cubs' regular season was concluded, the Giants were 1½ games behind Chicago and still had a three-game series with Boston to play. The Giants rose to the occasion and swept the series, thereby finishing in a dead heat with the Cubs with identical records of 98–55 and leaving the fate of the 1908 National League pennant in the hands of the board of directors.

On the morning of October 5, 1908, the position of the *New York Tribune* on the matter was printed in their morning edition:

> The disputed game between New York and Chicago is playing a far more important part than was expected at the time in the winning of the National League pennant. That game, so clearly won by the Giants and lost through a technicality on the decision of Harry C. Pulliam, president of the National League, will have cost New York the pennant if it is finally lost. There is a bare chance that the board of directors will reverse the decision of Mr. Pulliam when it meets to-day, in which case the Giants will be fairly safe. Mr. Pulliam is right in upholding his umpires on a question of fact, but it is a grave question in my mind whether he did not stretch a point in trying to protect his umpires from well merited criticism. An umpire has a duty to perform under the rules as well as a player, and it is not the duty of an umpire to leave the diamond, even if necessary to seek a place of safety, before rendering a decision on the facts. It is a rather lame excuse under the circumstances for O'Day, the umpire, to say that he did not declare the runner out and order the field cleared because in his opinion it was too dark to continue. It looks too much as if "calling the game on account of darkness" was an afterthought, and that no particular bearing on the case in point at the time. In as much as the umpire failed in his duty, the question resolves itself into whether New York should be robbed of a game won on the merits of the play on what is distinctly a technicality. If it were possible at this late day, it is safe to say that a number of games could be thrown out for the same reason, and while I am a strong believer in living up to the strict letter of the rules, there is such a thing as long custom in cases of the kind being worthy of some consideration under the conditions that existed in the now memorable game of September 23.[5]

Both the National Commission and the two leagues' board of directors worked in a quasi-judicial manner. Therefore, the decision in the Merkle controversy should have been made with precedent being considered. There had been a similar incident that had taken place during a game in the Eastern League between Wilkes-Barre and Buffalo on August 9, 1895. On October 5, 1908, at 9:00 P.M., Garry Herrmann and the National League Board of Directors met to determine the outcome of the September 23 game at the Polo Grounds. As usual, John T. Brush was late in arriving. The first order of business, following a lengthy discussion, was to excuse both Barney Dreyfuss and Charles W. Murphy from voting on the matter on grounds that the two had a vested interest in the outcome. However, other parties with a vested interest in the matter, including players and John T. Brush, would be permitted to submit affidavits. Therefore, Herrmann, Dovey and Ebbets met on the matter. Around 11:30 P.M. they adjourned for the night until 10:00 A.M. the next day.

The following morning, Herrmann, Dovey and Ebbets reviewed affidavits submitted by players from both clubs, both charging the other side with lying. In fact, Fred Merkle in his affidavit was now swearing that he touched second base. The reading of the affidavit of John T. Brush actually took over an hour and half. Over the past ninety-seven years, a lot of the facts in the Merkel fiasco have become ambiguous by various accounts. According to author Philip Seib, writing in *The Player — Christy Mathewson, Baseball, And The New Century*, one of the affidavits that peaked the interest of Herrmann, Dovey and Ebbets was submitted by Christy Mathewson, who stated that Merkel had not gone all the way to second base. Later, George Dovey was to remark, "You may not realize what that affidavit, offered to us voluntarily, meant to Mathewson. First of all, it meant a share in the World Series. Also, had the disputed game stood as it ended, without technicality, Mathewson would have led all National League pitchers for the season. Miner (Mordecai) Brown beat him out of the honor in the post-season game. We took all the other affidavits and threw them in the waste basket. Matty's word was good enough for us."[6]

Without a doubt, considering Mathewson's stature in the game at that time, his affidavit could have carried a lot of influence in the eventual decision of the board. There is, however, one small problem here. Following the Merkel controversy, Mathewson, who had been coaching at first base, gave the following account of the play to the *Sporting News*: "I had started from the field when I heard Evers yell to Hoffman, 'Throw the ball to second.' I remembered the trick they had tried to play at Pittsburgh, and I got Merkle by the arm and told him to go to second. In the meantime the ball had been thrown in high over Evers' head and fell near where the shortstop ordinarily stands. Merkle touched the bag, and I was near him when he did it."[7]

Umpires O'Day and Emslie, who had officiated the September 23 game, were on hand to present their evidence in person. Meanwhile, rumors were spreading that if the board of directors didn't rule in favor of the Giants, John T. Brush would bring a civil suit against the National League. Regardless of the conflicting evidence, the official decision of the National League Board of Directors in the matter would be the most important one delivered by the body since the National Agreement came into existence. So it was to be that the abbreviated conclave of Herrmann, Dovey and Ebbets rendered the following decision:

> In reviewing the entire matter, we realize the great importance that the game in question may be in determining as to what club is to be declared the winner of the championship in the National League. In considering the same, the thought has occurred to us as to whether or not, the New York Club can be deprived of their rights to play off the game in question, especially so in view of the fact that the game was not played off by reason of any action of that club. Our judgment and finding is that they can not be deprived of the right under the circumstances. As we have already stated, the evidence shows that the game was not played off on account of the estoppal of the Chicago Club under the constitutional operation of their first claim. The evidence, we repeat, also indicates in our judgment, that the New York Club would have played off this game on the only available day possible, had they not been informed by Mr. Pulliam that they would not be required to do so. This action on Mr. Pulliam's part can not be criticized by any one, because his hands were tied by the attitude of the Chicago Club. We therefore hold that the New York Club should in all justice and fairness, under these conditions, be given an opportunity to play off the game in question. For that reason we order that the game be played on the Polo Grounds on Thursday, October 8, or as soon thereafter as the weather conditions will permit, and both clubs are directed to govern themselves accordingly. We also require that the rules governing the World's Series in so far as they apply to the playing field, shall govern in this contest.
>
>   Aug. Herrmann
>   Geo. B. Dovey
>   Chas. H. Ebbets,
>   Directors of the National League[8]

With all the marbles on the line, an overflow crowd of 35,000 packed the Polo Grounds on October 8 as the Giants sent Christy Mathewson to the mound to once again face the Cubs' Jack Pfiester. However, when Pfiester struggled, he was quickly replaced in the box by Mordecai "Three Finger" Brown and the Cubs came from behind to win the game, 4–2. For the third consecutive year the Cubs had won the National League pennant. The shortsightedness of Fred Merkle in the September 23 game at the Polo Grounds that may have cost the Giants the 1908 pennant continues to live in baseball folklore as "Merkle's Boner." But following the game of October 8, Christy Mathewson volunteered to shoulder the blame alone, stating, "My part in the game was small. I started to pitch and I didn't finish. The Cubs beat me because I never had less on the ball in my life."[9] Fred Merkle went on to play sixteen years in the major leagues, playing on five pennant-winning teams, three with the Giants, one with Brooklyn and, ironically, one with the Chicago Cubs in 1918.

The 1908 National League pennant race had been a truly exciting one and for the first time since 1903, the National League (3,634,988) had out-drawn the American League (3,611,366) at the gate. It also had been a very profitable year for major league baseball. The New York Giants finished the season with a profit of $325,000. Nonetheless, owner John T. Brush was not a happy man, feeling that his team had been jobbed out of winning the pennant by the league board of directors. In the American League, the pennant race had been squeakier, too, with Detroit finishing ahead of Cleveland by just one-half game and ahead of Chicago by a game and half. A scheduling snafu involving postponements that allowed both Detroit and Chicago to play fewer games may have cost Cleveland the pennant.

The 1908 World Series was a repeat of the previous year with the Chicago Cubs once again facing the Detroit Tigers. Despite the superb hitting of Ty Cobb, who batted .368, the Cubs, bolstered by the fine pitching of Reulbach, Overall, Pfiester and Brown, once again repeated as world champions, defeating the Tigers 4 games to 1. In game two of the series, the Cubs' Joe Tinker hit a home run. It was the first home run hit the World Series since the second inning of the second game of the 1903 World Series.

By 1908, pitching had been become a dominating force in the major leagues. In the National League in 1908, Christy Mathewson won 37 games and "Three Finger" Brown 29. In the American League Ed Walsh won 40 games and pitched 11 shutouts. The American League also featured a young Walter Johnson and 41-year-old Cy Young, who on June 30 pitched a no-hitter against New York. In all, during the 1908 season there were four no-hitters pitched in the American League and two in the National League. In a game played on October 2, Ed Walsh struck out 15 batters in eight innings while losing the game, 1–0, to Addie Joss of Cleveland. In the National League in 1908, there were only six .300 hitters and in the American League four.

The era of major league baseball history from 1901 through 1919 has commonly been referred to as the "Dead Ball Era." The demise of the "Dead Ball Era" came about in the 1920 season with the introduction of a livelier ball and the abolition of the spitball. However, one baseball historian advanced the argument that the "Dead Ball Era" actually came to an end at the conclusion of the 1908 season. The late Lee Allen, writing in *100 Years of Baseball*, stated, "The Merkle play brought to a close the era of the dead ball, for in the following seasons concessions toward the batter originated, compromises that were not to cease until batting dominated the game to a degree beyond anything that had ever been known, but the change was to be a gradual one."[10]

X

1909 — A Year of Tragedies and Triumphs

In the presidential election of 1908, William Howard Taft was elected. Taft won the election over Democrat Williams Jennings Bryan with a plurality of 1,269,804 votes. The popular vote count was 7,679,006 for Taft as opposed to Bryan's 6,409,106. In the electoral vote, Taft won 321 to 162 over Bryan. There were also six other presidential candidates in the race, with Socialist Party candidate Eugene Victor Debs coming in third with 420,793 votes and Prohibitionist Party candidate Eugene Wilder Chapin placing fourth with 253,840 votes.

It was a special election for Cincinnati. For the first time in the city's history, one of its own was running for the presidency, and that made it just a little more than an ordinary political event. Although Taft professed that he loathed the political environment of his hometown, the Cox machine had taken care of business for him in Cincinnati. On election day, George B. Cox and Lew Kraft drove through the downtown wards, giving instructions to poll workers to dig and dig hard. So it was a surprise when William Jennings Bryan actually got more votes than Taft in Precinct A of the Tenth Ward, Garry Herrmann's precinct.

On election night at 5:30 P.M. when the polls closed in Cincinnati, the city was poised for a huge victory party. Every street-car entering downtown was crammed with riders and every street, Vine, Walnut, Fifth, Sixth, etc., was packed with people operating every kind of noise-making device known to man. By dusk at the Charles P. Taft residence, national election reports were starting to be received and all seemed favorable for the election of William Howard Taft. One of the first reports was from New York and it showed a clear plurality building in Taft's favor. By midnight the Taft gathering was sure that not only was New York in their camp, but likewise Connecticut, Massachusetts and New Jersey. As press bulletins continued to be read to Taft, a band could be heard outside of the house. William and Helen Taft opened the door to the blaze of bright, red fire burning out in the street. A band was playing that had been assembled by the Citizens Taft Club that had been organized by Cox, while a group of Cincinnati residents were cheering for the soon-to-be president-elect. Taft stepped onto the porch and with a hoarse voice gave a brief speech of thanks. Sure that he had won the election, around 3:00 A.M. an exhausted Taft went to bed.

Since Garry Herrmann became president of the Cincinnati Reds late in the 1902 season, the ballclub had never finished higher than third place. In the 1908 season, the Reds finished in the second division for the fourth straight year. The *Sporting News* referred to Herrmann as a "good loser," and that bothered him terribly.[1] Herrmann believed that the major element separating the Reds from succeeding was a winning manager. Following the 1908 World Series, rumors began to appear in the press that Herrmann did not intend to rehire John Ganzel for

The residence of Charles Phelps Taft, 316 Pike Street, Cincinnati. Photo by William A. Cook.

the 1909 season. Clark Griffith's name had come up as a possible successor to Ganzel. When Griffith was asked about his intentions, he simply ignored the question. But Herrmann told the press that until the stockholders met and discussed the question, no manager would be decided upon and no one approached with an offer for the job.

Clark Griffith had long been associated with the American League and was considered in the same vein as Charles Comiskey and Ban Johnson in the junior circuit. He had managed the Chicago White Stockings, where he won a pennant in 1901. When Ban Johnson established an American League franchise in New York, he was transferred to manage the team and protect the league's interest in the city. In fact, Griffith narrowly missed winning pennants in 1904 and 1906 with the Highlanders. Still, in early December 1908, Garry Herrmann hired Clark Griffith to manage the Reds for the coming season. As Herrmann was pursing Griffith, he had played cat-and-mouse with the Reds' president for over two months. Griffith had been noncommittal to Herrmann because he was holding out hoping to buy the Kansas City team. Herrmann, not knowing about the Kansas City connection, interpreted the aloofness of Griffith to mean he wanted more money to manage the Reds. In the end Fleischmann, Cox and the other Reds' investors had to open the club's purse-strings to an unprecedented width to sign Griffith. Although Griffith's contract called for $16,500 a year, the Reds' owners were hoping for big results from him.

Also in early December 1908, Garry Herrmann sat down with the other National League magnates for their annual meeting at the Waldorf-Astoria Hotel in New York. The American League owners were in town as well, holding their conclave at the Walcott Hotel. Both leagues were expecting rather innocuous sessions as most of the heavy lifting in routine, broad-sweeping policy administration was currently being done by the National Commission. At the conclusion of Thursday's American League session, president Ban Johnson suggested that the owners walk a couple of blocks up Fifth Avenue to the Waldorf and socialize with their National League counterparts. Minutes after arriving at the Waldorf, Johnson and Garry Herrmann had the corks popping. At that moment, the world could not have looked any brighter for Herrmann.

The National League meeting agenda included the re-election of Harry Pulliam as president and not much else. Pulliam was re-elected with seven votes, as neither John T. Brush nor his assistant Fred Knowles were present. Also, an agreement was expected to be reached on a rather mundane matter of closing each day's session by 6:00 P.M. to allow the magnates to partake in a hearty social schedule while in the big town. Suddenly, things got very serious. Rumors were circulating that in the Friday session, charges would be addressed that an attempt had been made to bribe Umpires Klem and Johnstone prior to the playoff game between the Cubs and Giants on October 8, 1908.

John T. Brush, the owner of the New York Giants, had been rumored to be ailing from rheumatism and stayed away from the National League meetings. More likely, the absence of Brush was a protest against the National League, as he was still smarting over the decision of the board of directors to not award the pennant to the Giants in the disputed game of September 23. However, when Brush was tipped off as to what was going to be said in the final meeting on Friday, he pulled himself out of bed — or whatever — and appeared at the Waldorf along with Knowles. Barney Dreyfuss, owner of the Pirates, remarked, "We had a rather sensational windup after several peaceable sessions. We had to attempt to fix Umpires Klem and Johnstone in our systems and we had to get it out. The entire matter will be laid before District Attorney Jerome. We had positive information about this matter and know beyond a doubt, the name of the men who made the offer to Klem and Johnstone."[2]

As the Friday meeting began, Harry Pulliam read affidavits from both Klem and Johnstone that categorically stated that prior to the game of October 8, both of them had been approached by an individual and offered a bribe to throw the game to the Giants. Immediately, the league decided to begin an investigation. Brush, Pulliam, Herrmann and Ebbets were appointed as a committee to look into the matter. The committee was given authority, if necessary, to report their findings to District Attorney Jerome. What seems a little inconsistent is that John T. Brush was named to chair the committee. To some observers this seemed a little like putting the fox in charge of guarding the henhouse. However, others held the opinion that it was sound policy to have Brush lead the investigation to avoid charges by him at a later date that evidence involving his club had been withheld from him by the committee.

Rational minds would have dictated that the National League owners go forward with a unified, determined effort that would result in flushing out the facts in the matter of the alleged bribe. But that was not the way that the National League owners did business. The reality of their relationship was that they were a group of anarchists sharing a common hotel and conference table and not much else. Immediately, commotion resulted and Harry Clay Pulliam was taking much of the backlash. Owners friendly to John T. Brush began to circulate charges that Pulliam had known about the bribe attempt for weeks and tried to sweep the matter under the rug. Others were charging that the whole matter was an erroneous charge concocted by Harry Pulliam, Barney Dreyfuss and Charles Murphy to settle past disputes with John McGraw. At the moment, everyone connected with the game was skeptical as to what evidence of the alleged bribe would surface in the committee's investigation.

While the National League owners had accomplished very little in their meetings, the American League owners introduced some significant changes at their meetings. Included in the new league policies and procedures for the 1909 season was a rule that required in all American

League parks scoreboards to be installed that contained the batting order of both teams, with changes made during the game. Other new rules agreed to included permitting the visiting team 30 minutes for practice and the home club 10 minutes, and requiring the umpires to be on the field 40 minutes before the game to supervise the practice.

The National Commission had been meeting regularly and, as usual, handling a considerable caseload of grievances from players and clubs, while addressing a few broad-sweeping policy issues. In fact, secretary John E. Bruce stated that by 1908, August Herrmann had been involved in making over 300 formal decisions of the National Commission. Major league baseball was becoming increasingly aware of the contributions that Herrmann was making to the game as chairman of the commission. Until that point, Herrmann had been administering baseball's high court gratis. However, it was the decision of Pulliam and Johnson that the time had come when Herrmann should be compensated for his participation and contributions as chairman, and voted him an annual stipend of $5,000 a year.

In early February, Harry Pulliam announced that a dinner was planned to honor August Garry Herrmann at the Auditorium Hotel Annex in Chicago and made the following remarks:

> Herrmann's unselfish attitude has helped baseball and the National League wonderfully. The National and American leagues never have been so prosperous as since the time Herrmann appeared on the base ball horizon. Garry, in a quiet manner, demonstrated the futility of the big organizations warring on each other and showed the benefits that would accrue by working in harmony. He did not harp on the financial possibilities for the club owners, but had an eye to the future and pointed out how the magnates would be able to better reimburse their skilled players and at the same time be sure of their services. As chairman of the National Commission, Herrmann has done incalculable good for base ball. Until recently, Garry was an unsalaried officer of the Commission. At the last meeting we voted him a stipend of $5,000 a year, which is about a quarter of the sum the position of chairman and the labor it entails is worth. If I had been selected to hold down this all-important job, I would figure that I ought to got just $5,000 and I don't know whether I would not have been too highly compensated at that. Herrmann should draw $20,000 a year from the National Commission and all the clubs in the domain of organized base ball should chip in and pay him his salary. When Herrmann first entered the ranks of the National League our franchises weren't worth much. Now they are so valuable none of our owners could be tempted to sell. There never will be any more wars in base ball between the big leagues and there will be fewer outlaw organizations from now on. Herrmann, as I said before, is one of the greatest men connected with the national game, and I tip my hat to Ban Johnson, president of the American League, for discovering Garry and inducing him to enter base ball. I had a row with Herrmann once, but that's past and I want now to tell the public how much it is indebted to him for the present high plane on which base ball is conducted. That dinner which John A. Heydler and I are to give in the Auditorium Hotel Annex, Chicago on February 16, is for the scribes only. Heydler and I both are former newspapermen and we thought we'd like to banquet the fellows who write base ball. Ban Johnson and Robert McRoy will be the only persons present at this dinner who are not newspapermen. Heydler and I pay the expenses of the entertainment and the National League has nothing to do with it.[3]

Recently there had been an increase in the commission's workload in addressing grievances between players and clubs over the reserve clause. Therefore, in order to bring clarity to the issue of when a player may or may not have an issue involving the reserve clause, Herrmann and the National Commission established written rules by which it would consider such a grievance. In September 1908, the following notice was sent to all players under jurisdiction of the National Agreement and also published in the *Sporting News*.

Notice to Base Ball Players

The National Commission will be governed by the following rules in cases coming before it in the future, when the rights of a club to reserve a player are questioned:

First — Where a contract contains a reservation clause, the player shall not be held to be free from reservation unless the clause is stricken out from the contract.

Second — Where a contract does not contain a reservation clause, every club nevertheless has a right to reserve a player, unless the player can produce a written agreement that he was not to be reserved, or a preponderance of evidence to the effect.

Third — On and after December 15, 1908, all written agreements releasing a player from reservation must be written on the same document as the contract itself, and no written agreement offered by a player releasing him from reservation will be considered unless it antedates that time.

> John E. Bruce
> Secretary
> Harry C. Pulliam,
> Ban B. Johnson,
> Aug. Herrmann,
> National Commission[4]

However, in January 1909, another matter found its way onto the agenda of the National Commission. After winning the 1908 National League pennant and World Series over the Detroit Tigers, Chicago Cubs president Charles Murphy approved a $10,000 bonus pool to be divided equally among his players. Some other clubs felt that improprieties were inherent in the matter. However, Murphy stated to the commission that he had never discussed the matter of a bonus with anyone other than Cubs manager Frank Chance, who was a minority stockholder in the club. Furthermore, Murphy stated that he would arrange for a delegation of Cubs players to meet with the commission. To that end, Murphy wrote to a relative in Cincinnati and asked him to call upon August Herrmann and request that the player delegation be permitted to speak before the commission.

Ban Johnson and Harry Pulliam found no fault in the bonus payment, considering it to be an internal matter among Murphy, Chance and his players. But August Herrmann was reluctant to rubber-stamp the decision, stating that he would not go on record as endorsing the bonus payment until he received a written statement from Murphy. In the end, it was a 2–1 decision in favor of the bonus and the matter was closed. Considering that Murphy and Herrmann were close friends, the dissenting action of Herrmann in the bonus matter should, but does not, lighten the historical notion that Herrmann allowed Johnson to dictate policy decisions of the National Commission.

Rumors also had been circulating that the 1909 season would be the last for August Garry Herrmann in baseball. Feeding the rumor mill was the upcoming banquet planned for him in Chicago by Pulliam and Heydler. The baseball community also had become increasingly aware of the fact that Herrmann had been quite busy of late with some of his new business ventures. Over the past year, Garry Herrmann had been named president of the Union Gas & Electric Company and as a director of the Cincinnati Gas, Coke, Coal and Mining Company. Rumors were swirling about that he would soon be selling energy commodities full-time.

It was true, Garry Herrmann, like his political partners George B. Cox and Rud Hynicka, was starting to make big money out of his political connections. However, that did not necessarily mean that he was ready to scrap his passion for baseball. The fact of the matter was that Herrmann needed extra income to support his lavish spending habits. By now it had become a spectator sport for people in Cincinnati to say that they had seen Garry Herrmann driving his green automobile around the city. He also was regularly meeting the annual deficits run up by the Laughery Club out of his own pocket. When the *Sporting News* put the question about leaving the game before him, Herrmann responded, "Retire from base ball? Sure, when I lay down the rest of life's burdens—when the Standard Oil Company comes across with the plea of 'Guilty' to every charge and indictment made against it, when base ball players tell me that I am paying them too much and request me to cut their salaries—when all these things happen, then I'll drop out of the game."[5]

While Garry Herrmann was being wined, dined and feted in Chicago by Harry Pulliam and John Heydler, rumors involving him in a coverup of the alleged bribe of Umpires Klem and Johnstone continued to circulate. It was being said that Herrmann and John T. Brush were attempting to whitewash the investigation. It was a fact that more than two months had passed since the National League established the investigation committee and so far no progress had been made in the matter. It was also being said that Harry Pulliam knew the name of the person who had made the alleged bribe, and that Brush and Herrmann were leaning on him to remain silent. On February 11, 1909, the *Sporting News* stated the following:

> Pulliam has the goods and in spite of the fact that Brush and Herrmann don't care for further publicity, it is up to the National League president to make the evidence in hand public, even if a criminal prosecution grows out of the question. It is up to Charles Murphy of the Cubs to demand that the whole case with names and facts be laid bare, so that the American public can place the blame where it belongs. It is not enough to say that Klem and Johnstone are honest, for everybody knows that they are. What we want to know is the name of the individual who did the tempting with the coin in his hand and when Pulliam has done that it will be an easy matter to connect certain underground wires. It will be an interesting matter to hear what excuses the suspected man will give when he is placed in the limelight and finds that he is against the wall.[6]

Throughout the final days of February, pressure was mounting from the public and press on the National League to be more energetic in pursuing the investigation of the alleged bribery charges in the October 8, 1908, game between the Cubs and Giants. Simultaneously, there were those who continued to place the blame for all the negative publicity in the matter squarely on the shoulders of Harry Pulliam for making the whole mess public information. There was no doubt in anyone's mind that Harry C. Pulliam cared deeply about the integrity of the game. Yet while he tried to hide it, Harry Pulliam was a troubled man. It seemed that his personal values were always in conflict with the way he was expected to conduct his business affairs. Pulliam once said, "Those of us who live up to our ideals may have some excuse for feeling high and mighty."[7] It was said of Pulliam that he refused to be a figurehead in his position as president of the National League, that he was not a pathfinder, but rather a pathmaker. He could be stern in his dealings and in one instance had ordered Barney Dreyfuss and Charles Ebbets out of his office. But now as the pressures of his office increased, Harry Pulliam's emotional stability seemed to be in jeopardy.

There had been a minor ticket-scalping incident in the 1908 World Series involving the Chicago Cubs that caused some ill-feelings between Pulliam and Charles Murphy. Now there was even a petty quarrel brewing between Herrmann, Pulliam and Johnson over an incredibly silly incident. Harry Pulliam had been showing visible signs of suffering from emotional stress, and Garry Herrmann sent him a personal letter of support. Being the astute politician that he was, Garry Herrmann was keenly aware of the fact that personal feelings were to be guarded and not issued as press releases. The fallout from his "Let 'em walk" comment during the Cincinnati municipal elections of 1905 was still fresh in his mind. When contents of his letter to Pulliam became public, published in the *Cincinnati Enquirer*, Herrmann went into a snit and demanded to know how it had become public. A meeting of the National Commission, along with all the club presidents from both leagues, was about to take place in Chicago when Pulliam told Herrmann that he had shared the content of the letter with Ban Johnson, and that it was he who had made it public. Now both Herrmann and Pulliam were angry with Johnson.

Meanwhile, Ban Johnson was ready to enter the meeting with a head full of steam angry at Chicago Cubs owner Charles Murphy for making disparaging remarks about him. Johnson had harbored ill-feelings towards Murphy as a result of the Cubs winding up in his control. When Cubs owner James A. Hart decided to sell the club in late 1904, he approached Ban Johnson in the lobby of the Pacific Hotel in Chicago. Hart advised Johnson to buy the Cubs, telling him the ballclub was a solid investment that would make a huge profit. Johnson knew that he could arrange for financing of the ballclub with various contacts he had in Chicago, but was having second thoughts. He was serving as president of the American League with a ten-year contract and had been indelibly associated with the American League since its inception. In the end, Johnson's loyalty to the circuit won out over the possibility of making a fortune.

In that sense, Ban Johnson may have been unique. It has long been the romantic notion of many that owners of major league teams, right up through the 1950s, were a breed of sportsman who cared more about the perpetuation of the game than securing profits from their investments. Of course, all of this is plain hogwash. All major league owners, beginning with William A. Hulbert, National League founder, the league's second president and owner of the Chicago White Stockings, right through current-day New York Yankees owner George Steinbrenner, have been dedicated businessmen. Sentimentality to the national game is a distant second in their motivation for owning a team.

When Johnson turned down Hart's offer to buy the Cubs, he approached Harry Pulliam. While Pulliam was on record as being opposed to syndicated ownership of teams, he realized the enormous monetary potential of the Cubs' franchise. One of the minority owners in the Cubs was Garry Herrmann. Pulliam conferred with Herrmann on whether or not he would have any interest in increasing his investment in the Cubs. In a letter, Herrmann advised Pulliam to seek backing elsewhere, but to go with the deal. Herrmann also indicated to Pulliam that he knew a wealthy man in Pittsburgh who might be interested in putting up some of the capital and to see him at once. Pulliam then took his time getting to the contact in Pittsburgh. Although the man was agreeable and found the investment to be sound, Pulliam found that he was too late to do business.

At that time, Charles Murphy was the press agent for the New York Giants. He came to Chicago in advance of the team, and while poking around for news, he became aware of the Cubs' availability while speaking with Hart. Several days had gone by since the team had been offered to Harry Pulliam, and Hart told Murphy that he wanted $105,000 for the club. Murphy knew the potential value of the Cubs, but had only a few thousand dollars of his own. Quickly, he caught the first train to Cincinnati. Murphy had previously worked in the newspaper business in Cincinnati for Charles P. Taft on the *Times-Star*. Taft listened as Murphy explained the potential value of the Cubs' franchise to him. Taft was aware of Murphy's keen sense of get-rich-quick schemes and was impressed with his presentation. He told Murphy to stay in town for a few days and he would get back to him. Taft then sent a trusted associate of his business affairs to Chicago to look into the matter. The report returned from Chicago to Taft was that the investment in the Cubs looked good.

Immediately, Taft sent Murphy back to Chicago to complete the deal. The price for the ballclub was $105,000, which represented the par value of the stock, with a $5,000 bonus going to James A. Hart for services involved in carrying out the deal. The first payment was for $65,000, which included 56 shares of the stock held by Hart and the $5,000 bonus. Taft and Murphy then set about acquiring the balance of the stock as rapidly as possible, including that owned by Garry Herrmann. Another $10,000 worth of stock was acquired from Cap Anson. The former major league star and manager had placed his stock in the Cubs as collateral on an outstanding loan of $10,000 with Charles P. Taft. As Anson was unable to repay the loan, Taft simply seized the stock as payment. The balance of the stock was acquired piecemeal until Taft and Murphy, along with player-manager Frank Chance, who retained his $10,000 investment in the club, became the sole owners of the club in November 1905. In 1906, the second year that Taft, Murphy and Chance owned the Cubs, they won the pennant. The successful season yielded a profit of $117,000, thereby paying for the club in one year. The following year the Cubs returned an even larger profit, allowing Murphy to quickly make payments to Taft until he became the majority stockholder. Going into the 1909 season, the Chicago Cubs had made a profit of $300,000 over the past three years and the franchise was valued at $500,000. As a result, Charles Murphy was enjoying the accruements of high living and Ban Johnson was more than just a little sensitive to any criticism originating from the Cubs' president. Perhaps Murphy's good fortune also fed the growing depression of Harry Pulliam, too.

The meeting of the National and American league magnates took place in Chicago the week of February 15–19, and for all intensive purposes was more civil than expected. However, Harry Pulliam wanted to make public the name of the perpetrator of the bribe in the Cubs-Giants playoff game, but there was some reluctance among the owners to do so. Pulliam was bordering on a state of paranoia, believing that the National League owners were persecuting him and that if the name of the perpetrator was not made public, it would doom major league baseball.

Toward the end of the week, Chicago White Sox owner Charles A. Comiskey gave a dinner for the National League owners. Harry Pulliam was scheduled to deliver an address at the banquet. When Pulliam approached the podium, within his mind the world seemed to be closing in upon him. Fighting hard within himself to maintain control as a panic attack consumed him, he struggled nervously to speak. He then lashed out at the owners in a bitter tirade. Out of control, he was momentarily quieted by some of the owners and removed from the hall. Hatless and coatless, Harry Pulliam left the hotel in the dark of a cold Chicago winter night and immediately boarded a train for St. Louis. Arriving in St. Louis the next morning, his bizarre behavior continued as he announced his engagement to a young lady.

When Garry Herrmann found

Charles Phelps Taft, publisher, political leader, major league magnate, brother of President Taft. Cincinnati Museum Center–Cincinnati Historical Society Library.

out where Pulliam had gone, he followed him to St. Louis and convinced Pulliam to accompany him to Kentucky, where relatives were waiting and he could rest. As the meeting in Chicago concluded, the National League owners voted Harry Pulliam an extended leave of absence with full pay in order to have the time to restore his mental health. In the interim, all the league's affairs, including those involving the National Commission, would be handled by John Heydler, the current secretary. After a brief respite in Kentucky, Pulliam left for Tennessee and then traveled to Florida to partake in some therapeutic sailing and fishing.

There were some owners in the National League that felt no empathy for Harry Pulliam's condition, and there was talk of a successor being named. One of the names being floated was former major league player and attorney John Montgomery Ward. Another was Albert G. Spalding. Still, some members of the press, including the *Sporting News*, were solidly behind the return of Pulliam to the National League's top post. The week following Pulliam's mental breakdown in Chicago, the *Sporting News* printed the following: "The National League can not afford to lose Harry C. Pulliam. The president of the National League commands the respect (which is the main thing), and to only a little less extent, the admiration of the entire base ball world. The writers on base ball topics and the people who go to see the games — the two classes upon which the National League, in common with all baseball, depends for its success — have a confidence in President Pulliam's integrity and ability which not even the National League upon its pinnacle of greatness can afford to lightly cast aside. Every trait of human nature points to the soundness of this assertion."[8]

On March 2, 1909, Cincinnati was the scene of much celebration as both the Young Men's Blaine Club and the Citizens Taft Club prepared to leave for Washington, D.C., to attend the presidential inauguration ceremonies of native son William Howard Taft. At 2:30 P.M., members of the Blaine Club, 280 strong, including Garry Herrmann, Rud Hynicka and Mike Mullen, met in front of the club's home. Judge William F. Lueders, president of the Blaine Club, presented both Herrmann and Hynicka with a bouquet of American beauty roses. Then falling in behind Weber's band of fifty pieces, the Blaine Club members marched down Race Street to Fourth Street, over Fourth to Pike, Pike to Pearl to Pennsylvania Station to the cheers of thousands of onlookers along the way. At the station, a train 1,000 feet in length, consisting of twelve sleepers, one commissary car and one baggage car and pulled by two monster engines, was waiting to speed Herrmann, Hynicka, Mullen and the other Blaine Club members to Washington.

Later in the day, the Citizens Taft Club, behind Smittie's band of thirty-five pieces, also marched from their headquarters at Fourth and Vine streets to Pennsylvania Station. During the last weeks of the presidential campaign, the membership ranks of the Citizens Taft Club, considered more of a civic organization than a political one, had swelled to over 28,000. When the Citizens Taft Club reached the Cincinnati Trust Company on Fourth Street, George B. Cox was standing outside with Norman G. Kenan. The band stopped, turned around and serenaded Cox before moving on towards the station. There was no reason for Cox to be traveling to Washington. His presence at the inauguration ceremonies would be controversial and troublesome to Taft. Anyway, both Herrmann and Hynicka were more suited for such hoopla, and Cox had better things to do in Cincinnati as his considerable business interests required his attention.

In the early hours of March 3, 1909, a fierce late-winter storm occurred, causing massive havoc along the Atlantic Coast, from New York to Norfolk. All communication links between New York and Washington were lost as telegraph, long-distance telephone wires and poles had been torn down all along the route. The blizzard had started at midnight and by daybreak, there was deep snow along the Atlantic Coast, snarling both maritime and railroad

William Howard Taft, 27th President of the United States, 1909–1913, and Chief Justice of the United States, 1921–1930. Author's collection.

traffic. By noon the next day, telegraph communication had been established between Washington and New York via Philadelphia, which was receiving dispatches from Cincinnati. In Washington a massive effort was underway to clear the snow from the city's streets for the inaugural parade.

U.S. presidents have traditionally taken the oath of office in ceremonies conducted out-of-doors, most often on the Capitol steps; however, the swearing in ceremony of William Howard Taft would have to be moved inside. The president-elect and Mrs. Taft arrived in Washington on Wednesday evening, March 3, under a driving rain and without attracting much attention. They were immediately taken by automobile to the White House, where they were to be the guests of President Roosevelt for the night. The Tafts' arrival at the White House was without demonstration, celebration or any fanfare, and upon being admitted by attendants, they were greeted without formality by President Roosevelt. The following morning, Helen Herron Taft, in defiance of the inauguration committee, demanded that her rightful place was by the side of her husband and became the first wife of a president-elect to accompany her husband to his inauguration.

At noon on Thursday, March 4, 1909, William Howard Taft stood before Chief Justice Melville W. Fuller in the Senate Chamber of the Capitol building and received the oath of office as the 27th president of the United States of America as Theodore Roosevelt, his cabinet, the members of the Senate and House and the Supreme Court were seated before him, while the galleries in the chamber were filled with friends of both Roosevelt and Taft. Taft then delivered his inaugural address, concluding by asking for support of his fellow citizens and Almighty God in discharging the duties of the office. Then, turning towards Roosevelt, Taft bid him farewell. Roosevelt promptly left the Capitol building for the railroad station, hoping to reach Oyster Bay despite the destruction left in the wake of the blizzard.

Following a quick lunch at the White House with brothers Charles P. Taft, Henry P. Taft and Horace D. Taft, and their wives and children, the next order of business for the new president was to view the inaugural parade. At approximately 1:30 P.M., Taft arrived on the reviewing stand. Seated with the president, his wife and their family were his three brothers, their ladies, Vice President Sherman and his wife, Governor Harmon of Ohio and Senator O'Connor Bradley of Kentucky. At once parade grand marshal, General J. Franklin Bell, Chief of Staff of the U.S. Army, gave the command to march while 150,000 to 200,000 spectators watched along the route. Leading the parade were the West Point Cadets, followed by military units of the marines and navy. Long lines of drum and fife corps, bands, troops from the Spanish-American War and the Philippine campaign and legions of Civil War veterans marched by saluting the president. Also, 300 Yale men representing the president's alma mater marched by. In all, 31,000 members of civic, political and military organizations marched in the inaugural parade.

President Taft stood tall on the reviewing stand, beating time to the music of the marching bands while lowering his hat time and time again. Suddenly, the high-minded new president was confronted with his political past as the Citizens Taft Club of Cincinnati marched by, stirring him to enthusiasm by chanting, "Bill, Bill, we'll have four good years of Bill."[9] Then the enthusiasm of Taft became subtle as the Young Men's Blaine Club of Cincinnati marched by the reviewing stand. Clad in new, tall, white hats and gray cravenette coats and carrying their flag over their shoulders were Garry Herrmann, Rud Hynicka, Mike Mullen and what seemed like an endless line of Blaine Club members proudly passing by the reviewing stand, all saluting the new president. Whether or not Taft cared to recognize it or not at the time, the fact of the matter was that the Citizens Taft Club and the Blaine Club and all of its political-animal members, from Cox to Herrmann to Hynicka to Mullen, were just as responsible as any other political entity in the country for making him president. It was a bitter pill for "Big Bill" Taft to swallow. Still, Taft knew he was obligated to them all. Therefore, political expediency required that Taft acknowledge that debt of gratitude and he agreed to receive Herrmann, Hynicka and Mullen the following day at a reception at the White House at 10:00 A.M.

The 1909 major league season was only a few weeks away. The National Commission met in August Herrmann's office in Cincinnati, with John Heydler representing the recovering Harry Pulliam, and went into high gear clearing up loose ends. In spite of the fact that the bribery scandal investigation that had been appointed by a National League special committee had nearly ground to a halt, there were many outstanding claims of free agency by players in the minor leagues and other personnel issues to be adjudicated. On March 31, a significant decision was reached by the commission as it ruled that players who jumped contracts would be suspended for five years. Furthermore, players who joined outlaw organizations (those not covered under the jurisdiction of the National Agreement) would be suspended for three years. Hal Chase was one of the players that had been reinstated before the recent edict was issued. During the 1908 season, Hal Chase had played for New York in the American League before departing the club in early September. The Highlanders had accused him of laying down on a recent western road trip, but Chase stated that his reason for leaving the club was ill health. Chase then played for an outlaw team in the California State League. In February, Chase was fined $200 and reinstated by the commission.

By 1909 baseball had moved ahead of horse racing and boxing in fan interest. Major league baseball, which everyone felt was in its infancy, was now ingrained in American culture. It was predicted that the 1909 season would be one of record-breaking proportions. The players were one of the chief benefactors from the rise of popularity in the game. In the 1885 world championship series between the St. Louis Browns of the American Association and the Chicago White Stockings of the National League, each player received $41.70. In 1908 World Series, each player had received $1,317.58. It was now projected that some major league ballplayers could soon make the handsome sum of $25,000 for seven months of work.

As gate receipts continued to rise, club owners began investing some of the profits from their enterprises into building modern infrastructure in which to play and showcase their teams. One of the hallmarks of modern major league baseball occurred in the 1909 season with the opening of two new steel-and-concrete construction ballparks in Philadelphia and Pittsburgh. Shibe Park, the new facility for the Philadelphia Athletics and named for the club's president, Benjamin Shibe, was the first to open. Shibe Park had seating for 23,000 and standing room for an additional 12,000 spectators. The ballpark had been built at a cost of $500,000 and contained state-of-the-art amenities.

Garry Herrmann's 1909 edition of the Cincinnati Reds opened the season on April 14 with the Pittsburgh Pirates providing the opposition. As usual, the opening game was a grand affair with Weber's band and 18,000 loyal fans on hand at the Palace of the Fans. Members of the Five Hundred Club were the guests of Garry Herrmann and his wife in their box, while Herrmann's daughter, Lena, was entertaining several persons in her box. Julius Fleischmann also had a box reserved, while his brother, Max, was seated in the upper box tiers. At exactly 3:00 P.M., the gong rang signaling the start of the game. Vice Mayor Galvin made a few brief remarks praising president Garry Herrmann and manager Calvin Griffith, and both teams received the command to play ball. The Pirates, however, spoiled all the fun by defeating the Reds, 3–0.

In mid–April, Harry Pulliam was still convalescing in the South from his nervous breakdown. John Heydler continued filling in as acting president of the National League and covering Pulliam's duties on the National Commission. Meanwhile, John T. Brush was making no effort to pursue the investigation of the alleged bribe of Umpires Klem and Johnstone. Major league baseball was starting to feel the heat from the inactive investigation. As a result, the National Commission began to pursue the investigation under the guise that the National League had referred the matter to that body. On April 19, the National Commission released a statement regarding their actions in the matter, which said in part, "We believe that statements made by the umpires are true and that an effort was made to bribe them with reference to their duties."[10] While continuing to withhold the name of the alleged perpetrator of the bribe, Herrmann, Johnson and Heydler notified all teams in both leagues of their decision, stating that the individual was forthwith banned from all major league ballparks. Later, umpire Bill Klem would reveal the name of the alleged briber as Dr. James Creamer, a well-known New York nightlife figure who had served as the New York Giants' trainer during the 1908 season. While the National Commission may have rendered its decision in the bribery matter under a cloud of suspicion, at least the process had taken place without the uneasy participation of Harry Pulliam. If the commission had waited for Pulliam to participate in the matter, they would have had to deal with a bundle of nerves and a man struggling with how to handle the matter publicly while maintaining political support as National League president.

On the afternoon of June 18, the Cincinnati Reds defeated the Philadelphia Phillies, 4–1, in a game played at the Palace of the Fans. That evening, Garry Herrmann's great experiment with night baseball took place in the ballpark. The towers necessary to hold the lights had been in place since opening day. Using George Cahill's plans, they were now outfitted with 14 flaming arch lamps. To participate in the experimental game, Herrmann invited two Elks teams to play, one from Cincinnati and one from Newport, Kentucky. Many of the Reds and Phillies players that had played that afternoon were in the stands for the night game. The Cincinnati Elks defeated the Newport Elks, 8–5, in a game that saw 18 errors committed. As for the results of the experiment, they were inconclusive. The lighting seemed to be adequate for the pitchers and batters. While there were shadows in the infield, it still did not seem to hinder fielding and throwing. However, in the outfield some balls were lost completely, and there was also a problem getting the proper line on a ground ball. It's possible that some of the poor fielding could have been a factor of the newness of the environment or the skills of the players. But it mattered little how much the experiment had succeeded, for the idea of playing night baseball was just too radical an innovation to be accepted by the major league owners at that time. Still, Garry Herrmann, always looking for ways to promote the game, had proved his point.

By late June, Harry Pulliam had been on a leave of absence for over four months and the league moguls were starting to request an update on his status. Harry Pulliam's support among the National League owners was divided, and a few of the owners were of the opinion that if he did not resume his duties soon, he should resign. Also, the name of John Montgomery Ward was still being mentioned as a possible successor as league president. Pulliam maintained the support of Garry Herrmann, Frank de Haas Robison, George Dovey and Israel W. Durham, president of Philadelphia Phillies. Barney Dreyfuss was conditional in his support, stating that if Pulliam was well enough to return, then he should remain as president. Finally, in late June, after visiting his brother, J. P. Pulliam, in Oshkosh, Wisconsin, and fishing around Eagle River, Harry Pulliam appeared before the National League board of directors in Cincinnati and notified them that he was ready to resume his post. Returning to Manhattan, he continued to reside at the New York Athletic Club at 59th Street, opposite Central Park, and assume his normal duties as league president.

Meanwhile, as Pulliam was leaving town for New York, the ever-fraternal Garry Herrmann was once again coordinating another huge event in Cincinnati, this time serving as chairman of the turnfest (or Turner Festival) of the National American Turner Bund. The Turners were a German social group dedicated to gymnastics and music. The Central Turner Hall, located at 1407 Walnut Street in Cincinnati, had been the site of many festivals and activities of the organization, going back to the middle of the nineteenth century. Many political conventions and rallies had also been held in the building. The 1909 National Turner Festival took place between June 19–27 and allowed Germans to maintain a sense of their heritage while being assimilated. The event involved track and field, gymnastics contests and much food and drink. To provide the correct mood for the event and frolicking, Herrmann temporarily retrofitted a great part of the city into a resemblance of a Bavarian village.

On Thursday, June 24, George B. Dovey, president of the Boston Doves, was on his way to Cincinnati to negotiate with August Herrmann for some of his surplus players when he died of a hemorrhage in the lungs while riding in a Pullman car between Cedarville and Xenia, Ohio. His body was returned to Boston and the burial was planned for Tuesday, June 29. He would be replaced as president of the Boston club by his brother, John S. Dovey. Immediately, a notice was sent out that all National League games would be postponed that day. With the Turner Festival extravaganza concluded, Cincinnati gracefully returned to the resemblance of an American city. Garry Herrmann, saddened by the loss of his friend George Dovey, packed his bags and with a large contingency in tow, was off to Pittsburgh for the opening of that city's grand new ballpark.

On June 30, 1909, Forbes Field, baseball's second all steel-and-concrete construction ballpark, was dedicated. The ballpark was named after British General John Forbes, who in 1758 had captured Fort Duquesne from the French, then renamed it Ft. Pitt. The steel gates to Forbes Field were opened at noon and immediately a standing room-only crowd of well over 30,000 was situated everywhere possible, including temporary wooden seats. The Forbes Field event was one that would be repeated over the next few years in more than a half-dozen major league cities. In fact, later that summer on August 15, 1909, ground would be broken in Chicago to begin construction on the White Sox's new ballpark. Modern major league baseball was now anchored in psyche of the nation and the days of wooden fences and firetrap bleachers were the stuff of folklore. Although another game had been scheduled at Forbes Field for the following day, on July 1, it was postponed due to the funeral of Philadelphia Phillies president Israel W. Durham, the second mogul to die in the last week.

In Cincinnati, popular Mayor Leopold Markbreit had been fighting off illness since late winter. In January the mayor had over-exerted himself during a visit to Cincinnati by naval hero Admiral Evans. On the night that Evans was scheduled to give his lecture, the weather in Cincinnati was at near-blizzard conditions and extremely cold. Still, the freezing conditions could not deter Leopold Markbreit from attending the gathering. However, the next day he was so ill that he could not go to his city hall office. As winter turned into spring, Markbreit's condition did not improve. He underwent surgery, but due to his weakened condition, his wound was slow in healing. As his protracted convalescence continued, he developed bed sores and had to continue his recuperation sitting up in a chair.

Eventually, Markbreit improved enough to leave the hospital and return to his home on Bedford Avenue in East Walnut Hills. But his condition was deteriorating rapidly. On July 8, acting mayor and council president John Galvin was away with the Elks in California. Markbreit, after being away from city hall for five months, made one last gallant attempt to resume his duties. Weak and having a look of pallor about him, Markbreit was carried from an automobile by an attendant and a nurse into city hall. However, his days at city hall were over almost immediately as symptoms of uremic poisoning developed. The end came for Leopold Markbreit a few minutes before 11:00 P.M. on July 27, 1909, while lying unconscious in his bed as his broken-hearted wife sat nearby keeping vigil over him. As the news of Markbreit's death reached Washington, President Taft sent the following message to the wife of the deceased mayor.

> Washington, D. C.
> July 28, 1909
>
> Mrs. Leopold Markbreit,
> Cincinnati, O,
>   I extend to you, on behalf of Mrs. Taft and myself, our sincerest
>   Sympathy in your great sorrow. Col. Markbreit was a brave soldier, a public-spirited citizen, a knightly gentleman, and one whose friendship and courtesy to those who came within the influence of his charming personality will always be cherished as a sweet memory.
>
> William H. Taft,
> President.[11]

On Friday, July 30, a grieving Cincinnati said its good-byes to Leopold Markbreit. His body laid in state from 10:00 A.M. until noon on the second floor in Memorial Hall on Elm Street. After the family members had viewed the flowers and position of the casket, the public was admitted to pay its last respects to the mayor. At 1:30 P.M., the funeral services began as scores of mounted police and others on foot appeared in front of Memorial Hall. The honorary pallbearers included August Herrmann, Julius Fleischmann, Charles P. Taft, J. G. Schmidlapp, Melvin Ingalls, J. T. Carew, W. H. Alms and others, who filed silently by on the stage of Memorial Hall and took positions facing the auditorium. As an organist began playing Boellmann's prelude, the grief-stricken widow and immediate family members of Leopold Markbreit entered the auditorium. Finally, Acting Mayor John Galvin and the city council entered and were seated along with judges, many distinguished private citizens, military orders and others, who filled all the seats in the balcony and below. Every seat was taken and no standing in the aisles was permitted. Acting Mayor Galvin, who would replace Markbreit as mayor, inspired the mourners with his stunning tribute to his friend and colleague. Glavin stated in part:

> Soldier, rest, thy warfare over. Dream of fighting no more.
> Sleep the sleep that knows no breaking. Morn of toll, nor night of waking.
> In Mark Anthony's oration at the funeral of his friend Julius Caesar, he said,
> "The evil that men do lives after them. The good is often interred with their bones."
>   If this were true, then Col. Markbreit would cease to be even a memory, after today, because I believe it can be said of him more truly than of any man I ever knew, that he did no evil and thought no evil.[12]

As Galvin concluded his remarks, a silence of respect reigned in the stale air of the old hall. Then Leopold Markbreit's body was carried from Memorial Hall to the strains of Chopin's Funeral March and placed in a hearse to be taken to Spring Grove Cemetery for burial.

In New York, Harry Pulliam had been back on the job for over a month and there were no visible indications of his depression or having suffered a relapse. He worked out regularly at Muldoon's Gym, and from all appearances, the leave of absence had been good for him. In fact, friends and colleagues remarked on how healthy and vigorous he looked. On the morning of July 28, Harry Pulliam arrived at his office around 9:30 A.M. and began to review a pile of correspondence on his desk. Then, suddenly he stopped and began starring out of the window. Around 1:00 P.M. he told a stenographer that he didn't feel well and left the office for the day.

That evening Pulliam finished his evening meal in the dinning room at the New York Athletic Club and went up to his room on the third floor. About 9:30 P.M., the telephone in the club office began ringing. When a club attendant answered the phone, there was no response from the caller. The light on the switchboard indicated that the call had come from Harry Pulliam's room. After about a half-hour with the line still open, Thomas Brady was dispatched to Pulliam's room to ascertain what the difficulty was. When Brady arrived at Pulliam's room, he discovered that the door was unlocked. He entered the room and found Pulliam, dressed only in his undershirt and socks, draped across a couch, lying unconscious and bleeding from the head. Next to Pulliam laid a revolver. Harry Pulliam had shot himself in the head. The force of the discharged bullet had put both his eyes out; the bullet came out through his temple and struck the wall. Apparently he had been standing at the telephone in his room when he shot himself, dropped the receiver and revolver simultaneously, and fell backwards across the couch. Dr. J. J. Higgins, the New York Athletic Club's physician, was summoned. Dr. Higgins arrived quickly and evaluated Pulliam's condition. He stated that Pulliam's situation was grave and that he would probably not survive more than a few hours.

The police also were summoned and shortly thereafter, Coroner Shrady arrived on the scene. Pulliam was now lying on the floor as Dr. Higgins attempted to aid him. The coroner asked Pulliam how he was shot. All that Pulliam could do was moan, although some news reports indicated he had attempted to say that he didn't know he had been shot. Soon after Harry Pulliam lost consciousness. He was too severely wounded to be moved to the hospital. Miraculously, early the next morning Pulliam became semi-conscious and said that he had a headache and asked the club attendants there with him to rub it. At 7:40 A.M. that morning, Harry Pulliam died. He had left no note or explanation for his suicide.

Family members in Kentucky and Tennessee were notified and Pulliam's brother-in-law, George W. Cain, immediately left Nashville for New York to make funeral arrangements. Meanwhile, the body of Pulliam was moved to a funeral parlor on Sixth Avenue where friends began calling during the afternoon. Slowly that morning, the baseball world became aware of Harry Pulliam's self-inflicted, violent fate. At that time, a shocked Garry Herrmann was 3,000 miles away in Los Angeles, California, attending the annual Elks national convention, where he had hoped to be named Grand Exalted Ruler. John Heydler was en route from Alexandria Bay to Montreal when he was handed a telegram notifying him of Pulliam's tragic death. Being the league secretary, Heydler immediately went to New York to assume charge of the league's affairs. When Pulliam's old mentor, Barney Dreyfuss, was notified in Pittsburgh, he was horrified. "Oh it's awful. It's awful, but I expected it. Poor old boy," said Dreyfuss.[13] Charles Murphy, the Chicago Cubs' president, called the league office in the St. James Building to ask if there was anything he could do for Pulliam's family.

On the morning of August 2, the body of Harry Pulliam arrived in Louisville, accompanied by his brother J. Page Pulliam and brother-in-law G. W. Cain. Pulliam's body was interred beside those of his father and mother in Cave Hill Cemetery. The following day, the *Sporting News* would report, "The services were held an hour later in the chapel at Cave Hill, and were conducted by Rev. T. M. Hawes, a Presbyterian minister. The floral designs were magnificent and came from all parts of the country. It is doubtful if any prominent man had more friends in Louisville than Mr. Pulliam. Printers and employees about the offices of the daily newspapers, the friends of his youth, never failed to receive a call and a pleasant word from him whenever he passed through Louisville. In consequence the florists were deluged with orders from those who desired to pay a last tribute to a man who did not forget his friends."[14]

Garry Herrmann was still making his way east from California as various dignitaries of major league baseball gathered in Louisville for the chapel services for Harry Pulliam at Cave Hill Cemetery. Honorary pallbearers representing major league baseball included Ban Johnson, member of the National Commission and president of the American League; John E. Bruce, secretary of the National Commission; John A. Heydler, secretary of the National League; John S. Dovey, president of the Boston Doves; Charles H. Ebbets, president of the Brooklyn Supebras; Barney Dreyfuss, president of the Pittsburgh Pirates; Charles W. Murphy, president of the Chicago Cubs; and James A. Hart of Chicago. Also several present and past managers came to pay tribute to Pulliam, including Fred Clarke of Pittsburgh and Frank Bancroft, who managed the Cincinnati Reds in 1902. Umpires attending included R. D. Emslie, Henry O'Day, J. E. Johnstone and William J. Klem.

Pulliam's last official act as president of the National League had been to notify club presidents that the time had expired for keeping the flags at half-mast in memory of Boston club president George B. Dovey and Philadelphia club president Israel W. Durham. About an hour after Pulliam was buried, a special meeting of the National League board of directors was held in Louisville, and John Heydler was appointed interim-president. Then the directors designated the remainder of Pulliam's salary for the season to his estate. Furthermore, a committee of Garry Herrmann, Barney Dreyfuss and Charles W. Murphy was appointed to have a monument erected to Pulliam in Cave Hill Cemetery. Lastly, it was directed that all players in the National League would wear crape for thirty days in Pulliam's memory.

Harry Clay Pulliam was 39 years old. Prior to entering baseball on a permanent basis, he had been a lawyer, served one term in the Kentucky state legislature, and was the city editor and night editor of the *Louisville Commercial*. His first position in baseball was in 1895 when he served as financial secretary for the Louisville club in the National League, having been hired by club president Dr. T. Hunt Stucky. By 1898, Pulliam had left both politics and the news business behind and become president of the Louisville club. Barney Dreyfuss later became the majority stockholder in the Louisville club and assumed the presidency, yet asked Pulliam to stay on as secretary and treasurer.

Harry Pulliam was a bachelor and a loner. His close friends in the game were few, still he was respected and loved by many and was probably one of the most interesting figures ever to be associated with the game. One of those who attempted to bring comfort to Pulliam during his intermittent mood swings was P. T. Powers, president of the Eastern League. The day after Pulliam's suicide, Powers told the press, "It always seemed to me that it was some deep personal trouble that bothered Harry, and Billy Murray and I used to go and get him, when he had one of those brooding moods on him, and take him to a matinee or something. He'd go along, hardly saying a word and just listen. He was always a square man. Of course, as a baseball executive, he naturally made enemies in backing up umpires, because that can't be helped, but he would stand behind his umpires through thick and thin. He took baseball matters too seriously, I think."[15]

It was a common belief at the time that what killed Harry Pulliam was baseball. It was a fact that Pulliam was a considerable worrywart, but he had nothing but good intentions for the game. He believed that the ultimate success of major league baseball was linked to the honesty of all participants, be they moguls, managers, players or umpires. Right up to the end, Harry Pulliam was staunchly behind his umpires, whether they were right or wrong. In fact, only a few days before his death, he had suspended Cincinnati Reds manager Clark Griffith for three games for disputing a call by Umpire Emslie in Philadelphia.

In some ways Harry Pulliam was decades ahead of his time. He had a holistic attitude towards labor relations in the game and saw ballplayers not just as hired athletes, but as total persons. He had been a strong advocate of providing a beneficiary system for players that became disabled or financially incapacitated in the years that followed their days as grandstand idols. He even envisioned a retirement home for decrepit former ballplayers and held deep empathy for their circumstances. It only added to Pulliam's overall melancholy to see former ballplayers such as Charley Jones, a veteran of eleven years in the major leagues (1876–1880, 1883–1888) living in New York, penniless and in squalor; former Boston shortstop Herman Long, who had 2,245 big league hits, penniless and dying from tuberculosis in Denver; and the bankrupt and broken spirit of superstar Cap Anson, attempting to organize a semi-professional league in Chicago.

Pulliam's high-minded principles often brought him into direct conflict with not only the personal values of his contemporaries, but also their goals and objectives for operating the game. Just how much his decision on the disputed Chicago vs. New York game of September 23, 1908, and the backlash that followed played a part in his demise is subjective. The reality of the circumstances surrounding the tragic suicide of Harry Pulliam was that he felt desperately helpless and inadequate in his position. His hands were tied and the only way he knew to get his point across was to do the unthinkable.

But now, John A. Heydler was on the hot seat and the politicking would go on for the rest of the year as the owners jockeyed for position with each other to promote their personal choice as Harry Pulliam's successor. One of those moguls who was not impressed with Heydler's selection as interim-president was Garry Herrmann. At least at the moment, Herrmann had doubts and strong opinions that he openly expressed, stating "that Heydler is not big enough to fill the position."[16] John A. Heydler had been the National League secretary since 1902. Born in Lafargeville, New York, on July 10, 1869, he began his working life as a printer in Rochester and later went to Washington, where he was employed by the U.S. Government. He entered major league baseball in the 1890s as a substitute umpire in the National League. Later, while working as a sporting editor for a Washington newspaper, he helped the American League gain a foothold in that city.

In mid–August, the *Sporting News* declared in an article that John Heydler was a capable leader who was both big and broad enough for the office of president of the National League.

> If Garry Herrmann really says that Heydler is not "big enough" to fill the position, what does he mean? Does he believe that Heydler is incapable of enforcing the rules and of commanding the respects of the club-owners? If he does, let me say that the Cincinnati magnate is entirely in the wrong. If the magnates have nerve and honesty of purpose enough to delegate absolute power to Heydler, they will soon learn that he is one of the great men that have ever taken part in the affairs of the National League.
>
> But they tell me that Herrmann, if quoted correctly, simply voices the opinion of several other club-owners who do not want to be bossed in the way that Ban Johnson rules the American League. John T. Brush is one of these club-owners and he is backed up by the esteemed Mr. Freedman. Brush has a candidate up his sleeve in the person of one who has truckled to the National League for years and who has made no secret of his desire to get the job. If this individual should happen to land in the presidential chair, it would not take long to convince the base ball public that the Giants were well protected against adverse decisions by the umpires and that visiting teams at the Polo Grounds were up against the rawest kind of a deal. Brush has been in the minority for several years and has been smarting from the yoke.[17]

The 1909 National League pennant race was a two-team affair, with the Chicago Cubs chasing the Pittsburgh Pirates all season long. On August 26, the Cincinnati Reds were in fourth place with a record of 54–55. With the pennant seemingly out of reach, Clark Griffith started planning for the 1910 season. Griffith was busy signing rookies that he intended to bring up to the big leagues in September for a look and the most promising would be invited to spring training in Hot Springs next March. By September, Griffith had signed 42 players. This practice of inflating the roster brought strong criticism from Brooklyn owner Charles Ebbets, who asserted that no team should carry more than 18 players, although he currently had 44 under contract. Still, both the Cincinnati and Brooklyn rosters paled in comparison by Connie Mack's roster in Philadelphia that included 100 names. When the 1909 season ended, the Cincinnati Reds finished in fourth place. In Clark Griffith's first year as manager, the Reds finished in the first division for the first time since 1904. The club also set a season's home attendance record with a draw of 424,643, a record that would stand for the next ten years.

Despite temporarily losing Honus Wagner in a mid-season injury, the Pirates won 110 games and the pennant, while the Cubs won 104, finishing 6½ games behind. Honus Wagner had won his third consecutive batting title. In the American League, for the third consecutive year the Detroit Tigers won the pennant as Ty Cobb won his third consecutive batting title. The 1909 World Series was billed as a hitting contest between the perennial batting champions Cobb and Wagner. However, it was Wagner who prevailed as the Pirates, led by the brilliant pitching of Babe Adams who won three games, defeated the Tigers, four games to three. The series batting honors went to Wagner, who hit .333, with Cobb hitting a lowly .231.

When the National Commission gathered at the Hotel Schenly in Pittsburgh for the 1909 World Series, a sense of sadness prevailed. Garry Herrmann obtained approval from the National Commission to pay lasting tribute to Harry Pulliam by having a memorial card printed each year on the day that the first World Series game was scheduled and distributing it to all the players on the opposing teams, the owners, the umpires, the scorers and business representatives. Also, each year on the same date a floral wreath would be placed on Pulliam's grave in Louisville. The arrangements for the floral wreath were made by Garry Herrmann and expedited by his friend Robert W. Brown of the *Louisville Times*. Brown had known Pulliam from his newspaper days in Louisville and served as a pallbearer at his funeral.

When the World Series concluded, Reds manager Clark Griffith headed west to his sprawling ranch in Montana for some rest and recreation. Meanwhile, Reds president August Herrmann had to momentarily sidestep baseball and turn to more pressing matters. It was an election year in Cincinnati and the Republican Party had its work cut out in attempting to retain city hall following the death of Mayor Leopold Markbreit. The *Sporting News* took notice of the sudden frozen state of the national game in the Queen City, stating in a late October edition, "This town has suddenly joined the 'dry' column so far as real base ball 'jags' are concerned, for with Manager Griffith on his way to the ranch in Montana, President Herrmann busy up to his classic neckties in politics, and Miller Huggins and Larry McLean the only Reds left in town, there is a decided famine of things base ballic to talk about."[18]

With the death of Leopold Markbreit, the Democrats recognized an opportunity to retake city hall in the November election and wasted no time. While John Galvin had been serving as mayor in the unexpired term of Leopold Markbreit since July, Dr. Louis Schwab got the party nod to head the Republican ticket in the November election. Dr. Schwab was a former county coroner and was well known from serving on the commission that was attempting to build a new city hospital in Cincinnati and from seeking a seat on the Board of Education in 1904. Opposing Schwab as the Democrat candidate for mayor was John Weld Peck, a resident of Mt. Auburn, the stately hilltop neighborhood of President William Howard Taft's boyhood.

Peck organized several coalitions of old-guard Democrats from the Judge Dempsey faction together with groups of Germans, Jews, lingering anti–Cox forces and independent

Boyhood home of William Howard Taft, 2038 Auburn Avenue, Cincinnati. Photo by William A. Cook.

Republicans. He made the ballooning municipal tax rate the burning issue of his campaign and ran a solid race. Peck was also supported by the anti–Republican *Cincinnati Post*. The paper, always ready to oblige in searching out lingering symbols of Coxism, trained its journalistic guns on Republican councilman Mike Mullen from the Eighth Ward. Mullen, a former detective-turned-politician, was a George B. Cox wannabe. Mullen sashayed around the Eighth Ward, with boundaries that extended to the banks of the Ohio River and were heavily populated with Negroes, offering himself as a Cox-type deal-maker, as well as a guardian and protector of citizens rights. But John Peck ignored the theatrics of Mullen and the temptation of the *Post* to make him an issue in the campaign. Perhaps that was a mistake, as Schwab won the election with a plurality of about 8,000 votes while carrying 18 of 24 wards.

While August Herrmann was sequestered in the political backrooms of Cincinnati helping in the election of Schwab, his National League colleagues were positioning for the coming election of the new league president. James A. Hart, the former owner of the Chicago Cubs, was denying rumors that he was a candidate. However, in Herrmann's absence, John Heydler had picked up some support. Barney Dreyfuss was supporting Heydler and stating that he should have a five-year term. Also, John S. Dovey of Boston announced that he, too, would support Heydler. Although he had earlier questioned Heydler's savvy for the job as league president, August Garry Herrmann was a seasoned and skilled politician. He knew it was not necessary to go out of one's way to make enemies, as they came naturally. Herrmann's earlier public comments on what he believed to be Heydler's administrative capabilities were out of character for him. Also, Herrmann knew his prejudice towards Heydler's candidacy was shallow and without proper foundation.

Herrmann did the rational thing, joined Barney Dreyfuss and threw his support behind John A. Heydler. In an attempt to spin his earlier remarks on Heydler, Herrmann told the *Sporting News*:

> I have found President Heydler to be an able and clear-minded man of affairs. I will admit that I have been much surprised at the showing he has made as a member of the Commission. I had thought of him as an excellent secretary, but had no idea that he would make good as an executive. He has done so, and I will be glad to vote for him next year, if he can't be elected. I am not out working or electioneering for him or for anyone else, but if Mr. Heydler can be elected by my vote, he can have it. He has shown great ability in a trying position, and I think he would make a satisfactory president of the league.[19] Furthermore, "Every Club-owner has a right to his opinion and if a majority of them decide that they don't want Heydler, the minority will have to accept the verdict, that's all.[20]

But from all appearances, a real donnybrook among the National League moguls was in the making over John Heydler. Charles Ebbets, Charles Murphy and John T. Brush, who recently returned to work after being ill for a year, where all adamant in their support of Ward. Therefore, the key to the election was in the two uncommitted votes. Stanley Robison of the St. Louis club was on the fence as far as Heydler was concerned. Meanwhile, Horace Fogel, the new president of the Philadelphia club, was indicating he was leaning towards the candidacy of John Montgomery Ward.

To make matters worse, American League president Ban Johnson, whom many felt was attempting to force the election of Heydler on the National League moguls, publicly stated that he would not sit as a member of the National Commission with Ward. Johnson's dissatisfaction with Ward had its roots in a matter that had taken place between the veteran major league shortstop and manager George Davis in 1902. Davis had been a star-quality player and a perennial .300 hitter with the New York Giants for nine seasons. Following the 1902 season, with the American and National leagues still at war, Davis had hired Ward to draw up a three-year contract for him with the Chicago club of the American League. Subsequently, Davis signed the contract with Chicago, then neglected to honor it after one season, signing instead with the New York Giants for the 1903 season. While Davis only played in four games for the Giants in 1903, and by the following season was back in a Chicago uniform, Ban Johnson took the breach of Davis' contract personally and placed the blame for the matter squarely on Ward.

> When asked about the Davis matter, Ward stated, John T. Brush, Charley Comiskey, John McGraw, Clark Griffith and Davis will tell you that I did nothing wrong. I drew up the Chicago contract for Davis and made it airtight, for which I received my fee. A year later Davis came to me with a contract signed by John McGraw as manager of the New York Nationals and asked me if he could collect money on it. I told him he could collect his salary from McGraw and Brush, even if he was prevented from playing by the courts. I also reminded Davis of the Chicago contract and told him that if he signed with New York he might get into trouble. He asked me how and I said that Comiskey could sue him for damages, but might not be able to enjoin him to the New York State courts. That was all the advice I gave and Davis paid me for it. I did not draw up the New York contract. Later Davis was enjoined by the Federal Courts, but he drew his salary from the New York Club just the same, afterward returning to the White Sox. If Mr. Johnson believes that I aided Davis in any way to violate his Chicago contract, he is mistaken. I simply answered Davis' questions to whether he could draw this stipulated salary in the New York Club contract in the affirmative, and as it turned out I was right in the matter.[21]

While Ebbets, Murphy, and Brush were advancing the candidacy of John Montgomery Ward for the National League presidency, he was not actively seeking the position, but rather keeping tabs on his busy New York City law practice and enjoying the company of a wide circle of friends in the city. Furthermore, Ward had nothing to say pro or con about John A. Heydler. When asked by Ebbets and Brush if he would take the presidency of the league, Ward simply remarked that if his election was assured, he would then consider the matter.

By now Garry Herrmann was beginning to realize that the current mess over the election of the new president of the league could have been avoided had he exercised leadership and not been aloof in his position on John Heydler when he was first elected interim-president in August. Herrmann, the man that forged the National Agreement, should have had the foresight to envision the infighting that would result among his colleagues over the election of a new league president. He knew how strong-willed Charles Murphy, Charles Ebbets and John T. Brush were and that each believed that he alone knew what was best for the game. It was Herrmann's responsibility to disarm the opposition and he had not.

As the drama surrounding the election of a new league president was coming closer to unfolding, Garry Herrmann was asked about his position on John Montgomery Ward and the rumors that he and fellow owner Barney Dreyfuss might desert the National League if John Heydler was not elected. Herrmann stated:

> There is absolutely no truth in the yarn that I'm to vote for Ward or anybody else as opposed to Heydler. I also wish to deny that there is any possibility of Cincinnati and Pittsburgh retiring from the National League, if Ward is elected. Understand me, Ward is a thorough gentleman and a fine sportsman, and neither Mr. Dreyfuss nor myself will speak any other way about him. We are looking, however, to the votes of Presidents Robison, Dovey and Ebbets, which, when added to by Barney's and mine will make enough to elect Heydler. We feel confident that he will win out, and are sort of counting on President Fogel of Philadelphia, though he has made no move nor has he said anything about how he will vote.[22]

For several weeks leading up to the meeting in New York where the battle over the election of a new National League president would take place, another matter also had been of major concern to the National League owners. A rumor had been circulating that the Philadelphia Phillies, which had been owned by the late Israel Durham, were going to be sold to the theatrical interests of the Keith's and Procter chains. Whether or not there was a connection in this proposed transaction with the deposed political boss of Cincinnati, George B. Cox, is speculation. However, it is a fact that at the time Cox was a major force in the theatrical world. Cox had been buying interest in the Keith vaudeville circuit for several years and, in 1909, he already owned Keith's theatres in Cincinnati, Louisville, Indianapolis and Dayton. Furthermore, Cox was a minority owner in the Cincinnati Reds.

The *Sporting News* confronted the rumor of the theatrical interests getting a foothold in major league baseball head-on. In its issue of December 16, 1909, the *Sporting News* stated, "Base ball is confronted with the most serious crisis it has faced since the Brotherhood, and no man can foresee the end. The kernel of the nut of the present agitation over the purchase of the Philadelphia National League club by syndicate interest in that league, is the side remark that a number of theatrical men are involved in the deal, and propose to operate base ball plants in connection with their circuit of open-air hippodromes. The hippodrome talk is merely incidental at present, but behind it lies the menace to the national game."[23]

Of course, most of the owners were outraged at the thought of baseball adopting a theatrical model to promote its product. As the Keith's theatre rumor dissipated, another emerged in late November when Chicago Cubs owner Charles Murphy suddenly made a trip to Philadelphia. Rumors began circulating that he was going to purchase controlling interests of the Philadelphia Phillies and thereby move major league baseball towards a model of syndicated ownership. In the end, both rumors proved be unfounded. Horace Fogel had controlling interest in the Phillies, and in regard to the visit of Murphy, he stated that the Cubs' owner was in town simply as a courtesy to him in an effort to assist with straightening out a few operational problems with his new enterprise. When Barney Dreyfus was asked for a comment on the state of the Philadelphia club, he remarked, "Until I received a wire from a friend of mine in Philadelphia I knew absolutely nothing about the sale and know nothing about this syndicate reported to have been behind the deal. I was greatly surprised to hear that Horace S. Fogel was elected president. I am unaware whether Mr. Murphy is connected with the new owners of the club or not and what is more, I don't care. Murphy's affairs fail to interest me in the slightest, and I take all reports from the Murphy domicile with a peck of salt."[24]

However, Charles W. Murphy went to Philadelphia for a reason. It is possible that Murphy's mission was to recruit the support of Horace Fogel in electing John M. Ward league president at the December meeting. It has also been speculated that Murphy came to Philadelphia on behalf of Charles P. Taft. Taft, it had been rumored, loaned the money to Fogel to purchase controlling interests in the Philadelphia Phillies, similar to an arrangement he had afforded Murphy in taking control of the Chicago Cubs. Still, it is possible that Murphy's business with Fogel may been a little of both issues.

On Tuesday, December 14, 1909, the showdown in New York began. An invigorated Garry Herrmann arrived early at the Waldorf-Astoria Hotel in New York for the National League meeting. He had regained his keen political senses and was ready for the fight. He openly courted the news media and clearly laid out his agenda. Realizing that there was little chance that John Heydler would be elected, prior to leaving Cincinnati for the New York meeting Garry Herrmann convinced his allies Barney Dreyfuss, George Dovey and the non-committed Stanley Robison that a compromise candidate was in order. The compromise candidate that Herrmann had in mind was Robert W. Brown, editor of the *Louisville Times*. Brown was a knowledgeable baseball man, a man who had known Harry Pulliam very well, and was a friend of both Herrmann and Barney Dreyfuss from his days in Louisville. Brown was an excellent choice and for all purposes a neutral candidate who seemed electable. Of course, over the years Brown has been vilified by the historians as simply being one of Garry Herrmann's cronies. Prior to the New York meeting, Robert W. Brown wrote the following note to Garry Herrmann.

December 8

Dear Garry,
    The chance may or may not come, but if it does, please don't forget me. You know I can make good at least and I think you feel that way about me; and already I have expressed my eagerness to you. The trouble with me is that all along, I fancied everything would be all right.
    Your friendship is one of my prize possessions that is why I ask you to do all you can for me if the chance comes.

Faithfully,
Robert W. Brown[25]

The first vote on the league president was scheduled for Wednesday, December 15. On the first day of the National League meeting, routine matters were discussed. The moguls took a close look at the profit and loss statement of the league and were all giddy over the fact that gate receipts in the National League were 100 percent more than in 1903, the first year of the National Agreement. Also, it was brought to the owners' attention that there was no need to construct a monument on the grave of Harry Pulliam, as the special committee had been directed in August, since the Pulliam family had independently placed one at the grave site. Therefore, the owners voted to bestow an unspecified lump sum on an invalid sister of Harry Pulliam and also give her the interest on $5,000 for her lifetime.

Meanwhile, the American League meeting was held at the Walcott Hotel. Ban Johnson told the press that his league meeting would be begin at 2:00 P.M. and that all business would be concluded by 5:00 P.M. The most important item on the American League agenda was to dismiss charges against the New York Highlanders that the team had maintained a covert group in the ballpark to disclose signals of opposing teams. While the charges against the New York club were dropped, the league board passed a unanimous resolution stating forthwith that if any manager or club official was found guilty of operating a sign-tipping operation, they would be barred from baseball for life. However, on the matter of the National League election, Johnson was still advancing strong anti–Ward feelings.

As the first day of voting in the National League meeting approached, the focus was on the potential vote of Horace Fogel of Philadelphia. Fogel told the press that, first of all, he didn't like the way Ban Johnson had been talking, stating it seemed to him that Johnson was attempting to run both leagues. He also stated, "I have no particular interest in the election of president. I was not in baseball when whatever the trouble is arose. All I want to do is to see what I can do for the best interests of the Philadelphia Club. It does not matter to me whether Mr. Heydler or Mr. Ward is elected. I will have no trouble with either of them."[26] However, Barney Dreyfuss did not put much faith in the avowed neutrality of Fogel and was also concerned about the announced neutrality of Robison. Therefore, Dreyfuss was seeking legal advice on what the Heydler camp could do in the event that Ward received four votes and Heydler three.

On the afternoon of Wednesday, December 15, the first vote for president of the league was taken. Three ballots were taken and each resulted in a deadlock, with four votes being cast for John M. Ward (Ebbets, Brush, Murphy, Fogel) and four votes for Robert W. Brown (Herrmann, Dreyfuss, Dovey, Robison). When showdown time came, the forces of Herrmann, Dreyfuss and Dovey were convinced that if they nominated John Heydler, then Robison would abstain, while Fogel would vote for Ward. So they withdrew Heydler's name and nominated Brown. Meanwhile, the speculation that Fogel's sudden break with neutrality was linked to some financial agreement with Charles Murphy and Charles P. Taft ran wild. The next vote was scheduled for the following day at noon. Outside the meeting room, the rather sad figure of Cap Anson was walking around the Waldorf-Astoria, offering himself as a compromise candidate for National League president. Anson had come to New York at the insistence of Charles Murphy, who led him to believe that he had a chance at being elected league president. It was to be a huge letdown for Anson.

That evening a dinner was held at the Waldorf-Astoria to honor Barney Dreyfuss. With the exception of Charles Ebbets, who would tell anyone within hearing distance in no uncertain words how dissatisfied he was with the anti–Ward comments of Ban Johnson, these affairs had a tendency to send a message of harmony in the game through the strange male-bonding that seemed to occur. Seated next to Ban Johnson was Pittsburgh manager Fred Clarke, and the two were involved in chit-chat that seemed to give the impression that they were lifelong chums. Seated near the head table was John M. Ward with Cap Anson next to him. When John Heydler was called upon to address the toastmaster, he was delayed for several minutes by wild cheering throughout the banquet room. Finally, Heydler made a few brief remarks, stating that honest men must govern the game or it would suffer greatly.

The following morning on December 16, with their business concluded, the American League owners began to leave New York. At the National League meeting, Garry Herrmann read a telegram to his colleagues that he had received. The telegram was sent by Ban Johnson from Syracuse on his way back to Chicago. It stated, "The American League club owners have left New York. This should indicate forcibly to you and your colleagues that we do not wish to influence or embarrass in the slightest degree your organization in the election of an officer."[27]

Immediately, John T. Brush proposed the following resolution, which was adopted unanimously. "Resolved. That the telegram received by Mr. Herrmann from Mr. B. B. Johnson last evening, which forms a part of the records for our minutes, in which he recedes from the position which he had advanced several days ago, that he would sit upon the National Commission in the event that a certain individual was elected president of the National League be given to all newspapers and press associations."[28] Regardless of the Brush resolution, the Johnson telegram seemed to say to most observers that the American League president was telling the National League moguls to go ahead and select whomever as president and they would deal with any personal feelings about the selection after the fact. In Chicago, American League secretary Charles A. Fredericks stated in regard to the Johnson telegram, "The National League has misinterpreted its meaning. I do not believe that Mr. Johnson meant to convey the meaning that he has withdrawn his opposition to Ward."[29]

Three more ballots were taken for league president that day with the results the same — a deadlock on every one: four votes for Ward and four votes for Brown. It was now apparent to the Herrmann-Dreyfuss forces that Robert W. Brown was not electable. Therefore, at least momentarily, they once again began to focus on advancing the candidacy of John A. Heydler. However, Charles Ebbets was still thinking deadlock and began to ask the necessary questions regarding what the league would do in regard to governance should they leave New York without having reached an accord. Subsequently, Ebbets felt that there were but two choices in the event of a perpetual deadlock: either appoint a regency or appoint one of the owners as acting-president.

When the voting continued on the morning of December 18, the results were the same. Three ballots were taken and the deadlock persisted — four votes for Ward, four votes for Brown. In lieu of a league president, the meetings were being chaired by Julius Fleischmann, former Cincinnati mayor and majority stockholder of the Cincinnati Reds. Ultimately, it may have been the action of Fleischmann that spurred the National League moguls to break their deadlock. The previous day, after the third ballot had resulted in a continuing deadlock, Fleischmann declared that until a new president could be elected, John Heydler would remain as interim-president of the league. This edict did not sit well with John T. Brush, and he was ready to negotiate. Overnight there had been some informal meetings between Herrmann and Brush, and some prearranged plans were activated. First, Charles Ebbets read a letter from John M. Ward stating that he had withdrawn from the race. Then Stanley Robison withdrew Brown's name from consideration. Brush then nominated Thomas J. Lynch, referring to him by his better-known moniker as the "King of Umpires." The seven other club magnates seconded the nomination and the election of Lynch was unanimous. Then Charles Ebbets, who had bitterly opposed the nomination of John A. Heydler, rose and nominated Heydler for secretary-treasurer. However, there was a condition that while the election of Lynch was for a one-year term, the election of Heydler would be for three years. The nomination carried with Heydler being elected unanimously.

Both Lynch and Heydler were paraded before the assembled press and both made brief speeches that seemed to indicate that an instant mutual admiration society existed between the two. Thomas Lynch had been known as the "King of Umpires" during his time officiating between 1882–1896 in the National League, American College Association, Eastern and New England Leagues. He told the press, "I know the game about as well as anyone and I think I have a pretty good reputation. The public, the players and the umpires will get nothing but a square deal from me and everything will be above board and open to the newspapers. I want to add that I refused to take the presidency until I was assured that my old friend Heydler, whom I broke in as an umpire, was elected as secretary and treasurer, as I could not get along without him."[30]

John A. Heydler demonstrated a great deal of humility in defeat and was high of praise for the election of Lynch, stating, "When I learned who had been elected president, the first thing I thought was that the National League has picked the right man. I started in base ball as an umpire associated with Mr. Lynch and he gave me splendid help when I needed it most. Some of the letters he wrote me to help me I have yet and they are the brightest spots in my life. No one will work harder now for the success of President Lynch and the National League than John Heydler."[31]

The dynamics of the selection of Lynch were, the evening before Garry Herrmann had spoken privately with John T. Brush and told him that if he would withdraw the name of Ward from consideration, his forces would do likewise with Brown as well as Heydler. He told Brush that he could come back with any candidate he might choose and that he would be elected on the first ballot. Brush took no time to consult with Ebbets, Murphy and Fogel, and immediately sent a telegram to Thomas J. Lynch at his home in New Britain, Connecticut, telling him to come to the Waldorf-Astoria immediately. With Lynch elected, Garry Herrmann walked out of the meeting room and the press surrounded him. Herrmann spoke to them, putting the best spin on the election of Lynch that he could muster. "I realized before I left Cincinnati that we had little chance of electing Heydler," said Herrmann, "and so we bent our energies toward preventing the election of Ward, who wasn't satisfactory to at least four of us. We succeeded in blocking the Ward program. Then we informed Mr. Brush that any other candidate he might name would be satisfactory and that we would vote for him on the first ballot."

Actually, Herrmann had been surprised at the nomination of Lynch. "The offering of Lynch's name in connection with the National League presidency was a great surprise to me," said Herrmann, "especially as I had never had the pleasure of meeting him as he quit the diamond before I became interested in the Cincinnati Club. However, I had heard enough of him to know of his reputation as an official, and was willing to accept Mr. Brush's estimate of him as the right man for the job. After I met Lynch and had a talk with him, I was convinced that we had made no mistake in choosing him to head our league. I believe that Lynch will make a good official, and that with Heydler as secretary and treasurer, our affairs will be as well taken care of as ever they were."[32]

Throughout the election process, John M. Ward had maintained a profile of quiet dignity. However, with the election of Tom Lynch complete, Ward let off some steam and let it be known that he was reserving the right to file suit against Ban Johnson for slander over comments he had made in regard to the contract matter of George Davis. Still, Ward supported the election of Lynch, stating, "The election of Mr. Lynch as president of the National League was a happy solution to the situation. He was a capable umpire and is a high class man. He has a mind of his own and will have something to say about the business of the National Commission." Then taking a parting shot at both Garry Herrmann and Ban Johnson, Ward added, "With him as a member of that body, the base ball interests of the country may rest assured that affairs will not be conducted in bar rooms and cafes."[33]

With the election of Tom Lynch concluded, there were still a few open items on the agenda before the meeting could be adjourned. For one, Charles Ebbets wanted to increase the season schedule to 168 games. He was even so bold as to unfold a proposed schedule of when the season would begin and when it would end. However, there was widespread concern among the National League moguls of what an extended season would do to the World

Series. Also, both Garry Herrmann and Barney Dreyfuss were adamantly opposed to the idea, stating that it was not a square deal with the players. Subsequently, the Ebbets' motion was defeated.

While Barney Dreyfuss was benevolent in his support of the players in the defeat of the extended schedule proposal, his sense of fairness was contradicted by being the prime mover behind a proposal to withhold 20 percent of the players' salaries to insure they remained fit during the off-season. Dreyfuss had banned any of the Pirates' players from playing winter ball, stating as an example pitcher Bill Powell, whom he alleged had reported to spring training in 1909 out of shape and exhausted. Garry Herrmann later told the *Sporting News*, "The proposition was squelched almost as soon as it was made, and next season as heretofore, the players will get everything that is coming to them on the first and fifteenth of each month."[34]

On December 19, Herrmann arrived back in Cincinnati battle-scarred but triumphant and perhaps a little wiser. The press gave him high marks for finding a harmonious ending to the league presidential battle. However, in a later day, Herrmann's vast army of historical critics would find temptation in suggesting that his efforts in naming a new president in New York in 1909 were more of an obsequious act than an exercise in statesmanship by simply kowtowing to the wishes of his friend Ban Johnson.

XI

Batting Kings and a Feud with Fogel

In the spring of 1910, the National Commission agenda continued to be bogged down with endless arbitration of disputes pitting major league and minor league clubs against players on such charges as tampering, compensation and contracts. But on March 1, the Commission's action rocked everyone out of a deep sleep when it handed down a ruling that prohibited the giving of various mementos to players on winning World Series clubs. The edict laid down by August Herrmann, Ban Johnson and Thomas J. Lynch stated, "The emblem of the professional base ball championship of the world shall be a pennant to be presented to the victorious club each year, and an appropriate memento in the form of a button to be presented to each player of the victorious club. Both shall be selected by the National Commission. The cost of the pennant and the button shall be paid by the Commission."[1] In years to come, this ruling would be set aside to allow for the traditional World Series ring to be distributed to winning players, coaches and selected others.

However, by 1910, the commercial advantages of baseball were apparent to all businesses with a product to market. Ty Cobb was already appearing in Coca-Cola advertisements, and other players were gobbling up endorsements as fast as they could. In January 1910, the Chalmers Detroit Motor Company approached Garry Herrmann with an offer of presenting a new car worth $1,500 to the player with the top batting average in the major leagues during the forthcoming season. At the time Herrmann wasn't sure how he wanted to handle the matter, or if he even wanted to handle it all. While Herrmann eventually agreed to table the matter with the National Commission, had he even remotely envisioned the calamity that would occur in regard to determining the eventual winner of the car, it is doubtful that he would have accepted the Chalmers offer. However, after the National Commission held a discussion on the matter in late March, Herrmann, Johnson and Lynch accepted the Chalmers proposition and established the following criteria for eligibility to win the car.

The conditions under which the award will be made are as follows:
1. Every player to be eligible must be a member of one of the clubs of either the National or American League.
2. The batting average of each player for the season of 1910 shall be the only thing taken into consideration. The player having the highest batting average in either league to be awarded the prize. The following stipulations to govern:
   A. If the player is an infielder or an outfielder, he must be credited with not less than 350 times at bat during the season.
   B. If the player is a catcher he must be credited with 250 times at bat during the season.
   C. If the player is a pitcher he must be credited with 100 times at bat during the season.

3. Players who are at bat less than the number of times above designated shall not be considered in the award of the prize.
4. A player playing more than one position on any team shall be credited by the joint times at bat under all positions that he plays.
5. The awarding of the prize to the winner will if possible be made during the playing of the World's Championship Series in the fall of 1910.[2]

Also in the spring of 1910, the National Commission ruled on the reinstatement of Chicago catcher Johnny Kling. Notwithstanding the career achievements of Lipman Pike, Johnny Kling is generally recognized as major league baseball's first Jewish superstar. Kling had changed his name from Kline to avoid anti–Semitism. With his timely hitting and rocket arm cutting down baserunners, Kling had played a major role in the Chicago Cubs' three consecutive National League pennants between 1906 and 1908. However, during the winter of 1908–1909, Kling won the world championship in pocket billiards. At the time this was a very lucrative affair. So Kling decided to retire from baseball and defend his championship. After losing his pocket billiards crown over the winter of 1909 and 1910, Kling decided to return to major league baseball and petitioned the National Commission for reinstatement. When the National Commission took up the matter in March 1910, the vote was split 2–1 in favor of Kling's reinstatement, with August Herrmann and National League president Thomas Lynch voting in the affirmative. Ban Johnson, still smarting over remarks that Cubs president Charles Murphy had made about him a year earlier and who never really came to terms with the fact that Murphy now owned the Cubs, took it all personally and voted no. The terms of Kling's reinstatement put forth by Herrmann were that Kling would pay a fine and play the 1910 season for his unexpired 1909 contract with the Cubs, calling for $4,500.

Meanwhile, the renaissance of major league baseball continued with two more new ball-parks scheduled to open in the 1910 season — League Park in Cleveland and Charles Comiskey's new home for the White Sox on the southside of Chicago. While Comiskey Park would not be finished for the opening game of the 1910 season, on St. Patrick's Day, March 17, a green cornerstone was laid. However, three weeks later on April 7, the park was threatened with destruction when a fire broke out. A house-wrecking company by the name of S. Krug Company was located next door to the Comiskey Park construction site. The company had stock-piled a large amount of lumber on their property that caught fire. The rising grandstand of Comiskey Park was only one hundred feet from the burning wood, and brisk winds started to carry sparks over the stands. Only prompt action by the fire department saved the structure from destruction.

On April 4, the Reds arrived in Cincinnati from their spring training camp at Hot Springs, Arkansas. They began the 1910 season on April 14 with 1–0 victory over the Chicago Cubs as Fred Beebe outdueled Orval Overall. During the past few seasons, the fans occupying the wired-off area under the grandstand at the Palace of the Fans, known as "Rooter's Row," had become increasingly obnoxious. There was a large bar located near this area and booze followed freely and vulgar language was the norm. At one point, Garry Herrmann, who liked a stein of beer or glass of wine as well as the next guy, threatened to stop serving alcohol in the ballpark. To put an end to the nonsense, beginning in the 1910 season Herrmann issued orders to his ballpark security force to evict any fan that verbally abused players or umpires. The Palace of the Fans was becoming an eyesore in major league baseball, and Garry Herrmann wondered just how long he would have to wait until he could build a new facility. However, for the moment, he had yet another one of his many social activities to tend to. Herrmann, as past president of the American Bowling Congress, was planning to accompany a delegation of Cincinnati bowlers to the 1910 American Bowling Congress Tournament in Detroit.

On the afternoon of April 14 in Washington, D.C., President Taft and Vice-President Sherman were escorted ahead of 12,000 fans through a portal at National Park and took their seats in the first-ever designated "presidential box." A specially reinforced, broad-seated chair had been installed to hold the chief executive's 330-pound frame. It was the beginning of a national tradition, and for the first time in the history of the game, the President of the United States was on hand to throw out the first ball on opening day. At the appointed time, President Taft was handed a ball and looked a bit confused as to what he was expected to do with it. However, on prodding by umpire Billy Evans, Taft launched a slightly sidearm toss out of the stands and into the waiting glove of Washington pitcher Walter "Big Train" Johnson. The moment seemed to solidify the bond between baseball and the nation. The Washington Nationals proceeded to defeat the Philadelphia Athletics, 3–0, behind the one-hit pitching of Johnson. The next day Johnson sent the ball that Taft had tossed to him to the White House for his autograph. Taft signed the ball and sent it back along with the following note.

> To Walter Johnson, with the hope that he may continue to be as formidable as in yesterday's game.
>
> William Howard Taft[3]

On July 1, Charles Comiskey's new ballpark in Chicago opened its gates having survived becoming a victim to fire and a five-week steel worker strike that delayed construction. For the inaugural game at White Sox Park, later known as Comiskey Park, 28,000 were on hand, including Chicago Mayor Russe and nearly all of the executives and moguls in the game. August Herrmann also brought a delegation of forty rooters from Cincinnati with him. However, the St. Louis Browns attempted to keep the celebration low-key as they defeated the White Sox, 2–0.

The Philadelphia Athletics and Chicago Cubs ran away with the pennants in the 1910 season. Toward the end of the season, the Cubs' Johnny Evers broke a bone in his right leg above the ankle while sliding into a base in Cincinnati. Consequently, Evers was lost to the Cubs for the World Series and would be replaced at second base by Heinie Zimmerman. The World Series was scheduled to begin on October 17 at Shibe Park in Philadelphia. However, at the moment there was more talk among the fans about who had won the American League batting crown and the Chalmers automobile than who would win the World Series.

As the pennant races in both leagues became runaways, the contest for the highest batting average in the major leagues and the coveted prize of the Chalmers automobile had captured considerable fan interest during the 1910 season. The early leader had been a big surprise, with weak-hitting Chicago Cub catcher Tom Needham breaking ahead of the pack after the first week. However, Needham was soon replaced behind the plate by Johnny Kling and would only play in 31 games during the season, hitting an anemic .184. It was only a matter of time before the cream of the major league hitters would quickly rise to the top, and for the next eight weeks Nap Lajoie of the Cleveland Indians held the lead. In the tenth week of the season, Fred Snodgrass of the New York Giants took the lead away from Lajoie. Lajoie jumped into the lead again and held it for the next three weeks prior to being caught by Ty Cobb of the Detroit Tigers. Cobb held the lead for two weeks before Fred Snodgrass suddenly charged into the lead again and held it for three weeks until Cobb grabbed the lead back for one week. But coming down the stretch in the final four weeks of the season, Fred Snodgrass did a nose-dive and would ultimately wind up as the fourth-leading batter in the National League with a .321 average. Meanwhile, Nap Lajoie, with Cobb nipping at his heels, once again grabbed the lead and held it until the final week of the season. Entering the final games, Lajoie and Cobb were in a virtual dead heat for the major league batting lead.

On the final day of the season, October 9, the unofficial statistics showed Ty Cobb in the lead. The Cleveland Indians were in St. Louis for a doubleheader and, surprisingly, Nap Lajoie had eight hits in eight at-bats in the twinbill. Immediately, the question was raised if perhaps Lajoie had a little help from the Browns in getting those eight hits. It was well known that most players in the American League liked Lajoie a great deal more than the fiery-spirited Cobb and would have preferred to see him win the batting contest. However, if in fact Lajoie had been given opportunities to make hits by the opposition, the act called into question the integrity of the national game. In attaining his eight hits off St. Louis pitchers Red Nelson and Alex Malloy, one of Lajoie's hits was a clean triple, but six of the hits were bunt singles. Although on several occasions Lajoie telegraphed his intention to bunt, it was alleged that Browns third baseman Red Corriden positioned himself defensively in short left field.

Following the final games of the season, the batting averages of Cobb and Lajoie were in dispute and every fan in the country had his own opinion regarding the winner. The *Chicago Tribune* listed the final averages as Lajoie .385, Cobb .382. *The St. Louis Republic* had Lajoie .38111, Cobb .38457 and the *Cleveland Leader* had Lajoie .382 and Cobb .381. The *Sporting News* was stating that an investigation had been held a week earlier when alleged discrepancies had been found in box scores around country that differed from those official scorers sent to league headquarters. Using the new data, the *Sporting News* reported that the final

Ty Cobb and Nap Lajoie win Chalmers automobiles in 1910. Author's collection.

averages were Cobb .38415 and Lajoie .38411. The situation was simply one big mess and would have to be decided by the American League office. Ban Johnson was outraged and called the play of Red Corriden and managing of Jack O'Connor dishonest. When Garry Herrmann was asked for a statement on the matter, all the chairman of the National Commission could do was shake his head, stating that he was not sure of the outcome of the batting leader. However, he was sure of one thing: there were not going to be any more prizes or bonuses permitted.

At the moment American League president Ban Johnson was on a hunting trip in Fienfeld, Wisconsin, with his on-again, off-again friend, White Sox owner Charles Comiskey. As the two chums were attempting to come to terms with their past differences, the Lajoie-Cobb controversy got in the way of the bonding process. Johnson was in a hurry to get the Lajoie-Cobb matter out of the way and out of the press so as to not overshadow the World Series. Consequently, he hurried back to Chicago and launched a cursory investigation. The results were that based upon the game statistics provided to Johnson by the official scorers, he declared Ty Cobb the batting champion and the winner of the Chalmers automobile. The Chalmers Automobile Company, realizing that they sold cars in Cleveland as well as Detroit, decided to award a car to both Cobb and Lajoie. The final statistics were published as those below:

Player	At Bats	Hits	Average
Ty Cobb	509	196	.384944
Nap Lajoie	591	227	.384084

While Johnson cleared both Corriden and O'Connor of any wrongdoing in the Lajoie hits controversy, he asked that St. Louis Browns president Robert Hedges launch an in-house investigation on the matter. While Hedges also found no wrongdoing in the matter on the part of either, he fired Jack O'Connor. O'Connor was probably fired more for his last-place finish and dismal record of 47–107 than the number of hits Lajoie had in the final games of the season. Both Cobb and Lajoie were satisfied with the official outcome adjudicated in the matter by Johnson. Ty Cobb stated, "I am glad that I won an automobile and am especially pleased that Lajoie also gets one. I have no one to criticize. I know the games were on the square and I am greatly pleased to know that the affair has ended so nicely." As for Lajoie, he remarked, "I am quite satisfied that I was treated fairly in every way by President Johnson, but I think the scorer at St. Louis made an error in not crediting me with nine hits. However, I am glad that the controversy is over. I have the greatest respect for Cobb as a batter and am glad of his success."[4]

The 1910 World Series was not the contest that major league baseball had hoped for as the Philadelphia Athletics battered the Chicago Cubs' brilliant pitching staff, defeating "Three Finger" Brown twice in the process. The Athletics won the first three games, 4–1, 9–3 and 12–5, while tapping the Cubs' pitching for 36 hits. The Athletics were on the verge of a sweep in the series, leading 3–2 with one out in the bottom of the ninth inning, when Frank Chance tied the game for the Cubs with a triple. The Cubs then scored the winning run in the tenth inning, defeating the Athletics, 4–3. In game five, the Athletics broke open a tight 2–1 game in the eighth inning by scoring eight runs and proceeded to wrap up the series with a 7–2 win as Jack Coombs won his third game. As Garry Herrmann was leaving the Cubs' West Side Grounds following game five, he remarked, "My sympathies were with the National League, but it wasn't the Cubs' year. The Athletics played grand ball and outclassed the Cubs in every respect, winning chiefly through superior batting and pitching. The Cubs are to be praised for the game they made."[5]

On July 15, the ever-fraternal August Herrmann had finally became the Grand Exalted Ruler of the Order of Elks. Herrmann had long coveted the office, and when the Elks held their 1908 national convention in Cincinnati, he had hoped to set the process in motion to be elected Grand Exalted Ruler the following year at the 1909 National Convention at Los Angeles. However, Herrmann's lavish spending spree at the Cincinnati convention had caused backlash among members of the fraternity. His opponents quickly raised the issue of whether the Elk's highest office should be obtained in exchange for good times showered on it by a free-spending millionaire brother. However, by the time of the 1910 Elks convention convened at Detroit, the gaudy spending of Herrmann in 1908 was a faded memory among the Elks' brotherhood and he was elected almost without any opposition. His term office would last until July 12, 1911.

When the good people of Cincinnati heard the news of Herrmann's elevation to the exalted post, there was much adulation heaped upon him. However, there was a considerable number also wondering what effect his election to the post would have upon the fortunes of the Cincinnati Reds. Serving as the Grand Exalted Ruler of the Elks was tedious responsibility. It required that one spend a lot of time on the road, traveling to all the lodges in the fraternity located in the backwater towns of America. It seemed to some that the best that could be hoped for would be that Herrmann's wanderings could serve a dual purpose in both taking care of his elected duties in the Elks while also serving as a scout for the Reds.

In 1910, Herrmann's Reds had finished another lackluster season in fifth place with a record of 75–79. Attendance slipped, too, by 11 percent in the fire-trap Palace of the Fans, to 380,622. While Herrmann would have to continue to wait for that elusive National League pennant, at the moment he had other matters much more dear to his heart to attend to. In late October, August and Annie Herrmann sent out invitations to the wedding of their daughter Lena. Lena was to be married to Karl Bendorf Finke on Wednesday evening, November 16, 1910, at St. John's German Evangelical Protestant Church, located at Twelfth and Elm streets. St. John's Evangelical Protestant Church was the oldest German congregation in Cincinnati, founded in 1839. As the German population started to move out of the Over-the-Rhine area, the church evolved in the 1930s into a Unitarian congregation.

The wedding began at 7:30 P.M. as a proud and staunch August Herrmann arrived at the church in a carriage alone with his daughter. As the bride was escorted up the stairs toward the church door, a small fox terrier ran between her and Herrmann. Immediately, a police officer intervened and began to wave the dog off, but Lena Herrmann politely asked the officer to withdraw. "Let him alone, it is a sign of good luck for a dog to follow one," she proclaimed.[6] The dog went as far as the church inner-door, then turned back. The inside of the church was nearly awash with festoons of Southern smilax hanging from the balcony, while each entrance bore a bouquet of yellow and white chrysanthemums. Herrmann then proceeded to walk Lena down the aisle behind the bridesmaids and groomsmen to the strains of Mendelssohn's "Wedding March," while the groom stood tall waiting at the chancel rail. For Garry Herrmann, the doting father, this was his finest hour.

For Lena Herrmann it must have been quite reassuring to know that by having the quintessential caterer in the United States as her father, it meant that her wedding reception would be an affair to be remembered. Following the wedding service, a reception line was formed and a caravan of automobiles and carriages pulled up along the street outside the church as the bride and groom, their relatives and guests were boarded and transported to the Herrmann home on Hollister Street, where an elaborate wedding dinner took place. The Herrmann home was a virtual flower bowl, and a velvet carpet was laid. On the veranda of the garage, a string band was playing among towering palms. As the bride sat down at the bridal table, she found a jewel box bearing an inscription "From Mama and Papa." As Lena opened the box, she let out a cry of sheer delight. She held up for all the guests to see a necklace of the finest pearls and diamonds that must have cost a small fortune. Garry Herrmann did indeed love his darling daughter. The bride then cut a huge wedding cake, and the menu was served by a corps of waiters in true Garry Herrmann tradition. It was a night to remember.

While Garry Herrmann had been taking care of his social, political and fraternal responsibilities in the fall of 1910, Reds manager Clark Griffith had tentatively worked out a trade with Phillies manager Red Dooin during the World Series, intending to exchange four players on both clubs. In the deal, Cincinnati would send Hans Lobert, Fred Beebe, Jack Rowan and Dode Pasker to Philadelphia in exchange for Johnny Bates, Eddie Grant, George McQuillan and Lew Moren. However, when Phillies president Charles Fogel was informed of the deal, he went ballistic. He charged Garry Herrmann of trying to pull the wool over his eyes and decimate his club by tampering with his players on his reserve list. Fogel stated, "I cannot help what McQuillan and Bates have done, nor am I responsible for anything unlawful in baseball President Herrmann may do."[7] But the salient questions were: What did Horace Fogel know about the proposed deal brokered by managers Griffith and Dooin and when did he know it? Was the deal done improperly and had Garry Herrmann tampered with players on the Phillies' reserve list, or was Horace Fogel simply attempting to get out of a deal he had approved and now had second thoughts about?

In the past, Herrmann would have probably relented and backed out of the deal, but suddenly there was a noticeable change in him. He was tired of losing and also tired of being held to a different standard in player transactions because of his status as chairman of the National Commission. Herrmann said that on a recent trip to Chicago to attend an Elks dinner, he conferred with Charles Murphy (who had often been accused of being the power behind the throne in Phillies hierarchy) and had gathered damaging evidence in regard to the business dealings of Fogel, and that if he continued to press him on the matter of the trade, he would use the evidence against him to sweep him out of baseball. Herrmann told the *Sporting News*, "Any time that Fogel is ready all he has to do is let me know and I'll be in New York with 24 hours. The case is looking better for us every day and I now see no reason why we should not have the privilege of keeping the players we drafted. You know it is peculiar that we have about 10 times as much evidence against Fogel as he thinks we have. For the past eight years I have been keeping low and have allowed as many as ten dozen excellent players to get away from the Cincinnati Club during that time, for the simple reason that I didn't want to make any fuss. But now I am tired of this and I'll fight Fogel till the hot place is a skating rink before I will give in one bit to him."[8]

Herrmann had already begun to sign the Philadelphia players; Bates and McQuillan were signed in Cincinnati after they had come to town to personally talk with him. Also, both Grant and Moren were due in town any day. The fact of the matter was that Herrmann was only offering each of the players a $500 raise to sign a Cincinnati contract. Still, that fact hadn't been a deterrent to any of them and they were all willing signers. Just as soon Herrmann had all the players' signatures on the contracts, he would be ready if necessary to go to the National League office in New York and lay all his evidence regarding the deal and charges in regard to Fogel in front of league president Thomas J. Lynch.

Of course, Herrmann knew that anything he put before Lynch was going to be rubber-stamped. Lynch had not been universally popular with the National League moguls in his freshman year as National League chief executive. Charles Ebbets had not spoken with Lynch since the season began, and Horace Fogel had been smitten with him because he failed to honor his request to fire umpire Bill Klem. The matter of Lynch's contract renewal as league president would be coming up on the agenda of the National League owners within the next month and he knew that having Garry Herrmann on his side certainly would enhance his chances of being retained. In fact, Lynch had recently gone on record, stating that in regard to Herrmann, "he's a just judge, and worth $50,000 a year, not the $5,000 he's getting."[9]

The trade matter became moot, however, when Horace Fogel decided to approve the deal without objection, or was ordered to do so by Charles Murphy. Whatever the case, the process by which the trade became consummated was a curious affair. First, Red Dooin was about to resign as manager of the Phillies over the trade flap and return home to Rochester when Fogel, with tears in his eyes, met with him and stated that he would approve the trade. Then it was being reported that Fogel had packed his bags for a trip to Chicago to talk with Charles Murphy and he would travel to Cincinnati to confer with Garry Herrmann and possibly offer an ordered apology. However, Fogel didn't go to Chicago or Cincinnati, but to New Orleans in search of spring training facilities.

While vacationing in French Lick, Indiana, Charles Murphy stated, "Charley Dooin certainly knows what he is about when it comes to exchanging the services of ball players. I think Griffith is a mighty good manager. As a trader, though, he is not so much. I guess he (Dooin) and Fogel will go through with the trade made with Cincinnati."[10] When Clark Griffith heard of Charles Murphy's assessment of his skills as a trader of players, he had a few comments for Murphy. He stated that the Cubs' clubhouse was a hog pen and unsanitary. Furthermore, Griffith asserted that he along with other National League managers would be willing to give Murphy $100 each to build a new clubhouse in the Chicago ballpark.

In the end it looked as if Charles Murphy had to approve the trade, and that raised questions as to who really owned the Phillies. The whole Phillies' ownership had been a bit of a mystery and no one seemed to know for sure just how much interest in the club was owned by Charles P. Taft or Charles Murphy. It was a fact that Taft's wife owned Baker Bowl, the Phillies' home park. In Cincinnati, Herrmann stated, "I am not surprised that Dooin will stay with the Phillies. I have felt sure all along that it would so result. We were absolutely in the right in the controversy and I was positive that Mr. Fogel could not get away with any such thing as a back-down to the detriment of our club, after the deal had been made by his manager and officially announced. I am glad to hear that Mr. Fogel has changed his mind on this subject, and will look for an official communication from the president of the league very soon. I think the deal is an excellent one for our club and am very glad that it is to be officially confirmed at once."[11]

Clearly the trade had demonstrated a sudden change in the administrative style of Garry Herrmann. Perhaps his lack of concern for due diligence in the matter was connected to the fact that the deal involved negotiating with Horace Fogel, who had become utterly adversarial in his dealings with Herrmann. Or perhaps it was a signal to the baseball world that Garry Herrmann was about to stop viewing the business of major league baseball through rose-tinted glasses. Herrmann was aware of the fact his ballclub was losing money and the interest of the fans in Cincinnati was beginning to wane. The downside of the deal, however, was that suddenly there was a little black cloud hanging over the impeccable record of fairness of the chief justice of baseball's supreme court.

While the trade was official, the process by which Garry Herrmann obtained the Philadelphia players had left a bad taste in the mouths of many observers. One such skeptic was the *Sporting News*, which stated in its edition of November 17, 1910,

> There was one thing about this affair which on its face had the appearance of such sensational features, that puzzled the people who were not in on the ground floor, was the utter indifference shown to the principles of organized ball. People hereabouts at least could not understand by

what right Mr. Herrmann had to do business with players whose names were on the Philadelphia Club's reserve list. If he really did so without the consent of Horace Fogel, which the latter has repeatedly said he did not give, the whole thing looks decidedly queer to say the least. No matter how strong Mr. Herrmann's case may have been, or how much he had "up his sleeve," the proper thing for him to have done was to have submitted his case to President Lynch, and if that had not been satisfactory, then to have taken it to the Board of Directors of the National League, and if the facts warranted it, the matter could have been settled in a very short time. It didn't appear to be necessary for such undue haste as had been shown in the matter, unless, of course, the facts are not as have been stated by Mr. Fogel. If the latter was sincere in his statements that he did not know anything about the deal until it had been consummated, then Mr. Herrmann has violated one of the essentials of organized ball, that is absolutely requisite to its success.[12]

In late December, Garry Herrmann and Julius Fleischmann represented the Cincinnati club at the National League meeting in New York. The first order of business for the magnates was to consider the re-election of league president Thomas Lynch. There had been some dissatisfaction with Lynch during the past season, and it had been rumored that Charles Ebbets might attempt to block his re-election. However, the real pressure to remove Lynch from office was external rather than internal. Robert W. Brown of the *Louisville Times* was aware that there was at least a remote possibility that a vacancy might exist in the league presidency and once again began lobbying for the job through correspondence with his close friend Garry Herrmann. In mid–November, Brown wrote the following to Herrmann.

> November 16, 1910
>
> My Dear Garry—
>   Send me the National League Presidency if you possibly can. Between (not legible) you can make terms with Ebbets & the others for a year. After I am in their will be no changes for a long time & I'll never forget it & pay you back in the honorable way. Write me.
>
> Faithfully,
> R. W. Brown[13]

For the most, Brown's lobbying for the job through Herrmann took on a rather mushy connotation. However, in a letter to Herrmann dated November 22, Brown suddenly became political, stating, "If you can get me the four votes I had last year, the fifth is already pledged and election is certain. Then we can work together & do big and splendid things for the league. You know the fifth man without me telling you. He has asked me to say nothing just yet. But it is all right."[14]

The pressure being applied by Brown to have Herrmann obtain the league presidency for him had the potential to place Herrmann in a most vulnerable position. First, while there was some vocal opposition to Lynch, mostly by Charles Ebbets, the issue had not become item number one on the league club owner's agenda. Charles Ebbets was a proud man who began his tenure with the Brooklyn club in 1883 and worked his way up from bookkeeper to club president. Herrmann knew that Ebbets loved baseball and that often his bite was not as bad as his bark. He knew how to deal with him. Furthermore, Garry Herrmann was still under the microscope of scrutiny by the press in regard to the Philadelphia deal, and his political mentor, George B. Cox, was being investigated for bank fraud by a Cincinnati grand jury. Herrmann was acutely aware that all he needed to do in order to seriously jeopardize his own status with the league was to undermine the compromise that he had brokered in bringing Lynch to the league presidency the previous year. He certainly did not want to have suspicion cast upon him of introducing patronage into his decision-making in major league baseball.

When the owners gathered at the annual league meeting at the end of December, there was full representation, with the only exception being that John T. Whalen, chief lieutenant of John T. Brush, represented the New York Giants. At the time Brush had become ill again and was recuperating in San Antonio, Texas, where he was expected to remain until spring. The first order of business was the re-election of Thomas Lynch as league president. Charles Murphy entered the name of Lynch into nomination for president and he was re-elected unanimously by the owners. Garry Herrmann then asked that the term of Lynch as president be extended for three years. However, six votes were needed to accept the proposal and Herrmann could only muster five. Surprisingly, Garry Herrmann thought he could convince Horace Fogel to support the extended term of office for Lynch, but failed to gain his support.

Before the magnates adjourned the league meeting, there were a few other proposals to consider, mostly in the area of scheduling. As usual there was widespread differences of opinion on this matter. Charles Ebbets still wanted a 168-game schedule, while Barney Dreyfuss wanted a 140-game schedule. Then Garry Herrmann made a radical proposal calling for inter-league play. The Herrmann plan called for the season to begin on April 10, with the two leagues playing a 112-game schedule within their respective circuits. The intra-league schedule would include two road trips east or west for every club and conclude in August. Then the schedule would call for a 64-game inter-league schedule from August through the remainder of the season. The players on the two leading teams in the inter-league schedule would receive a cut in the gate receipts. Herrmann actually attempted to sell this disjointed schedule to his colleagues in both the National and American leagues, but predictably a majority of the owners were simply dumbfounded by the idea and it crashed faster than a lead balloon.

XII

The Fat Lady Sings for a Boss and a Palace

In early January 1911, Garry Herrmann invited his National Commission colleagues, along with members of various commission committees to hold their annual reorganization meeting at the sanctuary of his beloved Laughery Club, thirty miles downstream from Cincinnati on the Ohio River. Following a lavish dinner provided by Herrmann, he read his annual report. In the report Herrmann stated that the commission's workload had increased annually by 300 percent above that in its first year. In fact, in the past season alone, the commission had to process 7,610 letters, issue 125 various findings and rulings, and still adjudicate in matters concerning over 100 minor league player cases and complaints. Clearly the commission's workload had outgrown Herrmann's ability to provide due diligence in each matter.

In its first eight years of existence, the National Commission had been less than perfect as a clearing house for baseball's administrative matters, but overall it had been efficient in processing matters that came before it and brought a sense of stability to the game. Therefore, the owners wanted to ensure that the commission continued to function in a robust manner and expedite matters in a timely manner. To that end, A. J. Flanner, a former editor of the *Sporting News*, was hired as an assistant to Garry Herrmann. The next item on the agenda was to hold the election for commission officers. There was absolutely no mention of the matter that had transpired earlier in the winter between Garry Herrmann and Horace Fogel, and the election took less than five minutes as there were only two candidates: Herrmann for chairman and John Bruce for secretary. The meeting was quick and Ban Johnson departed for a little rest and relaxation in Florida.

While it all may have seemed as if serenity was reigning in major league baseball during the meeting at the Laughery Club, that was far from the case. In Chicago, the ongoing war between Ban Johnson and Charles Murphy continued. In fact, Murphy was still making outrageous allegations toward Johnson, accusing him of trying to force him out of his ownership of the Chicago Cubs. In early 1911, the *Sporting News* caught up with Garry Herrmann and asked him to give them an assessment of the Murphy-Johnson feud. Herrmann stated:

> I haven't received a copy of Mr. Murphy's latest statement. In it, I am told, he makes a violent attack on Ban Johnson and me in particular. He also drags Barney Dreyfuss into the case and says that the Pittsburgh magnate is one of the American League faction in the National League, who is trying to force him to sell his base ball holdings. It's nonsense to suppose that I would stoop to such business as to attempt to cause Murphy to sever his connection with the game. There is an old saying, "Give a calf plenty of rope and he will hang himself." This applies to Murphy. He talks too much for his own good and the good of baseball. His own typewritten statements con-

vict him of being a man who isn't working for the uplift of the game. He is continually trying to stir up trouble and strife and to cause hard feeling between the club owners of the two leagues. If Mr. Murphy didn't have a chip on his shoulder for Ban Johnson and would listen to reason, the National League would be better off. Mr. Murphy wants to remember he has been an extremely lucky man in baseball. He came in on a shoestring six years ago and now is worth half a million. I feel sorry for him if this success has turned his head. By and by, when luck breaks against him, and the Chicago Club disintegrates, he will not feel so gay. When a magnate begins to lose money, he is willing to listen to reason. If Mr. Murphy would devote his entire attention for the next five years to building up the worn-out Cubs and trying to win back the world's championship for the National League, he would please all the magnates in that organization. We all wish him well, but we simply want him to tear the ribbon off his typewriter and agree to not buy a new one until he again is on top.[1]

With spring training looming on the horizon and the commission's winter business concluded, in early February Herrmann traveled to Boston where honors were bestowed upon him as the Grand Exalted Ruler of the Elks during a dinner at Faneull Hall.

The 1911 National League season opened on April 12. The New York Giants were picked as the favorites to win the pennant and 40,000 fans turned out at the Polo Grounds for the home opener. The old ballpark at 155th Street and Eighth Avenue shined brightly with its new coat of paint. Also, new ticket machines had been installed that allowed for rapid entry into the stands. However, the hometown crowd was disappointed as the Philadelphia Phillies defeated the Giants, 2–0. The following day Jack Rowan, one of the Philadelphia pitchers involved in the controversial trade with Cincinnati, beat the Giants, 6–1. Then shortly after midnight on April 14, the Polo Grounds caught fire and burned to the ground in a spectacular blaze. Around the time the fire started, Giants manager John McGraw was playing pool in a billiard parlor at 34th Street and Broadway. McGraw raced outside, jumped in his car and drove at threatening speeds to reach the ballpark. The flames were visible for miles around, and the fire was being fueled by the ample supply of wood from the stands. It didn't take long for the Polo Grounds to burn. Fire officials were convinced that the blaze was started by a lighted cigarette dropped in a pile of peanut shells under the grandstand. If the fire had started during the game with 40,000 fans in attendance, the loss of life would have been horrendous.

The Polo Grounds had originally been constructed for the New York club in the short-lived Players' League in 1890. At the time the Giants were playing their home games next door at Manhattan Field, and when the Players' League abruptly folded, they moved into the Polo Grounds. John T. Brush had become too ill to run the club, so John T. Whalen was handling the day-to-day operations. While the Giants decided what to do about replacing the Polo Grounds, arrangements were made for the club to play their home games at Hilltop Park, home of the Yankees. The National League constitution required that in order to transfer the games to another park, it required a consenting vote of two-thirds of the owners. Therefore, National League president Thomas Lynch set the process in motion by sending out telegrams, and authorization was quickly obtained for the Giants to play Brooklyn that afternoon at Hilltop Park.

Two years earlier, John T. Brush had been given an option on a piece of property near Long Island City. Although Long Island City was located just across the East River from Manhattan, at the time it was still considered a rural community without a bridge, and the Giants' board of directors preferred a site within easy reach of the city. Furthermore, the Giants had been leasing the land where the Polo Grounds was located from Mrs. James J. Coogan, daughter of the late William Lynch. The land had been in the Coogan-Lynch family for over 120 years. The Giants felt a sense of history about Coogan's Bluff and wanted to keep the team in that location. The bleachers and clubhouse had survived the fire and the Giants decided to have an engineering team assess the feasibility of rebuilding on the site while the team was on a forthcoming western road trip. Only a month earlier, a fire had occurred at the American League Washington ballpark and new stands were quickly constructed.

In early May 1911, the $50,000 slander lawsuit promised by John M. Ward against Ban Johnson was heard in United States Circuit Court in New York in front of Judge Hand. The suit had originated as a result of Johnson's comments made during the National League meeting in December 1909 in regard to Ward's handling of the George Davis matter. With a packed courtroom of observers, including Barney Dreyfuss, Charles Comiskey, John Heydler and others, the trial proceeded. The particular language that Ward took offense to was in Johnson's comments stating, "Ward is a trickster and he will never sit as a member of the National Commission, and I will not stand for Ward."[2] Ward, as a member of the bar, alleged that Johnson's statement had done great damage to his reputation.

Stephen C. Baldwin, the attorney for Ward, was largely basing his case on an article written by Ring Lardner and published in a Chicago paper on November 27, 1909. A deposition by Lardner had been taken in which he stated that he had indeed interviewed Johnson. Upon taking the witness stand, Lardner stated, "I wrote the facts as I remember them." Johnson had also been interviewed by Ernest Stout of the Newspaper Enterprise Association and in that article also referred to Ward as a "trickster." In his testimony before the court, Stout stated, "I prepared an article and asked Mr. Johnson to sign it. After looking it over, he signed it."[3] However, on the witness stand being questioned by Ward's attorney, Stephen J. Baldwin, Johnson denounced the alleged signature on Stout's article as a forgery, calling it a tracing. Mr. Baldwin asked Johnson if he realized that he was charging Stout with forgery. Johnson's reply was, "That's just what it was—forgery."[4]

Trouble nearly erupted in the courtroom with Stout leaping to his feet, objecting to Johnson's allegations, and court officers stepped between Johnson and Stout. The day's proceeding ended with Judge Hand ordering the deposition of Ring Lardner and two others thrown out. The single question left to the jury by Judge Hand was whether the signature of Johnson on the Stout document was a forgery. As the court was recessed for the day, many observers hung around outside the courtroom, waiting to see if Johnson and Stout might continue their disagreement with fisticuffs. On May 12, 1911, after one hour of deliberation, the jury awarded John M. Ward a verdict of $1,000 and the matter was closed.

In Cincinnati, Henry T. Hunt, the Hamilton County prosecuting attorney, was attempting to build a case of perjury against George B. Cox. Hunt's case alleged that in his testimony before a grand jury on May 31, 1906, Cox stated that he had never received any of the illegal interest money collected by Hamilton County treasurers from various banks. However, in front of a subsequent grand jury, the testimony of John H. Gibson, a former Republican county treasurer, alleged that various banks had returned $97,000 as a gratuity to him and that Cox had in fact received $48,500 of that sum.

Hunt was advancing a hidden agenda against Cox in that he planned to run for mayor of Cincinnati in the forthcoming municipal election in November and hoped to fuel voter apathy by resurrecting the old Democrat strategy of making George B. Cox the poster boy for bad government in the Queen City. As news of Hunt's investigation spread, Cox denied charges. In fact, investigating bank fraud in the early years of the twentieth century was widespread and almost fashionable among politicians.

Banking in the United State in 1911 was a vastly different enterprise than it is today, and bank failures, losses to depositors and fraud were commonplace. Of course, banking was not as regulated in 1911 as it is today and almost anyone with limited capital could open a bank. But as a result of the panic of 1907 and a continued epidemic of bank failures and fraud, change would come to the industry in 1913 with passage of the Federal Reserve Act by Congress. However, at the present time, Henry T. Hunt and other opportunists could play politics with the fragile banking system and attempt to use the issue for personal political gain.

George B. Cox knew that even the hint of his being investigated for perjury was a huge political liability to the Republican Party in Cincinnati. Furthermore, the possibility of the Republicans retaining the office of mayor in the coming election looked dim. In an effort to discredit Hunt's investigation of him, Cox decided to make a preemptive strike. He sat down with a reporter from the *New York World* for an interview in his office at the Cincinnati Trust Company. In the newspaper's Sunday magazine on May 14, 1911, Cox hoped to clear the air with his tell-all exposé "How Did I Make My Millions." In the magazine article, Cox admitted that he was in the classic sense a "boss." Cox told the *New York World*, "The term (boss) is purely relative. And nine times out of ten, it is applied by those who wish to vilify a successful political leader. This is true in my case. I have been so uniformly successful since I rose to the leadership of the Republican Party in Cincinnati and Hamilton County in 1884, that my enemies and vilifiers for twenty-seven years have been calling me a boss. They are at perfect liberty to do so. However I maintain that I am nothing more or less than the leader of the Republican Party in Cincinnati and Hamilton County."[5] Cox stated that a boss is a circumstance that is evolved, not self-made. He had no intention of becoming a boss when he entered politics as a young man, but because of his particular fitness, he evolved into a boss.

Cox was also asked how he made his millions.

> Principally in real estate and investments. I am interested in thirty-one different business enterprises, representing almost as many different kinds of business. For instance, I own half the Shubert Theatrical Company. Business with me comes first. About eight years ago I entered the banking business and since that time I have been president of the Cincinnati Trust Company, the second largest trust company in the city. But I have no personal or private interests when it comes to a question of doing that which is to be for the benefit of the party. While I have taken an active interest in politics since I was eighteen years of age, I have never neglected my business. I have always had business on my mind. That is one of the reasons why I have been successful. In political matters I have never allowed personal feelings to sway me. I use my own judgment as to the class of candidates most acceptable to the people. Whenever I have defaulted in that I have been unsuccessful. Cincinnati is the best governed city in the United States. There is less graft, less dishonesty among its office holders than in any of the large cities in the country. Why? Because I have prevented graft. The fact that all the investigations by self-styled reformers for the past twenty-seven years have not even resulted in the finding of seven illegal votes out of a total population of 400,000 is pretty good proof of my statement.[6]

Of course, Cox was exaggerating a bit on the matter of voter fraud. This circumstance was in fact a common occurrence among supporters for Republican candidates as well as Democrats at the time.

The Cox perjury trial continued into the summer. In the early going, Cox won an important victory when judge Frank Gorman, a partisan political cohort of the prosecutor, Henry T. Hunt, was removed from the trial. The defense attorneys for Cox asserted that Gorman was prejudiced against their client. Much to the disappointment of Henry T. Hunt, the Cox defense team was eventually able to have the indictment thrown out on the grounds that Cox's constitutional rights had been violated in 1906 when he testified before a grand jury on matters that may have incriminated him. While Cox escaped unscathed legally, in the end he had been mortally wounded politically in the trial, and it was the beginning of the end of his long, powerful, and sometimes misunderstood reign at the forefront of Cincinnati politics. Henry Hunt had Cox on the ropes and he knew it. So Cox quietly retired from politics. Charles P. Taft and Julius Fleischmann were convinced that the time was also right for August

Herrmann and Rud Hynicka to retire from the Cincinnati political scene, but both ignored the gesture.

John T. Brush wasted no time in rebuilding the Polo Grounds, and on June 28, 1911, the Giants went home to a new steel-and-concrete structure. The National League pennant race turned out to be a two-team battle between the Giants and Cubs. But with the Giants' superb pitching duo of Christy Mathewson and Rube Marquard and their blazing speed on the basepaths, setting a major league record of 347 stolen bases, New York went 20–4 down the stretch in September to outdistance the Cubs for the pennant by 7½ games. The American League race was also a two-team affair between the Philadelphia Athletics and the Detroit Tigers. While the Tigers had led most of the way, the Athletics caught them in August and kept the Bengals at bay down the stretch.

In Cincinnati, the Reds had another disastrous season, finishing in sixth place, 29 games behind the Giants. Fan interest in the Reds was waning. Barely 300,000 paying customers entered the Palace of the Fans in 1911, the lowest season attendance figure since 1902, when the club was still under the control of John T. Brush. Furthermore, the controversial trade that Garry Herrmann and Clark Griffith had engineered with the Philadelphia Phillies turned out to be a total bust. After three frustrating seasons managing the Reds, Clark Griffith was done with his National League experiment and was ready to return to the American League.

During the 1911 season, the way the game was being played was continuing to change with a sharp rise of many high-scoring games. The "Dead Ball Era," as it would become known, was dying a slow death. Between 1908 and 1911, the season ERA in the National League had risen from 2.35 to 3.39 and in the American League from 2.39 to 3.34. There was a growing concern among fans, newspaper reporters and baseball magnates alike that with the continued rise of the season earned run average (ERA), perhaps it had something to do with the manufacturing process of the balls. In fact, a common notion was that the ball used in the American League was more lively. The balls used in the two major leagues had different manufacturers. The National League balls were manufactured by A.G. Spalding & Brothers, while the American League balls were provided by the A. J. Reach Company. To address the controversy, a joint statement was drafted and signed by both company presidents Albert G. Spalding and A. J. Reach and sent to August Herrmann, who shared it with the National Commission, who in turn simply filed it. In the statement Spalding and Reach stated:

> Judging from newspaper comments there seems to be an impression in the minds of some that there is a difference in the construction between the official National League ball and the official American League ball. We take this method of assuring the commission that there is absolutely no difference in the quality of the material and construction of these two official balls.
>
> The best interest of the game not only demands this, but it is stipulated under the license from the owner of the patent on the "cork centre ball" that both the official National League ball and the official American League ball shall be made exactly according to the same specifications. The present official balls now in use by both major leagues and the balls that will be used in the world's series between the New York Giants and the Philadelphia Athletics will be the exact duplicates of the balls that were used in the world's championship series of 1910, and the same as have been used by both major leagues in all championship games during the entire season of 1911. We believe the official balls, as now constructed, are as near perfect as the art of ballmaking can make them.[7]

The year 1911 was also when Albert G. Spalding published his 600-page book *America's National Game*. Spalding was now baseball's elder statesman and a multi-millionaire sporting goods tycoon, and he never tired of fanning the flames of nationalism by equating the game of baseball with American values. The book was a huge success and widely read by everyone, from Kansas school boys to the mayor of New York, Robert Adamson, to Pittsburgh

Pirates owner Barney Dreyfuss. The book cost $2 and was published by American Sports Publishing Company of New York. In an effort to further promote the book, Spalding traveled from his home in California to attend the 1911 World Series. It would be in the 1911 World Series that the legend of "Home Run" Baker was born. In the second game of the series, Frank Baker, the Philadelphia Athletics' third baseman, broke a 1–1 deadlock between the New York Giants' Rube Marquard and Eddie Plank with a two-run home run in the 6th inning, providing the margin for an Athletics 3–1 victory. The following day, Baker hit a home run in the top of the 9th off of Christy Mathewson to break up a 1–0 shutout and send the game into extra innings, with the Athletics eventually winning, 3–2, in 11 innings. Baker had been the American League home run king for 1911, swatting eleven round-trippers. While the Giants were to make a determined effort behind Christy Mathewson, Philadelphia won the series in six games to give Connie Mack back-to-back World Series titles.

The position of Thomas T. Lynch as president of the National League was still fragile. The news media was now predicting that Lynch would not survive another election as he was edging closer to losing the necessary five votes to retain his office. The most vocal critic of Lynch was Barney Dreyfuss of Pittsburgh. However, both Charles Murphy of Chicago and Horace Fogel were also anti–Lynch. Meanwhile in Louisville, Robert Brown, the man that would be president of the National League, sensing that Lynch was vulnerable, seized the moment and began circling his prey. At the suggestion of August "Garry" Herrmann, Brown began an intensive letter-writing campaign to key National League magnates John T. Brush, Charles Ebbets, and Barney Dreyfuss, attempting to enlist their support in his quest to replace Lynch. In one letter, Brown even attached an Associated Press clipping that predicted the demise of Lynch at the next National League meeting. However, the major obstacle for Brown to overcome in advancing his candidacy was the fact that Tom Lynch was the hand-picked successor to Harry Pulliam of John T. Brush. In late September, Brown wrote a letter to Herrmann, asking him to make contact with John T. Brush on his behalf. In the correspondence he is even so bold as to suggest to Herrmann that if he were to extend some form of a golden parachute to Lynch by finding him a replacement job, it might placate the feelings of Brush on the matter and perhaps entice him to resign, clearing the way for Brown's election.

21st September 1911

Dear Garry:

My hope is that somehow you will find a way to edge a good word in for me with Mr. Brush. It will be so very much better if matters can be harmonized in my interest in advance.

This morning Mr. Ebbets called me by long distance from Cincinnati. He told me he had talked with you and was delighted with your position. Also that he would see Barney and that when he found out the latter was for me he thought there would be not much trouble.

You know Mr. Brush better than I do. He is going to win the pennant and be feeling good. Don't you think there is reason why he should be communicated with and relieved of any chance to imagine something is being done in which he is deeply interested, without an effort to get him? But as I say, you know him better than I, and whatever you think and do will be all right.

If you could help Mr. Lynch get something good or hold out a prospect to him, it might enable to ask Mr. Brush to favor you and be for me. This is only a suggestion, of course.

Faithfully,
Robert Brown[8]

Brown then went to New York and during the World Series continued his endless lobbying of various National League magnates. The primary target for his overzealous adulation was John T. Brush. However, Brush was still not convinced that it was in the best interest of the league to terminate Lynch, and avoided any contact with Brown. Furthermore, Brush was still dealing with his nagging health problems and didn't consider Brown's nonsense a priority.

Still, Brown kept imposing on August Herrmann to speak with Brush on his behalf. In the end, Thomas Lynch survived the *coup de tat* of 1911 and was reelected president of the National League, with Herrmann voting for him. But Robert W. Brown, still obsessed with his desire for Lynch's job, would remain lurking in the shadows and waiting for him to fail, all the while begging August Herrmann to help make him king.

At Cincinnati city hall, Louis Schwab, after serving one term as mayor, had become tired of the office and decided to not run for reelection. With George B. Cox retired, an advisory committee of Charles P. Taft, Garry Herrmann, Rud Hynicka and Julius Fleischmann, along with the consultation of the president of the United States, William Howard Taft, selected Albert Bettinger to run against Henry T. Hunt for mayor in the 1911 municipal election. Bettinger initially refused to accept the nomination. President Taft then asked Cincinnati dry goods magnate Joseph T. Carew to run for the office. When Carew also declined, the committee, knowing that Bettinger could not win the election, went back to him and he agreed to be the Republican Party's sacrificial lamb.

Hunt ran a nasty campaign, acting as if he had never aspired to the office, but rather the winds of reform had drawn him in. He ignored Albert Bettinger while drawing a parallel comparison between criminal elements in Cincinnati and the Republican Party. Rather than introduce new ideas for the city, he chose to rehash all the old issues and charges against the Republican machine, from the lack of competitive bidding on public contracts to its inability to keep the city's streets clean. With a disorganized Republican Party lacking any form of cohesive leadership to fight back, Hunt won the election 43,673 to 39,771 votes. George B. Cox looked upon the election of Henry T. Hunt with total disdain and began to wonder if perhaps he had retired prematurely.

In early January 1912, after taking the oath of office as Cincinnati's 17th mayor, Henry T. Hunt promised to make big plans for improving the infrastructure of the city, including its sewage system and park improvements. To reduce congestion in the basin area of the city, he advocated building a pathway for increased settlement of the suburbs via a rapid transit system. To accomplish his mass-transit agenda, Hunt stated that he would appoint a three-man Rapid Transit Commission and planned to build a rapid transit system that would encircle the city and become a subway in the basin area. The new mayor stated that it was his intention for Cincinnati to have the best urban transportation system in the United States. Thus began the planning for the belt rapid transit and subway system in Cincinnati that would eventually result in a $6 million public works boondoggle. When adjusted for inflation, the aborted Cincinnati subway system would become one of the country's most expensive failed urban public works projects of the twentieth century.

Following another disappointing season in 1911, Garry Herrmann knew he had to do something to improve the image of his ballclub. He couldn't demolish the team, so he did the next best thing by demolishing the ballpark. The Palace of the Fans was so woefully inadequate that there were not even any dugouts, and players sat on benches below the park's opera boxes. It took only 15 days to wreck the old stands and wooden bleachers of the Palace of the Fans and cart the debris away. Herrmann hired prominent Cincinnati architect Harry Hake to design a new state-of-the-art facility, and six months later, after 800,000 pounds of steel, 12,000 barrels of cement and 619,000 bricks had been forged together, construction was complete. Gone were the old distinctive features of the Palace of the Fans, with its entrance that looked like the Arch de Triomphe in Paris. The new park was built at a cost of $400,000 and could seat 23,000. However, according to Herrmann, the new park could actually accommodate up to 30,000 if necessary.

The ballpark would become known as Redland Field, but at the time it was actually unnamed. Most Cincinnati newspapers and many fans favored the ballpark being named after Garry Herrmann, as "Herrmann Field," to coincide with other new ballparks named after owners, such as Comiskey Park and Shibe Park. One notable distinction of the new Cincinnati home park was the size of the playing field. The dimensions were the largest in the major leagues. It was 360 feet down the left field line, 385 feet down the right field line, and 420 feet to straightaway center field. The fence was eight-feet high in left and ten-feet tall in center. There was immediate speculation that no one would ever hit a ball out of the park. In fact, it was not until 1921 that Pat Duncan became the first player to clear the left field wall. Among the amenities were a restroom for players along with a reading and billiard room on the second floor of the three-story building behind the home plate portion of the grandstand.

The new park was the pride of Garry Herrmann. While the official dedication of the new park was scheduled for May 18, the first game ever played there took place on opening day, April 11, 1912. It was grandest of events in the Queen City, with Weber's Band playing popular marching music of the day and an enthusiastic crowd of 26,336 (a new single-game attendance record in Cincinnati) was on hand. The Reds, sporting their crisp, new, white home uniforms, played host to the Chicago Cubs. Mayor Henry T. Hunt was on hand and posed for a photograph commemorating the event with Reds president Garry Herrmann and architect Harry Hake that was published in the *Cincinnati Enquirer* the following morning. Only a few weeks prior to opening day, Hunt had been playing politics with the new ballpark by floating the idea around city council of assessing a special tax of $1,500 a year for the Reds to use the new ballpark on top of the regular property taxes that could be assessed on a $400,000 investment of Herrmann and his partners. Such a tax was vindictive and political, and even more ridiculous when it was considered that Garry Herrmann often allowed various non-profit groups and clubs use of the Reds' former facility for free. The root of the problem was that Herrmann and his fellow investors had given something to the people of Cincinnati in which they could take pride in for generations to come. However, the fragile, over-inflated, politically partisan ego of Henry Hunt simply prevented him from being ceremonial about the park.

August Herrmann, chairman, the National Commission, 1903–1920, and president, Cincinnati Reds, 1902–1927. National Baseball Hall of Fame Library, Cooperstown, N.Y.

With Calvin Griffith having gone home to the American League, destined to become a major league legend, Garry Herrmann named Hank O'Day as the new manager of the Reds for the 1912 season. O'Day was a former pitcher with Toledo and Pittsburgh in the American Association (1884–1885), Washington and New York in the National League (1886–1889), and played with New York in the Players' League (1890). However, he was a rookie manager without any major league experience. But on opening day 1912, playing in their spacious new home park, O'Day's Reds beat the Cubs, 10–6. On May 18, the Reds' new ballpark was formally dedicated and named Redland Field. Dedication day was celebrated by the Reds and 28,000 of their giddy fans with a victory over the league-leading New York Giants. Suddenly, the whole town was "batty about Cincinnati" and it was simply bedlam at Redland with 70,000 fans attending the three-game Giants series.

That evening a huge dinner honoring the public service achievements of Garry Herrmann and the club's directors was given by the Cincinnati Commercial Association at the Sinton Hotel. Among the 350 guests in attendance were National League president Thomas Lynch, American League president Ban Johnson, Secretary Bruce and A. J. Flanner of the National Commission, the presidents of National Association and Blue Grass League, along with several major league moguls, including Charles Comiskey of the Chicago White Sox, Charles Murphy of the Chicago Cubs, Horace Fogel of the Philadelphia Phillies and Charles Ebbets of the Brooklyn Dodgers. Also, a touch of major league magic was added to the room with George Wright and Charles Gould, the shortstop and first baseman, respectively, on the legendary 1869 Cincinnati Red Stockings team, mingling among the guests. Both manager John McGraw of the Giants and Hank O'Day of the Reds were in attendance, along with many politicians, including Cincinnati Mayor Hunt, Governor Tener of Pennsylvania, and congressman Nicholas Longworth, Second District of Ohio.

While the local critics of August Garry Herrmann continued to harbor deep disdain for him, Redland Field, like the waterworks, was another monument to his ingenuity and untiring enthusiasm for his city. However, the story of Redland Field, like the story of Garry Herrmann, would be destined to that of a historical abyss. By the time the old ballpark was abandoned in 1970 and demolished two years later, to most observers it had become Crosley Field and heretofore had become associated part and parcel with the legacy of Powell Crosley, Jr. To most Cincinnatians, the old ballpark, like its builder, would lose historical relevance, while Redland Field would become a name of a place even more distant in the city's major league history than that of the Palace of the Fans.

XIII

Cobb Explodes and Taft Tumbles

The year of 1912 was a presidential election year and major league baseball was looking forward to a banner season. Fan interest was high and solid pennant races were predicted in both leagues. In addition to Redland Field opening in Cincinnati, two more new ballparks were opening for business in the American League. On April 20, Fenway Park opened in Boston. Mayor John F. "Honey Fitz" Fitzgerald, future grandfather of an American president, John F. Kennedy, threw out the first ball. Also, Navin Field opened in Detroit. The game was becoming ever-more fan friendly as the no-nonsense policies of Ban Johnson had done much to eliminate rowdiness on the playing field and in the stands. In Philadelphia, Connie Mack had plain-clothes cops in the stands to root out gamblers. Then, on May 15, 1912, major league baseball got a black eye that it neither deserved nor hardly anticipated that threatened to turn a landmark season upside down.

Crowds at New York's Hilltop Park had become increasingly unruly. Umpire Bill "Silk" O'Loughlin had been greeted by the New York fans with a fusillade of pop bottles as he stepped on to the field. The Highlanders' fans were claiming innocence in the bad behavior department, charging that such incidents were the result of the Polo Grounds' fans, who had been frequenting the American League park. But on May 15, the Detroit Tigers were playing the New York Highlanders at Hilltop Park when things suddenly turned very ugly. Several fans began harassing Ty Cobb from the stands. As the abuse escalated, one of the hecklers, Claude Lueker, a minor New York politician and former pressman who had lost both hands in an industrial accident, supposedly began shouting innuendoes, suggesting that Cobb was of a racially mixed genetic heritage. As the barrage of hateful remarks showered down upon Cobb from the stands, a New York policeman stood by totally unconcerned. Then in the 4th inning, Cobb could stand it no more. He mentally snapped, jumped into the stands, fists flying, and beat the handicapped heckler to a pulp. Upon being restrained, umpire Silk O'Loughlin promptly ejected Cobb from the game. Ban Johnson witnessed the assault from the stands and immediately suspended Cobb indefinitely.

Leaving New York, the Tigers were scheduled to continue their eastern road trip in Philadelphia on May 18. However, upon arrival in Philadelphia, the Tigers' players vowed that they would not play without Cobb and went on strike. The sentiments of both the Detroit fans and club president Frank Navin were with Cobb in the matter. Navin, who had the most to lose, told the *Sporting News*, "I am heart and soul in sympathy with the Tigers. As a matter of business, I must see to it that there are strikebreakers to take the place of the players who walked out or put myself liable to a fine of $5,000 a day for every day the Tigers don't appear."[1] The sentiments of a lot of players on other clubs were also with Cobb and the striking players. One unnamed Reds player stated, "Many a good player has been driven out of a city by abusive fans, and the quicker the magnates take action, giving better protection to players, the better it will be all around. Cobb may have violated a baseball rule by walloping that big stiff who insulted him, but there was a real excuse for it, and I believe I'd do the same thing under the circumstances."[2]

On May 18 in Philadelphia, the Detroit Tigers' players walked off the field and refused to play without Ty Cobb. Ban Johnson, in Cincinnati for the dedication of Redland Field, held firm on his decision to suspend Cobb. Furthermore, Johnson levied a fine of $5,000 for each day the Tigers did not field a team. Both Frank Navin and Ty Cobb urged the team to play, but it was to no avail. Consequently, Tigers manager Hugh Jennings did what he could to field a team. Jennings recruited Tigers coaches, 46-year-old Deacon Jim McGuire and 41-year-old Joe Sugden, both former major league catchers, to play, and added various amateur players and others from St. Joseph College to fill out the lineup. One of those players recruited by Jennings would hold an ominous place in major league history. Playing third base for Jennings' makeshift team was Philadelphia native, small-time gambler and pug-nosed prize fighter Billy Maharg. Maharg would eventually be implicated in the alleged fixing of the 1919 World Series. Also, one of the striking Tigers was pitcher "Sleepy Bill" Burns, who would become a cohort of Maharg's and also be implicated in the alleged plot to fix the 1919 World Series. Immediately following the players' strike, Burns would be cut from the team by Jennings and never pitched in the major leagues again.

With the makeshift Tigers' lineup in place, 20,000 curious fans showed up at Shibe Park, but the game was a farce as the Philadelphia Athletics won by a score of 24–2 while pounding out 25 hits. Connie Mack could not stand the circus atmosphere of the game and suspended the next contest, scheduled for May 20. Immediately, Ban Johnson, who was now imposing a $100 a day fine on the striking players, rushed to Philadelphia to verbally chastise the striking Detroit players. After missing two games, at the urging of Cobb, the Tigers returned to play at Washington on May 21. Regardless of the sentiments of the players, Ban Johnson realized the seriousness of the Cobb incident and what the implications were for major league attendance. Therefore, he quickly launched an investigation and issued the following finding in the matter.

> After a careful investigation into the causes and circumstances of the encounter between player Cobb and Claude Lueker, a spectator at the New York grounds, on May 15, I find that direct responsibility for the unfortunate occurrence rest upon the player.
> Evidence in the form of affidavits clearly shows that the player was the first to employ vicious language in replying to a taunting remark of the spectator.
> Cobb did not seek redress by an appeal to the umpire, but took the law into his own hands. His language and conduct were highly censurable.
> As a lesson to the accused and a warning to all other players, I fix the term of the player's suspension at ten days and impose a fine of $50. He will be eligible to play on May 26.
> Full protection will be afforded to all American League players against abuse or attack from patrons, but sure and severe punishment will be meted out to those who in disregard or discipline and of obligations to their club and league assume to act as judge and avenger of real or fancied wrongs while on duty. [3]

The reason a fine was levied on Cobb by Johnson for a lesser amount than his teammates was that officially he was not considered a striking player since he was under suspension. To enforce his edict, Johnson directed umpires to remove all unruly spectators from the grounds and also mandated that club owners increase police protection in the stands. Historically, Ty Cobb would be the big loser in the matter as it tainted his legacy. Future generations of Cobb

From the left: Ty Cobb, Shoeless Joe Jackson and Sam Crawford. Author's collection.

critics would offer the incident as definitive proof that his assault on Lueker was evidence of an overt display of psychotic behavior.

While there would not be another major league player strike until 1972, the Cobb incident triggered the formation of the first players union. Later in the year, the Ball Players' Fraternity would be formed, headed by Dave Fultz, a practicing attorney and former player with a seven-year major league career between 1898 and 1905, primarily with Philadelphia in the National League and New York in the American League. Fultz charged members a $5 initiation fee and annual dues of $18, payable in installments. A good number of major league players and those in the high minors joined the union, but hardly any change in the player-owner relationship resulted from the association.

Meanwhile in Cincinnati, the endless quest of the politically motivated forces to get George B. Cox continued. During the past year, the Cox-controlled Cincinnati Trust Company went belly up; the stockholders of the bank were suing the directors for mismanagement. Naturally, the administration of Mayor Henry Hunt advocated a full disclosure. Allied with State Attorney General Hogan, Hunt pressured Hamilton County prosecutor Thomas Pogue to begin a voluntary probe, calling for the liquidating committee of the Cincinnati Trust Company and the stockholders' protective committee to come forward and disclose all the facts they had uncovered in the failure of the bank. The preliminary allegations were that false bank statements were issued and signed by George B. Cox, that loans were made in excess of the statue limitations, and that a conspiracy existed to impair the integrity of the bank. Most of those affected by the bank's failure were of the mind that Pogue's probe would be a farce, citing that while the investigators were sincere, unlike proceedings under a grand jury, witnesses were being asked to appear voluntarily. Furthermore, Pogue and the investigators had no authority to prosecute any of the bank's directors, including Cox, for alleged misdeeds.

With members of the liquidating committee of the Cincinnati Trust Company, including grocery store magnate B. F. Kroger, shied away from the voluntary probe, the overzealous anti–Cox *Cincinnati Post* decided that prosecutor Pogue needed a little help in finding wrongdoing in the bank's failure. To make its case, the *Post* obtained and published a copy of a bank statement signed by George B. Cox on December 5, 1907, alleging it understated the bank's liabilities by $100,000. According to the report of the Cincinnati Trust Company that was published in the paper on June 1, 1912, the statement signed by Cox listed assets of $5,338,067.11 and liabilities of $5,338,067.11. However, according to the *Post*, the statement did not disclose an unpaid loan of $100,000 obtained from the Chase National Bank of New York on September 26, 1907, and still unpaid at the time that George B. Cox solemnly swore that the statement he signed was a true statement. The *Post* went on to state that it was highly unlikely that Cox didn't know about the loan since he was chairman of the executive committee that authorized the borrowing. In fact, it was disclosed that his name was signed to the resolution of September 26, 1907, authorizing the bank secretary and treasurer to borrow the money. While the loan was repaid on January 5, 1908, Cox had in the interim signed a bank statement that was inaccurate. Lastly, the *Post* alleged that similar loans had been obtained by Cincinnati Trust with Cox's knowledge in the recent past, including $75,000 from the First National Bank of Cincinnati and $125,000 from the Bank of Commerce of New York.

Much to the frustration of the anti–Cox forces, and despite the allegations of the overzealous *Cincinnati Post*, Thomas Pogue stated that at the moment the only evidence of wrongdoing he had was by innuendo and that nothing yet had been presented to warrant a grand jury investigation. All that Pogue could do was, in conjunction with the liquidating committee, seek an independent audit of the bank's books, then make a comparison of the report with those on file with the State Banking Department. Pogue also had to make sure that in the fervor of certain political entities in the city to get Cox, he did not compromise his own investigation by shooting from the hip. The Cox-led Cincinnati Trust was not the only Cincinnati bank that had recently failed. So had the Second National Bank. In fact, so distraught was its president, Elmer E. Galbreath, that only days before he had suffered what was reported as a nervous collapse and fainted on the platform of an Avondale streetcar.

With political pressure increasing on him daily to ignore due process and force a criminal prosecution of George B. Cox in the Cincinnati Trust Company matter, Hamilton County prosecutor Thomas Pogue turned to Charles P. Taft of the *Cincinnati Times-Star* for assistance. Pogue told Taft that he was being pressured to conduct an investigation of the Cincinnati Trust Company that was outside the bounds of his jurisdiction. Pogue wanted to ask a favor of Taft's half-brother, President William Howard Taft. He wanted to see if the federal government would appoint a bank examiner to oversee the examination of the state bank examiner in the investigation of the Cincinnati Trust Company affairs. On June 5, 1912, Charles P. Taft wrote a letter to the president on the behalf of Pogue, stating in part, "Mr. Pogue wants to secure a man thoroughly competent, and one who has had experience with National Banks, to make this examination; in other words, the State Banking Department will detail a man to make this examination and Mr. Pogue wants a Federal examiner to keep tab on the state officer."[4]

The entire crusade by the Cincinnati Democrats to get Cox had now reached a new height of absurdity as it became necessary for a local prosecutor to reach out to the president of the United States to ensure that the investigation would be conducted fairly. President Taft took immediate action and directed the matter to United States attorney general George Wickersham, who in turn dispatched Howard E. Rank to Cincinnati to assist Thomas Pogue in the matter of the Cincinnati Trust Company investigation.

President Taft was facing a tough reelection challenge in 1912 due to the lasting popularity of Theodore Roosevelt and Taft's inability to claim any major accomplishments made by his administration, particularly in foreign affairs. In 1911, Taft had negotiated and pushed through Congress a reciprocal trade agreement with Canada with lower tariffs that would have been extremely beneficial to his Eastern constituents. However, the agreement died when the Canadian Parliament failed to ratify it. While Taft actually had a firm grip on the inner-workings of the Republican Party's election machinery, he wasn't taking any chances. In an effort to secure New Jersey's 28 delegates in the Garden State's primary election, Taft made a 12-hour trip by automobile throughout the state on May 24 and delivered 15 speeches. Speaking at Plainfield, New Jersey, Taft stated that Roosevelt had recently declared, "I am the Republican Party." Taft expressed a concern for the safety of the institution of the presidency if Roosevelt were once again elected president. "I say to you in all conviction that were he allowed a third term in violation of the wise tradition, intoxicated as he would be with the sense of power, it would not be safe to have him in the White House. Those who love the Republic must see to it that no such risk is run."[5] Roosevelt was also in New Jersey on May 24 and told his faithful audiences that he intended to continue the fight if Taft was nominated in Chicago by fraud and corruption.

Meanwhile, the gamesmanship in the Cincinnati Republican Party had already begun. Without the strong organizational skills of George B. Cox, the Republican Party was discombobulating. Charles P. Taft, in an attempt to placate the sentiments of his brother, the president, was using his status as publisher of the *Cincinnati Times Star* to cast Garry Herrmann and Rud Hynicka as the last symbols of Cox influence and attempting to force them to resign from the Republican Party. In fact, both Herrmann and Hynicka had resigned, effective January 1, 1912. However, the Blaine Club forces remained steadfast in their loyalty to Herrmann and Hynicka and forced Taft to accept the co-leadership of the two. So infuriated were the Blaine Club members with Charles P. Taft that in retaliation they refused to endorse him for a delegate at-large to the Republican national convention, despite the pleadings of councilman Mike Mullen. Mullen pleaded his case to Blaine Club membership by stating, "Mr. Taft has done a great deal for the Republican organization. He has been of great assistance to me in the Eighth Ward in rolling up big Republican majorities. Mr. Julius Fleischmann asked President Taft for an endorsement of Mayor Schwab last year and the president gave it. Now we ought to reciprocate by endorsing his brother." Mullen, acknowledging that the party was in a state of disorganization, pleaded his case further by stating, "You are opposed to the organization and we haven't any now. Let us start a new one. I want to be in it."[6]

Despite the fact that Theodore Roosevelt had beaten President Taft by 47,000 votes in the Ohio primary election, at the first session of the Ohio Republican Party convention in June, of the total 758 delegates to the state convention, 349 voted for Taft, while 335 voted for Roosevelt, with 74 uncommitted. It had been the Cuyahoga County delegation that tipped the balance for Taft when it shifted 48 of its 53 votes to him as charges of robbery rang out from the Roosevelt camp. The Roosevelt delegation was also upset by the fact that the convention had elected six delegates at-large to the national convention and all pledged to Taft, including Charles P. Taft, Warren G. Harding and Theodore Burton. On June 4, the convention adjourned, scheduled to reconvene in July at Columbus for the purpose of nominating state candidates. Meanwhile, President Taft thanked Rud Hynicka, a member of the powerful state central committee, and Scott Small, editor of the *Cincinnati Commercial-Tribune*, for backing him.

Back in the Queen City, there was unrest at the Blaine Club. Garry Herrmann and Rud Hynicka were attempting to persuade the club's directors to invest $10,000 of the club's money in a reorganized Commercial Tribune Company. At the time the Blaine Club had a tidy surplus in its treasury of $24,000. Hynicka, chairman of the advisory committee, and Herrmann, chairman of the finance committee, along with Buck Schiebel, chairman of the campaign committee of the former Republican organization, had drafted and signed a letter sent to the directors recommending the Blaine Club make an investment in the newspaper to insure its continued operation in the interest of the Republican Party and the club. Both Herrmann and Hynicka were investors in the Commercial Tribune, and Hynicka was the president of the company. Hynicka blatantly stated that without the partisan backing of the paper, the Republican Party and the Blaine Club were vulnerable to the constant attacks of the *Cincinnati Post*, the occasional criticism of the *Cincinnati Enquirer* and the whims of publisher Charles P. Taft at the *Cincinnati Times-Star*.

Two of the directors, Dudley Sutphin and Geoffrey Goldsmith, both attorneys, didn't like the idea and balked. They sought to table the matter at a later meeting, and were considering filing a suit. Both felt that the money could be better spent making capital repairs and improvements to the club building without having to issue bonds, rather than dumping money into an enterprise that was on shaky ground. At the time the *Commercial Tribune* was losing money. The terms of its five-year lease for its operations building were $10,000 a year, including making specified improvements each year. At the end of the lease, the paper had the option to renew the lease or purchase the property for $500,000.

There was also concern among Blaine Club members of how expenses would be paid for the members attending the Republican National Convention. Many of the club members had fallen on hard times since losing their patronage jobs in the 1911 county and municipal elections that swept Henry Hunt into office. Many Blaine Club members felt that the $10,000 being requested by Herrmann and Hynicka to help the sagging *Commercial Tribune* should be diverted to financing the club's contingent to the convention. That matter was solved when Charles P. Taft agreed to pay $12,500 and Garry Herrmann and Julius Fleischmann dug deep in their pockets, too, thus ensuring the Blaine Club members would be adequately lodged and fed in Chicago while providing a cheering section for Taft's brother.

As the national convention neared, there were 241 disputed delegates and the count showed that Theodore Roosevelt needed at least 70 of them in order to be nominated. On June 1, the credentials committee began meeting in Chicago behind closed doors. The deck was stacked against Roosevelt, with the National Committee being loyal to Taft. The credentials committee consisted of 37 members who mostly represented the old boss system of politics with the likes of Senator Murray Crane of Massachusetts, Senator Boies Penrose of Pennsylvania and others. As a result, the credentials committee awarded 233 of the disputed delegates to Taft and 8 to Roosevelt. Immediately, the Roosevelt forces in Chicago notified T. R. that the nomination was in the process of being stolen from him, and he quickly boarded a train in New York bound for Chicago.

The Republican National Convention was scheduled to open on June 18 at the Chicago Coliseum, a building constructed in part with stone salvaged from the former Confederate Libby Prison in Richmond. There hadn't been a real donnybrook for the GOP presidential nomination since 1880, when Ulysses S. Grant and James G. Blaine nearly deadlocked the convention before James A. Garfield was offered as a compromise candidate. Theodore Roosevelt arrived in Chicago over the weekend and set up his headquarters on the top floor of the Congress Hotel. The apartment included a private telegraph wire that T. R. would use to keep in touch with his delegation at the coliseum. On Wednesday evening, June 17, Roosevelt, making one last attempt at turning delegates in his favor, went on the attack as he addressed a cheering crowd of 10,000 at the auditorium. Taking dead aim at the Ohio Republican convention, he called the Taft supporters at the convention who had stolen the six delegates at-large burglars.

The final lock in the nomination process for Taft was secured with the election of Senator Elihu Root as temporary chairman of the convention. A fellow New Yorker, Root had been a close friend of Roosevelt's in the past and oversaw the 1904 National Republican Convention that nominated him for president. However, over the past few years, issues had developed that had weakened the bond between the two. When the National Committee ruled that the 74 delegates could vote for temporary chairman while their status was under dispute, Taft suddenly had the necessary votes to elect Root, and his nomination was assured. Now the Roosevelt delegates were charging that the nomination of Taft was being railroaded through by the National Committee and the bosses were preventing reform from taking hold in the Republican Party.

Warren G. Harding had been selected by President Taft to make a nominating speech on his behalf. As Harding approached the podium, sounds of sandpaper being rubbed together to simulate the startup movement of a steam locomotive could be heard throughout the hall. Then pro-reform and pro–Roosevelt delegates began shouting, "Toot! Toot! All aboard! Choo! Choo!"[7] Still others began to chant, "We want Teddy!" As Harding spoke, throughout the hall boos and hisses rang out while sporadic fist-fights broke out in various delegations. A member of the Pennsylvania delegation who had been knocked out cold lay on the floor. Other delegates began to get up from their seats and leave the hall. In his words, Harding did his best to romanticize the Progressive movement and characterize William Howard Taft as a true champion of that cause. At times it seemed as if Harding might be driven from the podium, but he eventually entered the name of William Howard Taft into nomination for president. As Harding took a hasty exit from the platform, Henry J. Allen, a future governor of Kansas, turned to Senator Root and stated, "No radical in the ranks of radicalism ever did so radical a thing as to come to a National Convention of the great Republican Party and secure through fraud the nomination of a man whom they knew could not be elected."[8]

That evening in Chicago, Garry Herrmann, Rud Hynicka, Julius Fleischmann and Charles P. Taft sat down for a meeting. The writing was on the wall; President Taft was caught between the ideological forces of conservatism and progressivism, and the party was in complete turmoil. While his nomination was assured, the re-election of Taft seemed like an impossible task. Convinced that the situation was futile, both Fleischmann and Charles P. Taft refused to put up anymore money to finance the Blaine Club's delegation to the convention. Later that night, Gary Herrmann, Rud Hynicka and the other Blaine Club members boarded a train for home. Upon arriving in Cincinnati in the morning, the club members were converged upon by several members of the local press. Both Herrmann and Hynicka refused to speculate on the chances of President Taft being re-elected, and Hynicka immediately left the station for Camp Gass, his fishing haven on the Whitewater River. Many of the other Blaine Club members were expressing a belief that while Taft had the votes to be re-nominated, his defeat for re-election was inevitable.

Back in Chicago on Friday, June 22, the GOP platform was read and the roll call began. In the end Taft had 561 votes, Roosevelt 107, LaFollete and other candidates 60, while 349 remained present but not voting. With Taft nominated, Henry J. Allen led 344 delegates out of the convention to the sounds of hoots and hisses from the balcony. The uncommitted Roosevelt delegates met that evening at Orchestra Hall and Theodore Roosevelt inspired the crowd with a fiery speech. Roosevelt called the convention corrupt and asked the delegates to wash their hands of the Republican Party and join him in forming a new political organization, promising to run for president as a progressive if they would nominate him at a forthcoming convention.

The Democratic National Convention would take place in Baltimore, June 25–July 2, at the 5th Maryland Regiment Armory. It would take 46 ballots to finally nominate New Jersey governor Woodrow Wilson for president and Thomas R. Marshall of Indiana for vice president. On August 5, the Progressive National Party (a.k.a. the Bull Moose Party) opened its convention at the Coliseum in Chicago with 15,000 delegates and spectators on hand. Theodore Roosevelt was nominated for president and Hiram Johnson, former governor of California, for vice president. Now the stage was set for the fall showdown.

By June 23, the elation of the Cincinnati fans with the opening of Redland Field was over. The Reds had fallen to fourth place, nineteen games behind the league-leading Giants. The Cincinnati fans were heaping huge doses of abuse on manager Hank O'Day. In an attempt to shore up the club, Garry Herrmann was attempting to get Charles Comiskey to allow waivers to go through on Boston Red Sox pitcher Eddie Cicotte so Herrmann could claim him for the Reds. But Comiskey refused, stating in correspondence to Herrmann that White Sox manager Nixey Callahan thought very highly of Cicotte and wished to claim him for Chicago. The only thing left for Hank O'Day to do was simply tough it out with a starting rotation of Rube Benton, Art Fromme, Bert Humpries and George Suggs. As the dog days of August descended upon the 1912 major league baseball season, to no one's surprise the New York Giants were threatening to run away with the National League pennant. The Cincinnati Reds and Philadelphia Phillies were locked in a battle for fourth place. Rumors were circulating that Garry Herrmann and Julius Fleischmann, disappointed with Reds manager Hank O'Day, were throwing in the towel on the 1912 season.

Also, the annual soap opera among the National League moguls was being played out in grand style. Once again, Horace Fogel was accusing Garry Herrmann of violating the ethics code by attempting to make a deal with his second baseman, Otto Knabe, in using a couple of Cincinnati news reporters to feel out Knabe's position. Fogel told the *Sporting News*, "I wrote to Herrmann and told him to keep off my team and if he has any deals to make to arrange them with me and not have a couple of Cincinnati newspaper men do the dealing."[9]

However, a more serious situation existed that threatened to undermine the very integrity of the game. Chicago Cubs owner Charles Webb Murphy was making accusations that the New York Giants could not win the National League pennant without assistance. In particular, Murphy was aiming at manager Roger Bresnahan of the St. Louis Cardinals, currently in sixth place, indicating that Bresnahan might have a vested interest in seeing to it that New York won the pennant. According to Murphy, if the Giants won the pennant, following the World Series, John McGraw had plans to take the team on a world tour and Bresnahan would manage a team of all-stars to provide the opposition and thereby pick up a lot of extra cash. Murphy was even suggesting that National League president Thomas Lynch might be in on the conspiracy because he had recently suspended Cubs second baseman Johnny Evers for five days in an effort to weaken the club in an upcoming series against the Giants.

Somehow, Horace Fogel felt compelled to support the unsubstantiated accusations of Murphy, and in doing so, went way over the line, thus making himself a target for retribution by his fellow owners. In an interview with the *Sporting News*, Fogel stated,

If you will recall last season when the Giants hit St. Louis on their Western trip, Bresnahan, who had been using his regular team against the Cubs and Pirates, put in a lot of rookies. He used bushers in the infield and the outfield and instead of going behind the bat himself, he put in Wingo, a green one to catch. Did that look as though Bresnahan wanted to win a game for the Giants? Not much. There is only one conclusion to arrive at in that — Roger wanted to help McGraw and his team to win the pennant — and he did. That was not fair and you can bet it wasn't overlooked, although at the time there was little said of it. The Pirates and the Cubs were running neck and neck with the Giants at that time and if the Cardinals had grabbed off a game or two, things might have been different. Watch how things run this year.[10]

Whether or not Horace Fogel had been set up by his friend Charles Murphy or it was simply a factor of his compulsive personality forcing him to enter the fray, the fact was that he had just accused the 1911 National League pennant race of being fixed and was now indicating that a fix was underway in the 1912 pennant race.

As if Fogel was not in deep enough, in September a letter signed by him was published in the *Chicago Post* that accused the Cardinals of lying down against Giants and the National League umpires of favoring the Giants. Many historians have theorized that the letter was actually drafted by Charles Murphy, who had a hidden agenda in that he wanted to undermine National League president Thomas Lynch. Murphy was a part of a block of owners, including Fogel and Brooklyn president Charles Ebbets, who wanted Lynch out as president.

Regardless of who the actual author of the letter was, sportswriters around the country did not take the unsubstantiated charges of Horace Fogel lightly, and some called for his immediate expulsion from the league. Fogel's position was made even more precarious by the fact that most insiders and sportswriters were of the opinion that he was but a puppet-owner, serving in the place of Charles P. Taft. Harry Nialy, writing in the *St. Louis Times*, stated, "Either Horace Fogel must leave the National League or the club owners admit that the national pastime no longer is honest. Fogel Saturday made a signed statement alleging umpires robbed other clubs of 21 games and for the benefit of the Giants, and that umpires deliberately sought favor with the New York Club for the purpose of getting World's Series money. Fogel, to be sure, is but a weak echo of Charles Murphy of Chicago, but Murphy has property rights in Chicago of which he cannot be deprived, but Fogel is a mere figurehead and dummy president."[11]

While it was blatantly clear that Horace Fogel was going to have to offer proof of his charges or face expulsion, irony existed in the matter as it had also become a cause in which to criticize Thomas Lynch for not taking the bull by the horns in the matter. Ernest J. Lanigan, writing in the *Sporting News*, stated,

> Lynch should have acted earlier, squelched Fogel when he started to run amuck and not waited until Howling Horace got a chance to discredit the national pastime. Thomas J. possibly had been a believer in the theory of allowing a person sufficient rope with which to hang himself, but his friends haven't believed in that theory. Fogel may or may not be expelled by the National League (it is my theory that he won't be), but he has done the league harm and not the game, and the league is suffering, not the game. Lynch, as said before is square as a die, and he stands up for his umpires, but he ought to sit down on his magnates. Murphy made some startling accusations against Roger Bresnahan that were passed by without notice from the Metropolitan Tower and Fogel made some broad strictures against the National League umpires that were not passed by Thomas the Just. I see where Lynch says that he is glad that Fogel is against him, because it probably will reinsure his election as president. That is all right as far as it goes, but is shouldn't have gone that far. Lynch should have squelched Murphy and Fogel long ago and then he wouldn't have had to thank a most inopportune article by H. F. for the chance to make him campaign capital. The New Britain man is the man for the job all right if he once gets it into his head that the magnates as well as the players occasionally need disciplining and hands out the disciplining that the magnates need.[12]

In Louisville, Robert W. Brown waited in the wings. Brown had been ever vigilant as the latest Horace Fogel incident played itself out, testing the turbulent waters at times to see if the undertow would catch Thomas J. Lynch and carry him out of office. After coming to Cincinnati in mid–September while the National Commission was in session, Brown wrote the following to Garry Herrmann.

September 16, 1912

My Dear Garry:

    Was in Cincinnati a few hours Sunday afternoon, but the Commission was in session and I of course didn't want to intrude. Saw our good friend Tom Cogan and also Messrs. Murphy and Ebbets. Barney was not expected until later in the evening and Mr. Fogel was not around while I was there. Please write me when you have time if there are any developments about which I should know. I know your outing at the Club will be a joyous affair. With all good wishes, believe me.

Faithfully yours,
Robert W. Brown[13]

Shortly after Brown returned to Louisville, he contracted a mild case of malaria and was laid up for a short time. During his convalescence, he wrote to Herrmann and told him, "Barney (Dreyfuss) came to see me and told me about his position just as you had foretold me — that he would never again support Lynch and that his vote was mine whenever it would elect. At last it being my dream will be realized, thanks to you, and that I am to become your co-laborer. I know you will keep me advised and let me have any suggestions that occur to you for my guidance."[14] Brown was starting to feel confidant that Lynch would not be elected to another term as National League president and that with the help of Garry Herrmann, he would be a shoo-in as his replacement. Brown was hoping to be recovered enough to come to New York and lobby National League moguls for the job during the World Series. However, Brown was greatly underestimating the political savvy of Thomas J. Lynch.

The New York Giants, despite the cloud of controversy created by the innuendoes and baseless allegations of Horace Fogel, won the 1912 National League pennant by 10 games over the second-place Chicago Cubs. The Giants were led by a trio of strong pitching efforts from Rube Marquard (26–11), Christy Mathewson (23–12) and Jesse Tesreau (17–11), a rookie who threw a wicked spitball. Marquard had set a major league record that still stands by winning his first 19 starts. His consecutive game win streak began on April 11 and ended on July 8. The Giants also got strong hitting from first baseman Fred Merkle (.309), second baseman and captain Larry Doyle (.330) and catcher Chief Meyers, a Cahuilla Indian from Southern California who had attended Dartmouth. Meyers hit .358, a mark that still stands as the highest season batting average for a National League catcher. Larry Doyle was voted as the National League's most valuable player by a panel of baseball writers on the Chalmers Trophy committee and was presented with an automobile.

In the American League, the surprising Boston Red Sox won the 1912 American League pennant after finishing fifth in 1911. Leading the way for the Red Sox was a hard-throwing 22-year-old pitcher by the name of Smoky Joe Wood, who won 34 games and lost five, with an ERA of 1.91. The Red Sox pitching staff also included two other twenty-game winners in Buck O'Brien (20–13) and Hugh Bedient (20–9). Tris Speaker hit (.383) for the Red Sox, the third-highest average in the American League behind Ty Cobb (.410) and Shoeless Joe Jackson (.395). Speaker also was the 1912 American League winner of the Chalmers automobile after having been voted by a panel of sportswriters as the most valuable player. More surprising than the Red Sox winning the flag were the Washington Nationals, who under the leadership of new manager Clark Griffith finished in second place, improving over a seventh-place finish in 1911. Connie Mack's dethroned Philadelphia Athletics and his $100,000 infield of Stuffy McInnis, Eddie Collins, Jack Barry and Home Run Baker failed to repeat as American League champions, finishing in third place.

World Series seating was scarce despite the fact that the Polo Grounds had a seating capacity of 38,000. National League secretary John Heydler had issued a warning to fans that a lot of bogus tickets were known to exist. Therefore, Heydler stated that the only way to ensure that a fan had a legitimate ticket was to buy it at the ballpark and not from a scalper. Consequently, all 5,000 reserved seats were sold at the Polo Grounds, two to a purchaser. That made it difficult for Boston rooters since only two hundred tickets had been allotted to Red Sox fans for the first game in the series. Boston mayor John F. "Honey Fitz" Fitzgerald wired Ban Johnson, who in turn arranged for National League secretary John Heydler to reserve an extra hundred tickets for a Beantown club called the "Royal Rooters." Then New York mayor Gaynor invited the Boston mayor to sit with him in his box. As the series got under way in New York on October 8, the teams played to a less-than-packed house with just 35,730 fans in attendance. Mayor Fitzgerald and the other 300 rabid Red Sox rooters entered the Polo Grounds behind a big brass band, causing a shower of taunts to be rained down upon them from the Giants' fans. Boston prevailed in game one as Smoky Joe Wood outlasted Jesse Tesreau, 4–3, while striking out eleven Giants and holding off a ninth-inning rally. The Red Sox would go on to win the 1912 World Series four games to three over the Giants. However, the series was actually an eight-game affair. The second game was called after eleven innings because of darkness with the score tied 6–6.

The National League owners had met during the World Series and decided to put the Horace Fogel issue and the status of the Philadelphia Phillies ballclub on the back burner until the winter meetings. In the meantime, rumors were beginning to circulate that Thomas J. Lynch would force Horace Fogel out of major league baseball and that the Phillies would be sold. The Phillies were not a bad investment as they had made a profit in both 1911 and 1912. When Charles P. Taft bought Baker Bowl for his wife, he had given the club a lease on the ballpark for five years at a rental of $16,000 a year, with an option for 99 years at a rental of $20,000 a year. It was a fact that at the moment three possible buyers were feeling out Taft about his intentions. One was a Philadelphia banker, another a newspaper publisher and the third, Jefferson Livingston of Cincinnati. However, there were complications to closing any deal, mainly because of Horace Fogel. When the Taft family had bought into the Phillies, Fogel had a clause inserted in his contract stating that if the club was to be put up for sale, he should have the first option to buy. Furthermore, Fogel had an additional agreement that stated if the club was sold for a price above which it was acquired in 1909, then he should receive a bonus. So it appeared that if Horace Fogel was to be forced over a cliff by Thomas J. Lynch, he was going to land with a golden parachute.

As his campaign went into high gear, President Taft was feeling confident about his re-election. However, it was as if the president was facing the coming campaign with blinders on, totally ignoring the potential consequences of having a third-party candidate in the race. Taft was in a complete mental state of denial and had convinced himself that the Roosevelt campaign would not cause his defeat. Taft felt that with Roosevelt in the race, the total number of votes the Republican ticket would receive would be less than it had been in 1909. But by extension, the Democrats would lose an equal number of votes by the presence of the Bull Moose ticket. Therefore, the combined strength of the third party would not be enough to change the ultimate result in the election. In the end, it would prove to be a foolish philosophy.

Woodrow Wilson knew he had Taft defeated. Therefore, he focused his campaign on

Theodore Roosevelt, 26th president of the United States, 1901–1909. Author's collection.

adopting the issues of the Progressive movement as his own in an effort to weaken Roosevelt. Theodore Roosevelt began the Bull Moose Party campaign in late August with a barnstorming tour through New England. Then he headed west to Washington and California before campaigning in the Midwest and South during mid–September. By early October, Roosevelt was back at home in Oyster Bay. He had a conference with his campaign staff and it was decided that enough money was still available in the campaign coffer for him to make one last whirlwind campaign run through the upper Midwest, where Woodrow Wilson had been attempting to steal a lot of his progressive thunder. As a result, in mid–October Roosevelt was off to Michigan and Minnesota. He then stopped in Chicago and reviewed a parade of progressives before arriving by train in Milwaukee on October 14 to deliver a speech.

That evening Roosevelt had dinner at the Hotel Gilpatrick, then went up to his room briefly before leaving for the Auditorium to deliver his speech. Around 8:00 P.M. Roosevelt came out of the front door of the hotel to the thunderous cheers of hundreds of admirers. Accompanying Roosevelt was his entourage that included a young cousin, Philip Roosevelt; his stenographer, Elbert H. Martin; Captain Gerard of the Milwaukee Police Department, who had been a Rough Rider under T.R.'s command; Colonel Cecil Lyon of Texas; and Henry F. Cochems, a Wisconsin Progressive Party leader. His car was parked directly in front of the Gilpatrick and Roosevelt entered the open-top vehicle and stood up, waving his hat to the delight of the crowd.

Standing only a few feet away from the car was a shabbily attired would-be assassin, John Schrank, a former bartender from New York City. Schrank seized the moment and pushed his way through the crowd. When he had maneuvered just a few feet from Roosevelt, Schrank took dead aim with a .32-caliber pistol and fired a bullet into Roosevelt's right breast, just below the nipple. Although stunned by the shock of the bullet's impact, Roosevelt barely moved. With the immediate flash of the shot, Elbert Martin, a six-foot former football player, leaped over the automobile and directly on top of Schrank. As Martin put a chokehold on the assailant with his right arm, he grabbed with his left hand the pistol from Schrank's grasp. Martin then picked up the five-foot five-inch, 170-pound Schrank like he was an infant and carried him to the side of the car to face Roosevelt. "Here he is, look at him, Colonel."[15] Roosevelt, still standing, just gazed at the man who had attempted to kill him.

Within a few seconds, pandemonium broke out among the crowd. Hundreds wanted immediate justice and began screaming, "Lynch him, kill him!" As the crowd pressed forward, a contingent of four Milwaukee policemen using their nightsticks and four detectives using their revolvers began to fight back the crowd while Captain Gerard and Martin struggled to drag Schrank through the crowd into the hotel kitchen to safety. Roosevelt then intervened, raising his hand to the crowd and yelling, "Stop! Stop! Stand back! Don't hurt him!"[16] Then the wounded Roosevelt sat down in the car seat and started to speak to the crowd, "My good friends, I'm not hurt. I'm going on to the hall to speak. Good luck!"[17] Roosevelt then attempted to reassure the remaining members of his entourage that he was all right and in a remarkably calm voice issued an order to his chauffeur. "Now just run the car up to the hall. I'm not hurt, and everything is all right."[18] Immediately the car started, pulled away from the curb and proceeded to the Auditorium five blocks away carrying a bleeding ex-president with a bullet in his side who was determined to deliver his speech.

Actually, Roosevelt didn't realize the seriousness of his injury until he arrived at the Auditorium. He was staggering slightly, and as he unbuttoned his vest, he discovered that his shirt was covered with blood. Still, he was convinced that his wound was not fatal because he wasn't coughing up blood. The shot might have been fatal if it had not been slowed down upon entering his chest through his steel eye-glass case and heavy manuscript of his speech that was stuffed in his breast pocket. A couple of physicians quickly examined Roosevelt and attempted to persuade him to forgo his speech. However, Roosevelt was in no mind to entertain a suggestion of retreat. He glared at the physicians, stating, "I will make this speech or die, one or the other."[19] As Roosevelt's cursory consultation with the physicians was occurring, Henry Cochems had taken the podium and informed the large crowd that Colonel Roosevelt had been shot, but asked them all to remain calm.

As panic spread through the crowd, Theodore Roosevelt took the stage and staggered slightly to the podium. Then Roosevelt pulled the manuscript of his speech from his inside breast pocket. The bullet had penetrated the bulky paper and some of the pages were torn and blood-stained. Roosevelt held up the bullet-riddled pages and told the crowd, "It takes more than that to kill a Bull Moose."[20] Then he opened his vest, revealing his bloody shirt as the crowd gasped. Roosevelt began speaking at 8:20 P.M., and while continuing to bleed, he spoke for one hour and twenty-five minutes, concluding his remarks at 9:45 P.M. Several times during his address he seemed to be growing weak, and various members of his entourage would start to approach him, only to be scolded by the gruffy old warrior, "Let me alone, I'm all right."[21]

Although nearly a century has now come to pass since this incident occurred, it still seems incomprehensible to most observers that Roosevelt in such dire circumstances would insist on delivering a speech. Some historians have speculated that Roosevelt insisted on speaking that evening because he feared that the doctors would confine him to bed and that it would be his last chance to campaign before the election. However, the Milwaukee address was a minor one and was not a make-or-break affair for the Roosevelt candidacy. The answer to Roosevelt's insistence on speaking is really quite simple: he knew who he was. Although it would be several decades yet before his physiognomy would be eternally memorialized by being blasted and chipped into Mt. Rushmore alongside the likeness of Washington, Jefferson and Lincoln, Roosevelt already understood that he had become an American icon. He was T. R., the Lion, Theodore Rex, the Rough Rider. He knew there was no other option for him that night but to boldly stand up in front of a throng of supporters with a bullet in his side and address the cause he had championed. Furthermore, he was a soldier who had been battle-tested; he knew mortal wounds from superficial wounds. In the psychological makeup of Theodore Roosevelt, to not make that speech would have been tantamount to a taint on his legacy.

Following the speech, Roosevelt was immediately taken to the Emergency Hospital for an examination and treatment. An X-ray of the wound revealed that the bullet had lodged in muscular tissue in his chest wall and did not penetrate the lung. An antiseptic dressing was applied to the wound and at 11:25 P.M., Roosevelt walked unassisted out of the hospital. Before midnight he boarded a train for Chicago to undergo further treatment. Roosevelt arrived in Chicago at 3:00 A.M. Bystanders took off their hats when they saw the former president walking from his railroad car to a waiting ambulance as photographers began snapping pictures of him. Roosevelt yelled out to the onlookers, "Shot again."[22] Roosevelt was taken to Mercy Hospital, where the doctors decided to leave the bullet in Roosevelt's chest. After spending several days in the hospital under observation, Roosevelt was released and returned to Oyster Bay.

President Taft was attending a dinner at the Hotel Astor in New York with mayor John Gaynor, honoring the Atlantic fleet when he was informed of Roosevelt's plight. A penciled dispatch was handed to Taft. He fumbled for his eyeglasses and then read the half-dozen lines as his eyebrows began to slightly rise. Immediately the word spread throughout the ballroom, and naval officers in rank from admiral to midshipmen from Annapolis dressed in their finest blue and gold uniforms were asking what was the real story from Milwaukee. Governor Woodrow Wilson was in Princeton, New Jersey, when he received the news. Both he and Taft sent telegrams.

Under interrogation at the Milwaukee police headquarters, the would-be assassin, John Schrank, at first refused to talk. It was determined that Schrank's last address had been 370 East Tenth Street in New York. The police found in Schrank's possession scraps of hotel paper and envelopes with dates on them that suggested he had been following Roosevelt around for weeks. He had stalked Roosevelt in both Atlanta and Chattanooga, but had been foiled in his assassination plans because the former president had not come out of his hotel the way that Schrank expected. However, Schrank continued to follow Roosevelt throughout the Midwest, waiting for an opportune time to launch his assault upon him. He stated that he had intended to shoot Roosevelt the previous Saturday night at the Chicago Coliseum, but the crowds were so large that he couldn't get close enough to him. Finally the conditions were right in Milwaukee.

As the questioning continued, Schrank slowly began to reveal his motives for the assault on Roosevelt. Schrank stated he and his uncle had been in the saloon business in New York when Roosevelt was police commissioner in the 1890s. He said the Roosevelt had closed their bar, and ever since then, he had hated him. Schrank said that he considered Roosevelt's attempt at starting a third party and serving a third term as president a threat to the nation. He was deeply disturbed by Roosevelt's crying "Thief!" when he failed to garner the Republican nomination at the Chicago convention and was convinced that when he was defeated in the coming election, he would cry "Thief!" again and plunge the country into a bloody civil war. As Schrank continued to speak, his motives for shooting Roosevelt became bizarre. He told the investigating officers that the spirit of the late President McKinley had appeared to him in a dream. Dressed in monk's attire, the spirit told him to avenge his death. Schrank went on to say that McKinley's spirit stated that it was not anarchist Leo Czolgosz who had murdered him in Buffalo in September 1901, but rather forces sent by Theodore Roosevelt. "I have talked with the spirit of McKinley and the spirit told me to kill Roosevelt," declared Schrank.[23]

Theodore Roosevelt recovered speedily and the three-party campaign continued full tilt. It was predicted that 16 million votes would be cast in the 1912 presidential election and that a million of those votes would be cast by women. Then on October 31, with the presidential election only days away, Vice President Sherman died in Utica, New York. The Republican National Committee chose Herbert S. Hadley, the governor of Missouri, to replace Sherman. However, the official ratification would have to wait until after the election. With the presidential campaign at the end of the road, three days later Woodrow Wilson received a four-inch gash in his scalp when the car he was riding in hit a bump on a New Jersey road, throwing his head against a steel rib in the car's roof interior.

In Cincinnati during late October with the election eminent, die-hard Democrats in the city, including mayor Henry Hunt, kept alive their pipe dream that someday George B. Cox would be led out of a Hamilton County courtroom in handcuffs. A new grand jury had been seated in Hamilton County. Prosecutor Pogue was prepared to submit statements of the Cincinnati Trust Company signed by George B. Cox in 1906 and 1907 and obtained from the State Attorney General's office as the endless task of proving misappropriation of bank funds was renewed. Democrats in Cincinnati were feeling chipper and were convinced that they had neutralized the once-powerful Cox machine. On October 30, Hamilton County Prosecutor Pogue stated to the Taft Club of the Cincinnati Law School that Garry Herrmann was out of the Republican Party. He also stated that the same applied to George B. Cox, who he referred to as "an old man, broken down, not a pauper, yet a man who had recently lost a tremendous amount of money."[24] However, Pogue cautioned that Rud Hynicka was still very much active in party affairs.

Election day, November 5, 1912, finally arrived. President Taft spent his last day of the campaign in Buffalo and then boarded a train for Cincinnati where, as usual, he planned to spend election day at the home of his brother, Charles P. Taft, on Pike Street. When the train stopped in Conneaut, Ohio, the president went out on the rear platform of the car but refrained from speaking about politics. Instead, he stated, "I am on my way to Cincinnati to cast my vote. I hope all of you who have the privilege of voting will not forget to do so. I am not here to make a political speech. Your minds are already made up one way or the other, I doubt not."[25] Taft was right, the public had made up its mind, and when the votes were counted, he was a lame duck president as Woodrow Wilson won the election with a plurality of over two million votes.

The division of the Republicans and Progressives had made Woodrow Wilson a minority president. Wilson outdistanced the other five candidates in the race, receiving 6,286,214 popular votes and 435 electoral votes. Theodore Roosevelt finished with 4,216,020 popular votes and 88 electoral votes, William Howard Taft had 3,483,922 popular votes and 8 electoral votes, and Socialist candidate Eugene V. Debs, the strongest of the other three candidates in the race, received 901,551 votes. Taft won only two states—Vermont and Utah. It was a miserable showing for an incumbent president who was even beaten by Wilson in his hometown of Cincinnati by a vote of 31,221 to 30,588. Caught in the national undertow of the split in the party, Republicans lost 28 seats in the U.S. House of Representatives, and much to the consternation of Alice Roosevelt Longworth, her husband, Nicholas Longworth III, lacking a strong George B. Cox-led local Republican Party machine in Cincinnati, lost his seat in Congress by 97 votes to Stanley Bowdle.

In time William Howard Taft and Theodore Roosevelt would once again become friends. After leaving the White House and returning to private life, Taft would become a professor of constitutional law at Yale University, his alma mater. For a while Theodore Roosevelt would continue to attempt to ignite the Progressive cause. But the progressive movement in American politics had reached its zenith in 1912 and there would not be another Progressive Party candidate for president on the ballot until 1924.

XIV

National League Melodrama

The Chicago Cubs had finished in third place in the National League in 1912 and everyone was pointing fingers at Charles W. Murphy as the reason why. According to Webb Dunn of the *Chicago Post*, Charles Murphy had caused much dissension on the ballclub by hiring one of the players to spy and report on what Cubs players said about him. It was being reported that Murphy was regarded in the Cubs' clubhouse as tantamount to a scandalmonger and that none of the players had any use for him. Murphy's paranoia had become so intense that if a player was talking to a groundskeeper, he would become suspicious. Cubs' manager Joe Tinker wanted out of Chicago.

Frank Chance wanted out of Chicago, too, and he inquired with the Reds about becoming manager in 1913. However, neither Garry Herrmann nor Max Fleischmann were interested in Chance; they wanted Joe Tinker at the Cincinnati helm for the coming season. However, that would possibly lead to a confrontation with Charles Murphy. Joe Tinker was a stockholder in the Cubs and wanted to make a clean break from the club. He was proposing to sell his stock in the Cubs to Harry Ackerland, a Pittsburgh distiller, for $40,000. While Murphy could not block the transfer of the stock, he didn't want Ackerland for a partner. He vowed to fight any sale of Tinker's stock and refused to pay him what he wanted for it. Then Murphy reprised the tactic used by former Cubs owner Jim Hart to bilk Cap Anson out of his stock in the club several years before. Murphy promised to make the stock less desirable by not paying dividends and alleging that all the profits were being put into new players, capital improvements in the ballpark, and a higher salary for himself as president.

In early November, Murphy informed Garry Herrmann that he could have Joe Tinker for a price. That price, however, was costly. All Murphy wanted in exchange for the rights to Tinker were Bob Bescher, Armando Marsans and Eddie Grant, three of the Reds' best players, and a wad of Julius and Max Fleischmann's cash to boot. When informed of Murphy's demands, Herrmann stated, "I wouldn't let Bescher go even up for Tinker."[1] Still, Herrmann was determined to bring Tinker to Cincinnati and would fight for him if necessary.

But at the moment the annual battle loomed for Herrmann with his fellow National League moguls over the continued presidency of Thomas Lynch. Both Barney Dreyfuss and Charles Ebbets detested Lynch, although both would candy-coat the issue by taking a public posture that Thomas Lynch lacked diplomacy in his dealings with them. The two moguls were joined in their desire to unseat the National League president by Charles Murphy. There also was the matter of the allegations of Phillies president Horace Fogel that awaited adjudication.

A meeting by National League president Thomas Lynch had been set for November 26 to examine the evidence against Fogel. However, the cavalier Horace Fogel was telling everyone that when November 26 rolled around, there would be no trial because the matter was now a dead issue. In early November, Fogel was quoted in the press as stating, "You see, Lynch thought he had a chance to get square with me and he has been doing the most talking, but after all that he has said and done, it was impossible for him to get any evidence that was worthwhile. When Lynch discovered that both Ebbets of Brooklyn and Murphy of Chicago would never help him in his little scheme, he began to crawl, and this talk about getting affidavits against me is only a bluff."[2]

But Horace Fogel was wrong. On November 26, league president Thomas J. Lynch and the National League moguls met at the Waldorf-Astoria in New York City and reviewed the charges against Fogel. As Fogel arrived at the hotel, he was surrounded by members of the press, denying charges that Lynch had brought against him. He also was contesting that he was president of the Phillies in name only, adding that Charles P. Taft held the controlling interest in the club and that he had paid $15,000 for an option on stock. Lastly, he had a few choice words for Thomas J. Lynch.

Thomas J. Lynch and the club owners went into session at 2:00 P.M., witnesses were heard and a multitude of affidavits of everyone from umpires to book critics to clergymen to fans were reviewed in the charges against Fogel. Two sessions were held that day, the second ending after midnight with no decision reached in the matter. The first development of the day had been the announcement that Horace Fogel had resigned as president of the Philadelphia Phillies and that Alfred D. Wiler would become the new chief executive of the club. However, the selection of Wiler as president of the Phillies was looked upon with skepticism and mistrust by the other owners since Wiler was the attorney for Fogel and had been serving as vice president of the Phillies.

Developments became more complicated when a well-known criminal lawyer from Philadelphia by the name of A. S. L. Sheilds was presented in front of Lynch and the league moguls as representing Fogel in the matter at hand. Sheilds argued that since Fogel had resigned as Phillies club president, the league no longer had jurisdiction over him and could not pass judgment on him. In response, J. Conway Toole, personal lawyer of James E. Gaffney, president of the Boston Braves, who was representing the National League, stated that since Fogel had appeared at the meeting with a lawyer representing him, the owners should in turn investigate the charges and establish proof or disproof of them as they had a direct impact on the welfare of the game.

The most incriminating evidence produced by the league against Fogel occurred when Fogel and Charles W. Murphy took the stand to testify in regard to the statement signed by Fogel that had appeared in the *Chicago Evening Post* on September 28, attacking the league's umpires. W. G. Forman, the sporting editor of the Chicago paper, was present and provided the original copy of the statement with Fogel's signature attached. The document had been sent by Fogel to Murphy, who then gave it to Forman.

However, W. G. Forman was of the opinion that Horace Fogel was being made to hold the bag for the shortcomings of Charles W. Murphy. In a recent newspaper story that Forman had written on the Fogel letter, he stated the following:

> Charles W. Murphy authorized me to tell Fogel that Murphy had suggested writing the story. On this representation Fogel wrote it and signed it. He sent it to Murphy, who read it before I ever saw it. It came to me from Murphy's office, and if Murphy had not approved that story it never would have been published. The man who is morally responsible for that article and the charges it contained is Murphy himself, and I have Fogel's own word for it that he wrote it simply to help Murphy fight his battles in the National League.

It is not the first time Murphy has made Fogel the goat. Previously Murphy had sent me another article, signed by Fogel, and told me Fogel had written it, and wanted it published. It was printed in the *Evening Post*, on the understanding that Fogel was the author of it. Months afterward I learned that Murphy himself had written it, and Fogel had merely signed it because he was requested to do so by the Cubs' president. It was a defense of Murphy, who had been criticized in a syndicated article sent out by a Chicago baseball writer. We told Murphy to send it over and, if possible, we would use it. It was typewritten, but signed in ink by Fogel, and contained lavish praise for Murphy and his meteoric rise in baseball. We published it under the belief that Murphy was telling the truth when he said Fogel wrote it.[3]

When questioned by Lynch, Fogel insisted that he had authored the statement published in the *Chicago Evening Post* on September 28. However, Fogel alleged that the statement was not authorized for publication without first being perused and edited by Murphy, in case he found anything objectionable in the content. When Charles Murphy took the stand, he admitted that he had received the statement from Fogel. However, Murphy claimed that he had only read the first paragraph and made no changes before turning over the document to Forman. After the document was given to Forman, several letters were exchanged between Fogel and Forman in which some uncomplimentary characterizations of Murphy were made by Fogel. Forman told Lynch and the National League moguls that he considered this correspondence to be confidential between Fogel and himself. Nonetheless, Lynch and the moguls wanted to see the correspondence. Fogel was willing to turn over the documents, but his counsel advised against it.

Later during the evening of November 26, John T. Brush, owner of the New York Giants, died while en route to California by train. Brush had been ailing badly for several months from a condition diagnosed as locomotor ataxia. Earlier in the fall he had been in an automobile accident and suffered a broken hip, which further aggravated his condition. On Sunday evening, November 24, he was placed on a train in New York bound for San Francisco, where it was hoped the weather would be more conducive to a recovery. En route, Brush fell unconscious and died at Seeburger, Missouri. At Louisiana, Missouri, his private car was detached from the Burlington train and pulled back to St. Louis. The second day's meeting of the National League at the Waldorf-Astoria in New York was scheduled to begin at 2:30 P.M. However, immediately a committee was appointed that included Charles H. Ebbets, Edward C. Jones and Julius Fleischmann to draw up a resolution on the death of John T. Brush; the meeting was then adjourned for an hour to honor his memory. When the meeting was again called to order at 3:30 P.M., the resolutions honoring Brush were adopted by a unanimous vote.

Full representation of the league was present as the matter involving Horace Fogel resumed. Thomas J. Lynch, National League president, and secretary John A. Heydler were present as was Horace Fogel. A jury to hear the evidence was appointed that included August Herrmann, president, and Julius and Max Fleischmann, directors of the Cincinnati Reds; James E. Gaffney, president of the Boston Braves; Charles H. Ebbets, president of the Brooklyn Superbas; Charles W. Murphy, president of the Chicago Cubs; Cornelius J. Sullivan, director, and R. H. McCutcheon, secretary of the New York Giants; Alfred D. Wiler, president, and William Conway and A. T. Hogetez, directors of the Philadelphia Phillies; William Locke, secretary of the Pittsburgh Pirates; and E.C. Jones, president of the St. Louis Cardinals.

As soon as Thomas Lynch called the meeting to order, he gave up the gavel and Julius Fleischmann presided over the meeting. The charges against Fogel that had been put in writing by Lynch following the October meeting on the matter were read to the owners along with Fogel's reply. The charges made against Fogel implicated him in making egregious statements against Lynch and National League umpires. The charges included:

1. August 17, 1912, Horace Fogel declared in Pittsburgh that the St. Louis Cardinals, under the leadership of Roger Bresnahan, had "laid down" to let the Giants win the pennant in 1911.

2. September 6, 1912, Fogel declared in Philadelphia during a series between the Giants and Phillies that the race was "fixed" for the New York Giants to win.

3. September 7, 1912, Fogel wrote a letter to Thomas J. Lynch attacking the integrity of the umpires and reflecting on the character of the president.

4. September 28, 1912, Fogel authorized the publication in the *Chicago Evening Post* of a signed statement charging the umpires with being corrupt.

5. September 30, 1912, Fogel wrote a letter to each of the seven league presidents denouncing the umpires.

6. Lastly, that Fogel had given to the public press statements which defamed the character of William Brennan, one of the umpires.

After Fogel's written reply to the charges was read, he denied having made the statements attributed to him in charges one and two, those being the alleged statements of August 17, 1912 and September 6, 1912. Fogel declared that the letters and telegrams he had sent to Thomas Lynch, August Herrmann and others were to be considered privileged communications, those such as one executive might freely write to another. Furthermore, Fogel denied he had authorized the statement published in the *Chicago Evening Post*, declaring that his words were misinterpreted, as he was arguing for a change in the system of umpire assignments to games, rather than attacking the umpires personally. Lastly, Fogel denied that he had made any statements challenging the integrity of umpire William Brennan.

At this point, Fogel's attorney, A. S. L. Shields, rose and once again argued that the league had no right to pursue such an investigation and put Fogel on trial since he had resigned as president of the Phillies. In rebuttal, the league's attorney, J. Conway Toole, stated that since Fogel had appeared at the meeting represented by counsel, he was obligated to answer the charges as the integrity of the game depended upon it. The investigation then proceeded and Thomas J. Lynch called four witnesses to testify. The four — Grantland Rice, W. S. Trumbul and Sid Mercer, all three New York baseball writers, and D. Killafer, physical director of Trinity School — while not sworn, all categorically stated that Fogel, while leaving the ballpark following a doubleheader between the Phillies and Giants in Philadelphia on September 6, had "declared that the pennant race was fixed. This was said, they declared in a loud voice within the hearing of a number of fans."[4] While all four agreed that the umpiring in the second game of the doubleheader had been rather poor, with several close decisions going against the Phillies, they agreed that Fogel was upset, but hardly hysterical.

Horace Fogel then took the stand and denied making any such statements. Fogel alleged that a Methodist minister from Philadelphia who had been at the doubleheader on September 6 and who had declined to attend the National League meeting on the matter because he didn't want to be subject to the controversy it would generate, had passed the press stand and remarked that he was convinced that the pennant race was fixed. Fogel then went on to say that the New York newspapermen mistakenly attributed those words to him instead of the minister. Fogel stated, to the contrary, he had told the minister, "that it was impossible to 'fix' a pennant race because there were too many safeguards."[5]

Fogel was then asked if he had any evidence to substantiate his claim of any of the umpires being crooked, or of the president of the National League being crooked, or any other person connected with the league being crooked? Fogel's reply to each of the questions was "an emphatic no."[6] Next in the proceedings, seven witnesses from Philadelphia were asked to testify whether or not Horace Fogel had made the remarks stated in the indictment. All seven stated that they did not hear Fogel make any such remarks.

In the evening session of November 27, the jury took its first vote in the meeting regarding the issue of privileged communications that had been raised by Fogel's attorney. The motion carried with six votes, Chicago and Philadelphia not voting. Subsequently, several privileged communications written by Fogel to various league officials were read. The intent of reading the communication was to demonstrate the frame of mind and attitude of Fogel toward Thomas J. Lynch. Also, various newspaper articles were introduced to show that others besides Fogel had called the quality of umpiring into question. Fogel made an attempt to show that various players, managers and others had also used the words "crooked" and "fixed" without any charges being brought against them by the league.

Umpire William Brennan then took the stand. Brennan stated that he did not know anything about his appointment as an umpire in the World Series until six weeks previous to a public announcement being made. Horace Fogel had alleged that another umpire, Jimmy Rigler, told him about Brennan's appointment six weeks in advance of the public notice. When Rigler took the stand, he denied telling any such thing to Fogel. When all the evidence against Fogel and counter arguments were completed, Horace Fogel, no longer an officer with the Philadelphia Phillies club and no longer having standing in league meetings, was dismissed from the meeting. A vote was taken with new Phillies president Alfred S. Wiler abstaining. The result was the complete vindication of Thomas J. Lynch and the National League umpires. In the minds of the moguls, the integrity of the game was restored. Horace S. Fogel was forever banned from participation in National League baseball. However, the action of the league did not preclude Fogel from retaining his stock in the Phillies. Amazingly, Charles W. Murphy had emerged from the mess totally unscathed and totally unashamed.

For the next four hours, the league presidents argued over the wording of the resolutions to be drawn up regarding the specifics of the findings against Fogel and his subsequent censor from the league. One of the most significant points written in the resolution set precedent in establishing the jurisdiction of the league in the Fogel matter. In short, the league set precedent in stating that it did not undertake to say who could represent a club at a meeting, but the league reserved the right to say who could not represent a club. In regard to this matter the resolution stated:

> Whereas, the jurisdiction of this league to pass judgment upon the charges just disposed of has been brought to question. Therefore, be it further resolved, that this league is not a body of limited powers whose authority is restricted by the powers expressly enumerated in its constitution. As a voluntary association of the representatives of organized professional baseball we have the same unlimited powers that appertain to individual men and associations if any club falls short of those high principles which should be the standard of all modern businessmen and sportsmen it becomes the privilege and duty of this league to say to the clubs who shall represent them in the meetings of this league, but we do reserve the right to say who shall not represent them, when the person so excluded shall be proven to be unfit to discharge the high duties devolving upon him in our deliberations.[7]

Thomas J. Lynch, the man who had upheld the integrity of the game, had no statement for the press following the meeting. Around the corridors of the Waldorf-Astoria, it was being stated that the Fogel decision by the league's moguls had to ensure Lynch's re-election to another term as league president at the annual league meeting in December. However, with Barney Dreyfuss, Charles Ebbets and Charles Murphy all deeply opposed to the re-election of Lynch, his selection was far from a lock. In fact, Barney Dreyfuss, while not as outspoken as Horace Fogel, harbored the same opinion of Lynch's handling of the league's umpires.

Dreyfuss wanted a new man in the presidency and was openly campaigning for his friend from his Louisville days, the ever-available Robert W. Brown. Garry Herrmann was holding his cards close to the vest on how he might vote on Lynch. There was a growing speculation that Herrmann might join the anti–Lynch forces, and had even attended a closed-door meeting with Dreyfuss, Ebbets and Murphy to discuss who might be a possible successor to Lynch.

There was more scuttlebutt than just the Lynch presidency being discussed out in the corridors of the Waldorf-Astoria. Another hot topic was that if the Phillies were for sale, who would be the new owner? Charles Murphy was saying that he had offers ranging from $700,000 to $900,000 for the club. However, to most observers, such an outrageous sum was just normal exaggeration of "Chubby Charles." Another potential buyer for the Phillies that was being rumored was a syndicate that included banker Robert J. Balform and Pennsylvania governor John Tener. Another topic being discussed in the corridors of the Waldorf-Astoria was the deal between Garry Herrmann and Charles Murphy that would bring Joe Tinker to the Reds as the club's new manager for the 1913 season. In fact, Joe Tinker had arrived in New York and was staying at the Waldorf-Astoria.

Apparently, Tinker was ready to discuss the matter with Herrmann, Murphy and Johnny Evers, who was expected to pilot the Cubs should the deal be completed. Herrmann had known Murphy a long time, going back to his days as a modest newspaper reporter in Cincinnati when the two had on occasion played in the same poker game. Now Herrmann was in another poker game, with Murphy attempting to land Tinker. When the press converged on Herrmann, Murphy and Evers in the hotel bar, Murphy stated, "You can get all the drinks you want out of Herrmann, but you can't get any players." In reply, Herrmann stated, "Well, I haven't seen much coming out of Chicago. Let me talk with Evers and will have the deal all fixed in two minutes." As the crowd that had gathered around the men laughed, Murphy said, "That's what you would call airy persiflage, isn't it?"[8]

However, the Joe Tinker deal was not completed, and Garry Herrmann, Charles Murphy and the other moguls left New York for Indianapolis to attend the funeral of John T. Brush on November 29. At the time of his death, John T. Brush was considered as much a pioneer in major league baseball as Albert G. Spalding. Despite his legacy in the game, John T. Brush has yet to be elected to the National Baseball Hall of Fame. The Brush funeral was one of the largest for a private individual ever held in Indianapolis. In all, fifty various representatives from the major and minor leagues, including National League president Thomas J. Lynch and American League president Ban Johnson, attended the Brush funeral, held at St. Paul's Episcopal Church. Brush was eulogized by the Reverend Lewis Brown, who spoke of him as one of the most remarkable men in America because of his achievements while overcoming the handicaps of early poverty and later physical difficulties. Then Masonic rites were administered by ranking officers of the Indiana Grand Lodge.

Brush left the New York Giants in a trust along with his estate valued at $1.5 million. Brush had appointed two trustees of his estate — his wife and his 42-year-old son-in-law, Harry N. Hempstead — and directed them to sell the Giants. Hempstead, who ran Brush's clothing business in Indianapolis, would become president of the New York Giants until the club was sold. As the Brush estate was being settled, it was common knowledge that no women members in the family would undertake any actual duties or make policy on the running of the New York Giants. The irony in the Giants' circumstances is that Harry Hempstead, the son-in-law of John T. Brush, was named in his estate documents to run the ballclub. However, Hempstead knew practically nothing at all about running a baseball club at any level.

Mrs. Helen Britton had inherited the St. Louis Cardinals from her late uncle, Stanley Robison, who had died in 1911. While her husband Schuyler Britton was anointed with the title of president, which was little more than an honorary title. The fact of the matter was that Helene Britton was bound and determined to enter the male bastion of major league baseball and run the St. Louis club. While she admitted publicly that she found her male colleagues mean to a degree and lacking in chivalry and loyalty, nonetheless Mrs. Britton was serious about discharging her duties. In fact, she had put the kibosh on a big trade that would have sent two Cardinals to Pittsburgh. The American League magnates were simply aghast by the thought of a woman in the midst of their fraternity. Collectively, the junior circuit moguls were absolutely smitten when they viewed Mrs. Britton in a picture published in the *Sporting News* issue of December 19, 1912, proudly seated with the other National League owners at their New York meeting. The American League owners decided it was time to take pre-emptive action and they quietly agreed on an informal, non-written policy that no woman would ever be permitted to be left in control of an American League club through matters of probate.

On December 5, a letter penned by Garry Herrmann to Charles Ebbets in Brooklyn was mistakenly mailed to Robert W. Brown in Louisville. Before returning the letter to Herrmann, Brown read the content, which was in regard to the question of the continued tenure of Thomas J. Lynch as league president. With the annual National League meeting soon to take place, Robert W. Brown once again launched an intensive and more desperate campaign to be selected as league president by the moguls. Later in the day, Brown wrote the following to Garry Herrmann suggesting that he should convince Lynch to step aside.

December 5, 1912

My Dear Garry:

My earnest hope is but you and Mr. Dreyfuss will take a firm stand for me, in which event I am bound to believe the election will be all right for me. Don't you agree with me that Mr. Lynch has already been vindicated as much as he can be? Also, the club owners have registered themselves most emphatically for the control of the game. Still, in a National League administrative sense, the same conditions of dissatisfaction exist toward Mr. Lynch for reasons it would be improper for me to discuss. More than once remembering all you have done in the harmonizing way, I have wished that it might be so that you could speak to Mr. Lynch and convince him of the necessity for a change looking to the better adjustment of internal affairs, provided of course that gentleman is disposed to hear and heed. At all events, to judge from the public expression, a change is expected. Since the newspaper publications began, letters have been reaching me by the score, showing the interest that is taken. I know what I can do in co-operation with you, and all I ask is that you do for me as I would gladly do for you ever you in my place and I in yours.

— Your Friend,
Robert W. Brown[9]

While the American League owners had moved their winter meeting to Chicago, in mid–December the National League owners met as usual at the Waldorf-Astoria in New York. The first order of business for Garry Herrmann was to complete the Joe Tinker deal with Charles W. Murphy. On the morning of December 13 at 10:30 A.M., Garry Herrmann, along with his business manager, Frank Bancroft, met with Charles Murphy and Cubs manager Johnny Evers at the Waldorf-Astoria and began to hammer out a deal. In the end Herrmann got Tinker in an eight-player deal, with Cincinnati sending to Chicago Bert Humpries, Red Corriden, Pete Knisely, Art Phelan and Mike Mitchell in exchange for Tinker, Grover Lowdermilk and Harry Chapman. It was just a matter of time before the Tinker deal was going to get done. For weeks Chicago newspapers had been publishing cartoons showing Tinker with a suitcase in each hand. The key to getting the trade done was accommodating the insistence of Charles Murphy that he get a shortstop in the deal. To that end, Garry Herrmann got authorization from the Reds' directors to purchase Red Corriden for $6,000 from the

Detroit Tigers and then send him to Chicago in the Tinker deal. As a supplement to the deal, Herrmann passed on claiming Frank Chance on waivers to permit him to manage the New York Highlanders (who would become the Yankees in 1913). New York president Frank Farrell had been instrumental in arranging the Corriden deal with Detroit for Herrmann, so releasing Chance was a show of good faith.

The trade was very popular in Cincinnati and most fans believed that Tinker as manager could finally bring the pennant to Redland. The *Cincinnati Enquirer* characterized Tinker in the following manner, "Joe Tinker is extraordinarily bright, intelligent and accomplished. He can converse on any subject, and has a keen sense of humor. The scribes have ever found him their friend and helper, and the Cincinnati fans will find him a gentleman as well as a great ball player, and let us hope an A-1 manager."[10] Even Charles Murphy was telling all that asked that he believed Joe Tinker would over time make Cincinnati a contender. In between the horse-trading for Tinker, Garry Herrmann had sat down at the Waldorf-Astoria to play a little pinochle with "Hammy" Lichenstein of Montreal. Suddenly reports were published in newspapers nationwide stating that the card game was a high-stakes contest for $30,000. In reality, Herrmann and Lichenstein had agreed to play ten games of pinochle for the stakes of $100 each. In the end it was a wash with no money changing hands as Herrmann and Lichenstein each won five games.

As for the National League's business agenda at the annual meeting, much to the disappointment of Robert W. Brown, Thomas J. Lynch was re-elected unanimously and without a fight to another one-year term as National League president. In fact, two of Lynch's primary protagonists expedited the process when Charles Ebbets put his name in to nomination for president, which was then quickly seconded by Charles Murphy. John Heydler was then elected to another three-year term as league secretary. In the end, the owners realized that public perception of the league was at hand and Lynch's vindication in the Horace Fogel matter was just too overpowering to justify his dismissal.

Next, a vote was taken for the continuation of another year of pension money for Mrs. N. P. Johnson of Louisville, the sister of late league president Harry Pulliam. Herrmann then proposed inter-league play to replace the World Series. The radical proposal by the Cincinnati president generated almost no support from his contemporaries and was quickly squelched. Also, the league discharged an outstanding matter where a claim of $2,200 had been made against the Philadelphia Phillies by umpire Jimmy Rigler for services in getting pitcher Eppa Rixey to sign with the club. Alfred D. Wiler, the new Phillies' president, agreed to pay the fee. However, the league went on record as being opposed to umpires acting as scouts. Rixey would pitch in the National League for 21 years (1912–1933), winning 266 games for the Phillies and Reds prior to being elected to the Hall of Fame in 1963.

XV

The Teflon Boss

The Cincinnati Trust Company, with George B. Cox serving as president, had been organized on May 21, 1900, with $500,000 of capital stock. On election day, November 7, 1911, the day that former Hamilton County prosecutor and reform-minded Democrat candidate Henry Hunt was being elected mayor of Cincinnati, the state banking authorities declared that the Cincinnati Trust Company was in unsafe condition. Within weeks the bank was absorbed into the Provident Savings Bank & Trust Company and its depositors secured against loss of their funds. However, stockholders in the Cincinnati Trust Company took a heavy loss. At its highest point stock in the bank had sold at $320 a share. However, at the time of the takeover, the stock had plummeted to $94 a share.

On Saturday, January 4, 1913, the long-awaited findings from the grand jury investigation launched the previous June into the financial dealings of George B. Cox and others into the failed Cincinnati Trust Company were announced. Hamilton County prosecutor Thomas Pogue announced that three men were indicted. Nathaniel S. Keith, secretary of the Cincinnati Trust Company, and F. R. Williams, treasure of the Cincinnati Trust Company, were indicted on twenty-four counts of misapplication of funds. Also, A. D. Martin, manager of the Ford & Johnson Chair Company, was indicted on one count, and indicted jointly with Keith for making false statements. However, George B. Cox, the man that the entire politically motivated process had been set in motion to prosecute, escaped unscathed in the events that led to the bank's failure.

Although prosecutor Thomas Pogue had failed to secure an indictment of Cox, the *Cincinnati Post* was relentless in its pursuit of the boss and immediately began questioning the wisdom of the grand jury. The *Post* pointed out that the law specifically outlines in detail the duties and responsibilities of the executive committee of a bank. It stated that according to the state banking laws, the board of directors may appoint an executive committee which shall approve or disapprove all loans and investments. Furthermore, that minutes shall be kept of the meetings of the executive committee, including records of loans, or investments, to be submitted to the board of directors for approval at their meetings. Therefore, the *Post* reasoned that since George B. Cox was chairman of the Cincinnati Trust Company's executive committee and under the state banking laws he had to approve or disapprove all loans, not one dollar of the bank's money could be loaned without him knowing about it. That included misapplication of tens of thousands of dollars in bad loans to the Ford & Johnson Chair Company, a company in which Cox was an officer and knew its shaky financial condition.

In conclusion, the *Post*'s case against Cox stated that almost up to the week that the Cincinnati Trust Company closed, it continued to advance money in loans to the Ford & Johnson Company for its payrolls. Then after the Cincinnati Trust Company was dissolved, the Second National Bank, which was about to fail as well and had a close association with the Cincinnati Trust Company through relationships with its directors, attempted to take up the burden. Therefore, the paper reasoned, the Cox-controlled Cincinnati Trust Company continued sending the bank's good money after the bad money of the Cox-controlled Ford & Johnson Company. So it was the hope of the paper, the State of Ohio attorney general's office and the Hamilton County prosecutor's office, that based upon the outcomes in further legal proceedings against Keith and Williams, they might land the big fish that they so desperately sought to catch, George B. Cox.

Meanwhile, the state was advocating an early trial for Nathaniel Keith and F. R. Williams; attorneys for the indicted men were pleading for a delay so that the 24 counts charged against them could be studied in detail. Then the Second National Bank decided to jump on the legal bandwagon by filing suit for $10,000 against the Cincinnati Trust Company for alleged money due on two promissory notes in connection with loans made by the Second National Bank to the Ford & Johnson Chair Company. Suddenly the legal proceedings in the matter of the Cincinnati Trust Company were becoming a bundled mess.

On January 8, 1913, Keith and Williams appeared in superior court in the matter of the Second National Bank suit against the Cincinnati Trust Company. Also, George B. Cox appeared in court as a witness on behalf of Keith, but made almost no attempt to acknowledge his former colleague, not even making eye contact. Keith and Williams admitted that they had endorsed two notes on behalf of the Ford & Johnson Chair Company. However, they also stated under a prior agreement that the Second National Bank had been repaid and that they were dismissed from any liability. Attorneys for Keith and Williams stated there were records to that effect, but the records had been destroyed in a fire just four days earlier. On January 4, around 1:00 A.M., a fire began that destroyed the six-story Carlisle Building located on the southwest corner of Fourth and Walnut Streets (present location of the Dixie Terminal Building). An office in the building located on the first floor was formerly occupied by George B. Cox when he was president of the Cincinnati Trust Company. The books of the bank that were to be used in the trial of Keith and Williams were still being stored in the Carlisle Building when the fire occurred and were destroyed.

In early March, a new grand jury began hearing testimony against George B. Cox and the former directors in the never-ending matter of the Cincinnati Trust Company. On Monday, March 17, 1913, the second grand jury investigating the Cincinnati Trust Company returned two sealed indictments. On Tuesday, March 18, 1913, the second grand jury indictments were to be opened and read in the common pleas courtroom of judge Otway Cosgrove, a Democrat. Early that morning George B. Cox, Nathaniel Keith and Norman Kenan, a retired president of Union Gas & Electric Company who had served on the board of directors of the bank, appeared at the office of Prosecutor Pogue. Cox and Keith came together, accompanied by Garry Herrmann, Mike Mullen and attorneys Dinsmore and Shohl. When approached by the press, Herrmann stated in a jovial manner, "Bankers and financiers are having one hell of a time."[5] Herrmann and Mullen announced that they were ready to individually or jointly go Cox's bond. Then one by one, the other former directors of the bank began to appear in Pogue's office.

The courtroom of Judge Cosgrove was packed with spectators and friends of Cox and the other directors. There also were many familiar faces present from days when Cox and Herrmann held sway at city hall. The second grand jury investigating Cox and the former directors of the Cincinnati Trust Company had returned eleven counts in true bills naming George B. Cox and ten other men, including Nathaniel Keith and F. R. (Fletcher) Williams, in two indictments. The first indictment named Cox and the others on a charge of misapplying a $352,500 note and the other indictment was on a charge of misapplying a $115,000 loan to the Ford & Johnson Chair Company. Furthermore, the indictments of Keith and Williams in the prior grand jury on misapplication of funds were still pending. However, the new indictments of the second grand jury were serious business; Cox and the bank directors were now facing a possible fine of up to $10,000 or imprisonment of up to thirty years.

George B. Cox was the first of the bank's officials to be served with his indictment. Immediately, Garry Herrmann and Mike Mullen signed Cox's bonds, two of them contributing $5,000 each, covering the charges against him. Herrmann qualified for $20,000 worth of property on Cox's bonds, Mullen qualified for $35,000, while Max Burgheim also signed on, qualifying for $25,000 worth of property. All of Cincinnati was buzzing about the coming trial of the directors of the Cincinnati Trust Company, but the wise money was going down on a Cox acquittal. The trial was to be heard in the criminal court room of judge John A. Caldwell, a Republican who had been an office holder under Cox's tenure in city politics.

On Monday morning, June 2, 1913, in the courtroom of judge John A. Caldwell, jury selection began in the case against George B. Cox and other directors of the Cincinnati Trust Company. The charge was conversion and cancellation of a promissory note for $352,500 ordered placed to the bank's assets made by the State Banking Department. Looking confident, George B. Cox arrived in the courtroom early. He was dressed neatly in a vested suit with a red rose in the buttonhole, chewed on a toothpick, and took a seat between his lawyers. As perspective jurors were being polled, Cox wore a sphinx-like mask expression on his face, occasionally leaning forward while putting his hand to his ear to enable him to hear better.

Attorneys for both the defense and the prosecution asked pointed questions of perspective jurors. One potential juror was asked by Cox's lawyers, "Would it take any more evidence to convince you that these men were guilty than if anyone else was on trial here? Would the fact that you knew Cox embarrass you in the trial of this case?" A large smile appeared on Cox's face as perspective juror Michael Fox of Gabriel Street was dismissed. "I am a Republican and Mr. Cox is a good man," said Mr. Fox.[1] Nonetheless, one of the jurors seated was Thomas L. Evans, who had been the secretary to former Republican Mayor Schwab. Frank Dinsmore, attorney for Cox, and the other defense attorneys representing the former directors of the Cincinnati Trust Company planned to contend that their clients were not guilty of the charge of having abstracted the $352,500 note from the bank's assets because the Trust Company was not in existence at the time of the alleged offense.

As the trial got underway, testimony was given by a former deputy state bank examiner, Edward Romer, that it was at the suggestion of the directors that the note became part of the assets. On Tuesday, June 3, Edward Romer testified that the order of the State Banking Department had not been obeyed by the directors of the Cincinnati Trust Company. The witness for the prosecution stated that at a meeting of Trust Company directors at which his colleague, Deputy Bank Examiner Hindman, had been present along with George B. Cox, Norman G. Kenan, M.E. Mock, Keith Williams, and O.V. Parrish and others to the best of his recollection, those being Charles H. Davis, I.N. Miller and R.W. Neff, a general discussion took place in regard to the bank's condition and the Ford & Johnson loan. "We were to decide what should be done with the Ford & Johnson paper and our (the state banking department) request was that it be taken out."[2]

At this point Frank Dinsmore and the other attorneys for the defense began objections to the testimony of Romer. Dinsmore objected on the grounds that the witness was not giving specific conversation. Judge Caldwell then directed Romer to tell the substance of what had happened at the meeting. Subsequently, Romer stated, "We discussed Ford & Johnson matters for two hours. Everyone had something to say. I remember Mr. Cox said he would do anything we wanted him to. Mr. Moch said he didn't want anything from what the stockholders had paid into the bank's earnings. Another director had something to say and we told him he had a misconception of our presence and that we were not there to suggest, but wanted the Ford & Johnson papers taken out for once and all. They were told they would have to take it out." Romer went on to say that the bank directors then proposed "that $177,500 of Ford & Johnson Company first-mortgage bonds be left in the bank, that $225,000 be charged off to profit and loss and that the directors give their notes for $352,000 of Ford & Johnson securities, which were to be sold outright to the directors. That was the directors' final proposistion."[3]

Attorney Dinsmore then led the defense attorneys in a fight to have Romer's testimony expunged from the record, declaring that it was the vital feature of the case and that the defendants should not be bound to any conclusion of the witness. "We are not indulging in child's play," said Dinsmore. "It's not money out of the pockets of these men that is at stake, but their liberty. It seems there should be some kind of resolution that would show what action these directors are said to have taken."[4] At that point state's Attorney Jacobs stated it would be unfair to make Romer state each director's remarks during the meeting verbatim. Nonetheless, Judge Caldwell ruled that the testimony of Romer be stricken from the record. Then Attorney Jacobs asked Romer, "Who was the spokesman for the directors?" Judge Caldwell also ruled this question out on the grounds that it would bring out a conclusion.

Next Henry V. Sampson, who had been the auditor for the Cincinnati Trust Company, was called to testify by the prosecution. The lawyers for George B. Cox and other directors were attempting to show that the Cincinnati Trust Company went out of existence about November 21, 1911, when the Provident Bank assumed control of all the affairs of the Cincinnati Trust Company. On cross-examination Sampson testified that on about November 21, he began taking orders from officials of the Provident Bank and that he was now on the payroll of that bank. Cox's defense attorneys then pointed out that according to the indictment, the abstraction of the $352,500 promissory note was made from the assets of the Cincinnati Trust Company on December 11.

However, the prosecution then countered the claim of the defense that the Cincinnati Trust Company was already out of business by late November 1911 by producing a bank statement made to the Banking Department on December 5, 1911. The statement was made out in the form of an agreement between the Cincinnati Trust Company and officials of the Provident Bank because the title had been finally transferred and was signed by George B. Cox, president of the Cincinnati Trust Company.

Testimony continued for a few days before a motion was made by the attorneys for Cox and the other directors to Judge Caldwell that the jury return an immediate verdict of not guilty on the charge of abstracting the $352,000 promissory note based on the defense allegation that the note was not a credit, but merely evidence of a credit. Judge Caldwell concurred with the defense and subsequently instructed the jury to acquit Cox and the other directors of the charge. George B. Cox had beaten the rap in the first indictment.

Now the matter of the second indictment was at hand. This was the charge that Cox and six other directors had made excessive loans to the Johnson & Ford Chair Company of $115,000 when the company owed the bank between $150,000 and $750,000. On Monday, June 9, 1913, George B. Cox and the six other former directors of the Cincinnati Trust Company named in the indictment all entered pleas of not guilty before Judge Caldwell. Furthermore, each of the defendants asked for a separate trial and the motion was granted. The trial of George B. Cox was to be the first and set to begin on June 18.

The trial rambled on for a couple of weeks, but by the end of June it was apparent that the state could not prove what George B. Cox knew and didn't know about the Ford & Johnson Chair Company. Cox's lawyer, Frank Dinsmore, opposed introduction of the books of the chair company, which showed its profits and losses from 1905 to 1911. In the testimony of Robert G. McConaughy, national bank examiner, formerly president of the American Audit Company, he stated that he had charge of the Ford & Johnson company books and made up most of the data in the books. Hence the data showed only in summarized form the financial status of the company. Therefore, Judge Caldwell denied introduction of any such figures of McConaughy into evidence in the trial, holding that figures must be original and must be proved by the parties who were the originators. The state's case collapsed and, once again, Cox walked.

Hamilton County prosecutor Thomas Pogue and Ohio State Attorney General Hogan appealed the verdict in the first case against Cox and the other directors to the Ohio Supreme Court on the basis that Judge Caldwell had erred in his granting a motion for an immediate not guilty verdict to be rendered in the case. However, the Ohio Supreme Court upheld the ruling of Judge Caldwell. To George B. Cox, it was total vindication and he felt that his good name had been restored. Now working behind the front lines, he would train what ammunition he had left in his political guns on mayor Henry Hunt.

It had not been an easy year for Mayor Hunt. During the early months of the year, his administration had been bogged down in organizing flood relief as the Ohio River spilled its banks to record heights. The great flood of 1913 rose to a level of 80 feet before cresting and covered one-sixth of the city. Even the new waterworks was inundated with flood waters. In its wake were millions of dollars of destruction to property and secondary damage resulting from fires caused by the flood. As Hunt and his administration scurried about to provide the necessary services to restore the health and welfare of the community, the efforts were met with political scorn by the mayor's partisan detractors. There was also consider able labor unrest in Cincinnati during 1913. A building contractors' strike began in May and led to management locking out eight thousand workers. August would bring the traction company or streetcar strike that turned ugly very quickly when the traction company brought in strikebreakers. In counter action, strikers bombarded one streetcar with bricks, tools and pipes from the high up on the construction site of the 38-story Union Central Building at Fourth and Vine streets. At one point Mayor Hunt asked governor James M. Cox to send in the state militia. However, Cox refused and suddenly Hunt found himself backed into a corner, denying that he had ever made such a request. When the strike was finally settled, riders bombarded the streetcars with bouquets of flowers.

None of these conditions boded well for the mayor. Hunt had been elected in 1911 as a visionary socio-political reformer, a progressive who was going to break up the gang, i.e., the forces of George B. Cox and his disciples, Garry Herrmann and Rud Hynicka. Therefore, clergy in the city and others expected him as mayor to make broad-sweeping changes in cracking down on prostitution, closing seedy bars and dance halls, eliminating Sunday serving of alcohol and banning boxing exhibitions. Hunt, a genuine reformer, had made some progress in all these areas and more. He had closed down approximately sixty dives, cleared a shanty town that had grown along the banks of the Mill Creek, and implemented youth activity programs to reduce delinquency. However, it just didn't seem to be enough to satisfy considerable zealots of reform in the city. Now with the acquittal of George B. Cox, many were convinced that the whole process had been nothing more than an expensive political vendetta by Hunt carried out against Cox. Many even saw George B. Cox as a victim.

The residence of George B. Cox, Cincinnati. Photo by William A. Cook.

The Republicans sensed among the voters a wave of nostalgia in the air for the good old days of Coxism. They nominated for mayor Frederich S. Spiegel, a Prussian-born German Jew who had been active in Cincinnati politics since 1881 and who had also been a judge. In the waning days of summer, the Republicans threw a big, old-fashioned campaign bash at Chester Park, an amusement park on the north side of Spring Grove Avenue. On August 29, 1885, under the Maquis of Queensbury rules, world heavyweight champion John L. Sullivan had defended his title there against Dan MCaffrey of Pittsburgh. Chester Park was located just about a mile-and-a-half down Ludlow Hill from the stately residence of George B. Cox in Clifton. However, Cox was advised to remain at home and not let himself become an issue in the campaign. As Rud Hynicka was temporarily disabled from a swimming accident at his camp on the Whitewater River, the GOP looked to its bullpen and summoned Garry Herrmann, the old grand master of frolicking, to the mound to host the Chester Park bash. Herrmann didn't disappoint the party faithful, arriving with 37 quarts of champagne. Cabaret performers sang and danced as supporters gathered around Herrmann to discuss the good old days at city hall as well as the present. Everyone at Chester Park was feeling very confident that mayor Henry Hunt would soon be packing his bags.

On election day, Tuesday, November 4, 1913, the large German community in the city that had put Henry Hunt over the top in 1911 returned to the fold, rallied around Frederick Spiegel and offset Democrat strong holds in hilltop wards. The Republicans were swept back into city hall. Frederick Spiegel defeated Henry Hunt by 3,112 votes: 45,363 to 42,251. Machine-backed candidates had no problem winning election. In the Eighth Ward, party standard-bearer Mike Mullen defeated his Democrat rival and would now become the floor leader for Spiegel in the city council. In the Fifteenth Ward, the Republican candidate, Dan Bauer, the notorious proprietor of the Majestic Concert Hall, also won election to a council seat. That night the lights at the Blaine Club burned brighter and later than they had for several years as the vote count took place.

XVI

Herrmann's Joe Tinker Experiment

In early January 1913 as the grand jury findings in the Cincinnati Trust Company matter were being announced, the National Commission was in session at its annual meeting at the Sinton Hotel in Cincinnati. While American League president Ban Johnson was too ill to travel from Chicago to participate, the meeting was held, but the vote on commission officers was delayed. When the full commission did meet, all the officers were re-elected to another one-year term: August Garry Herrmann, chairman; John Bruce, secretary; and A.J. Flanner, assistant secretary. Herrmann had now served the commission as chairman for ten years.

In the 1912 season, with the opening of Redland Field and a fourth-place finish, attendance for the Cincinnati Reds had risen to 344,000. As the 1913 season approached, Garry Herrmann was sure that with Joe Tinker as manager, this year was going to be an exciting one for Cincinnati Reds baseball and he anticipated that attendance would be much larger than the previous season. That winter, before heading to Cincinnati, Joe Tinker had a contract to fulfill playing vaudeville on George B. Cox's B. F. Keith's circuit. Mrs. Tinker, who was very sports-minded and just happened to be a very good tennis player, too, had already arrived in Cincinnati to do the public relations frontwork for her husband. She was an excellent spokesperson for her husband's interests and told the press, "I am glad to be in Cincinnati this week, because I am going to begin housekeeping just as soon as my husband comes here in February to take charge of the team. No hotels for us. You see, we have the two boys, Joe is 8 and Roland 6. Their chief recreation is playing ball, and we have decided that a hotel corridor is not big enough to construct a diamond. We are not saying that we are going to land a pennant, but we will say that the prospects are good."[1]

Immediately after New Year's Day, Tinker wasted no time in laying out his plans for fielding a competitive Reds team. Before leaving on a trip to Kansas City to speak with veteran catcher and former Chicago teammate Johnny Kling about signing with the Reds, Tinker announced that he also wanted the former ace of the Cubs' pitching staff, Mordecai "Three Finger" Brown, in a Reds uniform. In the 1912 season Mordecai had been mediocre with a record of 5–6, the worst in his big league career. The Cubs came to the conclusion that Brown was washed up and released him, so he signed with the minor league team in Louisville for the coming season. However, Brown's ERA had only been 2.64 in the 1912 season and Tinker was convinced that he could still pitch. Furthermore, Brown was considered a smart pitcher and Tinker felt that he would be extremely beneficial in helping the other pitchers on the Reds' staff. So a deal with Louisville was quickly consummated, sending Grover Loudermilk to the Falls City in exchange for Brown and some cash.

Tinker also wanted to sign Jim Thorpe to a Reds' contract. In 1913, Thorpe was referred to as "the greatest living athlete." Thorpe had gained fame playing college football as an All-American back at the Carlisle Indian School in Pennsylvania. However, the previous summer at the 1912 Olympics in Stockholm, Thorpe had won both the decathlon and pentathlon, a feat that has still not been duplicated. Garry Herrmann dispatched Reds business manager Frank Bancroft to Carlisle to sign Thorpe. Despite the fact that at the time Thorpe was actually sick in bed, there were five other scouts in town besides Bancroft attempting sign Thorpe. Assessing the competition, Bancroft wired Herrmann, stating that he didn't think he could sign Thorpe. Bancroft offered Thorpe a contract for $4,500, but was turned down as he signed a three-year contract with the New York Giants, calling for $5,000 a year. Also at that time, Garry Herrmann was negotiating a contract with center fielder Armando Marsans, a Cuban national, who was holding out for an additional $800. In the 1912 season, Marsans had been the Reds' leading hitter with an average of .317. Eventually Marsans signed and former Cubs "Three Finger" Brown and Johnny Kling agreed to terms with the Reds. In early March, as spring training got under way at Mobile, Alabama, Reds manager Tinker had 13 pitchers to evaluate.

In Washington, D.C., on March 4, 1913, Woodrow Wilson was inaugurated as the 28th president of the United States of America. Inauguration Day began for Wilson at 10:30 A.M. when a Congressional delegation picked up the president-elect at the Shoreham Hotel and escorted him to the White House where he was greeted by the outgoing president, Taft. After exchanging brief pleasantries, within a few minutes the two left for the Capitol where upon arrival they were greeted by a crowd of 75,000 onlookers. Waiting at the Capitol for the ceremonies to begin, Taft took off his hat to test the weather and replaced it immediately, then continued to chat and laugh with Wilson. At precisely 1:11 P.M., Taft and Wilson stepped to the stand for the swearing in ceremonies. Woodrow Wilson was sworn in at 1:37 P.M. by Chief Justice White as president of the United States of America and delivered his inaugural address.

That afternoon as Wilson arrived at the inaugural parade, wild cheers rose from the crowd as the new president and family took the reviewing stand. Down Pennsylvania Avenue could be heard the sound of swelling voices coming closer as the aging members of the Grand Army of the Republic, dressed in fading blue uniforms, came into view of the new president. While they were fewer in number than just four years ago during the Taft inaugural parade, many of these same veterans had been there before as much younger men, having victoriously paraded past President Lincoln in April 1865. But now in 1913, many of them were just too infirm to march in step. Old wounds of the war between brothers were still very evident, however, as many in the crowd viewing the parade stopped cheering and turned away as the blue-clad veterans marched by. President Wilson was seen to swallow hard several times, and on one occasion had to wipe his glasses, which had become misty. In reality it was a harbinger of things to come for Wilson, as far across the Atlantic Ocean the distant sound of war drums could be heard starting to beat throughout Europe.

The 1913 major league season began on April 5 as Charles Ebbets opened Ebbets Field in the Flatbush section of Brooklyn. The new ballpark had 37,000 seats and was so large a project that Ebbets had to bring two partners, brothers Ed and Steve McKeever, into the team's ownership to finish it. In Cincinnati, Redland Field was inundated with ten feet of flood water and opening day was cancelled on April 11. As the flood waters started to recede, park superintendent Matty Schwab and his legion of grounds workers had to scoop and scrape mounds of mud and slime from the playing field. Schwab's troops were triumphant in their efforts and opening game was played on April 12. However, Joe Tinker's debut as Cincinnati skipper was spoiled by the Pittsburgh Pirates, who beat the Reds, 9–1. Tinker would have to wait until the third game of the season to get his first victory when the Reds beat the Cardinals, 5–0, in a seven-inning, rain-shortened game. Rain also spoiled the American League opening game scheduled at Washington between the Yankees and Nationals on April 12. When the game was played on April 14, President Wilson, following the tradition established by William Howard Taft, was in the stands to throw out the first ball.

As the first month of the 1913 season was coming to an end, Garry Herrmann and the National Commission was confronted with adjudicating yet another matter involving Ty Cobb. Cobb had been holding out for a contract calling for $15,000 from the Detroit Tigers and was suspended for failure to report to spring training. Cobb finally came to terms with the Tigers near the end of April, signing for $12,000 and now had to petition the National Commission for reinstatement into organized baseball. There was precedent for the matter set in the holdout case of returning billiard champion Johnny Kling in 1910. However, Cobb had been extremely boisterous during his holdout and rattled a lot of sensitivities of major league moguls in both leagues. But Cobb was the game's biggest star, and when the National Commission met in a special meeting at Chicago on April 30, they had little other choice in the matter but to reinstate Cobb. The Georgia Peach then went on to hit .390, playing in 122 games and winning his 7th American League batting title.

The Cincinnati Reds seemed to be about as good in 1913 with Joe Tinker as manager as they had been in 1912 with Hank O'Day at the helm. With the club fading fast in the standings, on May 22, Garry Herrmann and Tinker made a trade with the New York Giants in an effort to bring the club some much-needed pitching. The Reds traded third baseman/shortstop Eddie Grant and pitcher Art Fromme to the Giants in exchange for pitcher Red Ames, second baseman Heinie Groh, outfielder Josh DeVore and $20,000 in cash. The key player in the trade was Ames, who had been one of the mainstays of John McGraw's starting rotation since 1903, winning 108 games for the Giants, including going 22–8 in 1904. While Ames would immediately become an important part of the Reds' starting pitching rotation for parts of the next three seasons, he would have little impact on moving the club up in the standings. However, John McGraw had erred in letting young Heinie Groh get away. Groh would play in 117 games for the Reds in 1913, hitting a solid .282.

By September 2, 1913, the Cincinnati Reds were mired in seventh place, 34 games behind the league-leading New York Giants, with a record of 53–72. Joe Tinker had become frustrated in Cincinnati and was criticizing Garry Herrmann's running of the business side of the ballclub. The Reds' directors and Herrmann were both deeply offended by Tinker's demeanor and remarks. Herrmann stated to the press that Tinker had been consulted about every move made by the club. "The Cincinnati club has spent just $35,836 this year for players," said Herrmann. "Before the drafting season has closed we will have spent $50,000 this year for players. Our payroll is as high as that of any club in the league, and higher than the payrolls of most of them. We are paying higher salaries right now than the New York club. George Suggs is being paid $700 a month and he has won four games for us this season."[2] Joe Tinker's disappointment with the collapse of the Reds' season under his leadership was elevated further by the fact that he was no longer a part owner. Dealing with Garry Herrmann as an employee of the Reds was far different than dealing with wacky Charles W. Murphy as a business partner in the Cubs.

The riff between the Reds' manager and Garry Herrmann was apparent to everyone and it was becoming certain that the tenure of Joe Tinker in Cincinnati was going to be a short one. Under Tinker's leadership, Cincinnati finished in seventh place in the 1913 pennant race, 37½ games behind the first-place New York Giants, who had won the National League for the third year in a row. The Reds were also a huge bust at the gate under Tinker, drawing only

258,000 fans through the turnstiles of Redland Field, a decrease of 86,000 under the 1912 total. In the 1913 World Series, John McGraw's New York Giants met Connie Mack's Philadelphia Athletics and were quickly dispatched by the Mackmen, 4 games to 1.

On December 11, under pressure from the board of directors, Garry Herrmann fired Joe Tinker as Reds manager. Although he was no longer manager, Tinker was still under contract to Cincinnati for two more years and now Herrmann had to make a decision on how to dispose of him. Charles W. Murphy, who was in Europe at the time, stated that he would be interested in having Tinker rejoin the Cubs; however, he was leaning towards having "Three Finger" Brown manage the club in the 1914 season. When August Herrmann arrived at the Waldorf-Astoria Hotel in New York for the December 1913 National League meeting, he was faced with the most important agenda that had confronted him since 1903. The Fleischmann brothers and other Reds directors wanted Tinker out. Also, Herrmann was now cognizant of the fact that the rise of the Federal League meant a war was looming on the existing major league baseball establishment. Then there was the matter of electing a new National League president.

By December 1913, it was clear that Thomas J. Lynch lacked the powerful backing of his late mentor John T. Brush and would not be re-elected president of the National League. Consequently, Lynch had accepted his fate and decided to retire as president. There is even evidence to suggest that Lynch had quit acting as president of the league well before December 1913. During the previous season, he had visited only five of the cities in the league once for only a day, never setting foot in either Brooklyn or St. Louis at all. The only reason he was credited with being in New York was because his office was located there. While a rumor was circulating that Lynch had decided to join the Federal League, he categorically denied any such ambition, stating that he was a National Leaguer. The fact of the matter was that Lynch was battling fatigue, the Horace Fogel matter, constant sparing with Charles Ebbets and Barney Dreyfuss over his handling of the umpires and his personal crusade against rowdyism in the league had left him exhausted. He was determined not to become another Harry Pulliam. At the same time in Louisville, Robert W. Brown had abandoned his pipe dream of ascending to the National League presidency. For the first time in several years, Brown was not in New York for the league meeting and made no attempt to lobby his way into the office through his personal connections with Garry Herrmann and Barney Dreyfuss

On Tuesday, December 9, the National League moguls met at the Waldorf-Astoria to elect a new league president, and among an air of cigar smoke, civility reigned throughout the room. Maybe it was because Horace Fogel was no longer among them. Neither was Charles W. Murphy, who was a spectator in Europe to a world baseball tour occurring between the New York Giants and Chicago White Sox. With Murphy globetrotting, the Cubs were represented by Murphy's new business partner, Harry Ackerland, which may have added to the tranquility among the magnates. The first order of business for the cheerful moguls was an affirmative vote to extend the annual annuity granted to Cap Anson. Then they voted to extend the term of league president from one year to four years.

At that point August Herrmann announced that the election of officers was in order. Former police commissioner W. F. Baker, the new president of the Philadelphia Phillies, offered into nomination for the office of president governor John Kinley Tener of Pennsylvania. Charles Ebbets and Barney Dreyfuss then seconded the nomination of Tener. That was followed with a unanimous vote to elect Tener president. In fact, there was not one dissenting voice in the election. At the same time, John A. Heydler was re-elected league secretary for a two-year term. Following the tragic death of Harry Pulliam, if it had not been for the sale of the Philadelphia Phillies to Charles P. Taft, John Heydler could have become president of the league in December 1909. But when that event occurred, Heydler lost a crucial vote.

When the league had first approached Tener about the job, they offered him an annual salary of $15,000, but he felt the job was worth more than that. Subsequently, Tener demanded and was granted a salary of $20,000 a year. However, at the time Tener was still governor of Pennsylvania and his term had one more year to run. As he would receive $10,000 for his last year in office from the taxpayers of the Commonwealth of Pennsylvania, Tener agreed to accept just $10,000 in salary from the National League for his first year in office. To administer the league during the 1914 season while Tener was still holding public office in Harrisburg, it was agreed that John Heydler would run the New York office and handle routine business.

On his way out the door of the presidency, Thomas J. Lynch had a few remarks for the National League moguls that could be interpreted as a backhanded slap in the face. Lynch suggested that the moguls acquire some of the dignity that they expected John Tener to bring to the job. Lynch stated, "Gentleman, in choosing your next president you have gone on record as wanting a man who will lend dignity and prestige to the league. In your selection of Governor Tener you have the right man; but I hope that you will inject some of the dignity expected of him into yourselves and be a help instead of a hindrance to him. In leaving this office I want you to know that there is no ill-feeling on my part. I wish the National League and its new president all the success in the world."[4] Upon concluding his remarks, Thomas J. Lynch put on his hat and walked out of the room into the annals of major league history.

Not everyone following the game was satisfied with the selection of Tener as new league president. Some in the press, including the *Sporting News*, felt his election might be bad for the business of selling newspapers. Thomas Rice, writing in the *Brooklyn Eagle*, stated in part, "Governor Tener said that he proposed to run the league and that the owners would run the individual clubs, but in running the league he may feel it incumbent upon himself to be the sort of general fixer such as Ban Johnson is in the American League. We are personally convinced that the clubs, the newspapers and the fans would prefer to have more battling, within reasonable limits, and now and again a peck of blood on the moon rather than the excessive and oppressive close harmony which marks Johnson's circuit."[4] Regardless of John Tener becoming the new league president, the press would soon have pages of controversy to publish.

In between the business sessions at the meeting, the moguls were making merry in the Waldorf's bar and making several key player deals. Garry Herrmann had the Joe Tinker dilemma to handle. He knew that Charles Ebbets was interested in Tinker and in between business sessions went over to Brooklyn to chat with Ebbets and his new partners, the McKeever brothers. Herrmann was floored by what by what he learned. The Brooklyn magnates were willing to give the Reds a flat $25,000 for Tinker's release. It was an incredible offer, but Herrmann knew that the Reds' directors would want players in the deal, not just cash, not even an enormous sum like Ebbets and his partners were offering. So Herrmann said that he wanted players in exchange for Tinker. Brooklyn manager Wilbert Robinson was present in the meeting and said that he would draw up a list of players he would be willing to part with. Herrmann had other options in the works for Tinker, too. The Philadelphia Phillies were also interested in Tinker and Red Dooin was suggesting a possible three-team trade that would land Tinker in the Quaker City. In Chicago, Johnny Evers was advancing a deal that would send Roger Bresnahan to the Reds for Tinker. Even Pittsburgh manager Fred Clarke was considering a deal with Herrmann for Tinker.

However, Charles Ebbets really wanted Tinker and the next day came back to Herrmann with two possible offers. First, Ebbets once again offered $25,000 outright for Tinker and Herrmann again refused. The other was a possible deal that would send Tinker and outfielder

Bob Bescher to Brooklyn for $20,000 and Zack Wheat. Herrmann liked the second proposal and notified Ebbets that he would be willing to accept the deal. However, Ebbets then balked at the deal, telling Herrmann that he wanted more time to consider it. Zack Wheat had been in the majors for parts of five seasons and was developing into a very good player. Manager Wilbert Robinson was not about to trade Wheat's youth and potential for Joe Tinker's experience. So it was back to square one for Herrmann and Ebbets. Meanwhile, Herrmann had received permission from the New York Giants to talk with Buck Herzog about managing the Reds. The Giants were willing to trade Herzog and backup catcher Grover Hartley to Cincinnati, but they wanted Bob Bescher in return.

By December 11, Charles W. Murphy returned from Europe and dropped in at the Waldorf-Astoria. Suddenly there was a sense of a little less collegiality among the magnates. Murphy jumped right into the Tinker dealings and proclaimed to the press with a wink of the eye that he had offered Garry Herrmann $62,000 and four players for Tinker. The actual offer that Murphy had made to Herrmann for Tinker involved sending Roger Bresnahan, shortstop Al Bridwell and a pitcher to be determined to Cincinnati. However, Herrmann wasn't really interested in Bresnahan as a candidate to manage the Reds and was now talking with Mordecai Brown about the job. Still, Murphy proclaimed as he boarded the Twentieth Century Limited for Chicago, "I'll get Tinker after all this hullabaloo is over tonight."[5]

While Tinker's name was being bounced around by Garry Herrmann and the assembled National League moguls in the Waldorf-Astoria bar, Tinker let his feelings be known on the matter. Tinker told the *Cincinnati Commercial-Tribune*, "I want to play in Chicago, but if this is absolutely impossible, I suppose I will go East."[6] Tinker also let it be known that he was holding Garry Herrmann to the three-year contractual agreement that he had with the Cincinnati club and that any deal with Charles Ebbets or any other club would be responsible for compensating him accordingly.

The New York meetings were winding down and Garry Herrmann still had not made any player moves. So earlier in the day on December 12, he completed a deal with Harry Hempstead, son-in-law of the late John T. Brush, and John B. Foster, club secretary, sending Bob Bescher to the New York Giants in exchange for Buck Herzog and Grover Hartley. Now that Herrmann had his manager in Herzog, he had to move quickly to dispose of Tinker and his cumbersome contract. That evening around 6:00 P.M., Herrmann was sitting at a table in the cafe of the Waldorf-Astoria Hotel, throwing back drinks with Reds secretary Harry Stephens, Pirates owner Barney Dreyfuss and a few others, including a reporter from the *Commercial Tribune* of Cincinnati. When asked about Ebbets' offer, Herrmann stated that he believed that Charles Ebbets was only bluffing when he offered him $25,000 outright for Joe Tinker. At that time $25,000 would have been the highest amount ever paid to obtain a player. "If I had accepted Ebbets' offer he would have had heart disease," said Herrmann. Immediately the reporter asked, "Will you sell Tinker for $25,000?" "Find Ebbets and ask him if he will trade Wheat for Tinker, even up, and if he consents I'll make the deal," replied Herrmann.[7]

Charles Ebbets was also in the Waldorf café, and when the *Commercial Tribune* reporter located him and related what Herrmann had just stated in the bar, he became livid. Ebbets, hot under the collar, stormed over to Herrmann's table. "Mr. Herrmann, I never made a bluff that I would not go through with," said Ebbets. "You are not treating me fairly when you say my offer of $25,000 was not made in good faith." Herrmann quickly replied, "You can have Tinker for $25,000. Will you buy?" "I'm in no hurry after what you told me about Tinker," said Ebbets, "and furthermore, how do I know that he will agree to play in Brooklyn?"[8]

Harry Stevens (left) and Garry Herrmann. National Baseball Hall of Fame Library, Cooperstown, N.Y.

Herrmann then challenged Ebbets to state what he had told him about Tinker. Ebbets replied, "You said that he told the directors of the Cincinnati club last season that he would play wherever he felt like it." Herrmann still insisted that he would sell Tinker. However, Ebbets now raised the question of what would happen in the event that he purchased Tinker and that he refused to report to the Brooklyn club. Herrmann then told Ebbets, "If he does not sign with you, the deal is off and the Cincinnati club will return the $25,000 to you."[9]

Ebbets was starting to calm down and took notice that he and Herrmann were putting on quite a show for everyone in the café, including the reporters. He suggested to Herrmann that they go upstairs and talk the deal over in private. Maybe he had one drink too many, but there was no need for Garry Herrmann to humiliate Charles Ebbets in public over the Tinker negotiations. Ebbets had been a long-time friend and advocate for Herrmann. He had also been one of the few magnates to attend the wedding of Herrmann's daughter in Cincinnati. But for some reason, Herrmann's political side started to surface, and it was as if he was back at Wielert's cafe with Cox and Hynicka in the 1890s and his credibility was on the line. He blurted out, "Let's make this deal in public, Ebbets." At that point, Charles Ebbets walked away from the table to place a telephone call. Presumably he was going to call the McKeever brothers and Dodgers manager Wilbert Robinson. Herrmann, feeling that he had backed Ebbets down, said to everyone at the table, "I told you fellows that Ebbets would not put up the coin when he was called. He will back down sure."[10]

Soon Charles Ebbets returned to Herrmann's table with a serious look on his face and said, "Do you really mean business, Garry?" Now Herrmann had been backed into a corner. As the word spread around the room, the crowd was becoming larger at Herrmann's table. Herrmann looked at Ebbets with a pencil-thin grin on his face and said, "Do you?" Without hesitation, Ebbets replied in a hot, gruff manner, "Yes, and I'll make the deal here. I'll show you whether I am bluffing or not." Herrmann snapped back, "All right, get some paper and we'll put it in black and white. Just to clinch it, I'll agree to give $10,000 of the money to Tinker when he signs a contract." Barney Dreyfuss stated, "Reduce it all to writing, gentleman. That is the only way."[11] Immediately, George F. Kerr, a friend of Herrmann's that was sitting at the table, produced a sheet of paper and as Ebbets dictated the terms, he drew up the agreement. The agreement read as follows:

> It is hereby agreed and understood that the Brooklyn Baseball Club purchases the services and release of Joseph Tinker for the sum of $25,000 from the Cincinnati Baseball Club, this deal to hold on condition that the said Tinker accepts the term with the said Brooklyn Baseball Club and reports for service in the spring of 1914. It is further understood that out of this sum of $25,000 Mr. Tinker is to receive the sum of $10,000.
>
> AUGUST HERRMANN
C. H. EBBETS
>
> Witnesses:
> BARNEY DREYFUSS
> GEORGE F. KERR[12]

All at once all the baseball men in the cafe swarmed about Charles Ebbets, congratulating him, telling him what a great deal he had just made. In return, Ebbets was telling them that Tinker will make the Brooklyn Dodgers an immediate pennant contender. Ebbets further stated that he refused to include Zack Wheat, 1913 National League batting champion Jake Daubert or Nap Rucker in any deal with Herrmann because they were the core players on his roster and he hoped they would remain in Brooklyn their entire careers. While the prevailing attitude in the room was Ebbets got the better part of it all, Garry Herrmann laid out his reasons for making the deal. "We will clear $15,000 on Tinker and I can buy Sherwood Magee of the Philadelphia Club for $5,500. We will spend all the money for new players before spring. We won't miss Tinker now that we have Herzog. He can play shortstop." A reporter then asked Herrmann if he had the authority to make the deal. Would it have to pass muster with the Cincinnati Board of Directors? Herrmann quickly responded, "Yes, I have. And the deal stands too."[13] With that being said, Herrmann got up from the table and left the room.

When Philadelphia Phillies President Baker was asked about Herrmann's assertion that he could purchase Sherwood Magee for $5,500, he stated, "Herrmann never received an invitation from me that he could have Magee for that amount. In fact, we never discussed it."[14]

Joe Tinker had stranger things happen to him in his career than the Waldorf-Astoria agreement. In 1896 Tinker had been playing for the John Taylor team, an amateur club in Kansas City. At the end of the season his manager Eddie Oswald sold him to the Hager Tailors club for $1.50. The following year, with Tinker playing shortstop, the Hager Tailor team would win the league championship. From there Joe Tinker's odyssey to the major leagues would continue through Coffeeville, Kansas, Denver, Great Falls, Montana, and in 1901 Portland, Oregon, before becoming the regular shortstop for the Chicago Cubs in 1902.

When Joe Tinker was informed of the deal consummated in the Waldorf bar that sent him to Brooklyn, he quickly issued a statement that he did not want to play ball in Brooklyn and was still of high hopes that the coming season would find him employed back in

Chicago with the Cubs. Tinker stated that he believed his sale was conditional and that by remaining noncommittal he might force Garry Herrmann to rescind the deal. He said that he would not consider any offer from Charles Ebbets to sign a contract for $7,500 a year and a $10,000 bonus unless the offer was for three years.

At the moment nothing seemed to be going right for Joe Tinker. In Chicago, he got punched out by a *Chicago Tribune* employee. Tinker had gone to the paper to speak with the sporting editor in an effort to lay out his feelings over the sale of his contract to Brooklyn. However, when he arrived at the paper's headquarters, he was confronted by a doorkeeper who was not of the mind to let Tinker enter the office of the sporting editor unannounced. When Tinker attempted to force his way by the man, fisticuffs ensued and Tinker was quickly beaten into submission. Other Tribune employees separated the two, and hearing the noise outside his office, the sporting editor came rushing to Tinker's side, apologizing for the thrashing he had taken around the face. Tinker and the doorman agreed to drop the matter and he went into the editor's office and gave his version of the deal that sent him to Brooklyn. Meanwhile, Charles W. Murphy was in shock over the Tinker deal. He was telling all and probably exaggerating that he would have not only given Herrmann $30,000 for Tinker, but would have thrown in four players to boot.

After three days of meetings in New York, the National League magnates concluded their business by attending a huge banquet financed by Governor Tener. The following morning before boarding a train for Cincinnati, Garry Herrmann had a chat with Buck Herzog. Garry Herrmann was glad to get the Tinker matter off his mind. He said that he really never wanted to let Tinker go, but the other directors of the Reds didn't want him back. Addressing the press, Herrmann stated, "I sold Tinker for the best terms possible and the results will prove it. I could not trade him for players I wanted, so there was no other way out of it. When I secured Herzog I realized that Tinker's place could be filled."[15] Still, Herrmann knew that when he got home, he would have to convince Julius Fleischmann and the other directors of the club that in his Tinker deal he acted in the best interest of the club.

In fact, the Cincinnati Reds' Board of Directors were not impressed with Herrmann's Tinker deal and moved quickly to reverse it. The directors wanted players, not money, and they were also appalled at the generosity of Herrmann offering to give Tinker $10,000 of the purchase price as a bonus for signing a contract with Brooklyn. On December 15, without objections by a chastened Herrmann, the Reds' Board of Directors sent a telegram to Charles Ebbets that stated, "The Board of Directors absolutely disapproves of the agreement to sell Tinker for cash. They want an exchange. If you can make a deal with Tinker to play in Brooklyn submit to us a proposition which will include either Pitcher Yingling or Pitcher Ragan and Outfielder Moran or Outfielder Stengel with cash equivalent for the difference."[16]

In New York, Charles Ebbets refused to budge; he was standing pat on the Tinker deal. The situation had Garry Herrmann in a most uncomfortable position. He had signed the agreement with Ebbets in the presence of witnesses. Now he was simply ignoring the fact that he was being overruled by the directors and made no objections to the telegram being sent to Ebbets. It was the opinion of many that if Herrmann did not take a stand against his own board of directors and insist that the agreement be honored, then he should resign. While Herrmann may have felt in the Waldorf bar that Charles Ebbets was challenging his creditability and he needed to rescue it by completing the Tinker deal, it was at most a symbolic gesture. Herrmann knew all the wheeling and dealing was inherent in the art of baseball horse-trading, but he had let it go to far. Now his credibility was being challenged for real by his own allies, partners and friends. Consequently, if he didn't take action, the circumstances would escalate and his creditability would also be questioned in his duties as chairman of the National Commission.

It was brought to Herrmann's attention that National Commission Rule 12 stated all trades or sales must signed by the president of each interested club or its authorized agent. It was a fact that in the Tinker deal Charles Ebbets had consulted his partners before negotiating with Herrmann, and every baseball magnate outside of the Cincinnati Board of Directors believed that Herrmann as club president of the Reds had full authority to deal with Ebbets in the matter. It was a clean-cut deal done in full accordance with the rules of the National Commission and had the potential to really open up a Pandora's Box for major league baseball should it not be enforced. Some newspapers, including the *Commercial Tribune* in Cincinnati, were stating that if trades and sales done in full accordance with the National Commission rules can be called off by directors of a given club, the magnates could no longer insist that the reserve clause be enforced.

Charles Ebbets said in accordance with the rules of baseball it was impossible to call off the deal, and in response to the telegram received from the Cincinnati Reds' Board of Directors, he sent the following letter to new league president John Tener stating, "We have agreed to pay $25,000 for Tinker and we will go through with it. There will be no quibbling. After this deal has been settled by the signing of Tinker and the payment of the sum agreed upon, the Brooklyns will be glad to open new negotiations with the Cincinnati Club for a trade of players, subject to the approval of Manager Robinson. But this is a trifle premature. Tinker will play ball with Brooklyn next season or remain idle."[17]

For some reason Charles W. Murphy still was of the opinion that he had a chance to get Tinker to sign a contract. He was stating that he had received permission from the Cincinnati directors to attempt to sign Tinker and immediately sent Garry Herrmann a copy of the Cub reserve list with the request that he name the players he would like to have in exchange for Tinker. If all this wasn't bad enough for Garry Herrmann, this latest development had the potential of forcing him to declare where he stood on the Tinker matter — behind his deal with Ebbets or with a possible new deal with Murphy. It seemed like the whole mess was exposing how little control of the Cincinnati Reds baseball club Garry Herrmann really had and how much he had to kowtow to the desires of Julius and Max Fleischmann.

A few days passed and suddenly Joe Tinker began to come to his senses. He still admitted that he would prefer to play in Chicago. However, he was starting to realize that he could wind up without a paycheck in the coming season if the matter of his sale wound up in litigation. Tinker told the press in Chicago, "The chance to get a bonus of $10,000 does not come every day and I am not going to let this slip away from me, if I can arrange with Ebbets concerning my salary. I do not know what to say about the deal, as I have not heard a word from either Ebbets or Herrmann. If Ebbets would communicate with me or come to see me I would tell him what I want, but if he does not do that I will have to remain quiet and let the clubs settle their wrangle. Herrmann arranged with Brooklyn and according to baseball law, it should stand. If Ebbets comes to terms with me I think it will stand."[18]

Meanwhile, Charles Ebbets and the McKeever brothers had consulted New York attorney Bernard J. York in regard to the legality of the Tinker sale. It was the opinion of York that the signatures of Ebbets and Herrmann would stand according to the laws of baseball. While Charles Ebbets had sent a formal statement to National League headquarters, he was now stating that he felt that the Tinker matter would not wind up in the hands of the National League's board of directors or by appeal in the hands of the National Commission, but soon would be ratified by the Cincinnati directors.

Garry Herrmann paced the floor of his office wondering just what was going to come of all this. He was telling not only the Reds' directors, but anyone that would listen that while in New York he tried in every way possible to get something worthwhile in return for Tinker, but every club he spoke with wanted to unload a lot of dead players or untried rookies. Suddenly, Herrmann got help from a lot of people with clout. Newspapers around the country ran articles supporting Herrmann and a large contingent of his baseball colleagues, including new National League president John Tener, American League president Ban Johnson and most of the major league club owners, sent notice to Julius Fleischmann and the Reds' directors that they were adamant that the deal Herrmann had made for Tinker with Brooklyn should be carried out. Ban Johnson stated, "Herrmann is a man of his word and he will live up to his agreement to sell Tinker to Brooklyn, even if he is compelled to dig into his own pocket. He has been embarrassed, wholly without his fault, and I feel it is only justice to him to make this statement."[19]

Julius Fleischmann hadn't felt so much political heat since his days as mayor of Cincinnati. He knew the winds of public opinion were blowing in the opposite direction; it was time to go on damage control. Fleischmann released a notice to the press stating that August Herrmann would remain president of the Reds and the Tinker deal would go through as made. It was time to get on with business. The Reds had been successful in signing Buck Herzog and now were ready to use the cash obtained in the Tinker deal to buy other players.

The brief Joe Tinker tenure in Cincinnati had failed. However, Garry Herrmann was to learn at the New York meeting when approached by reserve outfielder Jimmy Sheckard, who had played with Tinker in Chicago during the pennant years 1906–1910, that Tinker had been set up by some of the Reds' players for failure. Sheckard told Herrmann that several of the Reds' players had been set in their ways of doing business on the field. Not that those players were dishonest or had thrown games, but they didn't like being harassed by Tinker to improve their skills and play the game his way. They mocked Tinker and refused to adapt to his fast-thinking, fast-acting style of play that he was so accustomed to in Chicago. Still, in years to come, the benefit of the deal that Joe Tinker had made to bring Heinie Groh from the Giants to the Reds would pay huge dividends. In the 1915 season he would switch positions, from second to third, and become captain of the Reds and a mainstay of the team's infield through the 1921 season. Groh would hit over .300 in four of the seven seasons he played in Cincinnati, and notwithstanding Pete Rose, he would become arguably the greatest player to ever play the hot corner in a Reds uniform.

While the fine points of the Joe Tinker sale were being worked out, Tinker threw the entire deal into a state of confusion. Tinker began haggling with Charlie Ebbets over his salary offer. When Tinker had played in Chicago, he commanded $7,000 a year. Despite the assurances of his $10,000 bonus from the Reds, he was demanding a higher salary to play in Brooklyn. Rather than continue the contract haggle, Tinker continued to negotiate with the Federal League. By January 1, 1914, it was announced that Tinker had signed a three-year contract to manage the Chicago franchise. A bonding company guaranteed his compensation regardless if the league failed. With Tinker in the fold, Chicago franchise owner Charles Weegham began the bidding process to construct a $125,000 ballpark on the north side of Chicago at Sheffield and Addison streets. In the not-too-distant future, this ballpark would come to bear the storied name of Wrigley Field.

XVII

War with the Feds Begins

By the mid-teens major league baseball had become a booming enterprise. New state-of-the-art concrete and steel stadiums had been built in both leagues and overall attendance had been increasing. Now other enthusiastic business-minded men wanted a piece of the action. However, there were only so many of the public's dollars for recreation to go around and the increasing popularity of the automobile permitted people to travel out of the city for recreation. Also, with the bulging popularity of movies and amusement parks, the boom in baseball was about to peak. Nonetheless, the market facts did little to discourage a band of entrepreneurs who decided it was time for a third major league to surface.

The Federal League had its genesis in 1912, being formed in Reading, Pennsylvania, as a minor league called the United States League, with franchises located in existing major league cities such as Cleveland, New York, Pittsburgh, St. Louis and Washington, as well as successful minor league cities such as Indianapolis. Initially it looked as if the United States League would fold before it started and, in fact, the league was in jeopardy of going out of business by June 1912. However, one of the franchises located in Pittsburgh had made a profit and that event gave hope to organizers that the league could rise to a state of financial equilibrium.

James A. Gilmore grew up in Chicago and was a White Sox fan. He had been a pitcher for Marquette High School on Chicago's West Side. He first learned of the Federal League while playing golf at the Chicago Golf Club in August 1913 with E. C. Racey, who was then treasurer of the Federal League. In September 1913, Gilmore was elected as new league president and he methodically set about to restructure the remnants of the United States League, now known as the Federal League, into a major league. Gilmore, known as "Fighting Jim," a reference to his service during the Spanish-American War as a member of the Illinois National Guard, had become wealthy through operating a stationary business. He had also been a Chicago coal dealer and brought much-needed professional business administration knowledge to the fledgling league.

Furthermore, Gilmore had vast contacts among the business community, and he quickly set about persuading some of them to join him in the new league venture. Gilmore's proposal appealed to the likes of Chicago restaurateur Charles Weeghman, Oklahoma oilman Harry Sinclair, St. Louis refrigeration magnate Philip De Catesby Ball and Brooklyn bakery operator Robert Boyd Ward, among others. Gilmore's business plan for the Federal League was similar to that of Ban Johnson when he founded the American League: attract potential owners armed with substantial cash to lure established star players away from other rosters onto Federal League teams, then immediately build new ballparks in the league's cities to house the teams.

For a while there was talk about placing a Federal League team in Cincinnati, and on October 19, 1913, Paul V. Connolly, a local attorney, wrote to August Herrmann informing him that he intended to travel to the state capitol in Columbus and file papers for incorporation of the new club to be known as the Cincinnati Baseball Club of the Federal League. However, to Herrmann, the suggestion of another team in the Queen City was rather ho-hum, and he paid little mind to it. The Feds did place a team in Covington, Kentucky, across the Ohio River from Cincinnati. However, the franchise could not compete with the Reds, lost money, and was moved to Kansas City at the end of the 1913 season. So, the franchises were set for the Feds' inaugural major league season, with eight teams scheduled to play in Baltimore, Brooklyn, Buffalo, Chicago, Indianapolis, Kansas City, Pittsburgh and St. Louis.

In early December 1913, the Federal League held a meeting in Pittsburgh and drew up a list of fifty existing major league players that they intended to lure away from the National and American leagues. When the press and fans began to accuse the Feds of crying wolf about their player shopping list, league secretary Lloyd Rickert, who had been lured away by James A. Gilmore from a similar job with the St. Louis Browns, produced the list. Among the players on the list were Mordecai Brown and Dick Hoblitzell of Cincinnati, Buck Herzog and Rube Marquard of the New York Giants, John Miller of Pittsburgh, Eddie Collins of the Philadelphia Athletics, Hal Chase of the Chicago White Sox, Smoky Joe Wood of the Boston Red Sox and Nap Lajoie of the Cleveland Indians, who had been one of the first players to jump from the National to the American League in 1901.

To obtain all the players on the Feds' list, it was estimated that it would require a cash outlay of more than $250,000. While Lajoie said he was satisfied in the American League and Smoky Joe Wood stated that he had no intention of leaving the Red Sox, the Feds were playing hardball and, in fact, Eddie Collins of the Athletics admitted that he had recently turned down a three-year, $50,000 contract to join the new circuit. Many other players on the list were exercising their right to remain silent, believing that by being named on the Federal League list, it would give them leverage in negotiating their 1914 contracts with their existing teams.

As the new year of 1914 began, the Federal League magnates stated that they would not honor major league baseball's reserve clause and began rushing to launch their outlaw league. With Joe Tinker signed to a $12,000-a-year contract to manage the Chicago Whales, Mordecai "Three Finger" Brown followed by taking the helm of the St. Louis franchise. Soon Hal Chase would jump from the Chicago White Sox for the Feds' Buffalo club, while Mickey Doolan and Otto Knabe would abandon the Philadelphia Phillies and Jack Quinn, the Boston Red Sox, all for the Baltimore club. Many others would follow, including Lee Magee and Steve Evans of the St. Louis Cardinals. Still, there was no great concern being expressed by either the American or National league magnates over ballplayers jumping their contracts. The prevailing attitude was that ballplayers were now paid so well that there was no incentive to jump to the Federal League. In fact, Ban Johnson issued a statement that 80 percent of the players in the American League the previous season had signed contracts for 1914. It was felt that the only players that would really sign Federal League contracts would be the disgruntled ones and the incompetents. In many cases, this attitude proved to be accurate. When pitcher Walter Johnson signed a Federal League contract, Washington Nationals manager and part-owner Clark Griffith offered Johnson a new contract with a marginal raise, and he agreed to stay put.

The American and National league magnates were advancing the theory that it would cost the Federal League at least $2 million to sign players, buy or lease property for ballparks, pay travel expenses, buy uniforms and equipment and have telegraph tolls. Therefore, it was necessary for each of the eight clubs to have a capitalization of $250,000 to cover all the liabilities before the first pitch was thrown. As the Feds were proposing 25-cent seats in their ballparks, it further indicated disaster. In addition, the Chicago franchise would have to compete with two other major league teams, the White Sox and Cubs, in the city for 77 days each year, and then play games in such cities as Kansas City, Buffalo, Baltimore and Toronto, where minor league ball had never been truly successful. However, undaunted Federal League president Jim Gilmore pressed forward in readying his league for opening day in April. A 154-game schedule was drawn up and he successfully completed the administrative oversight of constructing eight new ballparks in just three months.

By 1914, August Garry Herrmann was 55 years old, but life had not slowed down one iota for him. His life was still spent in the fast lane and he still occupied much of his time providing "Gasfreundschaft," i.e., hospitality for his fraternal brothers, political associates and major league colleagues. In a 24-hour period beginning at 6:00 P.M. on Friday evening, February 20, Herrmann would go through a taxing schedule of meetings and banquets. A number of Elkdom's highest hats were in Cincinnati, including exalted ruler Edward Leach of New York City, for a banquet and meeting of the Elks National Home Commission, of which Herrmann was chairman. Subsequently, at 6:00 P.M. on Friday evening, Herrmann entertained his brethren at a dinner. Then at 8:00 P.M., Herrmann attended a session of the Cincinnati Elks Lodge in which Cincinnati City Auditor Leimann was initiated into the fraternity. Finally, the Friday evening festivities concluded at 11:00 P.M. with an informal talk at the lodge.

At 9:00 A.M. Saturday, Herrmann was back on deck attending the meeting of the Elks National Home Commission. At 3:00 P.M. he went into session with the National League directors, which was followed by a league meeting. At the time Herrmann and the other league directors were keeping mum on a huge story about to break. Herrmann and the directors waited as National League President Tener talked with Charles P. Taft for six hours. Charles W. Murphy was about to resign as president of the Chicago Cubs and sell his interest in the club to Taft.

At 6:00 P.M., with Tener still talking with Taft, Herrmann went over to the Gibson House to attend the banquet in honor of Elks Grand Exalted Ruler Leach. The Leach banquet was one of the largest affairs ever held by the Cincinnati Elks. In between all these activities, Herrmann had to attend to several matters concerning the Cincinnati Reds, some National Commission business, some private business affairs, all while several hundred telephone calls had to be delegated with baseball writers looking for stories. To top it all off, there were a few matters to go over with Rud Hynicka in straightening out a few kinks in political job appointments. In early 1914, life was anything but dull for Garry Herrmann.

On Saturday, February 21, Charles P. Taft bought the stock held by Charles W. Murphy in the Chicago Cubs. With the deal finalized, Murphy officially resigned as president of the Chicago Cubs and his stormy tenure as CEO of the Bruins came to a close. However, with the majority of stock in the Cubs was now owned by two out-of-towners, Taft of Cincinnati and Harry Ackerland of Pittsburgh, fans back in Chicago were calling for local control of the ballclub. On Monday morning, a syndicate of six Chicago businessmen, through their attorney Louis J. Behan, made an offer of $750,000 to buy the stock from Taft. As a show of good faith, they were willing to deposit $100,000 in Taft's account. Then should Taft agree, three of the men representing the syndicate would take the night train from Chicago to Cincinnati to close the deal. Taft declined the offer and Chicago stockholders would still retain minority interest in the club.

Armed with abundant capital, James A. "Fighting Jim" Gilmore in April 1914 launched the Federal League in direct competition with the American and National leagues. Still, Garry Herrmann, Ban Johnson, Charles Ebbets and most of the other executives in major league baseball were not taking the new league seriously. They didn't consider Gilmore and his cohorts baseball men and felt that their only motivation for being in the game was to try and make an easy buck. However, at least two men expressed some anxiety over the Federal League, Cleveland Indians owner Charles Somers and National League president John Tener. Somers told New York baseball writer Frank G. Menke, "We're going to have our hands full. You fellows can spoof Feds if you want. But to me it seems they aren't going about this business with any fly-by-night methods. They are building for the future. We'd better give them real consideration right now before this matter goes to a point where we'll be forced into some ugly position."[1] In regard to the business skills of James A. Gilmore, Tener remarked, "I believe that man Gilmore, with a mixture of admiration and frustration, not only can convince a millionaire the moon is made of green cheese, but he can induce him to invest money in a cheese factory on the moon."[2]

By late June all the clubs in the American, National and Federal leagues were struggling for a scarce attendance dollar that was being spread thin as the result of three competing circuits. In the American League, the Philadelphia Athletics were leading the league as expected. In the National League, John McGraw's New York Giants, thanks to the brilliant pitching of Christy Mathewson and Jeff Tesreau, held a comfortable lead in the pennant race.

Then on June 28, the world suddenly changed. In Sarajevo, Bosnia, archduke Franz Ferdinand, heir to the Austrian throne, and his wife were ambushed and murdered by Bosnian activist Garvilo Princip, a member of an anti–Austrian Serbian society known as the Union of Death. Immediately the event sent a shockwave through the capital cities of the European nations. Old alliances were honored without question and a chain reaction of political events quickly ushered in the Great World War. Now the world would be on the borderline of political insanity for the next four years.

However, at the moment in America, the troubles in Europe seemed distant and vague. Even in cities like Chicago and Cincinnati with very large German immigrant populations, sentiments were guarded and there was no visible public display of support for the war one way or the other. In fact, there were other pressing matters to tend to. Following the presidential election of 1912, Theodore Roosevelt stated in a letter to James R. Garfield, "The people are sick and tired of reforms and reformers."[3] In Cincinnati, a new charter was unpopular with the voters, and on election day, it was defeated by a plurality of 25 percent, with 28,304 voting against and 21,304 for. Although defeated, the home rule charter was a harbinger of things to come, and in less than a decade, the issue of reform government in the city would be resurrected.

The 1914 season for the Cincinnati Reds and new manager Buck Herzog was a complete disaster as the team finished in the National League cellar for the first time since 1901. Part of the problem could be directly attributed to Garry Herrmann, who never really took spring training seriously for his players. The Reds now trained at Orlando, Florida, and some members of the press stated that Herrmann's spring training philosophy was that his players should have a good time. In the press the Reds were referred to as tourists and sightseers who did little running and conditioning. One writer following the Reds at Orlando in 1914 stated, "In fact, very few of the players are able to decide whether they were brought to Florida to get into playing shape or as a lot of prospective real estate buyers who might want to invest the extra money they confidentially believe will come their way as a result of the mixing up in the world's series next Fall. One hears stories galore of the 'joy party' this training trip of the Reds has been."[4]

The 1915 Boston Red Sox pitching staff; Babe Ruth is second from right. Author's collection.

In mid–August 1914, with the Reds hanging on to sixth place in the National League pennant race, August Garry Herrmann attempted to make a deal that would have changed the entire course of Cincinnati Reds franchise history. Providence of the International League was in hot pursuit of the pennant when southpaw pitcher Bill Bailey jumped to the Federal League. On August 1, Joseph J. Lannin, owner of the Boston Red Sox, informed the Providence club that he would send them a left-hander from the Red Sox to fill the void on their pitching staff left by the departure of Bailey. The pitcher that Lannin wanted to send to Providence was rookie left-hander Babe Ruth, who had only pitched in three games with the Red Sox since being purchased earlier in the year from the Baltimore club of the International League. However, in order for Ruth to be sent down to the minor leagues, he had to first clear waivers with the remaining 15 teams in the American and National leagues. Garry Herrmann was aware of Ruth's potential and threatened to claim him for the Reds. On August 13, American League president Ban Johnson wrote to Herrmann, informing him that there was no way that Lannin would release Ruth. The following day, Joe Lannin wrote to Herrmann, informing him that Ruth was to be protected. Lannin stated in his letter:

> I have been advised by Mr. Johnson's office that you held up Pitcher Ruth. I tried to get waivers on this man in order to send him to the Providence, International League club for the balance of the season, thus giving him a little experience and incidentally, help out the Providence club.

I have no idea of letting Ruth go, as he is a very good prospect, and the only reason I asked waivers on him is above explained. I have withdrawn Ruth for the present. May ask waivers on him again in a few days, as we are short of pitchers in Providence.[5]

As a result of further pressuring from Ban Johnson, Herrmann gave in and let Ruth pass on waivers. Lannin then wrote a thank you note to Herrmann, explaining more in detail his plans for Ruth. Still, one can only speculate about what the future of the Cincinnati Reds might have been had Garry Herrmann acquired Babe Ruth, and how much it might have enhanced Herrmann's place in baseball history. However, what history seems to have forgotten is the fact that the Reds could have had Babe Ruth before the season started, but the deal was killed by manager Buck Herzog. In early 1914, before the Baltimore club of the International League sold Ruth to the Boston Red Sox, he had been offered to the Cincinnati Reds along with another pitcher, Ernie Shore, for the purchase price of $12,000. However, Buck Herzog wasn't interested in Babe Ruth. Instead, he wanted to buy shortstop Claud Derrick and outfielder George Twombly from Baltimore. While Garry Herrmann really wanted Babe Ruth, he acquiesced to the wishes of Herzog and paid $15,000 for Derrick and Twombly. By mid-season 1914, Derrick was traded to the Cubs and Twombly wound up hitting .233 in 68 games for the Reds. Derrick would conclude his five-year major league career in 1914. Twombly, after playing one game for Washington in 1919, would finish his brief career with a lifetime batting average of .247 for 417 at-bats.

The New York Giants had won the last three National League pennants (1911–1913) and were once again the pre-season favorites to the win the pennant in 1914. As the season started, the Pittsburgh Pirates took the lead, then the Reds began an early-season move, but soon faded. By June 1, with Christy Mathewson and Jeff Tesreau absolutely dominating on the mound, the Giants had moved into first place and looked like they were on their way to a 4th straight National League pennant. However, a funny thing happened on the way to the World Series in 1914. The Boston Braves, who had finished in fifth place in the 1913 season, 31½ games behind the Giants, won the pennant. The chronicle of the "the Miracle Boston Braves of 1914" is one of the most amazing pennant stories in major league baseball history. The 1914 Boston Braves' roster was made up of mostly mediocre ballplayers, although two were future Hall of Fame members, second baseman Johnny Evers and shortstop Rabbit Maranville. Also, the catcher was Hank Gowdy, a player that should be enshrined in the Hall of Fame but is not. As the 1914 season got underway, the Braves quickly took up residence in the National League cellar, and after 22 games, their record stood at 4–18. On the Fourth of July, the Braves were still in last place with a record of 33–43, 15 games behind the league-leading Giants. However, at the time, no one had really noticed that in their last 44 games, the Braves had played .500 ball. The Braves were in fact beginning their move to the top.

In early July, the Braves won nine out of 12 games and on July 19 climbed out of the cellar. Then the Braves strung together a nine-game winning streak that included four shutouts in the five games they won at Pittsburgh and a sweep of a three-game series with the Giants. By August 14, the Braves had passed the Cubs into second place, and on August 23, they were in a tie for first place with the Giants. The Giants were having trouble. Giants pitching ace Christy Mathewson lost five out of six games in early August, including two to Buck Herzog and the sixth-place Reds in games played at the Polo Grounds. In early August, Mathewson's record was 18–4; however, by August 22 his record was 19–9. Also, Chief Meyers, Fred Merkle and Larry Doyle all were in a slump at the plate and Bob Bescher wasn't stealing bases. John McGraw went wild! He berated his players, challenged umpires on every close play and cussed at fans.

But the Boston Braves just kept coming on. Then as now, fans loved an underdog and the entire country was captivated by the rush of the Boston Braves as they kept winning and putting the pressure on the New York Giants. Fans all over the league turned out to see them, and in Boston, even Red Sox fans were rooting for the Braves. On September 8 after winning two out of three from the Giants, the Braves occupied first place alone. The next day at Philadelphia, Braves pitcher George Davis, who would win only seven games in his major league career, threw a no-hitter, defeating Grover Cleveland Alexander and the Phillies, 7–0. From that point it was a sprint for the Braves to the finish line, coming in 10½ games ahead of the Giants to win the pennant. Following their collapse in the 1914 season, the Giants played a lethargic post-season series against the Yankees. Disappointment among the Giants was pervasive. During the series, the Giants players often walked to their positions on the field with their heads bent down and eyes on the ground. This prompted one onlooker to remark, "What are you bums looking for? The pennant?"[6]

In the American League, the defending world champion Philadelphia Athletics won the pennant while the franchise took a bath, losing $60,000. If the baseball world had not been stunned sufficiently by the Miracle Braves' National League pennant, then it would get the necessary injection when the Braves met the Athletics in the World Series. Led by the heavy hitting of Hank Gowdy (.545) and Johnny Evers (.438), along with the brilliant pitching of a couple of average hurlers who would rise to the occasion in Dick Rudolph (2–0, 0.50 ERA) and Bill James (2–0, 0.00 ERA), the Braves swept the powerful Athletics four games to none in the 1914 World Series. Prior to the World Series, Braves manager George Stallings told sportswriter Grantland Rice that he expected his team to win the series in five games. When Rice asked him why, Stallings replied, "We are coming, and they are going."[7] In fact, Stallings' remarks were prophetic. Following the 1914 World Series, Connie Mack dismantled the Philadelphia Athletics, selling Eddie Collins to the Chicago White Sox for $50,000 and Frank "Home Run" Baker to the New York Yankees and trading Wally Schang, Amos Strunk and Joe Bush to the Boston Red Sox, while Eddie Plank and Chief Bender jumped to the Federal League. As a result, the decimated Athletics would go from first place in the American League in 1914 to last place in the 1915 season, winning only 43 games, less than half the number they had won (99) in 1914.

Although much of the baseball world was following the charge of the Braves in 1914, the Federal League had staged quite a pennant race, too. The entire 154-game schedule was played to conclusion without a single franchise shift. In the end Indianapolis won the pennant, getting by Chicago by just 1½ games, and there was only a seven-game separation between first-place Indianapolis and the fourth-place Buffalo club. Still, James A. Gilmore wasn't satisfied that his league had successfully completed its first season as a major league; he wanted all-out warfare with major league baseball. The Feds had wanted a club in New York in 1914 and even offered John McGraw a five-year, $250,000 contract to manage the club. McGraw declined and in the future often boasted that he was the one that had saved organized baseball in 1914 by declining the Feds' offer. To give the Federal League a near–New York presence for the 1915 season, the Indianapolis club was moved to Newark and oil magnate Harry Sinclair, who cared little for baseball and was in the game for profit only, took over as its president.

XVIII

Feds Fold and the Sisler Decision

The National League meeting at the Waldorf in December 1914 was a yawner. Newspaper reporters covering the meetings were hoping for stories of great alarm from the magnates over the Federal League, but hardly an eyelid was lifted. Barney Dreyfuss, owner of the Pirates, like most of his colleagues felt organized baseball had the moral high ground in the war with the Feds and that soon the public would see just how shady the dealings of the outlaw league had been. The National League meetings were so laid-back that even Garry Herrmann and Charles Ebbets were on friendly terms with each other again. Somehow the matter of the contested $15,000 in the Joe Tinker deal had gone away and no one really knew where. Herrmann and Ebbets both stated that an amicable settlement had been reached in the matter and that there were no details to announce. There were no big trades made and it was doubtful that Garry Herrmann could have made any, for even the Feds weren't expressing any interest in his ballplayers.

The biggest baseball news coming out of New York involved a Cincinnati politician, and it wasn't Garry Herrmann, but rather his cohort, Rud Hynicka. Rumors began to fly that Hynicka was trying to buy the New York Yankees. However, it soon was discovered that Hynicka was actually negotiating on the behalf of Jacob Ruppert and Captain Tillinghast L'Hommedieu Huston to buy the Yankees. Ruppert and Huston had wanted to buy a ballclub for some time. Both were multi-millionaires, with Ruppert making his money as a real estate financier and brewer of beer, while Huston, a retired army engineer, had made a fortune in public works in Cuba. Also, both Ruppert and Huston were close friends of John McGraw and huge Giants fans. When John T. Brush died, Ruppert and Huston had asked McGraw to inquire if it would be possible for them to buy the Giants. After speaking with Brush's widow, McGraw informed them that Brush heirs wanted to keep the ballclub in the family.

However, McGraw was aware of the fact that Yankees owners Frank Farrell and William S. Devery wanted out of baseball. The two were constantly arguing with each other and frustrated by the team's inability to win the American League pennant. McGraw informed Ruppert and Huston that they could buy the Yankees. At first, neither Ruppert nor Huston was interested in the Yankees, but McGraw convinced them that the ballclub could be a great opportunity for them. Jacob Ruppert, as did John McGraw, socialized among the New York theatre set. As the health of George B. Cox was declining, Rud Hynicka had been purchasing more and more control of the Cox theatre interests in New York and spending more time there. Hynicka already knew Huston, who had been a contractor in Cincinnati before departing for Cuba. Also through his theatre holdings, Hynicka had made the acquaintance of Ruppert. Hynicka also knew that American League president Ban Johnson intensely disliked John McGraw. So Hynicka was the natural go-between. Subsequently, Hynicka negotiated the purchase of the Yankees from Farrell and Devery on behalf of Ruppert and Huston. The negotiations started out with Farrell and Devery wanting $500,000 for the ballclub and Ruppert and Huston willing to part with $450,000. The negotiations would drag on through late February before the deal was done for $480,000. Over time Ruppert and Huston would realize a return on their outlay to acquire the Yankees by tens of millions of dollars.

The eyebrow-raising circumstances of the Ruppert-Huston purchase of the Yankees was that it clearly demonstrated how shaky the ground was for the Federal League. For a half-million dollars, Ruppert and Huston had purchased a perennial second-division American League team without any bona fide star players, that had no modern physical plant to play in, and that also was up against the New York Giants, the most popular franchise in the game for fan support. The two could have bought the Federal League's Kansas City franchise for a mere $50,000. Not only were Ruppert and Huston not interested in the Kansas City club, the club had also been peddled to people in Cleveland, Detroit and Toronto with no takers.

On January 9, 1915, the National Commission voted 2 to 1 to make George Sisler a free agent, with August Herrmann casting the deciding vote. At that time the commission's decision in the matter hardly got any attention in the press. However, the George Sisler decision would become a question mark on the legacy of August Garry Herrmann and weaken support for him as National Commission chairman. In 1910, Sisler, a high school pitcher, was signed by Akron of the Class C Ohio-Pennsylvania League. But rather than play professional baseball, he instead elected to enroll at the University of Michigan, where he was coached by Branch Rickey and had a brilliant college career. As a freshman in 1912, Sisler struck out 20 batters in seven innings. Meanwhile, while Sisler was attending college, the Akron team had sold his contract to Columbus of the American Association. In turn, Columbus sold Sisler's contract to Barney Dreyfuss, president of the Pittsburgh Pirates. With Sisler due to graduate in the spring of 1915, Dreyfuss was aware of Sisler's potential and laid claim to him before the National Commission.

When the commission heard the matter in January 1915, the result was a split decision, with John Tener saying Sisler belonged to the National League Pirates, while Ban Johnson sided with the American League Browns, who had now laid claim to him. The deciding vote was cast by Chairman Herrmann, who voted for Sisler to be awarded to the Browns. Upon graduation from college on June 10, 1915, Sisler signed with the St. Louis Browns, who were now being managed by his former college coach, Branch Rickey. Sisler then made his major league debut with the Browns, pitching in a game played on June 28, 1915.

Barney Dreyfuss felt like he had been cheated by the National Commission because of the close association of Herrmann and Johnson. The fact of the matter was that Herrmann and Johnson were good buddies and frequently enjoyed each other's company over cocktails, but whether or not that relationship influenced Herrmann's vote is conjecture. In rendering their decision to void the contract Sisler had signed with Akron, both Herrmann and Johnson reasoned that when Sisler signed the contract, he was a minor, therefore invalidating it.

Barney Dreyfuss, who had been a friend of Garry Herrmann's for nearly 15 years, never forgave him for the Sisler decision. Following the Sisler decision, Dreyfuss immediately began to criticize Herrmann and the National Commission, and started a campaign to replace both with a one-man chairman who had no interest in baseball. Branch Rickey would convert George Sisler from a pitcher to a first baseman and he would go on to become one of the greatest hitters in major league history, hitting over .400 twice and finishing a Hall of Fame career with 2,812 hits and .340 lifetime batting average in 15 big league seasons.

However, if there was a fix in the Sisler decision, it occurred long before the National Commission decision. What seems to have been historically ignored in the matter is that John E. Bruce, secretary of the National Commission, was a stockholder in the St. Louis Browns and had ties to the Cincinnati Republican Party machine. Future Mayor John Galvin was also a stockholder. If there was a hidden agenda driving the motivation of Garry Herrmann in casting his vote against awarding George Sisler to Barney Dreyfuss and the Pittsburgh Pirates, it is far more likely that the decision was a political one instead of the popular theory that he simply sided with his good drinking buddy Ban Johnson on the matter.

The American and National league owners had been filing numerous motions in various courts around the country to restrain players from jumping their contracts and signing with the Federal League. James A. Gilmore knew that he would need fresh talent from the established leagues to keep the Federal League competitive in 1915. So on January 5, 1915, Gilmore and Federal League owners filed suit in Federal court in Chicago under the Sherman Anti-Trust Act, seeking relief against the American and National leagues. The Federal League suit alleged, "that the National Agreement and the rules of the National Commission be declared illegal and the defendants enjoined from operating under them."[1] In short the Feds were asking the court to declare the National Commission null and void. They were alleging that the National Commission constituted a monopoly, with all but 300 professional players playing in the Federal League out of a total of 10,000 being controlled by the National Commission. Therefore, the Feds wanted all player contracts of the American and National leagues declared as bogus, while asking the court to dismiss all litigation by the commission against its players. In the suit the sixteen club presidents in the American and National league and the three members of the National Commission were named as defendants.

The case was to be heard in the United States District Court for Northern Illinois, presided over by judge Kenesaw M. Landis sitting in Chicago. In 1904, Landis, a practicing Chicago attorney, managed the Republican gubernatorial primary campaign of Progressive candidate Frank O. Lowden. Lowden would lose the nomination to Illinois state attorney Charles Samuel Deneen, who would serve as governor until 1913. However, Lowden would eventually be elected governor of Illinois and serve until 1921. Nonetheless, the efforts of Kenesaw Landis in the Lowden 1904 campaign attracted the attention of many in the GOP nationally, including President Roosevelt. As a result, in 1905, Roosevelt appointed Landis to a vacant seat on the United States District Court for the Northern District of Illinois.

In 1907, Landis would achieve national fame when he heard an anti-trust case against John D. Rockefeller and Standard Oil in his court. The trial lasted for six weeks and in the end Landis levied an unprecedented fine of $29,240,000 against Standard Oil. Although the United States Supreme Court would eventually overrule Landis and throw out the case, Landis had achieved a national reputation in the case as a flaming trust buster. Judge Landis had also been the jurist who had arraigned boxer Jack Jackson in 1912 on charges of violating the Mann Act (white slavery), in which he took an underage white woman across the state line for purposes of having sex with her. Later, in 1912, Johnson was convicted and sentenced to a year in jail. However, upon conviction, Johnson fled to Europe.

Landis was also a huge fan of the national game and regularly followed the Cubs and White Sox. The fact that the Federal League's case would be filed in the court of Landis was no fluke; it was a strategy planned by James A. Gilmore, Harry Sinclair and the other Federal League club owners. The hearing date set by Judge Landis was January 20. He then ordered summons to be issued against all the persons named in the suit and further ordered that they must answer to the Federal League petition before January 16. The fact that the hearing date was set only 15 days after the suit was filed suggested to many that a swift decision on the case was to be forthcoming from Judge Landis. Major league baseball knew that the war had now escalated and responded by hiring a team of expensive, high-powered attorneys to represent it. The National League hired George Wharton Pepper, who would later be elected to the United States Senate, from Pennsylvania to represent it, while the American League brought in George W. Miller, and the Federal League hired Edward E. Gates to represent its interest.

When the United States marshal delivered the court papers to Garry Herrmann, he had no trouble finding him. Herrmann was seated at his desk in his office in the Wiggins Block Building at Fifth and Vine streets in downtown Cincinnati. As Garry cordially greeted the marshal, it was almost as if he welcomed the Federal League suit. In fact, Herrmann was publicly stating that the suit by James A. Gilmore and the Feds was a last dying gasp for recognition from the outlaws. "The whole idea that Organized Ball is a trust, operated in violation of the Sherman law, and intended to crush all competition," remarked Herrmann, "has been all thrashed out before, and riddled again and again like a colander. The most ridiculous part of the whole Federal attack, perhaps, is the undisputed fact that the very things against which they complain have been solidly adopted by them and are now part and parcel of their own system — which will be easily shown at the trial."[2] All of the major league magnates were confident of victory over the Feds in court. Keeping with the order of Judge Landis that they must answer all the charges of the Federal League before January 16, the National Commission prepared a 47-page affidavit categorically denying the charges in the suit.

As proceedings got underway, Judge Landis stated, "Both sides must understand that any blows at the thing called baseball would be regarded by this court as a blow to a national institution."[3] That being said, Lee Magee (Leopold Hoernschmeyer), who had played for the St. Louis Cardinals in 1914, asked that he be included in the Federal League suit as a result of his being treated unfairly by the Cardinals, with whom his salary had only increased by $1,500 since coming up to the big leagues with St. Louis in 1911. When he tried to jump to the Federal League, he was restrained by a court order filed by the St. Louis club in the Cincinnati Circuit Court of judge Howard Hollister, a well-known reformer in the city. Subsequently, Judge Landis allowed Magee's case to join the big suit.

The contract circumstances of Lee Magee nearly brought him and Garry Herrmann to blows on Saturday evening, January 2. Magee, a native and off-season resident of Cincinnati, was socializing in a downtown cafe frequented by many of the city's politicians and baseball men. Magee was standing at the bar boasting that he was getting a big bonus by leaving the St. Louis Cardinals and signing with the Brooklyn Federals. Garry Herrmann was also standing at the bar along with a Hamilton County official, and became agitated by Magee's boasting. Then the county official drinking with Herrmann challenged Magee on the amount of money he would be getting by signing with the Brooklyn Feds. Magee proposed a $50 wager, stating that he could prove what his compensation would be. The county official accepted the wager, whereupon Magee reached into his suit jacket and produced his contract. All the witnesses to the wager broke out in thunderous laughter and Magee was immediately paid off by the county official. But Garry Herrmann was not amused by the antics of Magee and called him a contract-jumper. The remark infuriated Magee and friends of both had to jump in and separate Magee and Herrmann before fists started to fly.

Among the Federal League witnesses testifying before Landis and alleging that they had been abused by the National Agreement were Mordecai Brown, Joe Tinker and Otto Knabe. The Federal League lawyers used the case of Mordecai Brown as a centerpiece of their grievances against organized baseball. The Fed lawyers alleged that Brown was a victim of the monopoly. In particular it was stated that "he had been released by the Chicago Cubs to

Louisville and that part of the release agreement was a stipulation by Charles W. Murphy that Brown should never be allowed to play in the majors again — and in spite of that there was a clause in the agreement that if Brown should be sold or drafted, the Louisville Club was to pay a certain amount of money to the releasing Chicago Club."[4] However, the Brown situation was typical of incomplete arguments offered by the Federal League. How it could be stipulated that Brown should not be permitted to return to the majors and also be agreed that if he did return a bonus should be paid was something not explained by the Federal League attorneys. Furthermore, there was inconsistency in the Federal League testimony as on one hand they had painted Garry Herrmann as a tyrant and on the other neglected to mention that it had in fact been Herrmann who had rescued Mordecai Brown by bringing him back to the major leagues with the Cincinnati Reds.

After listening for four days to endless trivial testimony and legal babble from both sides, Judge Landis interrupted Federal League attorney Edward E. Gates, stating, "I have gone just about far enough in this case. The time has come when I should ask you gentleman just what you want me to do in issuing this injunction. Do you want me to stop the teams from going on spring training trips? Do you want me to break up the clubs or what do you want me to do?"[5]

Gates responded that it was never the intention of the plaintiffs to harm organized baseball. He stated that the sole purpose of their suit was to consolidate the litigation from all the other jurisdictions and bring them into federal court, and thereby prevent organized baseball from tying up Federal League players with injunction suits. On the other side, attorney George Wharton Pepper, representing the National League, stated that it was not the intention of the defendants to prevent the Federal League from finding and developing young players through a minor league system, as is done in with the National League. However, Pepper cautioned the Federal League wanted to accomplish and profit from in one year what the National League had done through ten years of labor. In short, the Federal League wanted to profit from the skill developed from the efforts and money of the National League owners. By the end of January, all the testimony had been heard and Judge Landis indicated that a decision would be forthcoming in the near future. Meanwhile, he announced that his delay was in the best interest of both parties. However, the baseball world would wait and wait and wait, and no decision would be announced by Landis.

There was fallout, however, in the aftermath of the Federal League anti-trust suit for Garry Herrmann. In their testimony the Federal League lawyers had painted a questionable picture of August Garry Herrmann, alleging that as a result of his being chairman of the National Commission, both he and his ballclub had personally benefited from the position. Regardless of the fact that it was difficult to determine how Herrmann had derived benefits from being chairman of the commission when his ballclub finished in last place in 1914, the issue raised by the Feds' lawyers seemed to stick. Also, at the time Herrmann was still suffering the adverse public relations effects throughout baseball from his public player transaction involving Joe Tinker and the subsequent troubles of being reprimanded on the deal by Julius Fleischmann and the Cincinnati Reds' Board of Directors. There were many who felt the actions of Herrmann in the Tinker deal demeaned the dignity of the position of National Commission chairman.

The Federal League suit had delayed the annual National Commission reorganization meeting usually held in early January. But now with Judge Landis calling an end to the testimony, a meeting of the commission was eminent and everyone was beginning to wonder whether or not Garry Herrmann would be voted out as chairman. Barney Dreyfuss was openly questioning Herrmann's ability to be fair in the wake of the George Sisler decision and Ban

Johnson was concerned. Although Johnson had known Herrmann since the 1890s when he was a sports reporter for the *Cincinnati Commercial Tribune*, he was all business and ready to sacrifice Herrmann for the good of major league baseball. Johnson was even suggesting that it would be in the best interest of the game to have someone as chairman of the commission who was in no way connected to baseball. For the previous few years, many throughout the baseball world were convinced that Ban Johnson was the actual head of the National Commission and called the shots, not Herrmann. So when Johnson began to openly suggest that a new chairman was needed, it was thought universally to be a done deal. The wild card in the scenario was just how National League president John K. Tener would vote should Herrmann's job be on the line.

In February, with the Feds' anti-trust suit in the hands of Judge Landis, the National Commission met in Cincinnati, and to everyone's surprise, Garry Herrmann was re-elected as chairman and John E. Bruce as secretary. Bruce was also serving the interest of the Republican machine in Cincinnati as a member of the Board of Park Commissioners. At the conclusion of the meeting, Herrmann issued the following statement to the press: "While we decided to reorganize, we likewise decided not to make any move for any of the players that are likely to be involved in any decisions that the court might make in Chicago."[6] While Herrmann, Johnson and Tener had felt it best to wait on the decision of Judge Landis in the Federal League suit before doing anything radical, there were many inside major league baseball, including Barney Dreyfuss and even Johnson and Tener, questioning if the National Commission was a useful entity any longer. Sources were stating that Johnson and Tener were of the opinion that the National Commission had outlived its usefulness and was becoming a financial burden to the two leagues. The fact of the matter was that the commission was processing volumes of activity each year, and in 1914 Chairman Herrmann had sent out 11,000 letters, telegrams and confidential communications while handing down decisions on 1,980 disputed baseball cases. While it would be another five years before the National Commission would be dissolved, the process had begun and Garry Herrmann would find himself on a slippery slope.

The Federal League had hurt organized baseball's bottom line in 1914, and as the 1915 season approached, there was talk among the magnates of how to keep the big fish from eating the small fish. No other entity in organized baseball had suffered more from the appearance of the Federal League than the minor leagues. Now Ban Johnson wanted to close many minor league parks. However, both Charles Comiskey and Garry Herrmann were ready to cross swords with Ban over this issue. While some minor leagues had already folded, Comiskey called closing down minor league teams a bad policy. He felt that all that some of them needed to do in order to maintain solvency was to overhaul their operations and cut some salaries to make salary levels consistent with gate receipts. If a club could not support $1,000 player contracts, cut back to $800 or $700 salaries in order to keep the gates open. Ban Johnson also felt that the major league teams could cut their costs by shortening the spring training season and cutting down or eliminating altogether spring training exhibition trips. While Comiskey was opposed to both of Johnson's suggestions, Garry Herrmann supported shortening the spring training season. Comiskey pointed out that the White Sox for several years had held spring training in California where the weather was beautiful, attendance at games was substantial, and the team had even made a profit from its spring training trips.

In March 1915, the National Commission released its 11th annual report in which it blamed sagging attendance in organized baseball on the Federal League and the war in Europe. In the report chairman Garry Herrmann summarized the 1914 season as follows: "The Federal League's aggressive activity in enticing players from the National Agreement clubs, to which they are under contract, loss of public confidence in the integrity of those who play the game because of these desertions, and the industrial and commercial complications which followed the European War, affected the patronage in practically all National and American League cities." Still, Garry Herrmann knew there was more to the puzzle of dwindling attendance in organized baseball and included the following qualifier to his remarks by stating, "This country-wide condition cannot be satisfactorily explained solely by the existence of an opposing organization, which employs questionable tactics in its futile efforts to sap the strength of the major and minor leagues to equip its teams with first class talent.[7]

The financial report given by secretary-treasurer John E. Bruce showed that the National Commission had only a slim war chest with which to continue to fight the war with the Feds. In 1914 the National Commission had receipts of $69,664.15, with its largest chunk of $15,000 coming from its share of the World Series receipts, and disbursements of $68, 270.15. The report stated that the commission had given financial assistance to the International League in 1914, with loans of $8,000 and $2,500. In addition, the report showed a refund for $3,218.65 to the Buffalo club had been authorized by Ban Johnson. The current balance of cash on hand was just $1,486.07. By comparison, on January 1, 1914 the bank balance of the National Commission had been $27,709.03 and at the same date in 1913 the balance was $46,906.70.

While a large chunk of the expenses of the National Commission were for salaries to its members, the war with the Federal League was causing the commission to dig deep in its pockets, and attorney fees were eating at the bottom line. While the commission's attorney fees for its defense against the Feds' anti-trust suit were not in the report because of the cutoff date of January 1, 1915, still for the year 1914 the report listed 22 separate items related to attorney's fees. Almost all of these were paid to Ellis Kinkead and John Galvin, the two Cincinnati attorneys who acted as counsel for the National Commission. John Galvin was a former associate of Senator Joseph B. Foraker and who as vice mayor had served out the remaining mayoral term of Leopold Markbreit following his death in 1909. Galvin, a Cincinnati Republican Party cohort of both Garry Herrmann and Rud Hynicka, would in a few years be elected mayor of Cincinnati.

As long as the war with the Federal League continued, it was a great opportunity for attorneys and ballplayers to fatten up their savings accounts. What the National Commission's financial report did not show was the enormous amount of money being spent by the individual clubs in both the American and National leagues defending their rights in court to ballplayers who had signed contracts with Federal League teams. Also, the elevated salaries for player contracts necessitated by the competition from the Federal League was draining the clubs' treasuries. If the war was a financial drain on the National and American league clubs, the Federal League clubs had the same expenses; it was a case of waiting to see who would collapse first. In fact, Federal League clubs were in such dire straights for revenue that they cut the cost of their bleacher seats to ten cents.

Federal League clubs were also paying the salaries of non-active players on their rosters who were being challenged in court. Such was the case with Armando Marsans, who had jumped the Cincinnati Reds for the St. Louis Feds. On June 22, 1914, a federal court issued an injunction against Marsans from playing in the Federal League. As a result, a year later the St. Louis Feds were still paying Marsans' $7,000 annual salary while attempting to get the injunction lifted. In late June 1915, judge Kenesaw Mountain Landis, now hearing the case of the Feds refused to permit Marsans to play and the injunction continued.

As the war with the Feds seemed to be reaching some sort of a conclusion in early 1915, the war in Europe was escalating. On February 4, Germany announced that it intended to use its U-boats for a blockade of Great Britain. In the United States, the German blockade brought a warning from President Wilson that any attack on U.S. ships by Germany would be considered a breach of neutrality. Then on May 7, the British liner *Lusitania* was sunk by a German U-boat off the Irish coast causing the loss of 1,198 lives, including 128 Americans. The *Lusitania* was the ship that only months before had brought John McGraw and the touring Giants and White Sox back to America from Europe.

Nonetheless, most activities of America in 1915 were still about business as usual. During the off-season in the winter of 1914–1915, manger Buck Herzog had scouted for new players and was doing all he could to make the Cincinnati Reds a competitive club. However, by August the Cincinnati Reds were once again out of the National League pennant race. By September, the Reds would be fighting off the New York Giants to keep out of the cellar as their ace, Christy Mathewson, was having the worst season of his career. There was also a lot of friction between Buck Herzog and his players, and sometimes Garry Herrmann, too. The Reds' players were complaining to Herrmann that they didn't like Herzog. They told Herrmann that Herzog was impartial, aloof and didn't hang out with them. Heinie Groh said that Herzog was so out of touch with his players that when they were on the road, he stayed in a different hotel than the team. Garry Herrmann would only say that Herzog was under contract to manage and play shortstop for the Reds in both 1915 and 1916. There was, however, a ray of hope among the Reds' pitchers in Fred Toney, who would finish the dismal 1915 campaign with a record of 15–6 and an ERA of 1.58.

While attendance at Redland Field was much improved in the 1915 season, the club was still hemorrhaging dollars and overall in financial dire straights due to the war with the Feds. The Reds tried to cut some costs. Rube Benton, ineffective and in manager Herzog's doghouse, was sold for $3,000 to the New York Giants, who needed pitching with Christy Mathewson having a bad year. With Ivy Wingo, who Garry Herrmann had plucked off a Federal League roster, doing most of the catching, the club took waivers on Charles Dooin, sending him to the Giants, thereby ridding the club of his $6,000 salary and ending the rumors that Dooin would replace Herzog as manager.

Then rumors began to fly all over the city that the Reds were going to be sold and that Garry Herrmann had authorized a friend by the name of Charles E. Bultman to negotiate the deal. The buyer being mentioned was a Pasadena, California, resident by the name of Warren M. Carter. When the press asked Garry Herrmann about the possible sale of the club to Carter, he stated, "When Warren M. Carter of Pasadena, California, was in the city not long ago, he asked me if I thought he could purchase some of the stock in the Cincinnati Club. I told him that I would consider the matter and confer with some of the stockholders and let him know later. At a subsequent meeting I told him it could be arranged, and he then asked me if I thought he could obtain controlling interest in the club, and I told him he could if he was willing to pay the price asked. He said he would like to consider it for two weeks or a month and it will be a month next Tuesday since the conversation took place."[8] Herrmann said that there was a figure mentioned and that if Carter purchased the club, it would mean a handsome profit for those who sold their stock and a good deal for those that did not. He also stated that there were three conditions for the sale. The first was that the club had to remain in Cincinnati, and second, assurance had to be made that the club would not wind up in the Federal League. Third, he had to remain as the head of the club.

Feds president James Gilmore quickly let it be known that his league considered Cincinnati a disaster area and that there was no interest whatsoever in obtaining the Reds. Still, there had been rumors in June that controlling stock in the Reds had been offered to Federal League Chicago Whales owner Charles Weeghman for $250,000. Weeghman said that Reds spokesman Charles Bultman had even showed him certificates amounting to 51 percent of the Reds' stock, but that he declined the offer. When Garry Herrmann was pressed for answers to the Reds' future, he dodged the questions about Bultman's authorization to sell the majority stock in the club and stated that as long as the current owners were in control of the Reds, they would play no place other than Cincinnati. Eventually, the 30-day option of Warren Carter to purchase majority ownership in the Reds passed and it was back to business as usual in the Reds' front office. But the rumors of Reds stock being up for sale would persist right through the rest of the season. In the fall, a rumor around the league was that Harry Ackerland was going to sell his 10 percent interest in the Cubs and buy Garry Herrmann's 10 percent interest in the Reds, then replace him as president of the Cincinnati club. When the press asked Herrmann about the Ackerland rumor, all he had to say was, "It's nonsense."[9]

The 1915 Philadelphia Phillies played in the Baker Bowl, one of the most rundown of National League parks. Sheep instead of groundskeepers were used to trim the grass at Baker Bowl and in center field there laid a noticeable hump. Under the hump ran a tunnel that carried trains of the Philadelphia and Reading Railroad. In right field was a tin-covered 40-foot-high fence that was all of 272 feet from home plate. Despite these facility disadvantages, the 1915 Philadelphia Phillies, under new manager Pat Moran, stormed out of the gate and won their first eight games. They hung on to first place as the Chicago Cubs challenged them until June, then fought off the Boston Braves as Phillies ace Grover Cleveland Alexander finished the 1915 season with a record of 31–10, including 12 shutouts and four one-hitters. Alexander also struck out 241 batters in 376 innings while compiling a stingy ERA of 1.22. Also, the Phillies featured National League home run king Gavvy Cravath, who set a new modern record with 24 home runs while driving in 115 runs and batting .285. However, the Phillies would be defeated by the Boston Red Sox in the 1915 World Series, 4 games to 1.

In April at Chicago's Weegham Park, mayor William Hale "Big Bill" Thompson threw out the first ball and the Chicago Whales took the field and the Federal League began its second season. Once again the Feds' pennant race was a squeaker as Chicago edged St. Louis by percentage points, .566 to .565. Furthermore, the third-place Pittsburgh club finished just one-half game behind. The Feds then sent out a challenge to organized baseball to have Joe Tinker's pennant-winning Chicago Whales play a series against the World Series champion Boston Red Sox. But the American and National league magnates ignored it. The Federal League had failed to convince the biggest stars in the American and National league to jump their contracts and now no one in organized ball was going to take a chance on validating the struggling Federal League's fragile talent.

Furthermore, in October when Brooklyn club owner Robert B. Ward died, the organized baseball magnates knew they had the Feds on the run. It was widely reported that Ward had pumped more than a million dollars into his Federal League franchise and hardly got a dime in return. Notwithstanding multi-millionaire oil man Harry Sinclair, it was doubtful if many of the other club backers had such a war chest to be squandered on saving the league. Nonetheless, the Feds began making plans for a third season. Sinclair announced plans to move his Newark club to New York. He hired an architect and drew up plans for a new ballpark in Queens.

In the fall of 1915, Mayor Spiegel declined to run for re-election in Cincinnati and the Republicans nominated 55-year-old George Puchta, president of the Queen City Supply Company. Puchta was another Cincinnatian of German heritage described as a self-made businessman not beholden to the machine. With Puchta at the head of the ticket, the Republicans won by a landslide. Puchta outdistanced Democrat Charles Sawyer by a total of 57,394 votes to 35,144. In fact, Sawyer only carried but one precinct. Also, the Republicans elected 31 out of 32 candidates for city council, including incumbent councilman Mike Mullen in the Eighth

Chicago mayor William Hale Thompson, Opening Day at Weeghman Park, Chicago, April 1915. Chicago History Museum.

Ward. At the Blaine Club, it resembled the grand old times of the Cox years with a crowd of about 10,000 waiting outside. Inside, Garry Herrmann, Judge Lueders, John Galvin and other standard-bearers of the old guard were on hand to count the votes. It was the biggest Republican victory in the municipal election since 1903, when Julius Fleischmann had defeated M .E. Ingalls by 16,000 votes.

As the year 1915 came to a close, Judge Landis still had not handed down a decision in the Federal League lawsuit. It was being reported that the Federal League had lost between three and five million dollars during its two seasons of existence and was interested in finding a way to end the baseball war. Something was definitely up. The National League had been the circuit hardest hit by the Federal League, and its attendance figures for all franchises but the New York Giants were down. The National League magnates had been negotiating with the Feds and thought they had a possible agreement to end the war. They dispatched Barney Dreyfuss to the annual American League meeting in Chicago to speak with Ban Johnson about the peace pact. However, Johnson was cool to the idea. He was of the opinion that soon the United States would be entering the war in Europe and that it would be the death knell of the Feds.

But in December at the National League meeting in New York, strange bedfellows seemed to be keeping company as peace talks were underway. Arriving from Chicago were American League president Ban Johnson and White Sox owner Charles Comiskey. Then Joseph Lannin came down from Boston and Ben Minor came up from Washington and were joined by New York Yankees co-owner Colonel Jacob Ruppert. At the Waldorf-Astoria Hotel, Barney Dreyfuss explained to the press why it had been necessary to silence the peace talk with the Feds. Meanwhile, Garry Herrmann was fraternizing in the hotel lobby with Harry Sinclair before John McGraw took him around and began introducing him to everyone. At the same time, James Gilmore, captain Tillinghast Huston of the Yankees and St. Louis Browns part-owner and National Commission secretary John E. Bruce were hanging out together in the cafe. In other areas of the Waldorf, a group of baseball writers were roasting National League president John Tener.

However, the Waldorf peace negotiations were threatened with a meltdown when Federal League owners insisted that the American and National league clubs should assume the contracts of all the Federal League players, which amounted to a tidy sum of $385,000. But when Charles Comiskey threatened to leave for Chicago and Jacob Ruppert indicated he would walk, too, the issue was withdrawn by the Feds. The reality of the situation was that peace was at hand. In between the meetings, Garry Herrmann had even bought pitcher Earl Victor Mosely from Harry Sinclair's Newark club for $5,000. The fact that Herrmann had been the first one to buy a contract jumper hardly raised an eyebrow. Mosely, a spitball pitcher, had pitched in the American League for the Boston Red Sox in 1914 before jumping to the Feds' Indianapolis club the same year.

A few days later on Tuesday, December 21, the baseball peace talks moved to Cincinnati where magnates from the Federal, American and National leagues gathered at the Sinton Hotel. There was a persona of cockiness among the Federal magnates as they arrived to sign the peace agreement. The reality was that these amateur sportsman and profiteers had almost derailed the national game. Now they were gathered with organized ball in an attempt to recoup their losses. Cincinnati fans were curious about all the hoopla and gathered at Fourth and Vine streets like groupies following rock stars to view the magnates as they entered the Sinton in a sort of a red carpet ceremony. The Federal League magnates didn't disappoint the onlookers, either. Charles Weeghman arrived at the Sinton dressed like an Ivy League college boy and carrying a cane. There was a certain swagger about Harry Sinclair, too, as he stepped through the doorway of the hotel with his derby hat tilted down over his right eye.

Meanwhile, in the Sinton lobby Harry Hempstead was surrounded by the press as he denied that the New York Giants were trying to sign Benny Kauff. Prior to the meeting, Garry Herrmann and Ban Johnson held a lengthy conference in Johnson's room, which was followed by two sessions with the magnates over a period of eight hours. The word on the street was that all the peace negotiations had really taken place the previous week at the Waldorf-Astoria in New York and that the Cincinnati meeting was simply for the purpose of ratifying the agreement that would allow for the disbandment of the Federal League and the purchase of two of the existing clubs in organized baseball by Federal League magnates. In fact, there had been an agreement drawn up by Judge George H. Williams, a St. Louis attorney on behalf of the American League, John M. Galvin, the Cincinnati attorney and politician for the National League, and S. L. Swarts, a St. Louis attorney for the Federal League.

On the morning of December 23, 1915, it was reported in the *Cincinnati Post* that the peace pact between the Feds and organized baseball had been signed. Signing for organized baseball were Garry Herrmann, chairman of the National Commission, Ban Johnson, president the American League, and John K. Tener, president the National League. For the Federal League, Jim Gilmore, president, Charley Weeghman of the Chicago club and Harry

Sinclair of Newark club signed. Also signing were International League officials J. H. Farrell, secretary, and Edward Barrow, president. For the American Association, Thomas Covington, president, inked the deal.

In the terms of the agreement, Charley Weeghman was permitted to buy the Chicago Cubs from Charles P. Taft and merge them with his Chicago Whales. Weeghman would be permitted to move the club to his new ballpark on Chicago's north side, which would eventually become Wrigley Field. Also, Phil Ball, owner of the St. Louis Federal League franchise, was permitted to buy the Browns from John Glavin and his partners and then play the club in Sportsman's Park. Both Weeghman and Ball would retain full control of players' contracts on both of the merged teams in Chicago and St. Louis. The children of deceased Feds Brooklyn club president Robert B. Ward were to receive 20 annual payments of $20,000, Harry Sinclair ten annual payments of $10,000 for his Newark club, and Ed Gwinner, the Pittsburgh owner, was given five annual payments of $10,000. In addition, since Harry Sinclair had assumed financial responsibility for about 80 player contracts in the Federal League as speculation, he would be permitted to sell his Newark players to the highest bidder, including those who had jumped contracts with organized ball teams. Sinclair, acting as sort of a ballplayer broker, was also given the sales rights to all players with binding contracts on the Feds' Buffalo and Kansas City clubs. All other Federal League clubs would be responsible for disposing of their players to any club in organized ball. Lastly, organized ball would have control of the Federal League ballparks in Newark, Buffalo and Pittsburgh to dispose of as they saw fit.

In return, much to the chagrin of "Fighting Jim" Gilmore, the Federal League officials agreed to drop all their lawsuits against organized baseball, including about a dozen cases of injunctions against players and the clubs that had been deprived of their services due to the suits. However, there was still a few bones of contention to be worked out, including one involving the Buffalo and Baltimore franchises in the International League. The Feds had sought to have the Buffalo and Baltimore clubs merged with the existing International League clubs in those cities; however, league president Ed Barrow was opposed. The biggest unanswered question in the peace agreement was what impact the merger of the National and Federal league clubs in Chicago and the merger of the American League St. Louis club with the Feds' St. Louis club would have on the outcome of the 1916 pennant race. Also, the National Commission had imposed player limits on clubs in organized ball, and now with the mergers, the Cubs and Browns would have 50 players under contract and have until 1917 to dispose of the surplus contracts. However, Garry Herrmann was confident that accord could be reached in these matters, and it was put into the agreement that a committee would be appointed to resolve the issue the first week of January.

1916 — Grief and Turmoil for Herrmann

Although the Federal League war was over, other matters threatened to upset the tranquility of organized ball. The most serious threat was coming from Barney Dreyfuss. The Pirates' mogul was still smarting over Garry Herrmann's deciding vote in the George Sisler matter and was determined to force change in the administrative structure of the National Commission. At the National League meeting in December 1915, Dreyfuss had introduced a resolution to replace the three-man National Commission with a one-man neutral chairman with no financial ties to baseball. However, Herrmann was still well-liked by most of the National League owners and the resolution did not carry. For now Herrmann had survived, but had the matter of the peace negotiations with the Feds not been the paramount issue on the agenda of the National Commission, it is possible that Herrmann's tenure as chairman may have come to an abrupt end at that time.

Still, as the new year of 1916 arrived, rumors of the dissolution of the National Commission persisted. Even Ban Johnson was supporting scrapping the National Commission and going through a reorganization that would still embrace the fundamental rules and regulations that had been established by the commission. However, it was more of a smoke screen. Johnson was getting pressure from some of the militant American League magnates who were waving the bloody shirt over the war with the Feds. A contingent of American League owners had wanted to see the Federal League franchises and owners not blossom, but rot on the vine. Furthermore, some of the American League owners were of the opinion that Garry Herrmann had been too chummy with the Federal League club owners and his fraternization bothered them to the extent that they felt it was best for Herrmann to be replaced. It was a fact that the ever-sociable Garry Herrmann liked Charley Weeghman, and it was also a fact that for almost a year before the Feds' peace pact was negotiated, Herrmann had been hobnobbing with Harry Sinclair and few other Fed circuit club owners as well. Also, the legal bills run up by the Federal League war had cost the National Commission over $400,000, and some mogul's wanted to make Garry Herrmann the fall guy.

Meanwhile in Cincinnati, Herrmann had to deal with the constant rumors that the Reds were being sold; the phone was constantly ringing at his office for confirmation. To dispel the rumors it was being reported that Herrmann was considering sending out New Year's cards with the inscription "From the Unsold Reds?"[1] The *Sporting News* was reporting that everyone and their little brother were being rumored as buyers of the Reds. Herrmann, tongue in cheek, was even telling people that he had received an offer to buy the ballclub from a syndicate comprised of General Joffre, Marshall von Hindenburg and Eva Tanguay. But at the moment, the fact of the matter was that the principle stockholders of the club remained Julius and Max Fleischmann and Garry Herrmann. George B. Cox had been one of the original investors in the Cincinnati Reds when the Fleischmann brothers and Herrmann bought the club from John T. Brush. However, Cox liked to make a profit and the Reds were continually losing money, so he sold out.

But as the year began, the sale of the Reds wasn't the only big league scuttlebutt. In the East rumors were circulating that Boston Braves owners James E. Gaffney and Robert Davis would sell their stock and join Harry Sinclair in buying the New York Giants from Harry Hempstead and the heirs of John T. Brush. The Boston Braves were for sale and purchased by Percy Haughton from Gaffney and Davis. Haughton was a very popular figure in Boston and had played second base for the Harvard varsity at the turn of the century. Immediately after taking control, he began exercising his authority as the 7th president of the Boston Nationals by issuing an edict to his players that there would be no basketball playing during the off-season. Haughton didn't want injuries resulting from basketball and sent a personal letter to his star player, Rabbit Maranville, informing him to forgo playing any games. Recently, Maranville had announced that he intended to join a team that included several players from the Red Sox, Nationals, and Yankees.

The first week in January 1916, Harry Sinclair and the former Federal League owners and the National Commission began to arrive in Cincinnati to finalize the peace proposal. On Wednesday, January 5, the delegations sat down and baseball history was made. The first order of business, however, for the commission was to elect its officers for the year. Although the rumors were still rampant that Garry Herrmann would be replaced, no other names were brought forward, and expeditiously, Herrmann was re-elected chairman, John E. Bruce, secretary, and Joseph Flanner, assistant secretary. One of the first items on the agenda was the approval for Charles P. Taft to sell his 90 percent interest in the Chicago Cubs to Charles Weeghman for $500,000. The remaining 10 percent of the Cubs' stock was retained by Harry Ackerland. Immediately, Weeghman stated that the Cubs would be moved to his Federal League ballpark on the North side and that Joe Tinker would be the club's manager. The sale of the St. Louis Browns to Phil Ball and the owners of the former St. Louis Federal League club had already been approved. C. J. McDiarmid of Cincinnati, one of the owners of the Browns, is reported to have gained control of the Browns before the peace proposal was negotiated and as a result made a tidy profit of $100,000 on the sale of the club.

However, there was no resolution by the commission to resolve the flap between the International and Federal League Buffalo and Baltimore clubs. Part of the problem was that Ed Barrow, president of the International League, was suddenly stricken with an appendicitis attack and returned home to have surgery. So the matter was to be tabled again at a later session. But as Barrow recovered, he was telling everyone that the peace committee had already blown the job and he planned to go on with business as usual in Buffalo, Baltimore and Newark during the 1916 season. According to Barrow, if the Feds didn't like it, they could yell plaintively.

On Saturday, February 5, organized ball and the Federal League attorneys representing every club in the circuit but Baltimore appeared in the United States District Court of Judge Kenesaw Mountain Landis in Chicago. Together, they made a motion for dismissal of the suit. It was plainly stated to Landis that the Baltimore club did not agree with the motion. Landis then stated that he felt it was in the best interest of the matter to postpone a ruling until Monday. Landis further stated that, in the meantime, the Baltimore officials should be notified by telegraph to appear in court on Monday.

On Monday, February 7, the dismissal hearing resumed with an attorney for the Feds'

Baltimore club present. The motion to withdrawal the suit was made by attorney S. L. Schwartz of St. Louis, representing the Federal League. Subsequently, attorneys representing organized ball, Harry P. Webber and George W. Miller, concurred with the motion for withdrawal. After notices from all the defendants in the suit consenting to the withdrawal were presented to Judge Landis by Attorney Webber, attorney Stuart S. Janney, representing Baltimore, made his appearance in the case but offered no objection to the dismissal. It was done, and Judge Landis dismissed the suit, stating:

> The motion for a preliminary injunction in this suit was presented to this court a little more than a year ago. The whole structure of Organized Baseball was immediately plunged into litigation. Aside from the interest of baseball fans there were two sides to the controversy: Organized Baseball and so-called outlaw baseball. There was a very full argument on every point involved presented to the court, and the problems appeared simple from a legal point of view. The court's expert knowledge of baseball obtained by more than 30 years of observation of the game as a spectator convinced me that if an order had been entered it would have been, if not destructive, at least vitally injurious to the game of baseball. No matter what decision had been made, neither side would have emerged from court victorious. After taking counsel with my own judgment, I decided that the court had the right, or at least the discretion to postpone decision in the case, and this was done.[2]

Later Landis was less candid in his remarks about the dismissal of the suit, stating that he hoped that the game would be free from would-be wreckers. The dismissal of the lawsuit had made Judge Kenesaw Mountain Landis, notwithstanding the feelings of Ban Johnson, a hero to the baseball world. The *Sporting News* in its February 10, 1916, edition called Landis "a loyal friend to baseball."

Following the official proceedings in court, Attorney Janney, representing the Feds' Baltimore club, put Garry Herrmann on the hot seat. Janney stated that Herrmann, acting in an official capacity representing the National Commission, had promised the Baltimore club ample remuneration for any damage it might have incurred as a result of being left out of the peace pact. Furthermore, Janney indicated that unless some sort of settlement came forth, the Baltimore club might file a new suit against the Federal League officials and key defendants of organized baseball, among them August Garry Herrmann. All of this rhetoric would only make the relationship between Herrmann and the American League owners more tedious.

With the dismissal of the suit,

Hal Chase, 1916. Author's collection.

Garry Herrmann and all the other National League magnates gleefully attended a big banquet on Wednesday evening, February 9, at the Waldorf-Astoria in New York to celebrate the National League's 40th anniversary. The largest ballroom at the Waldorf was not available for the event, so the guest list had to be limited to 350 rather that the 5,000 that would have liked to attend. National League president John Tener rolled out the red carpet for many notable persons from the senior circuit's glorious past that included Cap Anson, George Wright, Tim Murnane, John M. Ward, Alfred J. Reach, former president of the Philadelphia club, James A. Hart, former owner of the Cubs, James B. Day and James Murtrie, who organized the Giants. Even former National League president Nicholas E. Young and the first president of the league in 1876, Governor Morgan G. Bulkeley of Connecticut, attended.

However, the absence of American League president Ban Johnson at the National League's anniversary celebration was a bit conspicuous. Johnson stated that he had too much league business to attend to back in Chicago. However, Johnson, a devoted American League partisan, was aware of the fact that the event was tantamount to a National League lovefest, and furthermore, that some of the former Federal League magnates such as Harry Sinclair had been invited. While Sinclair failed to show up, it was no secret that Johnson was still more than a little disappointed over the peace settlement. Representing Johnson at the event was John E. Bruce, secretary of the National Commission. The American League was also represented by Yankees owners Colonel Jacob Ruppert and Captain Tillinghast L'Hommedieu Huston, along with president Joseph J. Lannin of the world champion Boston Red Sox.

The walls of the banquet hall were decorated with various flags and the actual championship pennants from the Braves, Giants, Pirates and Phillies. However, there was no trace of the Chicago Cubs' pennants from their championships of recent years. Apparently, former Cubs owner Charles "Chubby Charlie" Webb Murphy was peeved at not being invited to the celebration and forbade the display of the memorabilia. Also, at the time Charles Murphy was threatening to write a series of articles in a syndicated newspaper exposing the National League and many involved in it. However, at the moment Murphy was busy castigating Charles P. Taft for selling the Cubs to Charles Weeghman.

The featured speaker at the National League's big bash was former United States President William Howard Taft. Taft told the assembled magnates and others that their actions during the Federal League war had bored the public and he predicted that the peace settlement would reinvigorate public interest in the game during the 1916 season. Taft declared that rowdyism in ballparks should not be tolerated and that umpires should take swift action by banishing spectators who voice objections. Reminiscing about his days as the civil governor of the Philippines during the Roosevelt administration, Taft stated, "that baseball had been the means of civilizing the iggorrotes in the Philippines as well as benefiting the youth of this country." When a Philadelphia lawyer who had too much to drink attempted to interrupt the former president, Taft stood his ground and responded, "Give me half a chance and I'll drown you out."[3] Immediately, associates of the inebriate put a collar on him and Taft continued.

The dismissal of the lawsuit had thrown all the Federal League players onto the open market. Several National League club owners, including those in Chicago, Boston and New York, saw a chance to fatten up their rosters and wanted to increase the club player limit from 21 to 22. Garry Herrmann, on the other hand, wanted to reduce the roster limit to 20 players. The league moguls voted on the matter and decided to keep the current 21-player limit. Giants' manager John McGraw had long coveted Federal League outfielder Benny Kauff. He offered Harry Sinclair $30,000 for Kauff and got him. Then Germany Schaeffer, a close friend who had pitched in two games with Washington in his brief major league career, advised

McGraw to put in a bid on Newark outfielder Edd Roush. When McGraw asked Schaeffer why he should attempt to get Roush when he just got Kauff, Schaeffer told him that Roush was the best outfielder in the Federal League, and furthermore a better player than Kauff.

McGraw was stunned. He told Schaeffer that with Kauff in center field, George Burns in left and Dave Robertson in right, his outfield was set. What could he possibly do with Roush? Still, Schaeffer was persistent. "See what you can get Roush for," he urged. "I tell you he's the best buy in the lot and nobody knows it — not even Sinclair." McGraw approached Harry Sinclair and asked him what he would take for Edd Roush. Without batting an eye, Sinclair said $10,000. McGraw counter-offered $7,500. "He's yours," said Sinclair.[5]

McGraw had come to the conclusion that if Roush was as good as Schaeffer indicated, then he might be able to push Benny Kauff to peak performance by knowing that a talented kid was waiting in the wings for his position. It was classic John McGraw. Following the sale of Roush, Harry Sinclair announced that he was returning to his Oklahoma oil operations, saying, "I've sold all my players except one (Hal Chase) and I'm through with baseball."[6] Subsequently, Sinclair was off to establish the Sinclair Oil and Refining Corporation and the Sinclair Gulf Corporation. The following year in the wake of the Russian Revolution in 1917, Sinclair would go to Russia, meet Vladimir Lenin and attempt to negotiate the oil rights in Serbia.

Garry Herrmann had to prepare his weak ballclub for the coming season. The Reds had been hard-hit by the defection of their players to the Federal League. Herrmann needed ballplayers and he bought Buffalo Feds infielder Baldy Louden from Harry Sinclair. But pitching was still the Reds' biggest problem. So Herrmann bought a couple of Sinclair's Federal Leaguers to fill the gap, acquiring Earl Moseley from the Newark Feds and hard-throwing left-hander Al Schulz, who had won 21 games for Buffalo. However, Reds ace Fred Toney was holding out for more money. Garry Herrmann reasoned that the gold rush days of the Federal League war were over and he offered Toney a contract calling for $4,000, but Toney wanted $8,000. When Herrmann sent the contract to Toney at his home in Nashville, it was returned unsigned, but included a letter to the Reds' president. In the letter Toney reminded Herrmann about the great season he had in 1915, further stating that if he would have had a better team supporting him, he would have probably led all National League pitchers with the lowest ERA. In fact, Toney, with an ERA of 1.58, had finished second to Grover Cleveland Alexander, who led the league with an ERA of 1.22. With Herrmann and his ace pitcher at loggerheads, Toney's brother interceded and contacted Reds secretary Harry Stephens, inviting him to come to Nashville and hash over the salary dispute. A compromise was worked out and soon Toney was in the fold.

Another potential problem for the Reds was at first base. In 1915 the club's first baseman had been Fritz Mollwitz, a native of Kolberg, Germany, who had hit for an average of .259 while playing 153 games. Manager Buck Herzog was satisfied with the Teutonic as his first baseman for the 1916 season. But others in the Reds' front office were suspicious of Mollwitz's arm, saying that he had a bad shoulder, couldn't throw, and that he really wasn't a big leaguer. What was happening was that a contingent in the Reds' front office wanted to acquire Hal Chase. In 1916, Chase had played for Buffalo, where he led the Federal League in home runs with 17, was second in total bases with 267 and third in RBIs with 89, while hitting .291. However, he was not wanted back in the American League where he had a notorious reputation for allegedly fixing games, and Ban Johnson was stating that he felt Chase's career may be over.

As the Reds went through their spring training camp at Shreveport, Louisiana, stories began circulating back in Cincinnati that the Reds were going to sign the 33-year-old Chase. However, when sportswriters contacted Garry Herrmann or the Reds' treasurer, Louis Widrig, they would deny that there were any talks being held with Chase. But as the Reds began to play their way north to begin the season, Mollwitz developed a sore arm. It was then that Garry Herrmann decided to take a chance on Chase and bought the controversial, slick-fielding, hard-hitting first baseman from Harry Sinclair. Issuing a statement in regard to signing Chase, Herrmann said, "Duke Farrell talked to me at considerable length concerning Chase a few days ago and told me that Chase was much misrepresented — that he'd show the real stuff both as a ball player and a gentleman if given this opportunity. Well it's up to Chase now — we'll see what he does."[7]

As the season approached, baseball scribe Hugh Fullerton published his predictions for the 1916 National League pennant race. He picked Boston to finish first and Cincinnati to finish second, ahead of Chicago, Brooklyn, New York, St. Louis, Philadelphia and Pittsburgh. However, when Garry Herrmann acquired first baseman Hal Chase, Fullerton revised his predictions, moving Cincinnati from second place to a sixth-place finish. Although manager Buck Herzog didn't want Chase, the feeling among the baseball writers in general was that Chase was going to make or break the Reds' season.

The Reds opened the 1916 season at Redland Field on April 12 against the Chicago Cubs. Cubs' manager Joe Tinker sent George McConnell to the mound to face off against Fred Toney. In 1915, McConnell had led the Federal League with 25 wins pitching for Charlie Weeghman's Chicago Whales. But Fred Toney was wild, didn't have much on his fastball, lasted only five innings, and the Cubs won the opener, 7–1. Hal Chase had not yet arrived from his home in California and Fritz Mollwitz started at first base. The following day the Reds rebounded and mauled Cubs ace Hippo Vaughn, winning 8–1. On Friday, the Reds wrapped up the series with a 4–3 win over the Cubs. Hal Chase finally arrived on Saturday and got into his first game on Sunday after umpire Hank O'Day tossed Fritz Mollwitz out of the game.

On February 29, George B. Cox had suffered a massive stroke and his circumstances appeared grave. While Cox convalesced, he attempted to maintain a cheerful outlook for the sake of his wife. He fought hard and regained his speech and the use of his arms, but despite the struggle he put up, his condition weakened. Then in early May, he contracted pneumonia and gradually weakened. On Friday morning, May 19, Cox was resting comfortably in his bed in the quiet confines of his mansion located in Clifton at Brookline and Wentworth Avenues, just opposite Burnet Woods. Suddenly he slipped into a coma. At 4:40 a.m. on Saturday, May 20, death came to the Boss. George B. Cox was 62 years old.

The following Monday, under the direction of John J. Gilligan, Cox's funeral was held at his Clifton home, attracting a huge crowd. The Reverend Hugo Eisenlohr officiated. Silently, Garry Herrmann, former mayor and Reds attorney John Galvin, judge William Lueders, Rud Hynicka and Mike Mullin passed by the bier to say one final good-bye. Following the services, George B. Cox was buried at Spring Grove Cemetery beside the body of the mother he so dearly loved, who had died four years previously. Upon the demise of Cox, the *Cincinnati Post* stated in a front page article, "And so closed a career in which a newsboy rose until he became the most powerful man in the government of Ohio, virtually naming mayors, judges, congressman, governors, and having much to do with the fortunes of presidents."[8] The Democrats seemed more stunned than relieved as reality began to set in that this time George B. Cox had really quit politics for good.

As the summer of 1916 approached, the war in Europe had become a war of attrition as the senseless slaughter continued in the trenches with hundreds of thousands of French and German troops being killed at Verdun. Meanwhile, off the coast of Denmark, the British and German fleets engaged in the monumental Battle of Jutland that proved to be inconclusive.

Also, the British Naval blockade was wreaking havoc across the German homeland as sugar prices soared and potato blight set in, claiming the lives of 700,000 civilians. In the United States, safe from harms way by virtue of being separated from the conflict by the Atlantic Ocean, it all seemed surreal. But the saber-rattling was becoming ever louder in America, and war with Germany was eminent. In fact, the Wilson administration was mindful of the fact that the United States was in possession of one-third of the world's gold reserves. Consequently, a defeat of the Allies by Germany would cost the United States billions of dollars.

The year 1916 was also a presidential election year. At their national convention in St. Louis in early July, the Democrats would nominate Woodrow Wilson to run for a second term. While President Wilson had been preaching peace, he was really looking for a way to enter the war on the side of Great Britain and France. With Wilson assured the Democrats' nomination, the Republicans needed to select their candidate. That would take place at the Republican National Convention, held at Chicago on June 7–10, 1916. However, there were actually two conventions taking place in Chicago on June 7. The Republicans were meeting at the Coliseum and the Progressives were meeting at the Auditorium, hoping to once again nominate Theodore Roosevelt and re-ignite the Bull Moose cause. However, at the Coliseum it was the general feeling among the Republican delegates that the man who could bring the divided Republicans and Progressives together and prevent the Progressives from backing Woodrow Wilson was former governor of New York and current Supreme Court justice Charles Evans Hughes. On the third ballot Hughes was nominated nearly without any objection. Senator Burton of Ohio was offered the vice-presidential slot on the ticket but refused and the nomination went to former vice president Charles W. Fairbanks of Indiana.

The Progressives meeting at the Auditorium wanted to continue the good fight from 1912, and when Theodore Roosevelt's name was mentioned in the opening address, it brought forth a cheer among the delegates that lasted for 93 minutes. However, a couple days later when they learned from convention chairman Raymond Robbins and Progressive national committeeman Harold L. Ickes of Illinois that Roosevelt would not be a third-party candidate and had suggested Henry Cabot Lodge as a compromise candidate, they were outraged. They felt T.R. had abandoned the Progressive cause, and in anger tore Roosevelt campaign pins from their lapels and signs from the walls and trampled on them with their feet as they stormed out of the Auditorium.

As the Republicans met in Chicago and the Reds were struggling in sixth place, tragedy was again to descend upon Garry Herrmann. He did not attend the convention because his beloved wife, Annie, was ill and had become an invalid. As the condition of his stricken spouse deteriorated, Herrmann tirelessly remained by her bedside, refusing to attend any baseball or political meetings. Early Sunday morning, June 18, Annie Herrmann succumbed to her disabilities. Although Annie Herrmann didn't make the headlines that her well-known husband did in Cincinnati, as a result of her countless and tireless efforts in charity and benevolent events in the city throughout the years, she was held in very high esteem by a large circle of residents. At 3:00 p.m. on June 22, the funeral services for Annie were held at the Herrmann home at 47 Hollister Street. The floral arrangements that covered her casket came from every city in the major leagues and many minor league cities, too. The bereaved Herrmann never married again; Annie had been the love of his life and it was impossible for him to ever conceive of someone in her place. A few years later, a female fan or stalker of Herrmann's would proclaim that she and Garry were arranging nuptials. However, the woman and any such plans were unknown to Herrmann, who quickly called the newspapers, offering a blanket denial.

It was a discouraging year for Herrmann; the loss of his mentor Cox and now the love of his life Annie left him in a huge state of melancholy. As Herrmann struggled with his grief, by July 19, the Reds had slipped into the National League cellar with a record of 34–49, playing just .410 ball. Manager Charley Herzog was so disgusted with the state of things that he was offering to pay Garry Herrmann $10,000 to buyout his own contract and obtain his unconditional release. Suspecting that Herzog might be on the block, Charlie Weeghman caught the first train out of Chicago for Cincinnati and hunkered down for talks with Herrmann about acquiring Herzog. He offered Herrmann $25,000 and former Federal League outfielder Max Flack, who had hit .314 the previous season for the Chicago Whales. As always, Herrmann needed players, Flack was fast afoot and a left-handed hitter, and the twenty-five grand would give Herrmann the loot to buy additional players. So Herrmann gave Weeghman permission to speak with Herzog. Subsequently, Herzog told Weeghman that he had no objections about going to Chicago, but his first choice would be to go back to New York. John McGraw and the Giants were due to arrive in Cincinnati following their Boston series and Herzog eagerly awaited the chance to confer with the Giants' skipper.

The Giants were floundering in fourth place, barely playing .500 ball, and the National League pennant race was fast becoming a three-team race between Brooklyn, Boston and Philadelphia. McGraw was ready to have Herzog rejoin the Giants. When the Giants arrived in Cincinnati from Pittsburgh, John McGraw told sportswriter Sid Mercer to arrange a meeting with Herzog. Mercer was aware of the fact that the previous relationship between McGraw and Herzog in New York had been stormy. But while McGraw disliked Herzog personally, he respected him as a player. He told Mercer, "It's all right. Tell him (Herzog) I've already got Garry Herrmann's permission to talk to him. You know what that means. So will he. Tell him I just want to find out how he feels about it before I do anything."[9]

The Giants were staying in the Hotel Halvin in Cincinnati and the meeting was arranged in Mercer's room so as to not attract any attention from the press. McGraw was totally upfront with Herzog, telling him, "There is no use kidding ourselves. I don't like you and you don't like me. But I want you for my ball club because I think you can help me."[10] McGraw then went on to tell Herzog that with Harry Hempstead's permission, he had a tentative deal that would send Christy Mathewson, Bill McKechnie and Edd Roush to the Reds in exchange for him. McGraw then added that he had an understanding with Garry Herrmann that Mathewson would replace him as manager of the Reds. With that Herzog gave his approval to the deal, telling McGraw that there wasn't any need for the two of them to be friends, but he would do his best for the Giants.

The meeting had lasted only a few minutes and McGraw was to tell the press that it wasn't easy for him to part with Mathewson, but his days as a dominating pitcher were over and Matty agreed with him. It was time for Mathewson to enter the next phase of his career and become a manager. The Giants also acquired outfielder Red Killefer in the deal. There were mixed emotions about the trade in both Cincinnati and New York. Buck Herzog had become popular with the Cincinnati fans and, of course, Christy Mathewson was a legend in New York. Still, the prevailing attitude of the fans in both cities was that if there had to be any two players involved in the deal, they were all glad that it was Matty and Buck. Mathewson had Garry Herrmann put a clause into his contract that he could decide whenever and if he would ever pitch for the Reds. The proud Mathewson wasn't keen on taking the mound anymore. During his career in New York, he had appeared in 635 games, winning 373 and losing 188. Between 1903 and 1914, he had never won less than 23 games in a season and won over 30 games four times. Now he was coming to Cincinnati with a 3–4 won-lost record in a season that had seen him do most of his work out of the bullpen. While the Giants were convinced that Mathewson's days as a pitcher were over, they had a theory that he would become an outstanding manager. Also, as John McGraw was uncertain as to how much longer he intended to continue at the helm of the Giants, Harry Hempstead and McGraw insisted that Garry Herrmann include a two-year release clause in Mathewson's contract. Herrmann was strongly against the clause but conceded when it became clear that was the only way the deal would be done.

The official date of the trade was July 20 and it was the best deal that Garry Herrmann had ever made. Eventually all three players acquired by Herrmann in the deal would wind up in the National Baseball Hall of Fame — Mathewson through his pitching with the Giants, Bill McKechnie through being a manager who would eventually win two pennants and a world championship managing the Reds, and Edd Roush, who would become one of the greatest players to ever wear the Cincinnati uniform.

Announcing the deal to the press, Garry Herrmann stood with huge tears in his eyes and was almost apologetic about acquiring Mathewson, stating that he had requested the privilege of speaking with Mathewson. "I wish to announce the release of Christy Mathewson to the Cincinnati baseball club. My good wishes to his success are mingled with many regrets that he will leave the New York baseball club. For many years the New York public have enjoyed the games in which he participated and have given him their unquantified support, goodwill and respect. I certainly wish him well in his new line of endeavor, and trust that his name will stand as high as a manager as it has as a ball player and a citizen of the United States."[11]

On July 21 with a contract calling for a hefty salary of $20,000 a year, $8,000 more than he had been earning in New York, Christy Mathewson officially became manager of the Cincinnati Reds. For Mathewson's managerial debut, everybody that was somebody in Cincinnati was at Redland Field. The *New York Tribune* stated, "It was a highly suspicious occasion in Cincinnati, this debut of Manager Matty. Lots of officials attended the game and formally presented him the keys to the city. Prominent merchants presented him with the keys to their breweries, for which Matty has no particular use. Of course, this is a particularly fickle burg, but for the time being Christopher Mathewson late of New York, is emphatically Cincinnati's leading citizen. He is the McGraw of Porkopolis and then some."[12] But in his first game at the helm of the Reds, Mathewson took a 6–4 licking from the Philadelphia Phillies. However, Mathewson would insert Edd Roush in the lineup in center field, a position he would continue to hold down until 1927. Batting second in the lineup in his inaugural game with the Reds, Roush responded by going 3-for-5, including a two-run triple. On July 26, among much fanfare and ballyhoo, Mathewson made his return to New York as his Reds beat the Giants, 4–2.

In early September with the Reds in eighth place and out of the pennant race, Christy Mathewson would take the mound one last time in the second game of a Labor Day doubleheader at Weeghman Park in Chicago. The 38-year-old Mathewson agreed to face-off against his old rival, 39-year-old Mordecai "Three Finger" Brown, who had returned to the Cubs following a two-year stint in the Federal League. Charley Weeghman saw an opportunity to cash in on the Mathewson-Brown duel and advertised the forthcoming event extensively. One of the most extravagant promotional pieces produced was a poster, eight-feet by five-feet, that heralded the Mathewson-Brown pitching duel as the greatest event of the year for baseball fans and contained pictures of both hurlers and one of Brown's mutilated pitching hand.

On Labor Day, September 4, 1916, the two pitchers faced each other for the first time since 1912 and the largest crowd of the year turned out at Weeghman Park to indulge in the nostalgia. Prior to the game Mathewson and Brown were each presented with a bouquet of American beauty roses. However, the game seemed more like an exhibition than a league game and neither pitcher threw a masterpiece as the Reds beat the Cubs, 10–8. Mathewson, in prevailing

Christy Mathewson, manager, Cincinnati Reds. National Baseball Hall of Fame Library, Cooperstown, N.Y.

over Brown, went the distance, giving up 15 hits in the process, while Brown gave up nine hits, including several for extra bases. For Mathewson it would be his 373rd career win and his last.

On the last day of the 1916 season, the Reds, behind the six-hit, 11-strikeout pitching of Fred Toney, beat the Pirates, 4–0. In a field event prior to the game, Reds pitcher Pete Schneider had fungoed a ball 437 feet. Hal Chase won the National League batting title with an average of .339 and led the league in hits with 184. At the conclusion of the 1916 season, the Reds finished in a tie for last place with the St. Louis Cardinals with identical records of 60–93, 33½ games behind pennant-winning Brooklyn. Under Mathewson, the Reds went 25–43.

All through the dog days of August, the Braves, Phillies and Robins had been in a close three-way battle for the league lead. The Giants continued to flounder, and on September 5, the club was mired down in fourth place with a record of 58–60. Early in the season the Giants had put together a 17-game winning streak on the road. Now they went on one of most remarkable winning streaks in the history of the game. Between September 7 and September 30, the Giants won 26 straight games. However, it was inconsequential, and on October 1, the Giants were still in fourth place with a record of 85–63 and two games out of third place. While the Giants had won most of the games during the steak from second-division clubs— Chicago, Cincinnati, Pittsburgh and St. Louis— the four games the Giants had won from the Phillies would have an effect on the outcome of the pennant, allowing the Brooklyn Robins to edge out the Phillies by 2½ games.

The end came to the Giants' winning streak in the final home game of the year, played at the Polo Grounds against the Braves. The Giants then moved over to Brooklyn to finish the schedule with a mathematical shot at third place. However, it was not to be as the Giants returned to their pre–September lethargic style of play, with the Robins fighting hard to keep the Phillies at bay. On October 3, the Robins beat the Giants. John McGraw blew his stack leaving the bench in the 8th inning, accusing his players of not trying to win the game. All through the game McGraw had been agitated, and in the third inning had an on-field confrontation with shortstop Art Fletcher and pitcher Rube Benton. But in the eighth inning when relief pitcher Pol Perritt wound up with Mike Mowrey on first, and allowed the Robins' third baseman to take second with ease, it caused McGraw to explode. He rushed for the clubhouse, cussing and pushing players out of his way.

When reporters caught up with McGraw in the clubhouse, he told them, "That stuff was too much for me. I do not believe any of my players deliberately favored Brooklyn, but they simply refused to obey my orders and they fooled about in a listless manner. When Perritt wound up with a man on first base, allowing the runner to steal second, I lost my patience and left the bench. I have worked too hard this year to stand around and watch playing like that, and I refuse to be connected with it. I'm through for the year." As for his part in the fiasco, pitcher Pol Perritt told the press, "That game cost me a $100. I had that much bet that I would win twenty games, so you can see there was at least one reason why I would play square. I was out to win. I have too much self-respect and have been in the game too long to go before a New York crowd and do anything but my best."[13] A few days later, McGraw would be denying that anything crooked had happened in the game. National League president John Tener had been present at the game and called McGraw's charges absurd. Harry Hempstead, Giants president, said the incident was closed.

The Brooklyn Robins and the Boston Red Sox met in the lackluster and sparsely attended 1916 World Series, with Boston winning the series four games to one, thus becoming back-to-back world champions. The Red Sox's front office had once again anticipated a large demand for tickets and once again moved their home games in the series to Braves Field.

However, there were 6,000 empty seats for game one and just as many for game two as Babe Ruth beat the Robins, throwing a seven-hitter, 2–1, in a 14-inning duel with Brooklyn's Sherry Smith. After winning two consecutive World Series, Joseph Lannin decided to get out of the baseball business, and on November 1, sold the Boston Red Sox to New York theatre owner and producer Harry Frazee and his partner Hugh Ward for $675,000.

As the 1916 presidential campaign went into high gear, President Wilson was preaching peace and standing behind the slogan, "He Kept Us Out of War." However, the reality was that the Wilson administration was slowly mobilizing America for war, building new battle-ships and increasing the size of the regular army. While Theodore Roosevelt was rattling sabers, campaigning around the country for Republican candidate Charles Evans Hughes, Hughes himself was remaining vague on his position about war. The Republicans realized that in order to elect Charles Evans Hughes, they would have to transcend the war issue and demonstrate unity in the party among the progressive faction. So a reconciliation of William Howard Taft and Teddy Roosevelt was set in motion.

On October 3 at the Union League Club at Fifth Avenue and 39th Street in New York City, a reception was planned for Hughes, with both Taft and Roosevelt planning to attend. The timing was perfect. There was even talk about producing a Roosevelt, Hughes, Taft lapel button for the affair, but the idea was stricken by T. R. As the public knew in advance that the two former presidents would be meeting, a large crowd began to gather around the Union League Club and the police had to clear a path to the door. Taft was the first to arrive and was taken upstairs by an elevator to a reception line. Roosevelt arrived at the club to wild cheering from the crowd as he yanked off his felt hat and waved it while flashing that glistening broad-tooth smile of his. After being taken upstairs, Roosevelt began to shake hands with everyone in the reception line before he approached Taft. Taft stretched out his hand and Roosevelt clasped it. The two ex-presidents grinned at each other, engaged in a murmured greeting, and then Roosevelt passed on to take up his place in the reception line. But the brief meeting grabbed headlines that a perceived harmony in the party had been achieved. Later William Howard Taft downplayed the whole event. "Why, we shook hands as any two gentleman would," said Taft.[14] However, on election day, Tuesday, November 7, 1916, in one of the closest presidential elections in American history that took three days in which to count the votes, Woodrow Wilson was elected for a second term, defeating Charles Evans Hughes by a vote count of 9,129,606 to 8,538,221.

As Garry Herrmann's year of discontent neared the end, he kept busy at his job as baseball's supreme court chief justice and handed out fines of $50 to $100 to one hundred major and minor league ballplayers, including Ty Cobb and Babe Ruth, for participating in barnstorming post-season exhibition games. The National Commission also came under pressure from the Players' Fraternity and agreed to give injured players full pay for the duration of their contracts. Previously, the injury clause in players' contracts called for the suspension of players after 15 days pay.

However, Barney Dreyfuss was still after Garry Herrmann's scalp. The fact that George Sisler had batted .305 in his first full season with the St. Louis Browns didn't help matters much, either. Once again there was speculation as to whether or not Herrmann would be re-elected to another term as chairman of the National Commission. On Thursday, December 8, Herrmann traveled to Pittsburgh to attend an Elks function also attended by Dreyfuss. As the local reporters surrounded him, Herrmann stated that he was confident to let his tenure lie in the hands of league presidents John Tener and Ban Johnson at the next National Commission reorganization meeting in January. From Pittsburgh, Herrmann traveled to Boston and then to New York for the annual National League meeting at the Waldorf.

When it came to ownership, the National League was the circuit of equal opportunity between the sexes. Through inheritance, the majority stock in two of the National League clubs was owned by women. Mrs. Harry N. Hempstead had inherited the New York Giants from her late father, John T. Brush. However, Mrs. Hempstead immediately turned over the day-to-day control of the ballclub to her husband, Harry. But in St. Louis, Mrs. Helene Robison Britton, who had inherited the Cardinals from her father, Frank de Haas Robison, remained in control of the $400,000 franchise and played an active part in the day-to-day operations of the ballclub. As Mrs. Britton owned the majority of the stock in the ballclub and believed that she could run the business better than anyone else, she had elected herself chairperson of the Cardinals. The past season Mrs. Britton had demonstrated her business savvy as the Cardinals struggled, and she was constantly being badgered by Charles Weeghman and Charles Ebbets, who were attempting to purchase the Cardinals' talented rookie, Rogers Hornsby. While the Cardinals needed a cash infusion badly, Mrs. Britton refused to part with Hornsby, who batted .313 for the season, fourth-highest in the league. Had she dealt Hornsby, the future and history of the St. Louis Cardinals' franchise in the ensuing decade might have been drastically different.

As the National League magnates gathered in New York in December 1916, Mrs. Britton spoke with the press and elaborated on her duties, responsibilities and goals as the Cardinals' magnate. Mrs. Britton stated:

> You can reach me here most any morning at 9:30 and frequently I make it as early 9 o'clock. Unless I have an important appointment downtown in the afternoon you will find me here until past sundown. I want to succeed—why shouldn't I? I am not looking to success for personal prosperity. I am not so narrow-minded. Just look what it means to all of us to have a winning ball club. It will push St. Louis to the front. Cleveland is my original home but I'm in St. Louis and I'm proud to be here. My father and my uncle tried, and I will not give up. I know it can be done. Probably not today, maybe tomorrow; and I only ask the fans not to pass snap judgment. I could have sold years ago, but I love this game, just like my father and uncle. I could have sold last winter, and I could have sold last summer, but I have refused all the offers. A prosperous business is one that moves without a hitch. If there are any flaws in my club I hope to eliminate the defects, and then once operating successfully, I know that it will be an easy position for me.[15]

Upon concluding her remarks, Mrs. Britton entered the Waldorf meeting room and took a seat alongside her National League contemporaries—Tener, Ebbets, Weeghman, Hempstead, Haughton, Baker, Dreyfuss and Herrmann. The meeting's agenda would not produce any spectacular results. The magnates awarded the pennant to Brooklyn and agreed to raise the player limit for each club to 22 and abolish the disability list, thereby including every player under contract to the 22 limit. They also voted to reduce the number of 25-cent seats in parks having a large proportion of bleacher seats. The McGraw incident was hardly mentioned and no action was taken.

When Barney Dreyfuss, still gunning for August Herrmann, proposed to replace the National Commission with a one-man neutral chairman, there was complete silence in the room. Herrmann responded by calling Dreyfuss' hand. He offered to resign as National Commission chairman if it would bring peace to organized ball. However, the timing of Dreyfuss' proposal was bad. With the uncertainty of war with Germany looming and organized ball still in the process of restoring public confidence following the Federal League battle, all the magnates backed off, and soon Barney Dreyfuss did also. They agreed to support Herrmann for another year at the helm of the National Commission. While Barney Dreyfuss knew he had lost round one in his bout to restructure the National Commission, he was ready to fight on. Following the endorsement of Herrmann by the National League, Dreyfuss told the press that he had done his duty by stating his case to his colleagues, and that regardless of the fact that nothing was done in the matter, he had given the other club owners something to think about. For now Dreyfuss was going to concentrate on the task delegated to him by his peers of developing the 1917 National League schedule.

Out in the corridors and in the saloons of the Waldorf-Astoria, the largest banter was about possible trades and about what the future of the game might be if the country goes to war. Charley Weeghman announced that he was dumping Joe Tinker as manager after a disappointing season in the 1916 campaign that saw the Cubs finish in fifth place, 26½ games behind Brooklyn. While Weeghman would pursue Frank Chance to take over the job, in the end he engineered a deal with the Braves for Fred Mitchell, sending outfielder Joe Kelly to Boston, and Mitchell took over as the Cubs' field general. Christy Mathewson was at the Waldorf, too, and was the essence of elegance, dressed stylish and wearing a snow-white hat. The Cincinnati Reds' fans had not experienced a pennant in the Queen City since 1882. Mathewson was now telling Garry Herrmann the types of players that he would like him to acquire. In the 1916 season, the Reds had abandoned the scouting system. Matty, or "Big Six" as the New York press still liked to refer him, had Garry Herrmann agree to once again hire scouts and send them out about the country, beating the bushes for talent. Mathewson also had it written into his contract that he had the authority to discipline his ballplayers by handing out fines or suspensions. Finally someone was taking control of the ballclub.

The Great War and
the Great American Game

On January 2, 1917, the National Commission held its annual meeting in Cincinnati and once again re-elected August Garry Herrmann as chairman. At the National League meeting in December at New York, the moguls had voted affirmatively to abolish the disability list and include all 22 players under contract. Furthermore, the National Commission had approved a new major league contract for 1917 to be used by all clubs in both the American and National leagues that contained an injury clause. The clause stated that ballclubs were responsible for paying a player's full salary for disabling injuries that were sustained on the field of play for the full term of the contract. However, the payment period for the disability did not extend beyond the term of the contract.

Garry Herrmann pointed out that no club had the right to release a player during the period of the player's disability until that player had fully recovered and was once again fit to play. Also, Herrmann noted that the National Commission had never heard a disability contract grievance from a major league player. Still, Dave Fultz, president of the Players' Fraternity, wanted to continue to make the disability clause an issue with the National Commission by including the minor leagues. He pointed out that the National Association contracts did not include a disability clause and that three injured players were challenging National Association clubs. But Herrmann ruled that the National Commission could only get involved with those disputes should they come under appeal, and dismissed Fultz's appeal.

The National Commission ruling by Herrmann in the matter didn't sit well with Dave Fultz. He instructed players not to sign their 1917 contracts and threatened to shut down both major and minor league spring training camps by organizing a player's strike among the 700 major and minor league members of the Players' Fraternity. When New York Giants pitcher Slim Sallee signed his 1917 contract, Fultz, stressing unity as the absolute essential of the organization, immediately expelled him from the Players' Fraternity. National League president John Tener stated that there was absolutely no legal or moral basis for a strike on the part of the players. He remarked that the National League had granted every one of their requests. Tener further stated that the National Commission had no jurisdiction over the minor leagues and that those clubs had the absolute right to have their own relations with their players.

The word was circulating that Philadelphia Phillies pitcher Grover Cleveland Alexander and Boston Red Sox second baseman Harold Janvrin would not sign their 1917 contracts and supported the Players' Fraternity stand. On January 13, Garry Herrmann arrived in Washington, D.C., to attend the annual banquet of the Woodlawn Bards, a well-known baseball organization. He was immediately surrounded by members of the press and deluged with questions about a possible players' strike. Herrmann told the press that he was supported in his decision to not hear the Players' Fraternity request by American League president Ban Johnson, as well as Chicago White Sox owner Charles Comiskey and Chicago Cubs owner Charles Weeghman. He stated that organized baseball in Chicago was openly defiant in their opposition to the Players' Fraternity demands. Furthermore, he said that most of the White Sox players were signing their contracts and that Cubs players were telling Weeghman that they intended to sign just as soon as contracts were available. When asked about the Reds' contracts, Herrmann stated he expected no difficulty.

On January 16 in Chicago, about twenty members of the Players' Fraternity met with president Dave Fultz in a closed-door session. While reports were abounding that the entire Boston Red Sox team would support a strike, only about ten of the Players' Fraternity members that attended the Chicago meeting were major league players. None of the major league players in attendance were considered a star player, although Al Demaree of the Philadelphia Phillies had won 19 games in 1916. However, there was a report circulating that Ty Cobb was threatening to join a proposed strike. Detroit Tigers president Frank J. Navin called it nonsense, stating that Cobb's contract had two more years to run. When the press converged on Al Demaree following the meeting, he had little to say. "All I can say is that we pledged our loyalty to Fultz and the fraternity. We would be poor fraternity members if we didn't."[1]

But the facts were that behind those closed doors a plan of action had been formulated. Dave Fultz announced that February 20 had been set as the date for the players' strike to begin. The reason that February 20 was the date targeted was because on that date the Cubs' players had been instructed to report to Chicago to make the trip to their spring training camp in Pasadena, California, thereby being the first major league team to mobilize for spring training. Fultz was also threatening to have the major league players affiliate with Samuel Gompher's American Federation of Labor. Fultz said that his decision to have his members join the AFL occurred because of statements by American League president Ban Johnson threatening to crush the Players' Fraternity and stating that players in the major leagues must either resign from the fraternity or get out of the big leagues. Fultz said, "We needed something to bulwark us up, and there seems no doubt that affiliation with the American Federation of Labor will prove to be a great benefit. I believe such affiliation will strengthen us sufficiently to win the requests we now ask for without carrying this strike into the new season."[2]

American League president Ban Johnson and National League president John Tener believed that it was time to play hardball with the Players' Fraternity, and as a result of not allowing players to sign contracts, both severed relations with Fultz and the fraternity. Furthermore, when Johnson heard about the threat of Fultz to have the players affiliate with the AFL, he called it ridiculous, asserting that such a change would bring about a union scale of wages that would be paid to both star and average players. He recalled the attempts by the National League in the 1890s to standardize wages according to the positions that they played. He didn't foresee any support for such wage distribution in the modern era where certain star players would be willing to equalize their salaries with inferior players. However, Garry Herrmann, being mindful that he was not only a baseball mogul but also a politician, realized if he became perceived as defiant toward organized labor, it might cause a backlash at the polls in the next Cincinnati general election. Therefore, Herrmann was a little more formal and diplomatic in his response to Fultz's AFL proposition than Ban Johnson. Herrmann told the press, "I firmly believe that Samuel Gomphers is fair-minded and believes in the principles of equality and fair dealing. For this reason I do not think Mr. Gomphers, when he understands the ins and outs of the present baseball situation, will lend his aid to David Fultz."[3]

Regardless of the status of the flap with the Players' Fraternity, organized baseball was preparing for the 1917 season. Exhibition game schedules were being drawn up, trades were taking place, and players were signing contracts. Many major league moguls were stating that a players' strike for the most part existed only in Dave Fultz's mind. Ban Johnson, Barney Dreyfuss, John Tener and John Heydler, who made up the rules and schedule committee established by the National Commission, were headed for their annual meeting at Dover Hall, a hunting preserve in Brunswick, Georgia, that had been established by several moguls, including New York Yankees owners Colonel Jacob Ruppert and Captain Tillinghast Huston. Garry Herrmann was also part of the committee, but due to his busy, diverse civic and fraternal activities, he decided to remain in Cincinnati. Furthermore, when Herrmann had been asked to arbitrate between the owners and the Players' Fraternity, he flatly refused.

Herrmann had recently stated that there were three things that he absolutely needed to accomplish with the remaining years of his life. First and foremost was to bring a National League pennant to Cincinnati, but he also wanted to build a new Elks Temple in the city and wanted to save the Cincinnati Zoo. In 1901, the Cincinnati Traction Company bought controlling stock in the zoo from the Cincinnati Zoological Company. While operating the zoo, the Cincinnati Traction Company expanded it and even added a bandstand and theatre. However, by 1916, the emerging popularity of the automobile was eating away at the profits of the Traction Company and it could no longer support the zoo. It was then that Charles P. Taft and Mrs. Mary Emery, wife of Cincinnati industrialist Thomas J. Emery, agreed to donate $125,000 toward buying the zoo if a matching amount could be raised from public donations. Therefore, Garry Herrmann took up the challenge and began to personally administer the fundraising campaign.

In mid–January, several minor league owners were in Cincinnati to discuss the Players' Fraternity situation with Herrmann at his offices in the Wiggins Block building. Outside of the office building on Fountain Square, a band concert that Herrmann had organized to raise money for the zoo was taking place. During the concert, Herrmann arranged for several very attractive young ladies to pass the hat among the listeners for donations. When the young women came into Herrmann's office at the conclusion of the concert and dumped a few thousand dollars on his desk, the minor league officials were stunned. Herrmann's efforts at raising the necessary $125,000 were ultimately successful, and with the money raised and the matching donation from Charles Taft and Mary Emery, on May 1, 1917, the zoo was purchased from the streetcar company and began being operated by the Cincinnati Zoological Park Association. Under administration of the association, a place for opera within the zoo would be constructed, and beginning in 1920 and for the next forty-plus years, during hot, muggy Cincinnati summer evenings some of the most well-known virtuosos in the world would perform *Carmen* and *La Bohème* while being serenaded in the background by the squealing of monkeys and roars of lions.

On January 19, 1917, German foreign minister Arthur Zimmerman sent a telegram to the Mexican government proposing a German-Mexican alliance. In the communication that historically became known as "The Zimmerman Note," the German government promised financial support and to assist Mexico to recover lost territory of New Mexico, Texas and Arizona within the borders of the United States if it entered the war as an ally. Also, even though Germany had previously promised President Wilson that it would stop its practice of attacking neutral carriers on the high seas, it was stated in the Zimmerman Note that Germany was about to begin unrestricted submarine warfare in order to subdue England.

The Zimmerman Note was intercepted and published in many newspapers across the country.

Former president Theodore Roosevelt was pacing the floor at his home in Oyster Bay, criticizing President Wilson for not mobilizing for war and telling everyone that he did not believe that Wilson would go to war unless Germany literally kicked him into it. Meanwhile, former president William Howard Taft, who was teaching law at Yale, was leaning toward peace. Although Taft had served as Theodore Roosevelt's secretary of war, by nature he was a pacifist. In the late 1890s, Taft had after long, careful thought come to the conclusion that William McKinley had no other option but to enter war with Spain, but he still abhorred the nation's fervor for the conflict when it ensued.

Within a week Germany announced unrestricted submarine warfare. In an attempt to starve England into submission, the Germans announced that they would only permit one United States merchant ship a week with certain markings and signals displayed to enter the designated port of Falmouth. All other American ships were warned to remain within twenty miles of England, France and Italy or risk being sunk by German U-boats. Since May 2, 1915, over 200 Americans had been lost in ships attacked by German U-boats. President Wilson was now being forced to act, and on February 3, he broke off diplomatic relations with Germany.

By mid–February, the Players Fraternity had been beaten into submission. During a National Commission meeting, Garry Herrmann produced a strike bulletin, circulated to the players dated January 16, that contained the following message, "Hold all contracts sent to you. When we have won you will get the biggest salaries offered."[4] With the true motive for the strike exposed as a cash grab rather than a campaign to protect disabled players from greedy owners, the National League, following the militant lead of Ban Johnson and the American League, banished the Players' Fraternity. Fans all around the country gave their approval, the strike was dead, and so was the fraternity. The empty training camps promised by Dave Fultz never happened. Immediately Cubs players came sprinting to Chicago to sign their contracts and get aboard Charley Weeghman's special train to California for spring training.

The start of the 1917 major league baseball season was less than a week away when on April 6, at 11:00 A.M., President Wilson signed a joint resolution adopted by Congress declaring war on Germany. Immediately, 90 German ships with a value of over $148 million were seized in U.S. ports and attorney general Thomas W. Gregory ordered without warrants the arrest of German nationals residing in the country, accused of being conspirators in nearly every city in the nation, including Chicago, Cincinnati, Detroit, Indianapolis, San Francisco, even El Paso, Texas, and Terra Haute, Indiana. America was going to war, and across the land from coast to coast, patriotism spread like a giant brush fire.

In Albany, Georgia, 57-year-old confirmed pacifist and three-time presidential candidate William Jennings Bryan volunteered to serve in the U.S. Army as a private, telling the press, "Gladly would I have given my life to save my country from war, but now that my country has gone to war, gladly will I give my life to aid it."[5] When news of the declaration of war reached Theodore Roosevelt at the Langdon Hotel in New York, he stated that he wanted the War Department to allow him to recruit a division from New York and also allow him to join them in the field. However, the generals in Washington advised the secretary of war that allowing Roosevelt to raise a division would be a bad precedent. The secretary then let Roosevelt know that while he greatly appreciated his patriotic spirit, he had decided to decline his offer. As a result, the old lion would have to be content to sit out the war in Oyster Bay and acting as a critic of President Wilson's administration of the conflict.

With America mobilizing for war, a cloud of uncertainty suddenly hung over organized ball. But on April 11, Cincinnati opened its 1917 season with a 3–1 victory over St. Louis, with Pete Schneider holding Rogers Hornsby and the Red Birds to just four hits. The Reds' victory was preserved by Edd Roush, who made a long catch near the scoreboard that thrilled the crowd and prevented the game from being tied. As it was then and still is, opening day was a huge celebration in Cincinnati as 24,938 fans packed Redland Field to the rafters. The Reds then proceeded to win the second game of the season behind Fred Toney who was almost unhittable. It seemed that the tutelage of Christy Mathewson was already paying dividends. Mathewson had told both Schneider and Toney to pitch according to their own rhythm and forgo long bullpen warm-ups that had the potential to tire them.

On April 17, Garry Herrmann and the Reds' directors were all smiles when the voters of Cincinnati approved a $6 million bond ordinance to begin the long-delayed construction of the belt subway and rapid transit system that had been advocated when Henry Hunt was mayor. The final plans for the line included a station that was not too far from Redland Field, which would allow fans from far-reaching parts of the city to take the train to the ballgames. However, the ground-breaking for the line would be delayed. Soon after the election, the Ohio Supreme Court would invalidate the bond ordinance and then a prohibition for the issuing of capital bonds during the war would go into effect. As a result, the project would be withdrawn for the duration of the war.

To most observers, the 1917 Cincinnati Reds seemed improved over the previous edition. Then Edd Roush injured his leg and would miss several games. Christy Mathewson needed immediate help in the outfield and looked to his old team in New York for help. The deadline was fast approaching for teams to cut their rosters to the 22-player limit, and John McGraw, with his outfield set with Benny Kauff, Dave Robertson and George Burns, had decided to cut Jim Thorpe. Privately, McGraw had reached the conclusion that Thorpe couldn't hit a curveball. Still, McGraw told the press that he was sorry to see Thorpe go as he believed sooner or later that he would develop into a good ballplayer. The next day, on April 25, Christy Mathewson moved Greasy Neal into center field and Jim Thorpe played his first game with the Reds in right field, going 1-for-4 in a 8–4 loss to the Cubs. As Mathewson waited on Edd Roush to return to the lineup, he continued to sign players and acquired pitcher Scott Perry from the Cubs on waivers. However, after looking at him for 30 days, Matty came to the conclusion that Perry was probably going to be a good pitcher some day, but at the moment he wasn't going to contribute anything to the Reds, and sold him on waivers to the Boston Braves.

Over the winter, organized ball had lost the fairest of its moguls. Mrs. Helene Robison Britton was going through a bitter divorce from her husband, Schuyler

Jim Thorpe, 1917. Author's collection.

Britton, and as a result was forced to sell the Cardinals to a group of 110 local St. Louis businessmen, headed by James C. Jones, actor Al Jolson and others for $250,000. Soon after taking over the Cardinals, Jones and his partners signed Branch Rickey to a three-year contract to run the franchise. The club was now going to be run as a community-owned entity. To help celebrate the idea, Garry Herrmann and Mike Mullen led a large delegation of Cincinnati club officials, local politicians, civic leaders and businessmen to St. Louis for the Cardinals' opening day festivities. They were joined by many others, including John Tener and John Heydler, representing the National League, and were treated lavishly in the Mound City. At the Anheuser-Busch brewery in St. Louis, the largest in the world at that time, 6,000 employees stopped work to act as a reception committee for all the visiting dignitaries. The Cardinals avenged their opening day defeat at Redland Field in their home opener before a standing room-only crowd at rickety old Robison Field, winning 5–1 behind Bill Doak.

Following the St. Louis series, the Reds traveled to Chicago, where on May 2 at Weeghman Park the Reds' 6 foot-6 inch, 245-pound Fred Toney and the Cubs' 6 foot-4 inch, 215-pound James "Hippo" Vaughn faced each other in one of the most famous games in major league history by pitching a double no-hitter. Vaughn was a hard-throwing left-hander and Reds manager Christy Mathewson started an all right-handed–hitting lineup against him. After nine innings, Vaughn, backed by some slick fielding of his infielders, had held the Reds hitless, allowing but one baserunner to reach second. Likewise, Reds pitcher Fred Toney had held the Cubs hitless for nine innings, allowing only one baserunner to reach second. While Vaughn had ten strikeouts, Toney had but three. However, Toney would be the winning pitcher when in the top of the 10th inning with one out, Larry Kopf singled off Vaughn, advanced to third when Cy Williams dropped a fly ball hit by Hal Chase, and then scored when Jim Thorpe hit a slow roller back to the left of the mound and Cubs catcher Art Wilson seemed to become frozen, allowing the winning run to score. Toney then set down the Cubs in order in the bottom half of the 10th, striking out the last two batters he faced. Toney had previously pitched a 17-inning no-hitter in the minors on May 10, 1909, pitching for Winchester, Kentucky, against Lexington, Kentucky.

Meanwhile, the political landscape in Cincinnati continued to slowly change as another of Garry Herrmann's long-time political associates died. On May 10, former U.S. senator and governor of Ohio, Joseph B. Foraker, died at the age of 70. Since losing his bid to return to the U.S. Senate in 1914 when he lost a primary to Warren G. Harding while confined to a wheelchair, Foraker had been spending his final years writing his autobiography, *Notes of a Busy Life*. Earlier in his career, Foraker had been a teacher in the Cincinnati satellite city of Norwood. The street beside the railroad tracks that ran along the American Laundry Machine Company in Norwood was named in his memory.

The United States Government was estimating the cost of financing the war at $5 billion a year. Consequently, Congress was looking everywhere for revenue by taxation and reasoned that perhaps organized baseball should pay some of the costs. Therefore, a 10 percent tax on every admission was being proposed. In late April, August Garry Herrmann, as chairman of the National Commission, went to Washington and addressed various congressmen on the issue. Herrmann told the congressmen that organized baseball was willing to make sacrifices to aid the war effort, but that a 10 percent tax on gross gate receipts would put every minor league team out of business and possibly the majors, too. In fact, at least two minor leagues, the Southern Association and the Western Association, had already announced that if the tax was imposed, they would cease operations. Having heard Herrmann out, Congress decided to look at an amended proposal of taxing net receipts.

In early June, as America mobilized, Congress began a conscription system to provide manpower for the war. But it would be December before the first men were drafted. While mobilization was rapidly taking place, national cohesion over the nation's entry into the war did not exist. Many men were claiming exemption from the draft on the grounds of dependent families. Some members of the U.S. Senate were supporting pacifists in attempts to evade the draft. Both Senator Robert M. La Follette of Wisconsin and Senator A. J. Gronna of North Dakota were urging pacifists not to be intimidated by the threats of war traders. Among the nation's large German population, many naturalized Germans were resisting fighting in the war because of family ties to the fatherland. Also, the large Irish-American population had their druthers about becoming Great Britain's ally in the war. For nearly 300 years leading up to the World War, the British had held power over Irish sovereignty. On May 4, 1917, a delegation of prominent Irish-Americans led by former Boston mayor John Fitzgerald, called on the head of the British visiting mission, James Balfour. Fitzgerald and the delegation informed Balfour that overwhelmingly Americans of Irish extraction wanted an early resolution to the questions of Irish home rule. Balfour promised the delegation that he would immediately wire Prime Minister Lloyd George and Parliament in regard to their concerns and demands.

While no one was sure yet how the war would affect organized baseball, some in the game were already taking action on their own. In Brooklyn, Charles Ebbets announced that he would set aside gate receipts for one game to aid drafted players. However, some players couldn't wait to get in the conflict. When the Boston Braves made their first road trip to Cincinnati, catcher Hank Gowdy left the team, took the train up to his hometown of Columbus, and enlisted in the Ohio National Guard. Gowdy was the first major league player to enlist. He was given the rank of sergeant and ordered to report for basic training on July 1. During spring training, a lot of major league teams took the lead of White Sox owner Charles Comiskey and spent time practicing drilling. During the 1917 season, it was quite common to see teams prior to the game march side-by-side to the base of the flag pole in center field and stand at attention as a band played "The Star-Spangled Banner." Later in the season, Ban Johnson would state that he would agree to close the baseball season early and call off the World Series if the government found it helpful to the war effort. However, that idea was flatly rejected by Washington. In fact, the U.S. Army's big man in D.C., General McCain, stated that baseball meant too much to the country and was doing too much good to be suspended.

However, the war wasn't only posing a threat to organized baseball, but was also threatening the continuation of college football. Even the running of the Indianapolis 500 was uncertain. Most of the best drivers, including Eddie Rickenbacker, were enlisting in the army, and many felt that it was going to be difficult to recruit a field of starters. Also, there was a concern that with the war, there might be a shortage of cars. Most of the cars that were run in the race prior to World War I were modified production models produced by Marmon, Buick, Fiat, Stutz, Simplex, Mercedes and National. While the promoters considered reducing the Indy race to 250 miles and moving it to the Cincinnati Speedway for 1917, in the end they decided to cancel the race for the duration of the war.

Edd Roush was back in the lineup by early June, but the Reds had fallen to sixth place. Although the Reds were not in contention, the rivalry with the New York Giants was becoming intense. On June 6, at Redland Field, Fred Toney beat the Giants, 6–3, knocking them out of first place, one-half game behind the Philadelphia Phillies. The series was crucial for the Giants as they were battling the Cubs and Phillies for the league lead. The following day, the Giants took revenge on the Reds, beating them 10–1 behind Slim Sallee and regaining the league lead. However, the deciding game of the series, played on June 8, was a wild one with the Reds again knocking the Giants from the top by a score of 2–1. In the 7th inning, Heinie

Groh tied the game by scoring from third on a sacrifice fly by Edd Roush. John McGraw immediately confronted Umpire Quigley, claiming that Groh had left third before the catch and should be called out. McGraw's protest became so heated that he was ejected from the game. The Reds won the game in the bottom of the 9th on a single by Hal Chase and double by Jim Thorpe.

All during the game, John McGraw had been criticizing the calls of home plate umpire Bill Byron. Following the game as the players and umpires headed through the runway to the clubhouses, McGraw was waiting for Byron and began arguing with him. The argument soon got personal as Byron accused McGraw of being run out of Baltimore. That caused McGraw to explode and he punched Byron, splitting his lip. As he attempted to pummel Byron, the Reds' groundskeeper, Matty Schwab, grabbed McGraw, throwing his arms around him. Seeing this, Giants catcher Bill Rariden came rushing forward and punched Schwab in the side of the head. Players on both teams attempted to separate the combatants as police forced their way through the crowd.

Later that evening at the Havlin Hotel, McGraw downplayed the incident and told reporters that Byron had insulted him, that he had never been run out of Baltimore. At this point McGraw had come to his senses and was beginning to worry about how National League president John K. Tener would view the fracas with one of his umpires under the Redland Field stands. He said that the fight with Byron was a personal one and had nothing to do with the game. McGraw knew that he might be suspended along with his catcher, Bill Rariden, for throwing a haymaker on the Reds' agricultural attendant. The loss of Rariden could be devastating to the Giants as their other catcher, Lew McCarthy, was sidelined with a broken leg. That would leave only George Gibson to do the receiving and he hadn't caught for over a year.

Back in New York, Giants president Harry Hempstead was concerned that the incident might cause his club's season to implode. The Giants were headed for Chicago from Cincinnati and Hempstead immediately took the train to meet with his manager. McGraw told him that the fight with Byron was a personal matter and to stay out of it. On June 13, John Tener settled the personal matter by finding McGraw guilty of assault on Byron, fined him $500, and handed him a 16-day suspension. Rather than acting contrite, McGraw saw fit to criticize Tener in a statement to the press. McGraw blasted Tener's administration of justice in the matter and accused him of having been put in power in the National League by the Philadelphia club while continuing to run the team. Now Tener was taking the matter personally, and McGraw was in hot water. McGraw was called back to New York by Hempstead and forced to sign a statement drawn up by Giants legal counsel Cornelius J. Sullivan, repudiating his remarks about Tener to the press. In the statement, McGraw called the reporters liars who printed his remarks about Tener. The reporters were also upset with McGraw and called for an investigation. The matter was finally resolved when Tener held an investigation over the McGraw statement and ruled that he was convinced that McGraw had not been misquoted and fined him $1,000. All through the controversy, the Giants slipped in and out and back into first place in the pennant race.

Following his no-hitter in Chicago in May, Reds pitcher Fred Toney continued to be absolutely dominating. On July 1, Fred Toney would pitch complete game victories in both ends of a doubleheader against the Pittsburgh Pirates, throwing three-hitters in both games while winning by scores of 4–1 and 5–1. In the doubleheader, Toney would set a new major league record for fewest hits given up by a pitcher in a doubleheader. Toney had now won one-third of the Reds' victories. The day was supposed to be a celebration at Redland Field with Cincinnati fans honoring retiring Pittsburgh star Honus Wager, but in the end it was Fred Toney's day as he held Wagner to two hits in eight at-bats.

By August 1, with Fred Toney winning and Edd Roush challenging for the league lead in batting average, the Reds had climbed into third place and were challenging the first-place Giants and second-place Cardinals. However, the Reds had reached their high-water mark for the season. Earlier in the year they had beaten Brooklyn, the defending National League champions, five games in a row. Now in early August it was payback time and Brooklyn beat the Reds five in a row, sending them back into fourth place. After playing in 77 games with the Reds, Jim Thorpe was sent back to the New York Giants for the stretch drive. The Reds would finish with two twenty-game winners, Fred Toney (24–16) and Pete Schneider (20–19), while Edd Roush would win the National League batting championship with an average of .341. Christy Mathewson had improved the ballclub in the 1917 season and the Reds would finish in fourth place (78–76), but it was still a work in progress.

The New York Giants would win the 1917 National League pennant by 10 games over the second-place Philadelphia Phillies. In the American League, Charles Comiskey's Chicago White Sox would win the pennant by nine games over the Boston Red Sox. In the World Series, the White Sox prevailed 4 games to 2 over the Giants as Chicago's Red Faber won three games, two as a starter and one in relief. The final game of the series, played at the Polo Grounds, featured another one of those classic boneheaded incidents that had become the Giants' trademark in important games as Heinie Zimmerman chased Eddie Collins across the plate. In the 4th inning, Happy Felsch hit a high bounder to Rube Benton on the mound. Immediately, Benton threw the ball to Zimmerman at third, trapping Collins as Giants catcher Bill Rariden came up the line to close in on the play. However, Collins, alertly noticing that no one had moved to cover the plate, dashed past Rariden, scoring with Zimmerman in hot pursuit. Following the final game of the series, the victorious White Sox manager Clarence "Pants" Rowland walked towards John McGraw to shake his hand. McGraw simply snarled, "Get away from me, you goddam busher!"[6] Regardless of the low opinion that McGraw had of Pants Rowland, it should be pointed out that the Chicago manager had turned down a $1,000 offer to use his name over a series of articles that would be written about the 1917 World Series. When the victorious White Sox returned to Chicago and got off the train at LaSalle Street Station, Clarence "Pants" Rowland, a.k.a., the Busher, was hoisted atop the waiting shoulders of the screaming crowd and carried through the assembled mass at LaSalle and Van Buren streets.

With George B. Cox dead, the 1917 Cincinnati municipal election was a far different affair than those of the glory years of the machine. The Republican Party was successful in electing former mayor and National Commission attorney John Galvin mayor over two other candidates, Democrat and former congressman Alfred G. Allen and Socialist candidate Thomas Hammershmittthe with a decisive plurality. There was the usual vote count celebration at the Blaine Club and Garry Herrmann, Julius Fleischmann and Judge William Lueders were all there, but the election had a different feel about it. While Garry Herrmann and Rud Hynicka were making an attempt to keep the Republican machine rolling, clearly their other interests were drawing them away. In fact, on election day there was no Rud Hynicka counting votes at the Blaine Club. Hynicka was in Pittsburgh looking after his theatrical house interest and he sent Mayor-elect Galvin a congratulatory telegram. Also, at the polls the voters approved a new city charter that extended the mayor's term to four years.

The war in Europe was now looming ever larger over the baseball landscape. Cincinnati Reds manager Christy Mathewson was selling liberty bonds. In the west, Mathewson was being assisted in selling bonds by Hal Chase. One of the White Sox pitchers, Joe Benz, had used his entire World Series share of $3,666 to buy liberty bonds. Umpires Billy Evans and Silk O'Loughlin had each purchased a $1,000 of bonds. In mid–November, the National Association held its convention in Louisville and Washington manager Clark Griffith was given the floor. Griffith was at the forefront of advocating that 25 percent of gate receipts from organized ball in the 1918 season should go towards buying baseball equipment for the U.S. troops. The National Association agreed to hold a "Clark Griffith Day" in each of its ballparks to raise money for the Bat and Ball Fund. Griffith believed that it would be necessary to raise $100,000 to supply the troops and was hopeful the major leagues would follow suit.

Following the 1917 World Series, Ban Johnson traveled to Charles Comiskey's hideaway, Camp Jerome in Wisconsin, and told the "Old Roman" that he wanted to join the army and serve in France. Most people were not taking Johnson serious and many were accusing him of double talk. Johnson had recently advocated seeking exemption from the draft for 288 big league ballplayers. To counter the exemption, Johnson was advocating reducing the war-time rosters to an 18-player limit. The general public didn't agree with Johnson seeking exemption for what they considered high-paid ballplayers and was starting to refer to them as slackers. While athletes from other sports such as football, boxing and tennis were already serving in the army in large numbers, so far the only major league ballplayer of any notoriety that had volunteered to fight was Hank Gowdy, who was serving in France to become the first big league player to go over there.

Then Garry Herrmann was caught in the controversy when he was misquoted and the remarks were carried in many newspapers around the country. Herrmann was misquoted as saying that he approved of Johnson's exemption request and also felt that baseball should be given special consideration because the government could reap rich revenues from a tax on the sport. However, the fact of the matter was that while Herrmann agreed with Johnson in part on the 18-player roster limit, he did not agree that baseball should have a preferential status. As controversy and pressure mounted on Ban Johnson, by the end of November he had to drastically change course and issued a formal statement that advocated shutting down the major league ballparks for the duration of the war. Also, Johnson was now saying that if the War Department turned down his offer to serve in the army, he would then work for the Red Cross.

With organized baseball confused as to what would be the status of the game in 1918, it seemed logical to sort the matter out. Garry Herrmann spoke with Ban Johnson and suggested a joint league meeting take place in Chicago in early December. However, National League president John K. Tener was peeved at the notion that Herrmann had arranged a meeting without consulting him first and rejected the idea. Herrmann was in hot water over the matter with several of the National League moguls who viewed his action as an end run around Tener. But when the annual National League meeting took place at the Waldorf-Astoria in New York and Garry Herrmann showed up as usual toting a crate of his famous sausage, calmer heads prevailed and a joint meeting of the leagues in Chicago was approved. However, John Tener decided that this meeting was really for club owners and that it would not involve him. There were no actions of consequence to the war effort taken by the moguls. The decision was to stay with the 154-game schedule, but open the season later, on April 16. The 18-player roster was rejected and the war tax on admissions agreed upon. For 25-cent bleacher seats, the tax would be 3 cents, for 50-cent seats, a nickel, and for 75-cent grandstand seats, the fan would have to plunk down an extra 8 cents. Lastly, both leagues agreed to hold a "Bat and Ball Day" in June and contribute 25 percent of the gross gate receipts to Clark Griffith's appeal to buy baseball equipment for the troops.

While the major league moguls were still attempting to skirt the war issue, by the end of December reality was starting to set in as players were being drafted. In Cincinnati, Garry Herrmann lost his middle infield for the coming season as both second baseman Morrie Rath and shortstop Larry Kopf were drafted into the army. Meanwhile, in Nashville, Reds pitcher Fred Toney was arrested on charges that he was attempting to evade the draft. Toney was claiming his $5,000 a year salary as a pitcher for Cincinnati made him the sole provider of his wife and other relatives. However, investigators discovered that not only had Toney not lived with his wife for three years, but that she was employed as a telephone operator making $50 a month in salary. Still, Toney eventually beat the draft and pitched in 1918 for the Reds before being traded to the Giants in July for cash. Before the war would end in late 1918, a total of 247 players from major league rosters would serve in Uncle Sam's armed services.

The annual reorganization meeting of the National Commission, scheduled for January 8 and 9 in Cincinnati, was delayed because of a snowstorm. When the commission sat down a few days later, Garry Herrmann was elected chairman again. However, the bigger story coming out of the meeting was the commission's decision to restructure the players' share of the World Series receipts for the coming year. Under the new rules, 60 percent of the balance from the first four games was dedicated to a pool for the players of the teams playing in the series and of the teams finishing second, 3rd, and 4th in their respective league races. Two thousand dollars would go to each player on the winning series team and $1,400 to each player on the losing team.

As the 1918 season approached, unbeknown to Garry Herrmann, the beginning of the end in his long tenure as chairman of the National Commission was at hand. It all began in early April when Connie Mack, on the advice of catcher Ralph "Cy" Perkins, signed Scott Perry to play for the Philadelphia Athletics. At the Athletics' spring training camp in Jacksonville, Florida, Perry was pitching great ball and his fastball had batters spellbound in batting practice. Rube Oldring, long-time Athletics outfielder, was telling observers in Jacksonville that Perry had shown him more stuff that any pitcher he had ever faced. This was the same Scott Perry that only a year ago, on the advice of Christy Mathewson, Garry Herrmann had sold to the Boston Braves on waivers. However, after 17 days without ever pitching an inning for the Braves, Perry was sent back to the minors in Atlanta. Perry refused to report to Atlanta and instead pitched for a semi-professional team in Chicago in 1917 for $45 a game, posting a record of 27–1. When Connie Mack signed Scott Perry, he was not aware of the fact that Perry was still on the ineligible list of Atlanta after jumping that minor league team in 1917. As the Athletics arrived in Boston on April 15 to open their 1918 season with the Red Sox, things were becoming complicated as Atlanta was asking the Boston Braves for $2,000 for Perry's services.

Immediately Perry began to win games for Philadelphia and the Boston Braves wanted him back, claiming they had the rights to the pitcher as he abandoned them when he refused to report to Atlanta. On June 17, 1918, the Scott Perry matter went before the National Commission and Boston was ordered to pay Atlanta $500 for Perry and keep title to him, with Garry Herrmann and John Tener siding with the Braves and Ban Johnson voting against. In short, the National Commission reasoned that Connie Mack had negotiated with a contract-jumper without first getting permission from them. But Connie Mack was not about to accept the decision without a fight. He had lost 14 players to the draft and had considered giving up hope until after the war. But in Perry, Mack envisioned another Eddie Plank, a player with which to begin the rebuilding process and he was not going to let him get away. So Mack sought an injunction against the National Commission's ruling in a Philadelphia court seeking to keep Perry in an Athletics' uniform. Mack won and the National Commission was barred from enforcing its ruling in the Perry matter.

With Perry barred by court injunction from joining the Boston Braves, the fallout from the matter in the National League was horrendous. Barney Dreyfuss, still furious over losing

George Sisler to the American League, began to once again vilify the National Commission and make an issue out of it against Garry Herrmann. "Herrmann decides against us, and we have to take it; he decides for us, and the American League goes to court," stated a disgusted Dreyfuss. "We need a strong man to head the game, with no connections with any ball club."[7] Dreyfuss also blamed Ban Johnson for permitting the Athletics to go to court on the matter. While there had always been a theory that it was Johnson who encouraged Mack to take the matter to court, it is one that has never come to fruition. Furthermore, when Connie Mack sent the Scott Perry case to court, it was the first time that any decision made by the National Commission had ever been challenged by major league baseball outside the jurisdiction of the game. So it is highly unlikely that Ban Johnson would have wanted to see a challenge to his own authority.

National League president John K. Tener was so angry over the Perry matter winding up in court that he refused to sit on the National Commission unless Perry was handed over to the Braves. When Tener wanted to cancel the World Series over the incident and the National League moguls balked at the suggestion, he resigned as league president. Tener was replaced by John Arnold Heydler as acting president. Heydler then sought a compromise in the matter. The Athletics withdrew their injunction and paid Boston $2,500 for Perry. Scott Perry would have a pretty fair season for the Athletics in 1918, finishing with a record of 21–19 with an ERA of 1.98. However, after 1918, it was all downhill for Perry; he would conclude his big league career with the Athletics in 1921 posting a record of 3–6.

Acting National League president John Heydler, like Barney Dreyfuss, began to question the legitimacy of the National Commission. In the case of Garry Herrmann, there was a piper to be paid in the election of Heydler. This was the same John Heydler whose qualifications for the job as National League president had been questioned by Garry Herrmann in 1909 following the death of Harry Pulliam. Heydler viewed both Ban Johnson as partisan to the American League and Herrmann as partisan to whatever benefited the Cincinnati Reds, and like Barney Dreyfuss, he advocated a one-man commission. Suddenly there was a gathering cloud over Garry Herrmann's Wiggin's Block offices in Cincinnati. In late August, the National Commission would again be called upon to render a controversial decision in awarding the disputed services of pitcher Jack Quinn. In a 2–1 vote with Ban Johnson casting the deciding vote, Quinn, who had been pitching the 1918 season for the Chicago White Sox, would be awarded to the New York Yankees for 1919.

In late August, the *Sporting News* jumped on the bandwagon and ran an editorial calling for changes in the National Commission. In an article titled "Baseball's New Deal To Give Added Life, the paper stated, "The control of the game has been seriously endangered this very season because of the poor organization governing it. Undoubtedly the National Commission will undergo radical changes for the better, rendering internecine quarrels impossible in the future."[8] The fact of the matter was that organized baseball was starting to consider what its post-war plan for governance should be. The dye was cast for a radical change and everyone, including Garry Herrmann, knew it.

By late spring 1918, American troops were in France and Provost Marshall General Enoch Crowder had issued a work-or-fight order on the draft. Some local draft boards were acting liberal in the consideration of exemptions, others were not. In fact, one Philadelphia draft board member referred to baseball as an operation run for gambling purposes. When Washington catcher Eddie Ainsmith applied for a deferment, he was denied, with Secretary of War Baker declaring baseball as a nonessential occupation to the war effort. Nonetheless, Garry Herrmann was pointing out that since the end of the 1917 season, 30 percent of the big league players had been drafted or enlisted in the military. Furthermore, many players were leaving the game voluntarily and taking jobs in war-related industries. In late July, Erskine Mayer left the Philadelphia Phillies to work at the Hog Island Shipbuilding Company, a company that was already employing Chief Bender and Hans Lobart.

But baseball was unsure of its status. Ban Johnson was even advocating closing down the American League season in July; later he changed the date to August 20. In late June, Herrmann, members of the National Commission and several owners, including Barney Dreyfuss, Harry Frazee, Charles Weeghman and Harry Hempstead, traveled to Washington to submit a brief, hoping to convince Secretary of War Newton D. Baker to allow organized ball to finish the season. While Baker declined to meet with the delegation, General Crowder met with them and acted as their go-between. Herrmann, the commission and the moguls were arguing that baseball was a $10 to 15 million a year business that was necessary to the morale of the nation and to the troops at the front. It would be late August before the decision of Secretary Baker would be handed down, which extended an exemption from the draft to players in the World Series. A couple of days later, General Crowder followed suit and gave the National Commission official approval to play the World Series with the guarantee that 10 percent of the revenues would be allocated to war charities.

In early August, a meeting took place in Cleveland between Garry Herrmann, Barney Dreyfuss, representing National League owners, and American League owners, who had been called into session by Ban Johnson. In order to accommodate the war effort, it was decided to end the season early, on Labor Day, September 2, and immediately begin the World Series. National League president John Tener had previously gone on record as opposing any World Series in 1918; however, the National League owners overruled him. This circumstance, as much as the Connie Mack injunction over Scott Perry, led to Tener's decision to step down. But Tener wasn't the only one in conflict regarding when baseball should close up shop for the season. Ban Johnson was still advocating an early close to the season that included playing the World Series before September 1. Some club owners were concerned that fan interest in the pennant race had been killed by talk of an early closing, and overall attendance was down in 1918. With the Chicago Cubs leading the National League and the Boston Red Sox in the American, it was decided that the schedule would be played out as originally planned to Labor Day. While there were still some aspects of how players would be compensated for the early close of the season, baseball had survived 1918, but many observers were now wondering if it could survive 1919.

Garry Herrmann's Cincinnati Reds were much improved in 1918 and had been slipping in and out of the first division all season long. However, Fred Toney, his ace, wasn't winning, and John McGraw was desperate for pitching. Ferdie Schupp had hurt his arm and was no longer effective. Then McGraw lost Rube Benton, Jesse Barnes and Fred Anderson to the draft. On July 25, Herrmann sent Toney to the New York Giants for cash. Following the season on December 31, Toney would be sentenced to four months in jail after entering a plea of guilty to violating the Mann Act, a law which prohibits taking a woman across state lines for immoral purposes.

On August 9, Reds manager Christy Mathewson presented Herrmann with an affidavit of tampering with games by first baseman Hal Chase. The affidavit was in the form of a letter from pitcher Mike Regan, who alleged that Chase had offered him $200 in Boston to win or lose a game as instructed. There were also allegations that New York Giants pitcher Pol Perritt had been approached by Chase with an offer to let the Reds win. Mathewson's response was to immediately suspend Chase for the rest of the season. Garry Herrmann's response was more severe as he indicated that Chase was finished as a member of the Reds. However, Hal Chase professed his innocence and filed suit against the Reds to recover the balance ($1,650) of his season salary. The whole affair would drag on into early 1919. Then on August 27, with the shortened season a few days from conclusion, Christy Mathewson resigned as manager of the Cincinnati Reds and accepted a commission in the U.S. Army as a captain in the Chemical Warfare Service. Third baseman Heinie Groh managed the club for the final ten games of the season. Although the Reds finished in third place, 15½ games behind the pennant-winning Chicago Cubs, their placement was their best in the standings since 1904.

The Cubs and Red Sox were the pennant winners in the aborted 1918 season. The owners decided that in order to reduce train traffic, the first three games of the 1918 World Series would be played in Chicago, with the Cubs switching their home games to Comiskey Park due to its larger seating capacity, and the next three in Boston. The series was scheduled to begin on Wednesday, September 4, but due to rain the series opened the following day. In game one, Babe Ruth, who had previously pitched 13 consecutive scoreless innings in World Series play, added nine more to his total as he outdueled Hippo Vaughn, 1–0. In 1916, President Wilson had ordered that "The Star-Spangled Banner" should be played during military and naval services. During the 7th inning stretch of game one in the 1918 World Series, a band played the "The Star-Spangled Banner" as spectators rose to their feet. The song would not be adopted as the National Anthem until an act of Congress on March 3, 1931. During World War II, the anthem was played before the beginning of every game and became a tradition that continues to this day. The Cubs would win game two, then the Red Sox would win game three, taking a 2–1 edge in the series back to Boston. In game four, the Red Sox beat the Cubs, 3–2, increasing their lead in the series to three games to one. In game four, Babe Ruth's string of scoreless innings, dating back to the 1916 World Series, was stopped after 29⅔ innings.

Game five of the series was scheduled to be played September 10 in Boston. At the National Commission's reorganization meeting that past January, a decision had been made based on revenues from the 1917 World Series to give a cut of the first four games of future World Series revenue to all first-division teams in both leagues. But with lower admission prices and lower attendance in the first four games of the 1918 World Series, there was reduced series revenue. The gate for the first four games was only $179,619 and that meant with the other first-division clubs in both leagues getting a cut, the winning players would probably only get a winning share of about $900–1,000 each and the losing players perhaps $500–750 each. This was far from the projections advanced in January by Garry Herrmann and the National Commission, which more or less guaranteed winning players $2,000 each and players on the losing club $1,400 each. The Red Sox and Cubs players were quick to figure out the numbers. Led by a four-man committee consisting of Harry Hooper and Everett Scott representing the Red Sox, and Les Mann and Bill Killefer representing the Cubs, the players were threatening to strike and not take the field for game five.

A brief meeting was held in the morning with Garry Herrmann and the player representatives at Copley Plaza Hotel in Boston. The players demanded at least $1,500 for each winning player and $1,000 for each losing player. Herrmann knew that there wasn't much he could do, but still promised to respond to the players before game five started. The game was scheduled to begin at Fenway Park at 2:30 P.M. However, with 24,694 fans already in the stands, not one player had appeared on the field. At about 3:00 P.M. a park attendant with a megaphone appeared on the field and announced that the game would begin in 15 minutes. Meanwhile, the band playing on the field did all it could to keep the restless fans from escalating their discontent. The Boston police also positioned four mounted officers on the field.

When Garry Herrmann arrived at Fenway Park, he told the club owners, "I told Leslie Mann, the Cubs' left fielder, over the telephone that the commission could not change the rule, and that if the players did not propose to play, to inform the public at once at the gates. I further told Mann that we would end the series at this point and divide the money that was coming to the players equally among the club owners and that we would take the players' share of the Red Cross contribution."[9] Then Herrmann, Ban Johnson and John Heydler met with the players in the umpires' dressing room. J. G. Taylor Spink, publisher of the *Sporting News* was one of the official scorers and was present at the meeting. He stated that the meeting was a nasty affair and confrontational. Ban Johnson was already drunk, having stopped off for drinks with a friend at the Copley Plaza Hotel, and made no sense when he spoke. Garry Herrmann tried to play hardball by telling the players they were lucky that there was any World Series at all. Harry Hooper of Red Sox suggested that the entire gate be given to the Red Cross. However, his suggestion did not go over well. Johnson tried again, telling the players that public opinion was not going to support them with the war going on. In fact, news of the players threatening a strike was now beginning to spread into the stands and many were calling their actions "Bolsheviki."[10] Rather than disappoint the crowd, and for the sake of the game, the public and the wounded soldiers in the stands, the players gave in and played. Chicago won game, 3–0, behind the pitching of Hippo Vaughn. But the Red Sox won game six and the series, 4 games to 2. Each winning player received $1,102.51, the smallest winning share ever and each losing player $671.09, the smallest losing share since the 1906 series. Still, each player donated 10 percent of their share to the war charities.

Although it was the players that had caused the negative public reaction, the incident severely weakened the legitimacy of the National Commission. Herrmann and Johnson took a lot of abuse from the fallout over the incident, and it gave more ammunition to John A. Heydler and others wanting to dissolve the commission and replace it with a one-man neutral chairman. Reminiscing on the 1918 World Series years later, Heydler stated, "I can say now that our league went all out for the break up the old three-man Commission after that player's strike in Boston. From then on, we felt a strong one-man Commissioner was essential for the important post-war era of the game."[11]

On October 5, 1918, Eddie Grant, who had played 10 years in the major leagues between 1905 and 1915, was killed in action in the Argonne Forrest in France. On November 1, his 25th birthday, Alex Burr, who had played one game for the New York Giants in 1914, became a war casualty. Burr would be the third former major leaguer killed in the war. In all, five former players would die in action in France. Then on November 11, an armistice was signed and at 11:00 A.M. , it would be all quiet on the western front — the war was over in France. Now the burning question on the home front was whether or not major league baseball could survive. Theodore Roosevelt had made his last public speaking appearance in September. On November 11, the day the war ended, Roosevelt entered the hospital. He had been suffering from inflammatory rheumatism that was influenced by fever and infection he had contracted on his journey up the River of Doubt in South America in 1914. By Christmas Eve 1918, he was discharged from the hospital and at home in Oyster Bay. At 4:00 A.M. on the morning of January 6, 1919, Roosevelt died. Death came to T.R. as a result of a blood clot in his coronary artery.

XXI

1919 — Baseball's Achilles' Heel

When the National League moguls met at the Waldorf-Astoria on December 10, 1918, John A. Heydler was officially elected president of the National League. With Heydler at the helm of the National League, Barney Dreyfuss had gained a powerful ally in his quest to unseat August Herrmann as chairman of the National Commission and possibly even run him out of baseball. As the year 1919 was about to begin, there was a serious challenge mounting to Herrmann's leadership. In its edition of January 16, 1919, the *Sporting News* reported the following: "Some of Garry Herrmann's dearest friends and greatest admirers—so doth each and every one of them proclaim to be—have prepared a neat little exhibition of putting the skids under Garry as Chairman of the National Commission this week. With much regret and deep sorrow, they are going to shove the harpoon into his hide and turn it around, humble him, cast him out. But there is no jealousy, no personal feeling, no animosity in the execution—it is all for high principle. No charges are brought in his work as chairman. But the times demand a change."[1]

The *Sporting News* may have been a bit premature in predicting Herrmann's demise as chairman. As the National League meeting got underway at New York in January 1919, several of the owners were aligning with Heydler and Dreyfuss to replace Herrmann with Judge Francis X. McQuade of New York City. The New York press was also starting to get on the bandwagon by suggesting that Herrmann should be replaced. But the facts were that Garry Herrmann was becoming weary with the chairmanship and the fight to keep his job. Herrmann had arrived at a point were he was willing to step down. However, as a politician, his ego would not permit him to be pushed out by the New York press just so they could anoint Judge McQuade. But the owners' campaign to install McQuade became moot when on January 14, 1919; the heirs of the John T. Brush estate sold the New York Giants to Charles A. Stoneham, John McGraw and Judge McQuade. Of course, McGraw needed no introduction. McQuade was a well-known magistrate in New York who won favor in the baseball community in 1917 when he dropped charges against John McGraw and Christy Mathewson after they attempted to play a game at the Polo Grounds on Sunday in violation of the existing law. However, the man who was about to become the new president of the Giants, Charles A. Stoneham, was a bit of a mystery man. The facts on Stoneham were that he had lived most of his life in Jersey City, but had powerful connections with New York Tammany Hall politicians, such as Al Smith and Tom Foley. When the press asked Stoneham why he had purchased the Giants, he simplistically stated because he had been a Giants fan his whole life.

Now that Judge McQuade was an owner, it took him out of the picture as a potential candidate for chairman of the National Commission. Barney Dreyfuss and the other National League moguls that wanted Herrmann unseated were sticking to their guns for a new chairman who was not connected to any major league team. A year earlier the moguls had offered the job as commissioner to former president and current Yale law professor William Howard Taft. However, Taft literally embarrassed the moguls with his rejection. Simply stated, William Howard Taft believed it was one thing for him to have followed Theodore Roosevelt, the hero of San Juan Hill, into the presidency of the United States, but it was another to suggest that he should follow August Garry Herrmann, a man he considered little more than a political hack and lackey for the late George B. Cox, into the chairmanship of the National Commission. It was a supreme insult to Big Bill Taft and he let the moguls know it in no uncertain terms.

At the moment in January 1919, the American League moguls were still not in favor of a one-man commission. Ban Johnson went to bat for Garry Herrmann and got him elected to another term as chairman. While Barney Dreyfuss and John Heydler were chagrinned over their failed attempt to unseat Herrmann, the issue of restructuring the National Commission was far from dead. It was agreed that each league would appoint a committee of two men to study the matter of installing a one-man neutral chairman with no interest in the game. Both leagues agreed and no time limit was set to receive the committee's report on the matter. Serving on the nominating committee were Frank Navin, Detroit Tigers; Jacob Ruppert, New York Yankees; William F. Baker, Philadelphia Phillies; and William Veeck, Chicago Cubs. Almost immediately, the committee turned to judge Kenesaw Mountain Landis, but made no formal job offer. But it was official, the moguls knew who they wanted to replace Herrmann, and silent negotiations were under way. However, by the end of the year, forthcoming events in the 1919 World Series would be the death-knell of the National Commission and would fast-track the appointment of Landis as the first commissioner of baseball.

For now, with Herrmann still holding onto the chairmanship, the moguls faced the uncertainty of major league baseball in the post-war era. The sagging attendance at the 1918 World Series was fresh in their minds as they considered the coming season. Anticipating a downturn at the gate, the moguls decided to reduce the season schedule to 140 games and open the season late. The Boston Braves would open the season in a special "Patriots' Day" game scheduled for April 19. With Braves war heroes Hank Gowdy and Rabbit Maranville due to be released from the army in time for the opener, it had all the makings of a great event. Then, on April 23, the season would begin for all remaining teams in both the National and American leagues and the season would conclude on September 30.

However, the National League owners in their haste to recoup revenue losses created by the war were about to put the National Game in jeopardy even before the infamous 1919 World Series was played. In fact, Ban Johnson's biggest victory in the January 1919 league meetings was not in retaining Garry Herrmann as chairman of the National Commission, but by killing off a boneheaded proposal by tight-fisted National League owners who wanted to impose a salary limit on clubs for the 1919 season. The proposal actually passed in the National League, 6–2, with the Chicago Cubs' and New York Giants' owners voting against it. The proposal would have established a team salary cap of $12,000 a month. That meant that with a 140-game season schedule planned for 1919, the season payroll for each club would have been $57,000, or divided on the basis of a 21-player roster, $2,714 a player. With the proposed salary cap, it would have reduced players' salaries to the limits of the 1880s. This was all taking place at a time when it was being announced that heavyweight champion Jack Dempsey had just signed a contract to defend his belt on July 4th against Jess Willard for $27,500 and one-third of the motion picture rights to the bout.

John A. Heydler. National Baseball Hall of Fame Library, Cooperstown, N.Y.

It was certain that if Ban Johnson had not put the kibosh on the proposal by refusing to even consider it in the American League, a general players' strike would have resulted and possibly even killed the season or the game. Garry Herrmann's decision to vote for the salary cap was probably driven by the fact that despite a 3rd-place finish and improved ballclub, the Cincinnati Reds had only drawn 163,009 fans into Redland Field in 1918. In short, the ballclub had taken a bath financially, and in early January, it had been necessary for Herrmann and the club's stockholders to reorganize the Reds' company, reduce the value of the outstanding stock, and refund outstanding bonds to reduce debt. The Reds had also shaken up the front office for the coming season. While Herrmann would remain as president of the club and still be assisted by Frank Bancroft as business manager and his son-in-law, Karl Finke, he would now be joined by a trio of savvy businessmen on the board of directors that included Charles Christie coming over from the Fleischmann Company, former Cincinnati Safety Director and businessman Walter Friedlander, and C.J. McDiarmid, formerly one of the owners and directors of the St. Louis Browns.

Also, the Reds were unsure of the status of Christy Mathewson for the coming season. Mathewson was still serving with the army's chemical service in France and there was no indication that he would be discharged anytime soon. In late January, Garry Herrmann sent a cablegram to Mathewson in France asking for direction on the matter. When Herrmann did not receive a reply from Mathewson, he interpreted it as a sign that he didn't want to manage the Reds. The Philadelphia Phillies had recently released Pat Moran as manager, and he signed on as pitching coach for the New York Giants. Despite the fact that the Eastern press thought it would be a bad career move for Pat Moran, when Garry Herrmann contacted him and offered him the Reds' helm, he signed immediately. In March, Christy Mathewson would return home and rejoin the New York Giants as John McGraw's pitching coach, taking the job that Moran vacated.

On January 30, the same day that Herrmann was announcing that Pat Moran would be his new manager, the Hal Chase matter was being considered by John A. Heydler at the National League offices in New York. Chase had been suspended by Reds manager Christy Mathewson in August 1918 after it was alleged that he had been attempting to fix games. While both Herrmann and Mathewson were not present at the meeting, an affidavit was sent by the former Reds' manager. Pitcher Pol Perritt, who had alleged that Chase offered him the bribe, also sent an affidavit. However, several witnesses did offer testimony, including Reds pitchers Jimmy Ring and Michael Regan, Giants manager John McGraw and New York residents Sid Mercer, I. O. DePasse and I. E. Rich. John Heydler spent five hours listening to testimony before announcing that it would be two weeks before he would reach a decision.

However, it took only a week before Heydler announced his shocking decision clearing Hal Chase of all charges against him. In his official announcement on the matter, Heydler stated, "It is nowhere established that the accused was interested in any pool or wager that caused any game to result otherwise than on its own merits." Speaking informally, Heydler went on to say that the charges that had been filed by Mathewson were more or less a general complaint about Chase's careless manner on the field, a lot rumors and loose talk. In his testimony, Chase stated he had bet on only two games during his career. The first time was when he was a player in the American League and was a spectator at a National League game, and the second was when he made a bet in a post-season series in 1917. Wrapping up his remarks on the matter, Heydler stated, "I do not know where Chase will play during the coming season, but I wish to say now that he has been not guilty of the charges. I hope the fans and others will give him a fair chance to overcome the unpleasant impression which has been created."[2] Later, Heydler, attempting to cover all the bases while passing the buck, criticized Garry Herrmann for not overseeing a more thorough investigation of Chase.

Garry Herrmann quickly found a new home for Chase and traded him to the New York Giants for catcher Bill Rariden. Of course, this reunited Christy Mathewson and Hal Chase on the Giants and created a rather uncomfortable circumstance for both. The two would keep their distance from each other during the 1919 season. A story goes that when a bat slipped out of Larry Doyle's hands during batting practice and hit Mathewson in the stomach, all the Giants players rushed to his side. All but Hal Chase, that is, who stood by silently watching the commotion with a smirk on his face. While both Charles Stoneham and John McGraw were getting roundly criticized in the New York press for the trade, Garry Herrmann had made a pretty good deal. With Rariden joining Ivy Wingo, the Reds now had two first-class catchers. As for the void at first base created by the trade of Chase to the Giants, in March Garry Herrmann acquired Jake Daubert, 1914 N.L. batting champion from Brooklyn.

On opening day in Cincinnati, April 23, 1919, Major P. H. Hemphill arranged for six airplanes from Wilbur Wright Aviation Field in Dayton, Ohio, to fly over Redland Field prior to the game. Major Hemphill had also invited Garry Herrmann to fly to the game in one of the planes. At first Herrmann accepted, then his better judgment got hold of him. "After considering the situation thoroughly, I decided that I would make the trip provided I would be allowed to leave one foot on the ground," said Herrmann.[3] Mayor John Galvin told Garry Herrmann that he didn't intend to make a speech prior to the game. Galvin stated that he considered it stupid as people came to the ballpark to see the game, not listen to a speech. Instead, a large American flag was unfurled in center field as Weber's Band played the National Anthem. Lasting effects of the war were evident in Redland; ballplayers that had served in the armed services stood rigid at attention on the field and thousands of ex-soldiers in the stands did the same. But after Garry Herrmann tossed out the first ball, the Cincinnati Reds were off and flying high, beating the St. Louis Cardinals, 6–2, before a packed house of 22,462 fans.

While the moguls had some serious doubts about the popularity of baseball in the postwar era, on that sunny day in April 1919 in the warmth of Redland Field, all that really mattered was the game. The *Cincinnati Commercial-Tribune* stated the following day, "That baseball has come back stronger, cleaner and better than ever no one could doubt who witnessed the opening day's game. There may not have been the clown bands and there certainly were not the 'German' bands of yore; there may not have been the frothy frivolities that witnessed ante-bellum games, but there certainly was in evidence a big clean, healthy and overwhelming desire for the national game that bespeaks much for its brilliant future. 22,462 men and women paid to see the game, enjoyed the game and will come back for more."[4]

A little over two weeks later on May 11, the Reds were in second place, three games behind Brooklyn, when Hod Eller pitched a no-hitter, beating the Cardinals, 6–0, at Redland Field. In spring training, at the insistence of manager Pat Moran, Eller had added a fade-away pitch to his repertoire that already included a shine ball. Using this arsenal of dazzling pitches, Eller faced only 30 batters in the game, striking out eight. From that point on, the Cincinnati Reds only got better, and they had a pitching staff that was loaded. In addition to Eller, the Reds featured five more good starting pitchers, including Jimmy Ring, Ray Fisher, Dutch Ruether, Dolf Luque and Slim Sallee, who Garry Herrmann had plucked off the Giants' roster on waivers before the start of the season.

While the Reds had briefly been in first place in early July, the Giants quickly overtook them, but the Reds continued to hang tough and were nipping at the Giants' heels. On August 1, the New York Giants arrived in Cincinnati for a crucial three-game series, holding a halfgame lead on the Reds. There was high excitement in the Queen City as pennant fever was in the air. The Giants were hated in Cincinnati, and as they arrived at the railroad station, a cab driver refused to take any of the players to the Hotel Halvin. In the lobby of the hotel, one overzealous Reds fan hurled an insult at Giants second baseman Larry Doyle, prompting him to smack the fan in the face. In the first game of the series with Cincinnati, policemen posted at both ends of the Giants dugout were holding back 13,000 hostile Redland Field fans as the Reds defeated the New York Giants, 6–5, and took over first place. While the Giants' players took the loss with a grain of salt, John McGraw didn't. That evening at the Hotel Halvin, McGraw placed a telephone call to Boston Braves president George Washington Grant, and by the time he hung up the phone, he had swung a deal sending four players and $55,000 to Boston for Art Nehf, regarded as one of the best left-handers in the game. The Giants lost the second game of the series before winning the third game, 4–0, before a huge crowd of 20,000 fans in Cincinnati. As the Giants were about to leave town, Art Nehf reported to the team.

However, two weeks later the Reds arrived in New York to play three straight double-headers at the Polo Grounds, and they were about to make the Giants look small. This was the type of series that was tailor-made for the Reds with their superior pitching depth. In the first doubleheader, played on August 13, the Reds swept the Giants, 4–3 and 2–1. In second twinbill, on August 14, the Giants rebounded and swept the Reds, 2–1 and 9–3, cutting the Reds' lead to 4½ games. The next day, the rubber doubleheader was played and the Reds won both ends, 4–3 and 4–0, increasing their league lead to 6½ games. From this point on in the season, the Giants could only eat the Reds' dust. The pennant race was over; it was a formality of playing out the schedule. After sweeping the Phillies in a doubleheader on August 27, the Reds' lead ballooned to 11 games over the Giants with just 25 games left to play.

With the Reds pulling away from the pack, everyone was beginning to express sour grapes. New York writers, while not offering any specifics, were alleging that everything may have not been on the square in the Reds-Phillies series. Furthermore, Giants manager John McGraw was now questioning the fair play of both first baseman Hal Chase and third baseman Heinie Zimmerman. It is alleged that Fred Toney approached John McGraw and told him that Zimmerman had offered him $200 to lose a game. As September and the stretch drive loomed, McGraw suspended both Chase and Zimmerman for the rest of the year. With Chase in the doghouse, several after-the-fact comments were being made that his play in the Reds-Giants three-doubleheader series in August had been erratic. But the fact of the matter is that McGraw had a lot of player problems, including pitcher "Shufflin' Phil" Douglas, who went on periodic alcoholic benders. Going into September, with the Giants trailing the Reds by 9 games, Douglas suddenly disappeared from the team and was found by Cubs president Charley Weeghman drinking in Chicago.

The moguls' fears that attendance would be down in the post-war era had been unfounded and, in fact, 1919 turned out to be a banner year with over 6.5 million fans going through major league turnstiles. In New York, the Giants increased their attendance from 250,000 in 1918 to over 700,000 in 1919. In Cincinnati, the Reds increased their season attendance from 163,009 in 1918 to a franchise-record 532,501 in 1919. To recoup some of the lost revenue from the 140-game schedule, on September 2 the National Commission agreed on a cash grab by recommending a nine-game 1919 World Series.

As the Reds were just about to clinch the National League pennant, Garry Herrmann was summoned to the Federal Building in Cincinnati. At the meeting, Herrmann was informed by First Assistant United States District Attorney James Clark and Post Office inspector Morgan Grinswald that he would have to modify the plan for distribution of reserved seating World Series tickets that he had been publicizing. In the plan, Herrmann had intended to distribute tickets through a mail-in lottery drawing system, which was a violation of federal law

THE CINCINNATI REDS 1919
MAGEE, ROUSH, RATH, ELLER, SALLEE, GERNER, FISHER, RING, GROH
DAUBERT, SEE, RUETHER, MGR. MORAN, RARIDEN, ALLEN, WINGO, NEALE, BRESSLER
SMITH, LUQUE, DUNCAN, KOPF, MITCHELL, BATBOY.

Cincinnati Reds, 1919. Author's collection.

relating to prizes of chance. The Cincinnati Reds clinched the National League pennant on September 16 when Dutch Reuther beat the Giants, 4–3.

On September 24, 1919, at Comiskey Park in Chicago, the White Sox clinched the American League pennant when they defeated the St. Louis Browns, 6–5, on a single by "Shoeless Joe" Jackson in the 9th inning. On the same day at New York's Polo Grounds, Babe Ruth of the Boston Red Sox hit his 28th home run of the season off the Yankees' Bob Shawkey, breaking a 35-year-old major league season record established by Ed Williamson of Chicago in 1884. Babe's home run would be the only run the Red Sox scored while losing to the Yankees, 2–1. Between the 4th and 13th innings in that game, Boston rookie pitcher Waite Hoyt would pitch nine perfect innings.

All summer long as the pennant races in both leagues had been forging ahead, a drama had been unfolding in the American League that in September was reaching a high point. On July 13, Boston Red Sox pitcher Carl Mays was pitching in a game against the White Sox at Chicago when he suddenly quit and left the mound. Mays told Boston manager Ed Barrow that he didn't want to pitch for the Red Sox because his teammates were not supporting him and dogging it in the field. He then went to the locker room, dressed and left the ballpark, took a train to Boston, and went on a fishing trip. American League president Ban Johnson ordered that no action be taken against Mays until he was returned to good standing on the team. However, on July 29, Red Sox owner Harry Frazee traded Mays to the New York Yankees in exchange for two players and $40,000 cash. Johnson reasoned that Mays had jumped his contract and suspended Mays indefinitely. Then Johnson instructed the American League umpires to not let Mays pitch for New York. Quickly, the battle lines were drawn, and when the American League owners met in August, they declared that the suspension of Mays by Johnson had been unauthorized.

New York Yankees owners Jacob Ruppert and Tillinghast Houston were not about to take the matter lying down and tore a page out of Connie Mack's playbook in the Scott Perry matter. Subsequently, on August 6, the New York Yankees filed an injunction against Ban Johnson, the American League, Cleveland Indians and St. Louis Browns from interfering with Mays pitching for the club. Furthermore, Jacob Ruppert was threatening to oust Ban Johnson as president of the American League over the Mays matter. Some members of the press were fueling the fire in the controversy by printing misinformation, stating that Johnson owned $58,000 stock in the Indians and didn't want to face Mays pitching for the Yankees as the two clubs battled for the second- and third-place cut in the coming World Series revenues. However, the facts in the charges that Johnson had a financial interest in the Cleveland club were that in 1916, when the club was in dire financial straights, he had loaned $100,000 to James C. Dunn to purchase control of the Indians and keep them from folding. Dunn repaid $50,000 to Johnson and then handed over $50,000 to be held as collateral for the balance of the loan. Then in 1918, Dunn made a payment of $8,500 to Johnson on the loan. However, Ban Johnson was not the only person who bailed the Cleveland club out. At the same time in 1916, Charles Comiskey also loaned $100,000 to Dunn to keep the Indians from folding, and both loans were done with the full knowledge of the other American League owners.

In an attempt to hasten the removal of Ban Johnson, the only president the American League ever had, several owners, led by Ruppert, Frazee and Comiskey, were alleging that Johnson had not cooperated with the owners to keep gambling in check in American League parks. Furthermore, it was alleged that Johnson had withheld evidence he collected on gambling from the board of directors. In September, Johnson was given a further setback in the Mays matter when New York Supreme Court Justice Robert F. Wagner ruled that Johnson could not use any portion of the league's sinking fund to defend himself in the suit filed by the Yankees' owners. With the court's authorization, Carl Mays went on to pitch in 13 games for the Yankees in 1919, winning nine and losing three (for Boston, Mays had been 5–11). With dissident club members, Ban Johnson's iron-fisted control on the American League had come to an end. Soon this explosive matter would have Garry Herrmann in its cross-hairs, too, as he foolishly attempted to negotiate a peace treaty.

In mid–September, as Garry Herrmann was celebrating his most glorious moment in his 16-year tenure as president of the Cincinnati Reds by winning the 1919 National League pennant, his enemies were maligning him, making statements both on and off the record that they were determined to force him out of the chairmanship of the National Commission. Regardless of what his detractors were saying, the facts were that it was hard to argue that Garry Herrmann throughout his tenure had been an honest chairman of the National Commission and always put the best interest of the game above all other intentions in rendering his decisions. Herrmann himself stated that he had on occasion made decisions as chairman that were detrimental to his own club. Now in the light of his finest moment as a big league mogul, his enemies were stating that his status of being both chairman of the National Commission and president of the National League pennant-winning Cincinnati Reds created a huge conflict of interest in the administration of the World Series and therefore should step down.

On September 16, the committee named during the joint league conference in January to find a replacement for Herrmann as chairman of the National Commission met in Chicago. Immediately, Frank Navin resigned from the committee, leaving Jacob Ruppert, William Baker and William Veeck to handle the matter. However, there still wasn't any replacement named for Herrmann. There was an announcement by the committee that Judge Landis had been offered the job, but the next day that bulletin was withdrawn and replaced with a statement that four men were being considered. As the committee packed up and began leaving Chicago, William Baker read a statement that called for Herrmann to immediately resign as chairman of the commission, stating that it was not fit for the president of a club about to play in the World Series to also be in charge of the series. It was a low blow, and even Charles A. Comiskey, who opposed Herrmann as chairman, was red-faced rejecting such an allegation that Herrmann couldn't be trusted.

As the 1919 World Series was about to begin, most observers saw it as a close contest. Typical of the media predictions was that of John I. B. "Toney" Marsh writing in the *Boston Herald*: "I think it will be the closest World Series for a long time, as well as one of the best, but if I were asked to make a wager I would be compelled to put down my money on the Reds to win."[5] Marsh was basing his prediction on two factors. First, he thought the Reds were stronger at shortstop with Larry Kopf than the White Sox with Swede Risberg. Second, Marsh felt in the long run the Reds' pitching was more durable than that of the White Sox. The White Sox were in fact facing a pitching deficit in the series with Urban "Red" Faber, the hero of the 1917 World Series, scratched with injuries, thereby leaving the starting pitching in a nine-game series to fall on the arms of Eddie Cicotte, Lefty Williams and rookie Dickie Kerr against a Reds staff of six good starting pitchers—Hod Eller, Dutch Ruether, Slim Sallee, Jimmy Ring, Ray Fisher and Dolf Luque.

But on the morning of game one of the 1919 World Series, the White Sox's pitching deficit wasn't getting any headlines and they were 8-to-5 favorites to win the series. Manager Kid Gleason had been accused of overworking Cicotte and Williams during the season. In fact, all season long Eddie Cicotte and Lefty Williams had done most of the heavy lifting in the box for the White Sox, winning 59 percent of the team's 88 victories. Cicotte, with 29 wins, 35 starts and 30 complete games, had finished 1st in innings pitched (307) in the American League, while Lefty Williams, with 23 wins, 40 starts and 27 complete games, had finished 3rd in innings pitched (297). Kid Gleason was completely confident of a Chicago victory in the series. "I said last June that the Sox would win the pennant with only Cicotte and Williams in the box, and I'll say right here that my ball club will beat the Reds without being greatly extended. Why? Because we have the greatest hitting team that ever played for the title (.287)."[6] Well, almost. The facts were that at the time, the Philadelphia Athletics had the highest team batting average going into a World Series with a .296 average in 1911. Also, the Pirates had hit .287 in 1903 and lost the series to Boston. The Giants had hit .286 in 1912 and lost to the Red Sox, too.

The series began on October 1, 1919, at Redland Field. Garry Herrmann was happy as a lark as he had received 150,000 requests for 33,000 tickets. Hoping to cash in, Herrmann had even built a temporary bleacher over the left field wall to squeeze a few dollars out of eager fans. As game time neared, the White Sox, who a few hours earlier had been 8-to-5 favorites to win the series, were suddenly 2-to-1 underdogs to lose the first two games in Cincinnati. It didn't make sense. There were rumors flying all over the gambling community that a fix was in, but hardly anyone in major league baseball paid any attention to it.

The Sinton Hotel (formerly the St. Nicholas until 1911) in Cincinnati was the place where Garry Herrmann had hammered out the National Agreement, uniting the National and American leagues in 1903, and where the peace treaty ending the war with the Federal League had been signed in 1916. Now in October 1919, the Sinton Hotel was the place to be during the World Series. The visiting White Sox, most of the serious baseball community and the press were staying at the Hotel Sinton. Even U.S. Senator, presidential hopeful and huge Reds fan Warren G. Harding had checked in. Syndicated sportswriter Hugh Fullerton had arrived in Cincinnati the night before and also checked into the Hotel Sinton, where he was rooming with Christy Mathewson, who was writing a column on the series for the *New York Times.*

Years later, Fullerton would remark that the morning before the first game of the 1919 World Series, he and Detroit sportswriter Joe Jackson had gone to get an eye-opener at a speakeasy about a half-block from the Sinton. Fullerton went on to say in his 1935 article for the *Sporting News* that he was approached by a Chicago gambler he had an acquaintance with. When Fullerton introduced him to Jackson, the gambler was confused, not sure whether he was the White Sox outfielder. According to Fullerton, the gambler pulled him aside and quietly asked him if he had talked with Joe about the fix.[7] At the time Fullerton laughed it off.

The Reds won the first game, 9–1, with Dutch Ruether facing Chicago ace Eddie Cicotte. In the bottom of the first inning, Reds leadoff hitter Morrie Rath came to bat and took the first pitch from Cicotte, a fastball, for a strike. However, Cicotte's second pitch hit Rath square in the back. From that moment on it has been speculated — no one knows for sure — that Cicotte's second pitch hitting Rath was a signal to the gambling community that the fix was on in the 1919 World Series. Regardless, in the 4th inning, Eddie Cicotte was driven from the box as the Reds scored five runs and never looked back in the series. That evening Garry Herrmann celebrated in grand style by throwing a big bash at the Peruvian Club.

On the evening following game one of the World Series, the Sinton resembled a vaudeville house more than a stately hotel. Throughout the building's lobby, hallways and 600 rooms, ticket scalpers roamed freely, attempting to sell their wares under the watchful eye of undercover federal agents who were posted to make sure the government got its 50 percent war tax cut. Early in the evening, Chicago manager Kid Gleason, who had been hearing rumors of a fix, went ballistic in the Sinton lobby, yelling at some of his players, reportedly Eddie Cicotte and first baseman Chick Gandil, who seemed to be in too jovial a mood following the White Sox's loss in game one. Following his chastising of his players, Gleason beat a path for the room of Charles Comiskey for a conference. After game one, the odds had suddenly changed, making the White Sox no better than even favorites to win the series. Notorious gamblers were making book in the Sinton lobby, and it has been said that upstairs in a double room, the telephone rang every sixty seconds with updates from a guy by the name of Bennett in Des Moines. Well-known Eastern gambling figure and former featherweight boxing champion Abe Attell was standing on a chair in the Sinton lobby, clutching a wad of large denomination bills and wanting to make bets on the Reds with anyone that would take his money. It seemed as if a surreal sub-culture had transformed the stately Sinton Hotel into a den of debauchery.

That evening Hugh Fullerton had been at a speakeasy in Kentucky, across the Ohio River from Cincinnati, where talk of a fix in the series was freely discussed by everyone. When Fullerton got back to his room at the Sinton, he woke Christy Mathewson to tell him about what he had heard. According to Fullerton, Mathewson became livid, yelling, "Damn them" (meaning the club owners). "They have it coming to them. I caught two crooks (meaning Chase and Zimmerman), and they whitewashed them."[8] That morning Mathewson had written in his column for the *New York Times,* "I think we are about to see one of the best contested world's series that has been played in years. I look for it to go to eight games at least and, if it does extend that far, it will certainly be a fine battle."[9]

Charles Comiskey had been hearing the rumors of a fix from Hugh Fullerton, Barney

Dreyfuss and others. After game one, he was quite concerned, too. Comiskey felt that he couldn't approach Garry Herrmann for fear of crying sour grapes. However, the reality was that with Comiskey pushing for Judge Landis to become chairman of the National Commission, he felt uncomfortable approaching Herrmann. Of course, one of the lasting mysteries of the events involved in the 1919 World Series is just what did Garry Herrmann know about the reported fix and when did he know it? This was taking place in Herrmann's town and he was a man intimately in touch with everything that went on in the Queen City, politically or otherwise. Garry knew everyone, so it just seems natural that he had to know of the rumors. While Comiskey wanted to confront American League president Ban Johnson with the rumors, he couldn't do that, either, because the two were feuding over the Carl Mays matter. Unwilling to approach Herrmann and unable to approach Johnson, that night Comiskey spoke with National League president John A. Heydler and asked him to intervene on his behalf. When Heydler went to Johnson's room at the Sinton and woke him up, he was quickly rebuked as Johnson blurted out in regard to Comiskey's allegations, "That's the yelp of a beaten cur!"[10] It was back to square one for Comiskey.

With the Reds having four left-handed hitters in the lineup, the general opinion was that Claude "Lefty" Williams would win game two for the White Sox. However, when the dust had settled, the Reds had beaten Williams, 4–2. The decisive runs were scored in the

Claude "Lefty" Williams (left) and Eddie Cicotte. Author's collection.

fourth inning when Williams walked three batters and gave up a two-run triple to Larry Kopf. After the game, White Sox catcher Ray Schalk attempted to assault Williams, accusing him of throwing the game. One of the spectators at the game was Judge Kenesaw Mountain Landis, a guest of White Sox owner Charles Comiskey, whom the Old Roman was smoozing into becoming the new chairman of the National Commission.

Supposedly, the White Sox players in on the fix had been offered $100,000 to dump the series, payable in installments of $10,000 to $20,000 after each of five losses. However, over the years it has been stated that Eddie Cicotte was getting nervous after game two and demanded partial payment from the alleged fixers, White Sox first baseman Chick Gandil, former major league pitcher Sleepy Bill Burns and former boxer Bill Maharg. Also, Maharg had played two games in the major leagues, one as a replacement third baseman during the 1912 Detroit Tigers players strike in Philadelphia.

In game three, played at Chicago, the White Sox, behind the pitching of Dickie Kerr, shut out the Reds, 3–0. However, the following day in game four, the Reds, behind Jimmy Ring, shut out the White Sox, 2–0, to take a 3-games-to-1 lead in the best of nine series. After four games, the White Sox were only hitting .208, and in game five they were going to face Reds shine ball artist Hod Eller. Before leaving Cincinnati for Chicago, Edd Roush had been told by a man who approached him that the series was fixed. When the same guy approached him again and said that the gamblers had gotten to some of the Reds, Roush went to manager Pat Moran. Hod Eller was scheduled to pitch game five, and during the team meeting prior to the game in Chicago, Moran asked Eller if anyone had offered him anything to throw this game. There was complete silence in the locker room, and then Eller said, "Yep. After breakfast this morning, a guy got on the elevator with me and got off at the same floor I did. He showed me five thousand dollar bills and said they were mine if I'd lose the game today." Moran asked, "What did you say?" "I said if he didn't get damn far away from me real quick he wouldn't know what hit him. And the same went if I ever saw him again." Moran then told Eller, "Okay, you're pitching. But one wrong move and you're out of the game."[11] There was no need to worry about Eller as he pitched the best game in the series, continuing to cool the White Sox's bats by pitching the third consecutive shutout in the series, beating them, 5–0, while striking out nine, six in succession. The *Baseball Encyclopedia* states that there is no taint on Eller's six consecutive strikeouts because they include players not alleged to be in on the fix, such as Eddie Collins, Nemo Leibold and Ray Schalk.

At one point when Ray Schalk came to bat, he picked up a ball delivered by Eller and handed it to Umpire Nallin for inspection. "What's the matter with it?" asked Nallin. "It's a shine ball," exclaimed Schalk. "Just the same as Eddie Cicotte pitches," stated Nallin.[12] Indeed it was, and it was actually Cicotte who had taught the pitch to Eller when he had a brief trial with the White Sox before being shipped to Moline by Charles Comiskey because he didn't think he was worth $2,500.

Holding a four-games-to-one edge, the Reds had Chicago on the verge of elimination. But in game six, played in Cincinnati, Dickie Kerr beat the Reds again, 5–4, to give the White Sox life. The following day, Eddie Cicotte, using his best shine ball and knuckler, beat the Reds, 4–1, to cut the Reds' lead in the series to 4 games to 3 and send the series back to Chicago for game eight. Hugh Fullerton stated shortly after the 1919 World Series that about a half-hour before the start of game eight in Chicago, a man he had known for a long time came up to him and said, "Are you in?" Fullerton replied, "In what? On what's coming off. I'm not in on anything." As Fullerton was a bit angry, the guy stated, "You needn't get sore with me. I wanted to give you a chance. You're telling me this game is crooked? I ain't telling you anything. Only you'll see the biggest first inning that ever happened in a world's series."[13]

White Sox starting pitcher Lefty Williams lasted only one-third of an inning, giving up four hits and four runs as the Reds went on to win the game, 10–5, and the series, five games to three. The following day, back in Cincinnati at the Reds' offices in Wiggin's Block, Garry Herrmann parceled out the largest World Series winning share ever of $5,225 to each player. There would also be checks sent to the second- and third-place finishers in each league. However, Ban Johnson, still smarting over the court injunction that had permitted Carl Mays to play in New York, requested that Garry Herrmann hold up sending the Yankees owners their third-place share.

Meanwhile in Chicago, a sporting publication, *Collyer's Eye*, printed an article alleging a fix in the series and named eight players alleged to be part of a conspiracy: Joe Jackson, Chick Gandil, Claude Williams, Eddie Cicotte, Swede Risberg, Happy Felsch, Buck Weaver and Fred McMullin. At once Charles Comiskey offered $10,000 to anyone who could offer substantial proof that any of his players had thrown games in the 1919 World Series. Ban Johnson was suspicious about the series, too. During his newspaper days as sporting editor of the *Cincinnati Commercial Tribune* in the 1890s, Johnson had made the acquaintance of a Cincinnati policeman, Cal Crim, who now operated a private detective agency in the city. He asked Crim to begin an investigation of the World Series. At the moment, Johnson was saying nothing to Garry Herrmann about hiring Crim. That was just fine with Crim, who was a Democrat and had risen to the rank of lieutenant as a detective on the Cincinnati Police Force before losing his job in a patronage move engineered by George B. Cox, Rud Hynicka and Garry Herrmann after mayor Henry Hunt was defeated for re-election in 1913. However, Crim's investigation did little more than substantiate well-known rumors circulating throughout the nation's gambling community.

A year later, Ban Johnson would ask Cal Crim to launch a follow-up investigation. In this endeavor, Crim would follow the money in the Sinton Hotel during the 1919 World Series and connect some minor figures to the alleged conspiracy that would lead to grand jury indictments in Cook County (Chicago), Illinois in 1921. But Crim would have been giddy if somehow he could have uncovered evidence that Garry Herrmann knowingly allowed a fraudulent World Series to be played. By that means, Crim would have had the pleasure of driving the final nail into the coffin of George B. Cox and his Republican machine that had humiliated him. However, in his investigation, Crim was never able to get so much as a glove on Herrmann, much less connect him with any intent to defraud organized baseball.

Meanwhile, in the Carl Mays matter, Frank Navin, the president of the Detroit Tigers and a Ban Johnson ally, declared that since Mays had pitched for the Yankees and won, New York should be disqualified from receiving third-place money and the purse should be turned over to the Tigers, who finished in fourth place. On October 29, a strange alliance took place as John Heydler joined with Garry Herrmann in a National Commission decision to hold up the American League third-place money from the World Series shares. Because of the Detroit challenge to the purse, Heydler and Herrmann considered it a matter for adjudication by the American League. Meanwhile, the rebellion of the three American League owners— Charles Comiskey, Harry Frazee and Jacob Ruppert — against Ban Johnson continued and at one point the three proposed a new league, which fizzled out almost immediately.

Garry Herrmann still thought he was the great negotiator of days gone by. He made a silly attempt to patch up the differences between Comiskey and Johnson and tried to persuade Frank Navin to withdrawal his claim on the third-place money. In mid–November, without notice Herrmann arrived in New York seeking détente and set up a National Commission meeting at the Waldorf not knowing that Ban Johnson could not attend. John Heydler had no intentions of attending a peace meeting, either, having stated that he believed that it was an American League matter. While Herrmann meant well, immediately his critics went to work, declaring that he had been sent by Johnson to attempt to smooth over the dissidents — Ruppert, Frazee and Comiskey — when in fact Herrmann had acted on his own. The new owners of the New York Giants weren't pleased with his actions, either, and calls for both Herrmann and Johnson to retire continued.

However, Herrmann's sojourn had sent the right message, and toward the end of November, the American League magnates called a secret meeting in New York and began to hash things out. Suddenly, Garry Herrmann and John Heydler began supporting third-place money for the Yankees. Herrmann knew this would jeopardize his friendship with Johnson, but he also knew that his time as chairman of the National Commission was at an end. Johnson also knew that if he ended his friendship with Herrmann, any control he held on the National Commission was lost. At the New York meeting, Johnson survived a vote, 5–3, as president of the American League and his ally, Frank Navin of Detroit, was elected vice-president. This dealt a crippling blow to Ruppert, Frazee and Comiskey.

Also, ever since the World Series, sports columnist Hugh Fullerton had been producing a barrage of articles alleging a fixed series, including one published in the *New York World* on December 15 in which he named names that an investigating committee might want to speak with. Back in Chicago, a troubled Charles Comiskey turned his efforts to investigating the ever-growing charges of a fix in the World Series. Comiskey and manager Kid Gleason conducted what they concluded was a thorough investigation of all the charges, but came away with nothing that could link his players with a conspiracy with gamblers. Still, Comiskey kept open his $10,000 reward leading to conclusive information and hired private detectives to continue the probe.

Meanwhile in Cincinnati, Garry Herrmann announced that the National Commission would not begin a probe into the World Series, stating that the matter was for the discretion of Charles Comiskey, who was responsible for the conduct of his players. Herrmann told the press, "Why start another investigation of moth-eaten rumors?"[14] The night following the first game of the series in Cincinnati, sportswriter Hugh Fullerton had alleged that as he returned to his room at the Sinton Hotel, he was confronted by Reds manager Pat Moran, who accused him of getting a couple of his pitchers drunk. Fullerton denied the allegation of getting the pitchers loaded, but not the confrontation with Moran. With rumors still hanging around, in an effort to bring some sort of closure to the matter in late December, Pat Moran sent a telegram to Garry Herrmann, denying that he ever had any such conversation with Fullerton about the sobriety of his pitchers. In the wire Moran stated, "As to my own players and their conduct during the Series, I never had any conversation during the Series, with the writer who stirred up the scandal."[15]

XXII

Herrmann Quits and the Scandal Breaks

On January 8, 1920, the National Commission was all set for their annual meeting at the Hotel Sinton in Cincinnati and Garry Herrmann had done the math. In the National League, seven club owners wanted him out as chairman, while in the American League three of the eight owners (Comiskey, Frazee and Ruppert) wanted him out. With Herrmann abstaining, that made the tally 10 to 5 against if it came to a vote. His early stand on the third-place money issue in the 1919 World Series had tilted the balance of power and left him with a deficit of support. But Herrmann was tired of the bickering over his chairmanship. He had served as chairman since 1903, seventeen years, and done his best to serve the game. He decided to let both National League president John A. Heydler and American League president Ban Johnson save face and not have to vote one way or the other on his continuing as chairman of the National Commission. Instead, he took his fate in his own hands and resigned. As the meeting began at the Sinton Hotel, Herrmann submitted his final annual report. Then in written form, he submitted his formal resignation as chairman. Herrmann had agreed to serve until the league meetings took place on February 11. John E. Bruce, Herrmann's loyal secretary and long-time political ally, also announced that he would no longer serve on the Commission effective the same date.

The resignation read as follows.

Cincinnati, January 8, 1920,

Messrs. B. B. Johnson and John A. Heydler, Members National Commission:

Gentleman: Supplemental to my annual report submitted this morning, which has been approved, I desire now to notify you that I tender my resignation as Chairman of the National Commission, the same to take effect as at as early a period as possible, but with the distinct understanding that I can not serve you any longer after the joint meeting of the National and American Leagues, which it has been agreed to this morning, should be held in Chicago on February 11.

Respectfully,
Aug. Herrmann, Chairman.[1]

During Herrmann's final meeting, the commission did have a cursory discussion about the influence of gambling on organized ball. But the final decision was to just handle charges as they happened. The same day in Chicago, Charles Comiskey called off his investigation of the 1919 World Series. Major league baseball was relieved; they accepted Comiskey's decision as final and announced that there would be no public investigation. At the moment baseball was more concerned with making the peace between Ban Johnson and the dissident American

League owners, even to the point of proposing that judge Kenesaw Mountain Landis should be appointed as a referee to determine if Johnson had been acting fair and should continue as president of the league.

Now that August Garry Herrmann was out as chairman of the National Commission, a vigorous campaign began, primarily led by John Heydler, to appoint Landis as his successor. Heydler led a masked campaign for Landis in the press while swiping at Garry Herrmann with back-handed compliments. A few days after sitting with Herrmann at the National Commission meeting in Cincinnati, Heydler told the *Sporting News*, "From now on the chairmanship of the Commission will be a real job, not a sinecure. I do not mean to cast any reflection on the diligence of Herrmann, as he has been a wonderful man for the game. I really regret to see him step out of the position, but times are changing in baseball and therefore changes are required to the governing body of the sport. The position is a tough one. The man who takes it will be required to stand for a lot of criticism, because he is going to get it, no matter what he does. That has always been the history of the job, but Herrmann weathered it nicely and, I believe has always been fair."[2]

On February 11 in Chicago, the day Herrmann's resignation became official, club owners from both leagues met in a joint session to receive nominations from the Joint Nominating Committee to be his successor as chairman of the National Commission. The names submitted included: Judge Kenesaw Mountain Landis, Chicago; William Edwards, New York; State Senator J. E. Walker, New York; Harvey T. Woodruff, sporting editor of the *Chicago Tribune*; and J. Conway Toole, New York. Surprisingly, Judge Landis was not the preferred candidate of the moguls, but he was still the favorite of John Heydler. When Garry Herrmann was asked which candidate he preferred, he stated Woodruff. A resolution was drafted and adopted, commending the work of Herrmann during his tenure as chairman. The resolution was a formality and it candy-coated Herrmann's resignation, stating in part, "We regret the decision of Mr. Herrmann that to remain at the head of his club in his own city had made it impossible for him any longer to give his time and attention to the affairs of the Commission."[3] No successor for Herrmann was agreed on during the meeting. A split between the leagues still existed, with the National favoring a one-man commission and the American favoring the existing three-man commission. So it was agreed that in the interim the two league presidents would decide disputes in the game.

The bigger news coming out of the Chicago meetings was that peace between the warring factions in the American League had been achieved. It all started when Frank Navin, the Detroit Tigers' owner, made a move in the name of sportsmanship by awarding third place and subsequently, the third-place World Series share, to the New York Yankees. Then the dissidents—Comiskey, Frazee and Ruppert—agreed to drop their three lawsuits against Ban Johnson and one against each of the five club owners loyal to him. Then the American League owners agreed to appoint a two-man committee to review all fines over $100 levied by Ban Johnson. Making up the committee would be one of the dissidents, Jacob Ruppert, and Clark Griffith, one of the owners loyal to Johnson. Finally, it was agreed that the reinstatement of Carl Mays was automatic because past precedent ruled that no player's suspension had ever carried over from one season to the next. Suddenly all factions were claiming victory and Johnson was still president of the American League.

The year 1920 was a presidential election year. The American public was tired of the World War fallout and tired of two-term incumbent Democrat president Woodrow Wilson. Ohio Republican Warren G. Harding was a strong possibility as a successor. In Cincinnati, on January 28, mayor John Galvin, operating a steam shovel on the surface of the canal at Walnut Street, broke through the ice and raised the first load of dirt for excavation and construction of Belt Rapid Transit and Subway System. But Garry Herrmann was all baseball now. He had lost his passion for politics and municipal infrastructure. He was president of the world champion Cincinnati Reds and was determined to repeat in 1920. During the meeting in Chicago, he was making a strong bid for Philadelphia left-hander Eppa Rixey, offering pitcher Ray Fisher and another player. The Giants and Cubs were also after Rixey, who would remain in the Quaker City for the 1920 season. Eventually Herrmann and manager Pat Moran decided to stay pat with their 1919 roster, which in the end would not prove to be a wise decision.

April 14, 1920, may have been the proudest day ever in the life of August Garry Herrmann as the Cincinnati Reds raised the 1919 world championship flag in center field at Redland Field and then proceeded to beat the Chicago Cubs and Grover Cleveland Alexander, 7–3, in the opening game of the 1920 season before a packed record house of 24,822 fans. John D. Rockefeller, Jr., the richest man in the world, was sitting in a box near third base. After Reds starting pitcher Dutch Ruether's first pitch, the ball was taken out of play and given to Rockefeller to autograph. The ball was then presented to Garry Herrmann, who stated that it would be placed on exhibition in his Wiggin's Block office. In the 1920 season, major league baseball returned to the 154-game schedule, and during the off-season, the spitter and shine ball had been banned. However, several pitchers throwing the spitter were grandfathered in, including Carl Mays. On May 31, Dutch Ruether won his 8th straight game, beating the Cubs, 6–5. The Reds were in second place as they battled the Dodgers in a two-way race. Captain Heine Groh was hitting .359, third in the National League behind Rogers Hornsby at .403. Then after a slow start, the Giants got hot and by July made it a three-way race.

In Chicago, from June 8 to12, 1920, the Republican Party gathered for its national convention. Mayor William Hale Thompson encouraged all Chicago residents and businesses to honor the convention by flying the American flag. It was the fifth consecutive time that the Republicans had met in the big town by Lake Michigan to nominate their candidate for president. With the pending passage of the 19th Amendment, for the first time women had been elected as delegates, and 27 were present at the 1920 convention. But there was no August Garry Herrmann in Chicago; he had for all intensive purposes washed his hands of politics. But Rud Hynicka was present, having been elected a delegate to the convention from Hamilton County. However, Hynicka was not backing Warren G. Harding for his party's nomination for president. Hynicka considered Harding a dark horse candidate and was backing General Leonard Wood, a comrade in arms of the late Theodore Roosevelt and a man who many considered T.R.'s political heir and the logical challenger to Woodrow Wilson. Why Hynicka would support a progressive candidate is not known; most political bosses considered it unthinkable. The best guess is that it was a personal matter. The old Cox machine never had much regard for Harding and considered him a small-town political maverick and a piker.

The field of candidates seeking the nomination was crowded, seventeen in all. Besides Wood and Harding, some of those included were such formidable candidates as U.S. Food Administrator Herbert Hoover, Massachusetts governor Calvin Coolidge, progressive Wisconsin U.S. Senator "Battling Bob" La Follette and favorite son, Governor Frank O. Lowden of Illinois. The nomination process dragged on through nine ballots, and on each Harding kept gaining strength as Wood and Lowden went head-to-head, with each refusing to step down and accept the nomination for vice president. All through the succeeding ballots, the Ohio delegation had been split, with the majority of the 48 votes going to Harding with the exception of nine, which were controlled by Hynicka. But on the ninth ballot, the New York block of 66 votes switched to Harding. When Hynicka continued to withhold his nine Ohio delegates from Harding, there were loud hisses, boos and catcalls among the Ohio delegation that could be heard throughout the Coliseum. Still, Harding, with 374½ votes, went ahead of both Wood, 249, and Lowden, 121½ votes. Rud Hynicka was no longer in touch with the political times; the Cox machine had been dead for several years and he no longer wielded any serious political power. Furthermore, for the past few years Hynicka had been busy making tons of money running his theatrical empire in New York City and was an absentee Cincinnati politician.

That night the Republican leaders met in room 404 of the Blackstone Hotel in the infamous smoked-filled conference rooms and agreed on Harding as the Republican candidate. Hynicka was acting as if Cincinnati wasn't part of Ohio and Cincinnati mayor John Galvin was tired of the embarrassment. Galvin took command of the delegation and blocked any further attempts by Hynicka to persuade Ohio delegates to switch to Wood. The next day, on the tenth ballot, the galleries in the Coliseum were rocking, with supporters screaming for Harding. Hynicka finally gave in and made the Ohio vote unanimous for Harding. Now Harding had 440 votes and needed 53 more to be nominated. Then Pennsylvania came over, casting all 61 votes for Harding. It was all over. At the end of the roll call on the tenth ballot, Warren G. Harding had racked up 692½ votes and the Republican nomination. Then Calvin Coolidge was nominated as the vice-presidential candidate. A chastened Hynicka returned to New York.

The Democrats nominated Ohio governor James M. Cox for president and Assistant Secretary of the Navy Franklin D. Roosevelt for vice president. Warren G. Harding decided that he wanted to campaign from his front porch in Marion, Ohio. So he had his front yard covered with gravel to prevent crowds from turning it into a sea of mud. Subsequently, he began making speeches from the porch as brass bands played, Al Jolson sang "Mammy" and every fraternal organization conceivable — the Elks, the Moose, the Ohio State Dental Association — and hordes of women and children tromped across his gravel-laden property. Films of Harding playing golf were shown in local movie houses and no one applauded. Then letters began to pour in to Marion from around the country, accusing Harding of supporting a rich man's game. Harding loved baseball and he was a huge Cincinnati Reds fan. So in order to neutralize Harding's perceived link with the bourgeois golf scenario, his campaign staff decided that he needed to identify himself with the national game. In late August, the assistant chairman of the Republican National Committee, Albert D. Lasker, a millionaire advertising executive (Puffed Wheat, Pepsodent, Lucky Strikes) who owned some stock in the Chicago Cubs, decided he needed to bring baseball to Marion. Lasker knew how passionately Harding felt about the Reds and was friends with Walter Friedlander, a fellow Republican, Cincinnati Safety Director and Cincinnati Reds vice president. So Lasker wrote to Friedlander asking if the Reds could play an exhibition game at Marion against the Cubs.

By the end of August, the defending world champion Cincinnati Reds were holding a slight lead over the Brooklyn Robins (or Dodgers) and New York Giants while fighting hard to repeat as National League champions. They had not had a losing streak of more than three games all season long. But the schedule didn't favor the Reds. They were faced with playing 25 of their 36 remaining games on the road, and in early September the trouble started. Notwithstanding Friedlander, Garry Herrmann was of no mind to play a useless exhibition game for political purposes with the National League pennant on the line, and for Warren G. Harding of all people. So Lasker tried the Cleveland Indians and the New York Giants and was met with the same rejection. Soon Lasker realized that he was going to have to settle for the Kerrigan Tailors to play the Cubs.

The Cubs agreed to foot the bill for the game and club president Bill Veeck arranged for the club to stop over in Marion after playing at Pittsburgh. Then Lasker got Hugh Fullerton to cover the event to make it look less staged and more of a tribute to Warren Harding's love of the game. The game was arranged for September 2, 1920, to be played at Lincoln Park in Marion. With club president Bill Veeck, manager Fred Mitchell and pitcher Grover Cleveland Alexander all in attendance, Warren G. Harding threw out the first ball and then the Chicago Cubs beat the Kerrigan Tailors, 3–1. Hugh Fullerton wrote, "In 1885 Harding had played first base 'barehanded' in a game to benefit the Johnstown flood survivors. Harding was a stockholder in the Marion club, which was a member of the Ohio State League, and attended every home game. He often attended games in Washington when his work would permit and even passed up work for baseball on occaision."[4] Harding in his remarks from his front porch that day pitched an analogy between President Wilson's failure at Versailles, his failure with the adoption of the League of Nations and the great American game, stating, "You can't win a ball game with a one-man team. No one can dispute the American team played badly when it got on a foreign field. There was a meeting of league officials when they sought to change the rules. The contending team tried a squeeze play, but the American Senate was ready with the ball at the plate."[5]

Meanwhile, the Reds began a September swoon. On Labor Day the Reds won a doubleheader from Cardinals, 5–3 and 4–2, moving back into first place. However, by September 16, they were fighting the New York Giants for second place and reeling fast as Brooklyn went on a tear after Labor Day, winning 16 out of 18 games. After the Reds lost a doubleheader at Pittsburgh on September 22, they were mired in third place; there was no longer any hope of repeating as champions.

On that same day in Chicago, a Cook County grand jury under administration of judge Charles A. McDonald, a friend of Charles Comiskey, began hearing testimony in regard to an alleged fix in a game played between the Cubs and Phillies on August 31. When Cubs president William Veeck testified, he stated that he and the Cubs had been duped by gamblers, who sent him a telegram stating that the game between the Cubs and Phillies had been fixed. Veeck reasoned that what the gamblers wanted was for the Cubs to replace the announced starting pitcher, Claude Hendrix, believed to be a comparatively weak pitcher, with hardthrowing Grover Cleveland Alexander.

As the grand jury probe continued, on September 23, New York Giants pitcher Rube Benton testified that during the 1919 season, teammates Buck Herzog, Hal Chase and Heinie Zimmerman had offered him an $800 bribe to lose a game played on September 10, 1919, between the Giants and Cubs. Later Benton exonerated Herzog. Then in a separate statement, Benton told the grand jury that following the 1919 World Series, a man from Cincinnati named Philip Hahn, a.k.a., "the betting commissioner," visited him at his home in Clinton, South Carolina. During that visit, Benton stated that he asked Hahn about the past World Series and was told that the series was not on the square. According to Benton's testimony, Hahn stated that "certain players on the White Sox team had visited Pittsburgh before the series was played and made arrangements to throw the games for a price. He said that the players demanded $100,000 to lay down so that the Sox would lose and this was paid them. Four players were mentioned by Hahn in the course of the conversation. The four are Eddie Cicotte, Lefty Williams, Chick Gandil and Hap Felsch."[6] Immediately, the focus of the grand jury probe changed. At the time there were many in the press that held the belief that if Judge McDonald had not instituted the grand jury probe into the alleged fixing of the game between the Phillies and Cubs on August 31, 1920, then it is likely that the alleged scandal of the 1919 World Series might never have come to light.

As the news spread around Chicago and the nation, reporters rushed to speak with Charles Comiskey. The Old Roman told them that immediately after the 1919 World Series had begun in Cincinnati, he had heard rumors of a fix. He said that he sent for manager Kid Gleason and told him to immediately pull any player out of the game that didn't look like he was giving his best. Comiskey went on to say that on the morning of the second game, he had spoken with National League president John Heydler about the rumors he had heard, because he had no confidence in American League president Ban Johnson. Furthermore, Comiskey stated that since the series, he had paid out more than $4,000 to private detectives to investigate rumors and for a while held up the players' share of the series money. Getting back to Ban Johnson, Comiskey intimated that perhaps a cover up had taken place in regard to a conspiracy: "At no time since the playing of the World's Series did I have any cooperation from Johnson or any member of the National Commission in ferreting out charges of crookedness. Johnson now says that an official investigation was made (meaning the Cal Crim investigation)—if so, it was made unknown to me, my manager or any ball players. The results of such

Rube Benton. Author's collection.

alleged investigations have never been communicated to me or to the league."[7]

But the fact is that Charles Comiskey knew all the details of the scandal shortly after the World Series and had systemically covered the whole affair up. Harry Redmon was a resident of St. Louis and ardent Chicago White Sox fan. In October 1920, Redmon testified before the grand jury that after he had he had lost $3,500 betting on the White Sox in the first two games of the series, he overheard Carl Zork, also of St. Louis and the former manager of Abe Attell when he was boxing professionally, state that the series was fixed. However, after the White Sox won game three with Dickie Kerr pitching, the gamblers took a bath as they had pyramided their bets from game to game. Immediately the gamblers thought they had been double-crossed by the bribed players and began a campaign to raise $25,000 to bet and recoup their losses. Redmon went on to state that the St. Louis gamblers asked he and another man by the name of Joe Pesch to attend a conference at which he learned of the whole plot directly from the conspirators. Redmon said that he refused to furnish any money to continue the scheme and they began telling others about the plot. Following the series, White Sox manager Kid Gleason came down to St. Louis and Redmon told him all the details. Gleason said that Redmon should come up to Chicago and tell Comiskey.

Redmon stated that, at their own expense, he and Pesch went to Chicago and met with Charles Comiskey, his attorney Alfred Austrain and club secretary Harry Gabriel. According to Redmon's testimony, at the conference, Austrain began making a speech about how the White Sox were the apple of Commy's eye and how he was anxious to learn about any crookedness on the ballclub. Redmon stated he and Pesch told the story of the World Series plot to Comiskey and his associates thoroughly, although Austrain didn't seem very interested in what Pesch had to say. Next Redmon stated that he told Comiskey, "I guess now you will fire one or two players and whitewash the rest; it's probably the first offense of some of them and firing the others will teach them a lesson."[8] Instead, Comiskey began telling Redmon how much the players he had named were worth; Joe Jackson alone had cost him $78,000. Comiskey then offered to reimburse Redmond for his travel expense and Redmon refused, stating that he didn't want any reward money, either. Redmon said that he and Pesch went back to St. Louis and waited for something to happen, but nothing did. Charles Comiskey had begun a cover up on the 1919 World Series scandal. Then a check arrived at his home in St. Louis for $30 to cover his expenses during the trip to Chicago. It was at the request of Ban Johnson that Redmon came back to Chicago to testify to the grand jury.

Within a few days of the Benton testimony, the grand jury named two more White Sox players, Fred McMullin and Buck Weaver, as part of the conspiracy. McMullin was alleged to be the go-between with gamblers and players. Weaver's family dentist, Dr. Raymond Prettyman, told investigators that Weaver's mother-in-law had told him that Fred McMullin had brought a mysterious package to the Weaver home which Buck refused. Within a few days the list of players accused of being conspirators would rise to eight with the additions of Swede Risberg and Shoeless Joe Jackson. Charles Comiskey immediately suspended all eight of his players named in the conspiracy, even though the White Sox were in a heated battle down to the wire with the Cleveland Indians for the 1920 American League pennant.

None of the Cincinnati Reds' players was implicated in the alleged fixing of the 1919 World Series. However, Garry Herrmann received a telegram from the grand jury and state attorney in Chicago requesting that he appear on October 1 and asking him to bring whatever evidence he had of gambling in the game. Herrmann told the press, "Of course I heard a world of rumors and gossip. Of course I am intensively interested in the present investigation, as bearing so directly upon the series won by our ball club last fall. Therefore I'll cheerfully go right up to Chicago and assist the grand jury in every way possible. I have never had much information as to the doings of American League players. My testimony, therefore, may not be of much assistance to the present case, but I'll help all I can."[9]

The fact of the matter is that Garry Herrmann, like Charles Comiskey, knew a lot more about the scandal than either ever revealed, and both took most of their knowledge of the series scandal to the grave. On September 25, 1920, Garry Herrmann sent a letter to Ban Johnson that stated, "I am somewhat surprised at Mr. Comiskey's statement published broadcast, that he never had the co-operation of any member of the Commission in the investigation of the stories pertaining to the World's Series last year. If you will look at the files you will find that I not only wrote him but sent the Fullerton and other articles when the same were received at this office; in fact, I gave him the lead to call on the gambler in St. Louis, whom he claims he tried to secure some information from." Furthermore, when Rube Benton testified before the grand jury on September 23, he had stated that after the 1919 World Series, Philip Hahn, a.k.a., "the betting commissioner," had visited his home and revealed the plot to him, naming the perpetrators. In the same letter from Herrmann to Johnson, it is stated, "I am positive that statements made by Benton are absolutely incorrect in many instances. I know Philip Hahn, of this city, the betting commissioner to whom he refers, very well, and when Heydler comes here, as I understand he intends to do within the next few days, I will have him meet him in person, and I know Mr. Hahn will give him a correct and straight story of everything that he knows."[10] If indeed Herrmann, as he alleges, knew Hahn so well, it would follow that he, like Benton, knew of the series plot in the fall of 1919.

Suddenly the blame game was being played. Comiskey was blaming Johnson for the series scandal and now John Heydler was blaming White Sox manager Kid Gleason. Heydler stated, "Gleason could have done much to avoid all this. From the information that I gathered in the East, from a baseball writer, Gleason openly accused some of his players while the series was being played. Ray Schalk was called into the conference and he supported Manager Gleason in his contention. If this is true Gleason should have taken the players under suspicion out of the game."[11] Of course, this was the same John A. Heydler whose due diligence in the investigation of Hal Chase the year before had allowed him to walk away totally unscathed when Garry Herrmann had presented affidavits to the contrary.

In New York, gambler Abe Attell was passing the buck on the alleged fix to big-time gambler Arnold Rothstein, stating that, "You can say that the story placing responsibility upon me for passing the $100,000 to the White Sox is a lie. It looks to me that Arnold Rothstein is behind the stories, and I'm surprised at this because I have been a good friend of Rothstein. He is simply trying to pass the buck to me. It won't work."[12] Rothstein's name had come up early in the grand jury investigation. It was stated that some of the alleged fixers had approached Rothstein to back them in the deal and when he refused, they used his name to put it through. At the moment in New York, Rothstein was telling everyone that he was through with gambling and was going to devote his time to his real estate business and his racing stable.

On September 28, the grand jury voted indictments against all eight named White Sox players: Cicotte, Gandil, Williams, Felsch, McMullen, Weaver, Risberg and Jackson. Eventually the grand jury would also indict five of the gambling associates of the players, too. That same day, the grand jury heard testimony from pitcher Eddie Cicotte, who had waived immunity. With tears in his eyes, Cicotte stated that he received $10,000 for his part in losing the series. He said that he never saw the man that paid him the money, but found it under his pillow in his room at the Sinton Hotel before the first game of the 1919 World Series. He then stated that in the first game he had made an intentional wild throw and muffed a play in the fourth game by deliberately intercepting a perfect throw to the plate from left field by Joe Jackson that may have cut off a run. Cicotte was repentant as he broke down in tears during his testimony, stating, "My God, think of my children. I've lived a thousand years in the last year."[13] Cicotte's testimony had been corroborated the night before by Billy Maharg in a Philadelphia newspaper interview. In the article, Billy Maharg had also stated that Abe Attell was at the head of the gambling conspiracy and eventually double-crossed the players in the alleged conspiracy by withholding the promised $100,000 to dump the series. Late in the series, Attell told Maharg that he was withholding payments to the players because he needed the money to bet.

Cicotte testified that four days before the series began there had been a big meeting in his room at the tiny Warner Hotel on the southside of Chicago to discuss dumping the series. It was because of this meeting that the Cook County prosecutor reasoned that he had jurisdiction in the case. Cicotte stated, "Risberg, Gandil and McMullin were at me for a week before the Series started. They wanted me to go crooked. I needed the money. I had the wife and kids. They don't know this and I don't know what they'll think. I had bought a farm. There was a $4,000 mortgage. I paid that off with the crooked money." Then, after going further into his motives, Cicotte seemed to contradict his intent to dump the series by stating, "The first ball I pitched I wondered what the wife and kiddies would say if they ever found out I was as a crook. I pitched the best ball I knew how after that first ball. But I lost because I was hit, not because I was throwing the game."[14]

Shoeless Joe Jackson also signed an immunity waiver and testified before the grand jury on September 28. Jackson had a brief conversation with Judge McDonald, then before enter-ing to testify before the grand jury, he turned towards the assembled newsmen and said, "I am going to reform."[15] Jackson shed no tears during his two-hour testimony, but often cov-ered his face with his hands. It is alleged that Jackson stated that throughout the series, he either struck out or else hit easy balls when hits would have meant runs. However, in 32 at-bats in the series, Jackson only struck out twice. The only testimony of Jackson's that corrob-orated the testimony of Cicotte's was that players had been offered a bribe. Jackson stated that the go-betweens with the gamblers were Chick Gandil, Swede Risberg and Fred McMullen. He stated that he had been offered $20,000, but received only $5,000, which he too found under his pillow. Somehow he trusted the gamblers that the rest would be paid after the series. However, not once in his testimony did Jackson corroborate Cicotte's testimony that any of his plays were intentional or questionable. As for his throw in the fourth game, Jackson testified that while he was angry about Cicotte cutting it off, if he hadn't, it would have gone to first base. The only play in the series that Jackson said appeared irregular was in the first game when shortstop Swede Risberg only got one out on what appeared to be a perfect double-play ball. As for his own play, Jackson stated that not once in the entire series did he attempt to make an intentional error. In fact, in both the 1917 World Series and the 1919 World Series, Jackson had a fielding average of 1.000 while playing in 14 games. He also led all hitters in the 1919 World Series with a .375 average.

Happy Felsch and Lefty Williams signed statements that they had conspired to throw the series, and the next day Williams told his sad story to the grand jury. Williams stated that while the series fix had actually been hatched at the Ansonia Hotel in New York, he corrob-orated the testimony of Eddie Cicotte about the meeting at the Warner Hotel in Chicago where gamblers by the name Brown and Sullivan from New York were present. Williams fur-ther testified that at the Warner Hotel meeting, Chick Gandel told him that the series was going to be lost whether or not he wanted to be in on the action. He further testified that he was supposed to receive $10,000 after he pitched and lost the second game. Williams went on to say that after he didn't receive the payoff, "I figured then that there was a double-cross some place. On the second trip to Cincinnati, Cicotte and I had a conference. I told him that we were double-crossed, and that I was going to win if there was any possible chance. Cicotte said he was the same way."[16] The most interesting aspect of Williams' testimony was that Gandil had told him at the Sinton Hotel upon the return to Cincinnati that Bill Burns and Abe Attell were also doing an independent fixing of the series and the players stood to get a lot more money.

White Sox third baseman Buck Weaver was on a hot seat. He was contemplating going before the grand jury and telling them that he had been present in Cicotte's room at the Warner Hotel when the decision to fix the series had been made, but he did not join in the plot and didn't receive any money. However, Weaver had been advised that if he followed through with this, then he would be indicted for perjury. In the end, Weaver refused to tes-tify, as did McMullin and Risberg. Weaver stated, "What can I confess? Look at my record in the World Series. I fielded 1.000 and batted .333. That doesn't look much as if I was fixed, does it? I am going to hire the best lawyer in Chicago to defend me and I'm going to be cleared."[17] Happy Felsch stated in his confession that he had bet the $5,000 he received in the plot on the Reds to win the series. Felsch went on to say that after the second game of the series in Cincinnati, he sent a telegram to his wife, May, in Milwaukee and told her to meet him in Chicago. When she arrived in Chicago, Felsch gave her $15,000 that he said he had won betting on the Reds and told her to deposit it in the bank. Subsequently, May Felsch deposited the $15,000 in the Franklin Trust and Savings Bank at 35th and Michigan in her own name. Chick Gandil did not return to play for the White Sox in 1920. As the scandal broke, Gandil was recuperating in a Lufkin, Texas, hospital from an appendicitis operation, and stated that he intended to clear his name.

If anyone was taken by surprise with the breaking scandal in the Chicago court room, it was the Cincinnati Reds. As the story broke, the defending National League champions were in Pittsburgh playing out the string in the 1920 season. When they heard the news of the confessions from Cicotte, Felsch, Jackson and Williams, they were stunned. Reds manager Pat Moran stated, "If those fellows were stalling in three games to us, then they must be consummate actors and they have missed their calling. They seemed to play their heads off against us and it never entered my head that they were not trying. However, it does not alter my firm opinion that we had the best team and would have won any how." Edd Roush then said, "Cicotte had everything on the ball when he pitched to me and I did not make a safe single off him at any time in the games he worked in. His pitching was just as hard to connect with as any other pitcher during the season."[18] Edd Roush would maintain until his dying day on March 21, 1988, that the White Sox played hard in every game of the 1919 World Series. Meanwhile, Heinie Groh was praising the fielding of Swede Risberg in the series, citing as an example of how Risberg had speared a ball with the bases full that almost caused the Reds to collapse. To the Reds, the scandal just didn't seem possible.

As the grand jury probe continued in Chicago, a blast from the past reappeared in the presence of Horace Fogel taking center stage in Philadelphia, with the press alleging among other things that Garry Herrmann and Ban Johnson routinely and openly made bets on the World Series and that they should be summoned at once to tell why they did this. On October 1, August Garry Herrmann did appear before the grand jury in Chicago; however, there was no probing into the allegations of Horace Fogel or further discussion of Herrmann's alleged association with Philip Hahn. In essence, Herrmann arrived to testify with what really amounted to an empty satchel. What Herrmann had brought were the historic affidavits that had been submitted by former Reds manager Christy Mathewson, Reds players Earle "Greasy" Neale and Jimmy Ring, and Giants manager John McGraw in the Hal Chase matter. These documents were of little interest to the grand jury and were yesterday's news. When Herrmann left the grand jury room, he told the assembled press that he was still convinced that the best team won the 1919 World Series. Although Herrmann had been through many political scandals involving alleged fixed votes in elections and alleged rigged public contract bidding, he was deeply hurt by the acquisitions that his team's world championship was tainted. When sportswriter Hugh Fullerton first published reports of the scandal in an article in the *New York Evening World* on December 18, 1919, according to the *Cincinnati Commercial-Tribune*, Herrmann had referred to Fullerton's writing as the vaporings of an unsound mind.

To make its case, the State of Illinois brought before the grand jury a resident of Chicago by the name of Samuel W. Pass as one of its primary witnesses. Pass complained that he had been cheated out of gambling money in the World Series by Abe Attell. Then, one by one, major league executives, managers, some players and members of the gambling community came before the grand jury to testify: Charles Comiskey, John Heydler, John McGraw, Kid Gleason, Rube Benton, Fred Toney, Larry Doyle, Benny Kauff. Ban Johnson found Sleepy Bill Burns hiding out in Mexico and convinced him to return to Chicago to testify. Harry Redmon testified. Even gambler Arnold Rothstein came to Chicago to testify and quickly placed the blame for the scandal on Abe Attell. Subsequently, the grand jury wanted to hear from Attell, but at the moment he was missing.

On October 26, 1920, Arnold Rothstein would be exonerated of any blame in the scandal by the Chicago grand jury. Rothstein testified that Abe Attell and Bill Burns had approached him with the scheme to fix the series. According to the testimony of Rothstein, the two told him that it could be done for $100,000. However, Rothstein stated that he turned them down as he was so sure that a series could not be fixed. Then he personally bet $6,000 on the White Sox to win. For years following the scandal, J. G. Taylor Spink, late publisher of the *Sporting News*, liked to embellish his role with uncovering the scandal by insinuating that he had expedited the investigation launched by Ban Johnson in providing him with names of informed gamblers Redmon and Pesch in St. Louis.

However, a great many people did not take the grand jury probe seriously. Such was the case with Chicago Chief of Police John J. Garrity. Chief Garrity referred to the investigation launched by American League president Ban Johnson the previous year, including his previous Cal Crim Detective Agency probe, as a joke. According to Chief Garrity, the detectives from the local Pinkerton detective agency and the Cal Crim agency in Cincinnati refused the assignment on the grounds that the probe would take them deep into Chicago official and political circles, so deep into dangerous territory that they refused to get involved. Such an investigation would have involved the probe of such notorious Chicago machine politicians as the quintessential odd couple of Michael "Hinky Dink" Kenna and Democrat Alderman "Bathhouse John" Coughlin. Between 1897 and 1938, Kenna and Coughlin partially ruled the Chicago's First Ward, known as the Levee, by controlling scores of office holders in every level of government — city, county, state and federal — as well having many city inspectors and police officers also beholden to them. In addition, Kenna and Coughlin consolidated their power by consorting with notorious criminals such as Big Jim Colosimo and his nephew, Johnny Torrio (later Al Capone), who controlled a string of saloons, brothels and gambling dens on the South Side.

While Colosimo and Torrio made appropriate payoffs to Kenna and Coughlin, they were also beholden to Chicago's popular Republican mayor, William "Big Bill" Thompson. In fact, both Colosimo and Torrio were life members of the William Hale Thompson Republican Club and ready to grease the palm of the mayor whenever he demanded it. No detective agency hired by Ban Johnson was going to risk life and limb poking around this den of thieves on Chicago's Levee. Chief Garrity told the press, "Baseball gambling in Chicago is no more under official prosecution than the stick-up business, burglary or any other form of crime. In the present circumstances, it cannot be stopped.

Arnold Rothstein. Author's collection.

I would have to put a policeman in every building in Chicago. I had better say in every room in Chicago, in order to eradicate gambling on baseball games or on the horse races."[19]

Nonetheless, suddenly everyone was jumping on the bandwagon to clean up baseball. In Cincinnati, Hamilton County prosecutor Louis Capelle said he would wait to see what the Cook County grand jury discovered about gambling in Cincinnati during the 1919 World Series to determine if any Ohio state laws had been broken and, if so, he might request a grand jury investigation. Judge Edward T. Dixon, a Democrat who was running for re-election to the Court of Common Pleas, used the coming series probe to enhance his re-election. Judge Dixon stated that the probe was, "for the sake of America's youth, if for no other reason, a clean, wholesome pastime should be kept free from any contaminating influences."[20] Congressman Sidney E. Mudd of Maryland was stating that as soon as Congress reconvened, he would introduce an anti-gambling bill that would call for jail sentences from two to five years for ballplayers convicted of throwing ballgames played in interstate commerce.

Now rumors were circulating that the forthcoming 1920 World Series between Cleveland and Brooklyn would be a fixed affair. The Cleveland Police Department began raiding gambling dens in that city, and in Brooklyn, District Attorney for Kings County Harry Lewis announced that he would immediately examine Brooklyn manager Wilbert Robinson and some of his players, among them Zack Wheat, Otto Miller, Burleigh Grimes, and Hy Myers. "If there is anything wrong with this World Series we are going to find it out before it's too late," said Lewis.[21] John Heydler kept banging the drum harder in an effort to scrap the National Commission, calling it the only hope for the game. Also, he was stating that anyone who even insinuates that the 1920 World Series has been fixed ought to be shot.

Albert D. Lasker, a Warren G. Harding backer, advertising executive and minority stockholder in the Chicago Cubs, devised a plan to scrap the National Commission and govern baseball using a tribunal comprised of men with no financial ties to the game. The proposal would historically become known as the Lasker Plan. Names being floated by Lasker to serve on the tribunal included General John Pershing, Judge McDonald, Judge Landis, Senator Hiram Johnson and, once again, former president William Howard Taft, among others. Three days before the start of 1920 World Series, Lasker met in Chicago with Bill Veeck, president of the Chicago Cubs, Charles Comiskey, president of the Chicago White Sox, and John A. Heydler, president of the National League, and submitted his proposal to them. At that same time Barney Dreyfuss, president of Pittsburgh Pirates, was in town, and John McGraw, vice president of the New York Giants, was in Chicago to testify before the grand jury. Lasker discussed his plan with them, too. Although both Garry Herrmann and Ban Johnson were also in Chicago, Lasker ignored them. Although Herrmann's snub by Lasker probably had more to do with his snub of Warren G. Harding than baseball.

The revelation of a scandal in the 1919 World Series had no effect on the 1920 World Series, as fan interest had never been higher. On October 5, 1920, the series between the Dodgers and Indians opened in Brooklyn with every seat in Ebbets Field occupied. In fact, Brooklyn president Charles Ebbets had to return $60,000 in checks and currency for ticket orders that he could not fill. The scheduled nine-game series went seven games, with Cleveland defeating Brooklyn, five games to two. The only controversy in the 1920 series was the involvement of Brooklyn pitcher Rube Marquard in ticket scalping. Consequently, Marquard had his share of the losing player's money attached in Municipal Court in New York. Eventually, Marquard would be fined one dollar in a Cleveland court, be reinstated to baseball, and be acquired by Garry Herrmann in a trade with Brooklyn for Dutch Ruether and would win 17 games for the Reds in 1921.

While mounds of historical doubt have been piled on Garry Herrmann's 1919 world champion Cincinnati Reds, mainly due to the long-ago whining of Hugh Fullerton, the legitimacy of the Cleveland Indians' 1920 American League pennant has been given a pass. Nonetheless, a huge question mark does in fact loom over the conclusion of the 1920 American League pennant race, too. It is a fair question to ask what might have been the ultimate outcome in the 1920 American League pennant race had Charles Comiskey not suspended seven of his best players in the last week of the season while being one game behind Cleveland in the standings.

As for August Garry Herrmann, he never attempted to draw any parallel conclusions between other events and the Reds' 1919 world championship. Herrmann was above playing the sour grapes card, and during the 1920 World Series, it was business as usual. It was as if Garry Herrmann was in a complete state of denial that anything had happened at all. There was no World Series scandal swirling about, no grand jury probe in progress, and he had not been pushed out as chairman of the National Commission. At the moment he was having a grand time at the 1920 World Series in that familiar, grand Garry Herrmann style. In the 1920 season, the Reds had set a new attendance record with 568,501 fans paying at Redland Field. Herrmann was already putting everything behind him and focusing on 1921.

While in New York, Herrmann obtained catcher Bubbles Hargrave from St. Paul of the American Association for $10,000 cash and his overcoat. The St. Paul Saints were playing in Baltimore and Mike Kelly, manager of the club, quickly came up to New York and got together with Herrmann at his suite in the Waldorf-Astoria Hotel. While the two talked about the deal for Hargrave, Kelly noticed Herrmann's overcoat. Herrmann told him it was tailor-made and his favorite coat. To close the deal, Kelly told Herrmann that not only did he have to part with $10,000, but also his overcoat. "It won't fit you," said Herrmann. Kelly told Herrmann to put the coat on him, and when he did, the sleeves were way too short. "So, I told you it wouldn't fit. I'll give you $10,000 and a player for Hargrave," said Herrmann. To which Kelly replied, "It's no deal unless I get the overcoat too."[22] Herrmann relented, threw the coat into the deal, and then coatless, he shivered all afternoon at Ebbets Field while watching game three of the 1920 World Series. It was just Garry Herrmann still being Garry Herrmann.

Following the resignation of Herrmann as chairman, John Heydler and Ban Johnson could not reach accord on how to restructure the National Commission. As a result, major league baseball had essentially been governed on automatic pilot during the 1920 season. After the 1920 World Series, a joint meeting of the American and National leagues was scheduled for October 18 in Chicago to discuss the Lasker Plan. While the National League moguls, with Herrmann agreeing, gave the plan a thumbs up, American League president Ban Johnson gave it a thumbs down. Johnson opposed the plan on the basis that his authority would be reduced in administering the league, and he felt that in the long run a tribunal of persons with no practical knowledge of running the national game would ultimately fail. Lastly, Johnson felt that with the grand jury in Chicago still investigating the 1919 World Series and with the Baltimore Federal League suit still unresolved, the time was not right for such a radical change in governance of the game as the Lasker Plan. However, the most compelling opposition offered by Johnson was his contention that if the National Commission could not prevent gambling influences from penetrating major league baseball, how would it be any different with the tribunal proposed in the Lasker Plan?

Joining Johnson in his opposition to the Lasker Plan were American League Board of Directors Phil Ball, St. Louis Browns; Frank Navin, Detroit Tigers; Calvin Griffith, Washington Nationals; and Thomas S. Shibe, Philadelphia Athletics. Collectively they became known as the "loyal five." However, with three American League clubs — Boston, Chicago and New York — supporting the Lasker Plan, an ultimatum was given to Johnson, threatening that if he didn't get on board with the plan, they would withdraw from the American League and join the National League, and one new team would be added, making the senior circuit a 12-team league. A November 1 deadline was issued for Johnson and his five American League supporters to get on board. On October 29, in Chicago, Ban Johnson met with the five American League club owners dissenting against the Lasker Plan. Johnson told the five moguls that he believed that Comiskey, Frazee and Ruppert were bluffing. Johnson decided that they needed to consider a counter proposal, and he devised a plan calling for a nine-member commission, consisting of three members from each league and three from outside baseball.

That same day, October 29, 1920, the grand jury in Chicago issued conspiracy indictments on five counts for fixing the 1919 World Series, naming Chicago White Sox players Eddie Cicotte, "Shoeless" Joe Jackson, Claude "Lefty" Williams, Oscar "Happy" Felsch, George "Buck" Weaver, and Charles "Swede" Risberg. Also indicted were former major league players Arnold "Chick" Gandel, Hal Chase and Bill Burns, along with gambling figures Abe Attell, Rachel Brown and Joseph "Sport" Sullivan. Subsequently, extradition papers were being prepared. Named as the series fixers in the indictment were Abe Attell, Hal Chase and Bill Burns. When the scandal broke, Abe Attell had fled to Canada. From his residence in Montreal, Attell was accusing the grand jury of not indicting Arnold Rothstein, whom he referred to as one of the master minds of the scheme because of his financial position. Attell was alleging that Rothstein had made a profit of $60,000 to $70,000 on the series.

With the indictments in the series scandal handed down, the nation's attention turned to the presidential election, now only a few days away, between Warren G. Harding and James M. Cox. What was left of the Cincinnati machine would play no part in deciding which way the state of Ohio went in the election. Garry Herrmann had distanced himself from the party and Rud Hynicka had severely weakened his influence with his shenanigans at the GOP's national convention in Chicago. For some reason, though, Hynicka still envisioned himself as a kingmaker in local elections. The local Republicans in Cincinnati were waging a bitter election campaign against incumbent juvenile court judge Charles W. Hoffman. From New York, Hynicka was attempting to give orders to the local Republican campaign, and it was resented. As the election neared, Hynicka arrived in Cincinnati to personally take charge of the effort to unseat the popular Judge Hoffman, whom the *Cincinnati Post* has called "the woman's and children's judge."

On election day, November 2, 1920, Republicans Warren G. Harding and Calvin Coolidge defeated Democrats James M. Cox and Franklin D. Roosevelt in a landslide for the White House, 16,153,115 to 9,133,092 votes. However, in Cincinnati, Democrat Judge Charles W. Hoffman defeated the Hynicka-backed candidate Frank R. Gusweiler by 1,500 votes. While many of Hynicka-backed candidates had won in county office races, including long-time George B. Cox associate Judge William Lueders in the probate court race, the Hoffman victory was considered a moral victory and proof positive that Rud Hynicka was no longer a force in Cincinnati politics. Republican mayor John Galvin knew the winds of reform government were starting to blow hard, and the day after the election, announced that he intended to implement reforms in the police department.

On November 8, the National League clubs and three American League clubs supporting the Lasker Plan met in Chicago. They had enough of the gamesmanship of Ban Johnson and made a decision to formally disband the National League and form a new circuit to be called the National-American League. They selected John A. Heydler as the president-secretary of the new league and voted to place a 12th team in Detroit. They went on to formally adopt the Lasker Plan and selected judge Kenesaw Mountain Landis to be the chairman. When Johnson heard the news of the meeting, he stated that he would simply put new franchises in Boston, Chicago and New York.

The support for Johnson and his resistance to the Lasker Plan among the five remaining American League clubs were starting to wane. On November 9, Johnson traveled to Kansas City to address the annual meeting of the American Association. He continued his fiery rhetoric against the Lasker Plan and attempted to build support for his nine-man commission. Organized baseball was potentially coming apart at the seams, and most of the major league moguls, including Garry Herrmann of Cincinnati and Frank Navin of Detroit, rushed to Kansas City to hold private meetings in hotel rooms. The following day, on November 10, as Garry Herrmann was addressing the National Association convention, he was handed a note. The note stated that all the major league club owners had agreed to meet in Chicago on November 12. However, the meeting would be owners only, without the presence of Ban Johnson or John Heydler, who might attempt to rush the process to an inconclusive agreement.

After several weeks of innocuous threats by Charles Comiskey, Harry Frazee and Jacob Ruppert to start a 12-club league, countered by equally banal threats by Ban Johnson to put new clubs in New York, Boston and Chicago if they did, on November 12, peace was at hand. In Chicago, the moguls, without any attorneys or league officials present, went into a closed-door meeting that lasted four hours. They decided to scrap both the Lasker Plan and the Johnson proposal and instead develop a plan with one man acting as the supreme head of major league baseball. They unanimously agreed to offer the job of governing major league baseball to judge Kenesaw Mountain Landis in a contract calling for seven years at a salary of $42,500 a year. Later in the day, Herrmann and all the owners but Phil Ball of the St. Louis Browns, who still opposed the plan, took taxi cabs to the Federal Building in Chicago and called upon Judge Landis. While he immediately accepted the position, the judge demanded $50,000 a year. Since he was still serving as a federal judge, he announced that his current $7,500 annual salary would be deducted from his commissioner's salary. Landis stated his office would be in Chicago and that he was ready to start immediately.

Landis had been appointed a judge to the United States District Court for the Northern District of Illinois in 1905. President Theodore Roosevelt wanted to appoint what he considered a tough judge to the post and one he considered supportive of his progressive agenda against big business. Landis was a progressive ideologue. He had been champing at the bit to become baseball's commissioner. He believed that the reformation of baseball was an extension of the social and political reform movement begun in the Teddy Roosevelt era. Other than Connie Mack and Calvin Griffith, Landis had very little respect for the owners, and he smarted at them as being referred to in the press as moguls. But the prevailing mindset of Judge Kenesaw Mountain Landis was that by bringing an end to the National Commission, outing Garry Herrmann and limiting the power of Ban Johnson, whom he considered a dictator, was bringing an end to "bossism" in the national game, and he relished the role.

In the interim, organized baseball needed to draft a new national agreement to replace the National Commission. To accomplish the task, a drafting committee was established and John A. Heydler named August Herrmann, Charles Ebbets and Barney Dreyfuss to represent the National League. Ban Johnson, being careful not to name any of his detractors, named Thomas Shibe, Frank Navin and James C. Dunn to represent the American League. Judge Landis would preside as chairman of the committee and Heydler and Johnson would serve as ex-officio members of the committee. But oddly enough, the man that major league baseball had kicked out as the leader of its governing body, August Herrmann, would be the man they would look to for the task of drafting the major points of the new agreement. Historically, John A. Heydler has been given credit for drafting the new agreement, which is incorrect. The facts are that Heydler made two contributions to the new agreement. The first was that the term of the agreement should be for twenty five years. The second was that the chairman should be named Director General of Baseball. Landis rejected the title.

On Monday, December 6, 1920, a court of appeals decision was handed down, upholding the reserve clause and holding that major league baseball is not interstate commerce or subject to antitrust laws. The court's decision reversed a 1919 judgment that had awarded $264,000 in damages to the Baltimore Federal League club. In 1921, President Harding would appoint William Howard Taft as chief justice of the United States Supreme Court. In 1922, the Supreme Court headed by Taft would uphold the 1920 court of appeals decision in the Baltimore suit. With the old Federal League baggage seemingly out of the way, major league baseball could breathe easier.

For several days, Garry Herrmann had been laboriously working on a draft of a new charter for major league baseball. It was a familiar labor for Herrmann, and considering the circumstances, it could have been his finest hour. But in the end, the new agreement closely followed the old. There were some changes in the new agreement, such as the restoration of the minor league draft, but only one major change was included — the one-man commissioner's decision was to be controlling, and he was given the authority to fix penalties in player rule infractions. On Wednesday, December 8, 1920, Garry Herrmann departed Cincinnati for New York carrying the draft document with him. The joint meeting of the leagues lasted three days. The draft of the new agreement was accepted by both leagues and then sent to the lawyers for perusal.

Before departing for New York, Herrmann began to close out his business with the National Commission. He packed up all the commission property that he had and sent it into storage, placing it in a large room of the upper grandstand at Redland Field (later Crosley Field). Then Herrmann prepared a memorandum listing the articles for Judge Landis that included a crate containing a roll-top desk, a crate containing a Smith-Premier typewriter, a crate containing a letter-press stand, press and cabinet, along with many boxes containing papers relative to the Federal League war and more than 45,000 personal papers, letters and records. The only articles that Landis was interested in were documents relating to the 1919 World Series. The rest would continue to sit in their Redland Field/Crosley Field tomb for the next 40 years, until 1960 when then Reds owner Powell Crosley, Jr. would donate them to the National Baseball Hall of Fame in Cooperstown. However, archiving of the Herrmann papers would not begin for another 46 years, in 2006. For many years Garry Herrmann had been sailing on a major league baseball world that was flat, and in 1920 when he stepped down off the ship as chairman of the National Commission, he slid off the side of that world into an historical abyss.

XXIII

The Black Sox Trial

On January 12, 1921, the major league moguls gave their final approval to a seven-year agreement with judge Kenesaw Mountain Landis, making him the first commissioner of major league baseball. Landis was given broad sweeping autocratic authority and began his new duties nine days later. Surprisingly, Judge Landis had not shown an inclination to want to prosecute the eight indicted players in the 1919 World Series scandal. After the scandal had broken in September 1920, Ban Johnson had asked Landis what he intended to do about it and was told, "Nothing."[1] This rankled Johnson, who despised Landis. The press was now referring to the indicted players as the Black Sox, and according to Illinois law, the perpetrators of the series scandal had to be brought to trial within 18 months of the act that had occurred in October 1919. With time running out on bringing the players to trial, on March 13, 1921, Landis exercised his authority and placed the eight players indicted by the grand jury on baseball's ineligible list. However, charges against Fred McMullin would eventually be dropped due to lack of evidence. Five of the gamblers were also indicted.

The previous fall there had been a change in the District Attorney's office and District Attorney Crowe inherited the Black Sox case from former Assistant District Attorney Hartley L. Replogle. Now, in early 1921 with the clock ticking against the prosecution, there was an aura of uncertainty of whether or not the state could make a case against the players. It was revealed that confessions of Eddie Cicotte, Shoeless Joe Jackson and Lefty Williams were missing. District Attorney Crowe notified Ban Johnson that without the confessions, the state didn't have a case and, consequently, the charges might have to be dropped. Johnson accused Arnold Rothstein of paying $10,000 for the stolen documents. However, Rothstein denied the charge and threatened to sue Johnson for libel. Suddenly, the stolen confessions were offered for sale to various newspapers as stories. In fact, the *New York Herald* offered copies of the confessions in eight installments to the *Chicago Tribune* for $25,000. District Attorney Crowe needed to quickly rebuild his case without the stolen testimony. Furthermore, Crowe and his assistant, John Tyrell, would need to bring new evidence to the grand jury to extend the time limit. In order to have any chance at convicting the players, Crowe needed to directly connect the players to the gamblers. To that end, Ban Johnson traveled to Del Rio, Texas, and convinced "Sleepy Bill" Burns, who had been hiding out Mexico, to return to Chicago and testify. Burns would become the prosecution's chief witness.

The Cook County grand jury had indicted Abe Attell on charges of bribing the White Sox players in connection with the 1919 series scandal. When the series scandal broke in late September 1920, Attell was telling all that he would name the fixers and blow open the scandal.

However, Attell suddenly had a change of heart and abruptly left New York to hide out in Montreal. But Attell soon missed the bright lights of Broadway, and in early 1921, returned to New York. When news of Attell's return to New York reached District Attorney Crowe in Chicago, he set the legal wheels in motion to extradite him to Illinois. But Attell decided to fight extradition and filed a writ of habeas corpus in the New York supreme court. He claimed that he was not the Abe Attell that had been indicted in Illinois in connection with the 1919 World Series scandal.

On June 6, 1921, a hearing on Attell's writ was heard in the New York supreme court. A Chicago resident by the name of Samuel W. Pass had complained loudly before the Cook County grand jury in September 1920 that he had been bilked by Attell in the 1919 series scandal. Subsequently, Illinois District Attorney Crowe sent Pass to New York to identify Attell. When Pass took the stand and was asked to point

Judge Kenesaw Mountain Landis, commissioner of baseball, 1920–1944. Author's collection.

out Attell, he stated that he had never seen him before. Pass also went on to say that the testimony that he had given to the grand jury in Illinois was hearsay. Other witnesses that had been brought in by the New York district attorney to identify Attell failed to show up in court. Then the attempt to extradite Attell fell apart when Justice Tierney, who had been hearing the case, went on a month's vacation. Attell's attorney informed the new justice, Martin, that because of the change in jurists, he would need to delay the hearing for at least a month. Meanwhile, all of the indicted White Sox players kept a safe distance from New York, fearing that they might be sworn in as witnesses and have to state whether or not they had ever met or dealt with Abe Attell. Even without Attell, District Attorney Crowe was still able to rebuild enough evidence to secure new indictments of the original eight players and five gamblers as well as the indictment of five additional gamblers who worked out of the Midwest.

The defense had also been building its case and was certain that it could quash the indictments. There was still a lot of uncertainty as to what law existed on the books in Illinois covering the charges against the eight players. Was playing crooked baseball in Illinois a crime? Were the defendants actually guilty of a conspiracy to throw games? The confessions of Cicotte, Jackson and Williams were key to the prosecution's case and they no longer existed. If the prosecution attempted to reconstruct them by having any of the grand jurors or even Judge Charles A. McDonald testify, charges of perjury could be filed. Furthermore, without a definitive law existing that covered the alleged actions of the players, the testimony of Abe Attell, and the confessions of Cicotte, Jackson and Williams, it was going to be very difficult for the prosecution to connect the dots in the scandal.

Other states were aware of the loose legal grounds that the Illinois Attorney General was working on in building his case and were determined to make sure that should a subsequent event occur in their jurisdiction, there would be an appropriate legal foundation on which to secure convictions. Such was the case in Ohio, where the alleged fix of the series had been made operational. On April 27, 1921, the Ohio State General Assembly passed a bill to make it illegal in the state to attempt to bribe a professional baseball player or manager or participant in any other sport to lose a game. The bill contained tough penalties for such acts, including fines of $10,000 and prison terms of one to five years.

It was now early July and as his ballclub was fighting to stay out of the second division, Garry Herrmann was spending a few weeks relaxing at the Laughery Club in Aurora, Indiana. While Herrmann was still attempting to keep Laughery operating out of his pocket, Prohibition was slowly sounding the death knell on the retreat. Ban Johnson contacted Herrmann and informed him that District Attorney Crowe might want to secure some testimony from him about his duties as Chairman of the National Commission during the 1919 World Series. Herrmann did go to Chicago and testify, but it was all formality. Just as with the testimony of Charles Comiskey, the prosecution played softball with Garry.

Thirty-eight-year-old judge Hugo Friend was assigned as the Black Sox trial judge. Then after two weeks and the examination of 600 potential jurors, the panel was seated on July 15 and the trial began. But it would be a travesty; the defense threatened to disrupt the pennant races by calling large numbers of current players to testify. Fans in Chicago sent a petition to Kenesaw Landis with 10,000 names on it asking that Buck Weaver be reinstated. Dutch Ruether had beaten the White Sox in the 1919 World Series and was now pitching for Brooklyn. Ruether showed up in the courtroom and shook hands with the accused players. Likewise, White Sox manager Kid Gleason and several players, such as Eddie Collins, Red Faber and Ray Schalk, frequently showed up in the courtroom and were openly friendly with the indicted players, slapping them on the back, joking with them and wishing them good luck. This outraged the press, but others saw it from a fraternal perspective. Christy Mathewson was analytical in his reasoning, stating that the act could be condemned but the individual forgiven. Matty professed that Gleason, Collins and the other White Sox were deeply saddened by what had happened, but they didn't want to see their ex-teammates sent to the slammer for two-to-five years. While Gleason, Collins, Faber and Schalk were openly glad-handing players that might have cost them a world championship, the reality was that not a single other major league player was expressing outrage or disgust at what had happened. In regard to the eight White Sox players on trial in Chicago, a flannel wall of silence prevailed among the big league players. The nation as a whole had lost interest in the Black Sox trail and most newspapers printed reports of it deep inside their daily editions.

The prosecution called "Sleepy Bill" Burns to the stand and he was examined by Assistant State Attorneys Edward Prindville and George Gorman, then cross-examined by defense attorneys James "Ropes" O'Brien, Michael Ahearn, Max Lusker and Ben Short. Burns alleged that the players had first approached him about fixing the series. During examination by Gorman, Burns stated that he had met Eddie Cicotte and Chick Gandil at the Hotel Ansonia in New York City on September 16, 1919. Burns testified that at the meeting he was told by Cicotte that the White Sox were going to win the pennant and that he had something good for him. Then at a follow up meeting with Cicotte and Gandil at the Ansonia on September 18, he was told by Gandil that if he could get $100,000, the White Sox would throw the World Series. Burns also stated that present at one of these meetings at the Ansonia were New York Giants pitchers Fred Toney and Jean Dubuc.

Prindville asked Burns who was at the meeting at the Sinton Hotel in Cincinnati the night before game one of the World Series. Burns stated Gandil, McMullen, Williams, Felsch, Cicotte, and Weaver. He was asked by Prindville if Jackson was in the meeting, and he replied that he didn't see him. Prindville then asked Burns about the conversation he had with the players and he stated that he told them he had $100,000 to cover fixing the series and that the financiers were Arnold Rothstein, Attell and Bennett. Prindville asked Burns if Bennett was in the court room and he said yes. He was then asked to identify Bennett. Burns rose from his chair and pointed toward a man in a yellow shirt and said that was Bennett. The man identified by Burns as Bennett was actually David Zeilser. Bennett, a.k.a. David Zeilser, was one of the indicted gamblers and the alleged confidential go-between of Arnold Rothstein.

In their cross-examination of Burns, the prosecution screamed at him and threw one insult after another. The abuse of the witness became so intense that Judge Hugo Friend eventually intervened. The prosecution had set up a scenario for Burns as a go-between of the fixers and players, who were supposed to receive $20,000 from Abe Attell after each Cincinnati win. However, the prosecution attempted to make it appear that Burns was a double-crosser and on his own demanded a cut from the players to be paid to him by Chick Gandil. Under cross-examination by defense attorney Max Lusker, Burns was asked where he was going to get his reward for fixing the series. Burns replied from the players and Attell. When asked by Lusker if he thought that was double-crossing, Burns replied, "No." Then defense attorney Ben Short asked Burns if he had threatened Chick Gandil with revealing the fix if the players didn't come through with their share for him. Burns stated that he didn't double-cross the players until they double-crossed him. The players, suspecting a double-cross, had decided to switch the order in which they lost games. Short then accused Burns of testifying against the players because he was double-crossed when they didn't cough up their payment to him, not for the purity of the game, and Burns concurred.

On Monday, July 25, the prosecution was given a ray of hope. Judge Hugo Friend removed the jury from the court room. Then Judge Friend heard testimony from Eddie Cicotte, Shoeless Joe Jackson and Lefty Williams in regard to their confessions. The three accused players all admitted making confessions, but said that they had done so under duress. Furthermore, Cicotte, Jackson and Williams all swore that they had made confessions under the promise of immunity before signing some sort of paper that each did not know was actually a waiver of immunity. Judge McDonald and former District Attorney Replogle followed the three players to the stand and both swore that there was no promise of immunity made to Cicotte, Jackson or Williams on their statements.

The defense called Charles Comiskey's attorney, Alfred Austrain, to the stand with the intent to prove that he had called Harry Redmond a blackmailer when Redmond told him what he knew of Comiskey's attempt to cover up the series scandal. Austrain denied the charges. They questioned him on his alleged promise to the players to get off easy in return for their confessions. Once again, Austrain testified to the contrary. The defense sought to cast Austrain as an unreliable witness, one who was working as the club official who was charged with prosecuting the case against the players as well as acting as the attorney for one of the persons accused of planning the fix. The defense accused Austrain of acting as an attorney or advisor for Arnold Rothstein when he came to Chicago to testify before the grand jury. Austrain denied the allegation. However, it was revealed by the defense during the testimony of Austrain that the missing confession of Lefty Williams had been in his office, not the office of the state's attorney.

Judge Friend ruled that the confessions of Cicotte, Jackson and Williams could be used as evidence against the three players, but not others named in their statements. However, as the original confessions no longer existed, the jury would be given a transcript. The prosecution was filled with joy, and out in the halls during court recess, they began talking tough, telling the press that nothing less than sentences to the penitentiary for all the players and gamblers would satisfy them.

The prosecution had intended to put former St. Louis Browns second baseman Joe Gedeon on the stand to testify that Carl Zork had been instrumental in setting up the secondary fix of the series. However, as the trial proceeded, the prosecution became antsy about having Gedeon testify in regard to Zork's part in the conspiracy because they weren't sure he would be a reliable witness. So the prosecution turned to Harry Redmon to make its case that the 1919 series scandal was actually a two-part fix. According to the testimony of Redmon, the fix arranged by Abe Attell and Bennett fell apart when the players decided to double-cross the gamblers and switch the order in which they lost the games by winning one. At that point, according to the testimony of Redmon, a second fix was arranged by Carl Zork and Ben Franklin of St. Louis, who were called in to finance it. In the new scenario arranged with the players, they agreed to drop the last two games of the series for $20,000. Redmond also testified that Carl Zork often boasted that he had the players under his thumb and he had fixed games during the regular season. Redmond stated that Zork told him that it was just as easy to fix big games as ordinary games. However, evidence of other games being fixed by Zork was not allowed since only the games in the 1919 World Series were involved in the trial.

The defense was very skillful in not putting any of the accused players on the stand and have them face cross-examination by the prosecution. However, near the end of the trial, the defense summoned Kid Gleason, Eddie Collins and a few other present members of the White Sox to testify. At the time the White Sox were playing in Washington, so Gleason and the others were forced to leave the club and return to Chicago. In their testimony for the defense, they would provide alibis for the accused players on the Monday before the World Series started. Kid Gleason, Eddie Collins and Ray Schalk testified that it would have been impossible for "Sleepy Bill" Burns to have met with any of the accused players on the Monday before the first game of the World Series, because the whole team practiced that Monday morning at the Cincinnati ballpark from about 10:00 a.m. until noon. Furthermore, Collins testified he and Buck Weaver had gone to the horse races that afternoon. However, Schalk did testify that he was aware of a meeting between several of the accused players in a room at the Sinton Hotel previous to the series.

In the end, the defense had allowed the prosecution to paint itself into a corner by not helping them prove a weak case. In its summation, the prosecution focused on the confessions of Cicotte, Jackson and Williams, stating that all three had sold out the American public for a paltry $20,000. But their consciences would not let them rest and when the scandal broke, they sought out the state's attorney office to make their confessions and repeated them to the grand jury. Calling for the most severe punishment of the law, five years in the penitentiary and fines of $2,000 for each defendant, state's attorney Edward Prindville stated that the evidence showed that a swindle and a con game had been worked on the American people, and unless a verdict of guilty was returned, legislation would be passed to stamp out corruption in not only baseball, but also boxing and horseracing.

The defense in its summation stated that the state had failed to establish that a criminal conspiracy had taken place or that the players had any intention of defrauding the public or bringing ill will upon the game. The defense questioned why Arnold Rothstein had not been indicted. The defense pointed out that when Rothstein came to Chicago to testify before the grand jury, he was chaperoned by Alfred Austrain, who later boasted that he had prevented him from being indicted. The defense questioned why Abe Attell, Hal Chase and several other gamblers remained unindicted, while under-paid ball players and a few penny-ante gamblers from Des Moines and St. Louis were being made the goats in the case.

The hardest hitting summation, however, came from defense attorney Michael Ahearn, who stated that Ban Johnson had been the directing genius of the prosecution. Ahearn stated that it was Johnson who had hired "Sleepy Bill" Burns and Bill Maharg to gather evidence. Ahearn also said that Johnson used his money to send Maharg to Mexico to find Burns, and that Maharg had come into the court room as an auto worker, but he had enough diamonds on his fingers to buy a fleet of autos. Ahearn then characterized the prosecution's chief witness as a liar. Ahearn stated that Burns had testified that he had talked to the players on the morning before the first game, but had not. Then he accused Burns of lying about meeting with Chick Gandil in Chicago after game two. Ahearn concluded by comparing Burns to moonshine, stating that it looks good, but when one drinks it, the result is a stomachache.

On Tuesday, August 2, 1921, Judge Friend instructed the jury "that the state must prove that it was the intent of the Chicago White Sox players and others charged with conspiracy, through the throwing of the 1919 World Series, to defraud the public and others, and not merely to throw baseball games."[2] Judge Friend then put the case in the hands of the jury and it retired from the courtroom to deliberate. Outside the courtroom, the accused players and gamblers nervously paced back and forth, sometimes gathering in little groups to discuss the case. Then after two hours and 47 minutes of deliberation, three loud knocks were heard on the jury room door; a verdict had been reached. Everyone raced back into the courtroom. Anticipating that the jury would take considerable time to reach a verdict, Judge Friend had left the court. Consequently, it was forty minutes later before court was back in session and the jury brought in. Then nine verdicts of not guilty were read, acquitting not only Eddie Cicotte, Happy Felsch, Chick Gandil, Joe Jackson, Swede Risberg, Buck Weaver and Lefty Williams, but also Carl Zork of St. Louis and David Zeilser of Des Moines.

Hundreds of spectators had packed the courtroom and immediately following the verdict, pandemonium ensued. The air in the room was filled with shouts of "Hooray for the Clean Sox!"[3] Hats were tossed in the air and papers thrown around. Buck Weaver grabbed Swede Risberg and the two embraced. Eddie Cicotte rushed toward the jurors and grabbed William Barrett by both hands, shouting, "Thanks!" Likewise, Joe Jackson and Lefty Williams dashed toward the jurors behind Cicotte. The jurors then lifted the players on their shoulders and flashes from photographers' cameras exploded like fireworks in the courtroom. Bailiffs began slamming gavels on the bench, calling for order. However, when they noticed Judge Friend smiling, they dropped their judicial hammers and began whistling as loud as they could. Happy Felsch just stood at the defendant's table and smiled. Chick Gandil got up, shook hands with a few friends, and quietly slipped out of the courtroom. When the press caught up with Gandil, he gave what he said was a sailor's farewell to Ban Johnson, stating, "Goodbye, good luck and to hell with you."[4] That evening the acquitted players, their defense attorneys and several members of the jury, celebrated at an Italian restaurant in Chicago's loop.

However, the holiday from justice for seven acquitted White Sox players and non-indicted player Fred McMullin would be very short. The day following the verdict, baseball commissioner Kenesaw Mountain Landis issued his famous edict banning all eight players from ever playing professional baseball again. There were those that thought Landis should have acted sooner and not let major league baseball take such an enormous black eye over the scandal. Prominent among the Landis critics was Cincinnati sportswriter Bill Phelon, who stated that it was a gross mistake for Judge Landis to ever let the Black Sox affair go to court. Phelon felt that Landis should have followed the precedent set in 1877 by National League president William A. Hulbert when he banned for life from baseball four members of the Louisville Grays for throwing games.

It did seem that the trial had left more questions open about the alleged conspiracy than it had answered. The result was there was no guarantee that baseball was any more honest than it had been before the trial. It is even possible that the full story of the 1919 World Series has never been told. In an article published in the *Sporting News* on October 17, 1935, Hugh Fullerton wrote in regard to the 1919 World Series, "the full story never has been told and never will be, because Johnson, Comiskey, Herrmann and Alf Austrain, the only ones who knew it, are dead."[6]

Following the trial, most of the other players in the major leagues held no contempt towards the acquitted White Sox players. When a *Sporting News* reporter questioned several players, he was told, "Aw well; that isn't any worse than the magnates have done, only the magnates are so strong you can't punish them."[7] In Cincinnati, most fans were more interested in an exhibition game between the Reds and New York Yankees featuring Babe Ruth than the trial. The day before the verdict was reached, in Cincinnati, 16,265 fans paid their way into Redland Field on a Monday to see Ruth hit two scripted home runs in the exhibition game. It was pointed out to Garry Herrmann that if he could get Ruth and the Yankees booked again, they'd draw 30,000. Pat Moran, manager of the 1919 Cincinnati Reds, and first baseman Jake Daubert still held the belief that while the acquitted White Sox players had taken money from the gamblers, they still played the series on the square. Former Reds pitcher Dutch Ruether supported that belief as well. Ruether said he only saw one play in the series that was questionable, that coming when Cicotte slapped a ball away from him instead of fielding it properly.

The Black Sox scandal soon became old news. A post-war economic boom brought widespread prosperity to America in the early years of the 1920s. Major league baseball was never more popular with the home run-hitting feats of Babe Ruth capturing the imagination of the nation. Upon becoming the commissioner, judge Kenesaw Mountain Landis wasted no time in showing everyone who was in charge of the national game. On the federal bench, Landis had developed a reputation for his enjoyment of pushing people around, and his authoritarian style followed him into the commissioner's office.

In 1921, Landis blacklisted former Cincinnati Reds pitcher Ray Fisher for requesting his release from the club after Garry Herrmann wanted to make a $1,000 cut in his salary. Fisher had pitched in the major leagues from 1910–1917 with the Yankees, then served in World War I before being picked up in 1920 on waivers by the Reds. After pitching for the Reds in 1920, Fisher never pitched professional ball again. He took the job as varsity baseball coach and freshman football coach at the University of Michigan. In fact, one of Fisher's freshman football players was Gerald R. Ford, 38th president of the United States. Landis also added Benny Kauff to the ineligible list following the former Giants outfielder's acquittal on charges of auto theft.

Prior to the 1921 season, Cincinnati Reds third baseman Heinie Groh became aware of the fact that John McGraw had attempted to acquire him. Tired of playing in Cincinnati, Groh attempted to exploit the situation by demanding a raise from Garry Herrmann and becoming a holdout. When Groh was still a holdout beyond opening day, Judge Landis suspended him indefinitely. In June, Groh came to terms with Herrmann with the stipulation added to his contract that he be traded to the New York Giants. Although Judge Landis lifted the suspension on Groh, he ordered that in the 1921 season, he could play only for the Reds. Landis continued exercising his authority following the 1921 World Series when he suspended Babe Ruth and Bob Meusel of the New York Yankees for barnstorming. Ruth and Meusel were suspended from playing until May 1922. The owners knew what they were getting in Landis and stood behind his decisions.

Herrmann's Last Stand

When the New York Giants were on the road, John McGraw's favorite stop was Cincinnati. On nights following the games, he enjoyed going to the Peruvian Club and Curly's Place on Delhi Turnpike. However, McGraw had been a friend of Garry Herrmann for a long time and his favorite post-game haunt was the Laughery Club on the Ohio River. Often following games at Redland Field, McGraw would gather up some of the New York newspapermen traveling with the Giants, such as Frank Graham, Ford Frick, Sam Crane, Murray Robinson and others, then headed out to the Laughery. When they arrived, Herrmann would be waiting for them and already have the charcoal grill burning and a corps of waiters serving broiled sausages, limburger cheese and rye bread. As the night progressed, there would be much singing, home brew swilling and baseball talk. So, it was a certainty that eventually McGraw would get around to discussing a deal with Herrmann for Heinie Groh. On December 6, 1921, Judge Landis approved a deal for Herrmann to send Groh to the New York Giants in exchange for two players and $150,000 cash.

In the 1922 season, the New York Giants got off to a fast start, wound up with a .295 team batting average and won the National League pennant. However, the Giants didn't go unchallenged in the 1922 campaign. Garry Herrmann had assembled a strong pitching staff that featured starters Eppa Rixey, Dolf Luque, Pete Donohue and Johnny Couch and provided the firepower to allow the Reds to make a run at the Giants, finishing second by seven games. The World Series in 1922 was once again a subway series as the New York Giants defeated the New York Yankees four games to none. It was actually a five-game series as the second game ended in a 3–3 tie when umpire George Hildebrand called the game at the end of the 10th inning on account of darkness. Judge Landis was so outraged by the decision to call the game that he ordered all the funds donated to charity. In the series, Heinie Groh hit .474 and Frankie Frisch .471, while the Giants' pitchers held Babe Ruth to a paltry .118 batting average.

During the 1922 World Series at the Polo Grounds, Garry Herrmann was virtually ignored by the press and he walked freely and unpretentious to his box. According to one reporter, not one of the five hundred members of the press present who used to follow his every move found it important enough to interrupt their work long enough to say hello to Garry. As chairman of the National Commission, Herrmann had been showered with affection and given regal-like attention by the press. But now reduced to the role of Reds magnate, Herrmann's presence at a World Series was not considered newsworthy.

Following 1919, the Cincinnati Reds never won another National League pennant under

Garry Herrmann's tenure. But in 1923, the Reds would make things very interesting. Herrmann was aware of how having depth in starting pitchers had helped the Reds win the 1919 National League pennant, and despite the controversy, the 1919 World Series, too. For the coming 1923 season, Herrmann wanted to add a fifth starter to his staff. On July 30, 1922, he had reacquired pitcher Rube Benton from the New York Giants for pitcher Cliff Markel and cash. This was the same Rube Benton — pitcher, gambler and whistle-blower — whose testimony in front of a Cook County grand jury in September 1920 had opened up a Pandora's box in the alleged fix of the 1919 World Series. Benton also had a reputation for drinking copious amounts of beer, and it had been exposed that he bet $20 on a game in 1919. Being subjected to an unofficial blacklist by the National League moguls, Benton had been pitching for St. Paul of the American Association in 1922. However, in 12 years in the major leagues, including a previous stint with the Reds from 1910 to 1915, Benton had won 126 games, including 22 shutouts. Now for the 1923 season, Garry Herrmann wanted to sign the hard-throwing southpaw to a major league contract, and National League president John Heydler was livid.

John Heydler announced that he could not approve the signing of Rube Benton unless all of the National League club owners approved it. Although retired and farming cantaloupes in Maryland, Buck Herzog had not forgotten the fact that he, along with Hal Chase and Heinie Zimmerman, had been implicated in a game-fixing scandal by Benton in his 1920 grand jury testimony. Herzog had also made counter charges against Benton, accusing him of getting a tip on the fix of the 1919 World Series from "Sleepy Bill" Burns and then profiting from bets on the fixed games. Although Herzog had later been cleared of any charges by Benton, he was determined to file a suit if Benton was permitted to pitch again in the National League.

In February 1923, the National League meeting in New York was about to take place and Garry Herrmann knew that he would have to fight for Benton. Herrmann knew he had supporters among the moguls; he and Barney Dreyfuss were once again on the best of terms and he knew that he could count on support from John McGraw and the Giants. In addition, Herrmann was somewhat confident that he had the Braves' moguls in his corner, too. So Herrmann and Lou Widrig let it be known that they intended to sign Benton. Addressing the circumstances of Rube Benton, *Cincinnati Times-Star* sports reporter W. A. Phelon argued, "If players can be barred from the National League simply because some one club in the league objects to such players, a dangerous precedent will be established, and pennant races can be wrecked through spite, fear or petty envy."[1]

Arriving in New York was the Garry Herrmann of old. He checked into his suite at the Waldorf-Astoria, and while he would not talk about the pending Benton matter, he held an open house for the moguls and press, serving dill pickles, liverwurst, Kentucky hams and frankfurters, all imported from Cincinnati. On Tuesday, February 13, 1923, behind closed doors at the Waldorf-Astoria Hotel, the moguls took up the Rube Benton matter. It was apparent immediately to the assembled moguls that the 64-year-old Garry Herrmann, addressing the Benton matter, was not some cartoon-like characterization of himself, or "Ban's man, or "Cox's man." This was the Garry Herrmann of the 1890s — Cincinnati City Hall demeanor, tough, articulate and determined to have his way.

Herrmann presented a great argument in the defense of Benton's right to sign a major league contract. In a somewhat belligerent mood, Herrmann blasted his colleagues, pointing out the absurdity of allowing Benton to pitch in the American Association while being barred from the National League. Herrmann argued that it undermined the legitimacy of the minor leagues and prevented Benton from advancing himself. The moguls argued the pros and cons of Rube Benton for an hour and a half. In the end, by a majority vote, the moguls supported

John Heydler's ban of Benton from the league. But then in a unanimous vote, it was decided that the whole affair should be put in the hands of Commissioner Landis.

Somehow John Heydler and the National League moguls, attempting to bar Rube Benton from the league, were confident that Commissioner Landis would issue a lifetime ban from baseball for the pitcher. But when the decision of Landis was announced, they were thunderstruck! Landis ruled that Benton should be permitted to sign with the Reds. In rendering his decision, Landis came down hard on Heydler and the others who sought to bring charges against Benton more than two years after they had occurred. Following his grand jury testimony, Benton had pitched for the New York Giants in 1920 and 1921, while the moguls looked the other way. Also, Landis upheld the contention of Garry Herrmann that the moguls were attempting to interfere with the pitcher's livelihood. In short, if Rube Benton could pitch in St. Paul, then he should be permitted to pitch in Cincinnati, too. At first John Heydler, who did not like losing a decision to Garry Herrmann, resisted the decision of Landis in the matter. Heydler even wired Herrmann that he would fight the decision based on a long-standing precedent that existed in the league of deciding who was and who was not fit to play. However, after Heydler had a private meeting on the Benton decision with Landis in Chicago, he quietly acquiesced and announced that Benton would be permitted to play for Cincinnati in the 1923 season.

The 1923 National League season offered a thrilling three-way pennant race between the New York Giants, Cincinnati Reds and Pittsburgh Pirates. On August 2, behind the pitching of Pete Donohue, the second-place Reds shut out the Philadelphia Phillies, 2–0. That same day, President Warren G. Harding died at the Palace Hotel in San Francisco. Harding had been ill for a few weeks and the night as he succumbed, he was sitting up in bed as his wife, Florence (a.k.a. "the Duchess"), read to him from the *Saturday Evening Post*. But Harding's thoughts were with the pennant race. He asked Florence, "How did the Reds come out?"[2] A few hours later the President was dead, and the following day Calvin Coolidge was sworn in as the 30th president of the United States.

Although Harding enjoyed a booming post-war economy, appointed former president William Howard Taft as Chief Justice of the U.S. Supreme Court and added 10,000 miles of paved roads to America's highway system, his presidency would be historically riddled with scandals. The most notable was Teapot Dome that involved former Federal League magnate Harry Sin-

Warren Gamaliel Harding, 29th president of the United States, 1921–1923. Author's collection.

clair, who had now become filthy rich in the oil business. In 1909 and 1910, President Taft had begun to acquire tracts of land that were public domain and believed to have contained oil. Subsequently, Taft, seeking to keep the tracts from private oil prospectors, turned them over to the navy for future use. However, there was a hitch in the deal. If any private drilling took place on the lands, the money went directly to the treasury, not the navy. So the navy was against any private drilling. Albert Fall, Harding's Secretary of the Interior, devised a scheme to get the navy's support for drilling by arranging for private operators to pay royalties in certificates rather than in money. Using royalties allowed the private driller's payments to bypass the Treasury and go to the navy, who could then use them when they wanted. So the navy supported Fall on the arrangement. Then Secretary Fall did a little finagling with the Department of Interior to bypass public bidding and cut-in his friend, Edward Doney, a California attorney, in on the deal, allowing him to drill in Elk Hills, California. Fall also arranged a similar deal for Harry Sinclair near Casper, Wyoming, on a sandstone formation known as Teapot Dome. The government properties that Doney and Sinclair had been granted drilling rights on were estimated to be worth $100 million each. President Harding defended the actions of Secretary Fall, stating that he had given his approval.

Following Harding's death, a Senate hearing on the matter took place in October 1923 and Fall was forced to resign. Nonetheless, Fall left public office a wealthy man. In October 1927, Harry Sinclair was tried for conspiracy to defraud the United States Government. But the trial ended prematurely in a mistrial when it was revealed that Sinclair had hired a detective agency to follow the jury. Consequently, Sinclair was tried for criminal contempt of court and sentenced to six months in prison. Harry Sinclair would continue to run his oil company and died in Pasadena, California on November 10, 1956.

On August 3, as the Harding funeral arrangements were being made, the Giants arrived in Cincinnati for a five-game series. The New York Giants were in first place, leading the Cincinnati Reds by two games. However, Commissioner Landis announced that all major league games would be called off in honor of President Harding. Regardless, before Landis had issued his instructions, Garry Herrmann had contacted John McGraw and it was agreed that the first game of the series would be delayed out of respect to Harding. When play resumed, the Reds lost five straight games to the Giants and fell behind the Pirates into third place. In the fifth game of the series, Reds pitcher Dolf Luque left the mound, charged the Giants' dugout and attacked Casey Stengel, whom had allegedly been hurling racial epithets at Luque, a Cuban national. John McGraw was later to state that the insults to Luque came from reserve outfielder Bill Cunningham, not Stengel. Nonetheless, for his actions Luque was immediately suspended by National League president John Heydler.

Struggling to regain momentum, the Reds finished up their homestand playing Boston and a quick exhibition game against Babe Ruth and the Yankees. Then the Reds staggered East to play a 16-game road trip, beginning with a do-or-die five-game series with the Giants in New York. It was announced that Dolf Luque would be reinstated by John Heydler in time for the Giants series to the delight of the large Latin community in New York. On August 16, Luque got his revenge, beating the Giants, 6–3, at the Polo Grounds in the first game of a doubleheader. In the second game, Eppa Rixey beat the Giants.

Then on August 18, an article appeared in the Chicago racing sports weekly *Collyer's Eye* which alleged that Reds second baseman Sam Bohne and left fielder Pat Duncan were offered $15,000 each to throw games in the recent Giants series played in Cincinnati where the Reds lost five straight games. Immediately, John Heydler interviewed the two players in New York with members of the Cincinnati press present. Both Bohne and Duncan swore under oath that they had not been approached by any gamblers. Furthermore in the Giants series, Duncan had hit .350 and made no errors, while Bohne hit .286 and made two errors. The only questionable play in the series had been a mix-up on a fly ball that involved left fielder Duncan and shortstop Ike Cavaney. Heydler believed Bohne and Duncan, and he suggested they file a suit against *Collyer's Eye*, and furthermore, Garry Herrmann should take action against the paper, too. When the *Collyer's Eye* article hit the newsstands, Herrmann was at the Laughery Club. He immediately sent a telegram to Commissioner Landis, who replied within an hour, impugning the integrity of the racing publication and stating that at the moment Herrmann should wait and see if further articles were published.

Burt Collyer, publisher of *Collyer's Eye*, was recuperating from an illness in Toronto, Ontario. He declared that his paper did not accuse the Reds' players of throwing games and sent a letter to Commissioner Landis, urging him to begin an investigation into existing gambling cliques in baseball. Collyer pointed out that it was John Heydler who called the reports by his paper false, months before others picked up the story that the 1919 World Series had been fixed. Collyer went on to say that if Heydler didn't know about the existence of gambling cliques in baseball, he ought to resign.

On Friday, August 31, 1923, Pat Duncan and Sam Bohne met with Garry Herrmann and the Cincinnati Reds' board of directors—Louis C. Widrig, Walter J. Friedlander, James P. Orr and C. J. McDiarmid. The directors decided that Herrmann should depart that night to file suit in U.S. Court in Chicago against publisher Burt Collyer on behalf of the players. However, it didn't take long for the whole affair to reach a settlement as Collyer was unable to get any members of the gambling community to substantiate his paper's allegations in court. In the end, an out-of-court settlement was reached, with Collyer to pay $100 and court costs. Commissioner Landis put a positive spin on the matter, stating that both Bohne and Duncan had been vindicated before the American public.

Although the Reds set a home attendance record of 575,063 in the 1923 season as Dolf Luque won 27 games, Eppa Rixey 20, Pete Donohue 21 and Rube Benton 14, they were never able to catch the Giants. New York won their third consecutive National League pennant by 4½ games over second-place Cincinnati, and for the third year in a row the Giants played a subway World Series against the Yankees. The following spring, manager Pat Moran died on March 7 at the Reds' spring training camp in Orlando and was replaced by Jack Hendricks. However, prior to his death, Moran and Garry Herrmann would bring another controversial pitcher to the Reds' staff by signing Carl Mays. While Mays would win 20 games for the Reds in 1924 and the club would finish in 4th place, it was he who had played a part in Herrmann's losing control of the National Commission.

By 1923, the remnants of the Cox Republican machine in Cincinnati were referred to as the Hynicka machine. But this machine was about to putter out. The City of Cincinnati was in dire financial condition. Street lights were being turned out at night, there were plans to close a tuberculosis hospital, and funds for the construction of the rapid transit system had run out. Rud Hynicka was running the Republican Party by telephone from New York, and his answer to the financial woes of the city was to put a tax increase on the ballot. One of the long-time advocates of changing the form of government in the city was 45-year-old Cincinnati native and Harvard-educated lawyer Murray Seasongood. Although Seasongood was a former Republican executive committeeman, on October 9, 1923, he delivered a dynamic speech at the meeting of the Cincinnati Association against the tax increase, pointing out among other things that Cincinnati had the fourth-largest per capita expenditure of any city in the United States. In Cincinnati political history, Seasongood's speech became known as the "Shot Heard Round the Wards." Seasongood's speech is given credit as a rallying point for the reformers to take action in Cincinnati city government. Seasongood pounded away

Carl Mays signs with the Reds. From the left: Pat Moran, August Herrmann, Mays, Lou Widrig, January 8, 1924. Cincinnati Museum Center–Cincinnati Historical Society Library.

at the city's woes as being the result of the bossism it had suffered from the days of George B. Cox until the present under his lieutenant, Rud Hynicka. Reform for better or worse, depending on how one conceptualized it, immediately took hold in Cincinnati and on June 6, 1924, the City of Cincinnati formed the Charter Committee to draft a new city charter based on modern management principles. The charter proposed an arguable shift of power away from popularly elected politicians to an elitist professional who is trained in municipal bureaucracy to be known as the city manager.

On November 4, 1924, at the general election Cincinnati voters approved a change to the city manager form of municipal government by a 2–1 majority, 92,510 for, 41,015 against. Henry Bentley, chairman of the City Charter Committee, proclaimed, "A new day has dawned in Cincinnati. The era of machine politics is dead."[3] Indeed it was and former reform-minded mayor Henry Hunt, who had advocated a new charter more than a decade earlier, had been vindicated. August Garry Herrmann now had to suffer a second indignation to his life's work. Just as his diligence as chairman of the National Commission had been undermined when the governing body had been dissolved and replaced with the one-man commissioner, now his work in municipal government was being scrapped out by the voters in the guise of the need for a city manager to bring professional management to civic operational affairs.

The old guard in Cincinnati city government had made their last stand. On February 5, 1925, one of its brightest stars, Julius Fleischmann, died at the age of 54 and was buried at Spring Grove Cemetery. A few years before his death, Fleischmann and his brother, Max, had sold their interest in the Reds and also their distillery and inventory, now under control by the government during prohibition to the "King of the Bootleggers," George Remus.

Later that year in the November general election, Murray Seasongood's Charterites would take control of Cincinnati City Council. With 39 candidates on the ballot running for nine council seats, the Charterites would win six, and the Hynicka Republicans would hold on to three. To ensure that the ward system, which fueled the machine, would be broken up, the Charterites introduced an irregular form of vote counting into the new city charter called "proportional representation" or "PR." This bifurcated system of vote counting allowed for what was known as surplus votes to be distributed. In PR voters list their choice for council seats by rank: first, second, third and so on. The candidate receiving the most first-place votes is declared elected. Then the same happens with the second-place candidate and on down the line. The candidate receiving the lowest number of first-choice votes is declared out of the running, and that candidate's choices on all of his ballots are transferred to those candidates of the same party. This confusing and questionable system of vote counting obliterated the machine, and it continued to exist in Cincinnati municipal elections until the late 1950s. Murray Seasongood received over 15,000 first-place votes in the election, but came in second behind fellow Charterite candidate Edward T. Dixon. Under the new city charter, the mayor was elected by the City Council, and on December 29, 1925, Murray Seasongood was chosen by the other elected councilman. He would begin his official duties on January 1, 1926. To fill the position of city manager, the council hired Colonel Clarence Sherrill, who had been superintendent of parks and public buildings in Washington, D. C.

In the 1925 season, the Reds finished 3rd. Meanwhile, Garry Herrmann was becoming a visionary. Attendance had been solid at Redland Field since 1919 and he believed that the Cincinnati club needed to position itself for growth. Also, although professional football was still somewhat of a barnstorming sport, Herrmann was impressed with the growth and popularity of the new National Football League. Recently, the Chicago Bears, featuring Harold "Red" Grange, had played a cross-country 18-game exhibition tour and crowds of 70,000 had attended the games in both Los Angeles and New York. Herrmann saw opportunity for professional football in Cincinnati, too. On December 2, 1925, at a luncheon meeting at the Sinton Hotel with 306 leading citizens of Cincinnati in attendance, Garry Herrmann announced plans to build a new 50,000-seat multi-purpose stadium for baseball and other events.

Herrmann was aware of the fact that if construction was completed on the politically and financially beleaguered Belt Rapid Transit System, it would allow for the transport of fans to all of the ballpark sites he was proposing in less than 20 minutes. Three sites were under review. The first would involve a land swap with the City of Cincinnati Park Commission for the property currently occupied by Redland Field at Findlay Street and Western Avenue in exchange for the property currently being occupied by the city workhouse on Colerain Avenue in Camp Washington. The Cincinnati Workhouse was a fortress-like Civil War-era prison that by 1925 was grossly inadequate and archaic. Prisoners serving municipal sentences in the prison for violations such as drunkenness and prostitution still defecated in buckets in their cells. The second choice for a land swap would be 67 acres situated in the rear of Paddock Road on the city's north side. The third site was 100 acres behind the workhouse. By trading for the space with the Park Commission, the ballclub was willing to improve the former Redland Field tract for a park. However, if the land was sold by the Park Commission to the ballclub, it would involve a formal process of a sealed bid and the funds for the purchase would go into the city's general fund rather than into a park improvement project. But the Park Commission was against the Camp Washington site, having previously promised residents of the community park land. Herrmann explained that although the new stadium project would cost in excess of one million dollars, the ballclub would foot the entire bill and no financial aid would be necessary from the city. It seemed like a win-win situation for the city and for the Reds.

But there was a huge problem. There was a new political power structure in Cincinnati city hall with Murray Seasongood and the Charterites and one that wanted all vestiges of the former Cox machine historically buried. To the Charterites, Garry Herrmann was a living, walking, breathing reminder of the Cox era that they detested and loathed. Therefore, no matter what grand plans Herrmann might have to improve the quality of life in the city, those now in power were going to find a way to nullify those plans. Whether or not dissension was orchestrated by the Charterites is speculation; nonetheless, within days of Herrmann announcing his plans for the preferred site to build his new stadium near the workhouse, various groups and individuals began to complain. On December 10, 1925, both the Camp Washington M.E. Church and Sacred Heart Church sent communications to the Board of Park Commissioners protesting the sale of the workhouse land to Herrmann and the Reds. That was followed by a protest from the Young People Society of Camp Washington Evangelical Church and from the Valley Playground Mother's Club.

The Park Board decided to send the matter on the workhouse land swap with Herrmann and the Reds to the Cincinnati Chamber of Commerce for study. Then on February 18, 1926, the Cincinnati Board of Park Commissioners held a hearing on Herrmann's land swap proposal and several citizens protested against selling the workhouse property to the Cincinnati Baseball Club, including the Camp Washington Tennis Club. However, Herrmann and the Reds had support, too. A petition signed by 88 residents of Estes Avenue and Sassafras Street was received by the Park Board, recommending that a land deal be worked out with the Reds that was advantageous to the city. On February 25, the chairman of the Park Board, Levi Ault, sent a request to Herrmann and other officers of the Reds to meet with the commissioners on March 1, 1926, at their office at 2005 Gilbert Avenue.

At the time Garry Herrmann was with the ballclub at spring training in Orlando, Florida, staying at the San Juan Hotel. Despite the bureaucratic process that was taking place in regard to his plans to build a new ballpark, he had been busy with other things. Herrmann had been paying attention to the huge farm system that Branch Rickey had been building for the St. Louis Cardinals and saw it paying dividends to the franchise. So Herrmann purchased the Columbus club of the American Association from Thomas Wilson for $75,000. He intended to use the club as a feeder club for the Reds and installed Ivy Wingo as manager.

Still on March 11, 1926, Herrmann, Walter Friedlander, C. J. McDiarmid, Lou Widrig and the Reds' attorney met with the Cincinnati Board of Park Commissioners. Board president Levi L. Ault and fellow commissioners Frederick W. Hinkle and Irwin M. Krohn stated that the workhouse property had not yet been turned over to the Park Board. But in the event that it was, the commissioners wanted to retain a tract on it, extending along Colerain Avenue 300 feet in depth for park and playground purposes. Herrmann knew that with the easement rider of a 300-foot tract being retained by the commissioners, it would make the construction of the ballpark very difficult. While the Reds could swap the Redland Field property for the workhouse property, the Park Board had now upped the ante by wanting to keep the tract extending along Colerain Avenue. Herrmann and the Reds' Board of Directors knew that the Park Board, by keeping the tract along Colerain Avenue, was looking to make a big profit on the deal as well. It was apparent that the fix had been put in by the Seasongood administration to prevent the Reds from obtaining the workhouse property with a simple land swap.

The 1926 Cincinnati Reds were a very strong team led by the pitching of Pete Donohue (20–14), Carl Mays (19–12) and Eppa Rixey (14–8). Also, the team featuring National League batting champion Bubbles Hargrave (.353), the first catcher to ever win a batting title, Cuckoo Christenson (.350), Edd Roush (.323), Curt Walker (.306) and Wally Pipp (.291), led the league in hitting with hit a .290 mark. The Reds finished two games behind the pennant-winning St. Louis Cardinals, who caught them from behind. It was the first St. Louis team to win a pennant since 1888. However, the good news was that once again the Reds had made a big profit in 1926, drawing a record 672,987 fans. Garry Herrmann was now more confident than ever that he could build a 50,000-seat stadium in Cincinnati and fill it. So Herrmann attempted to make a final push with the Seasongood administration for land to build his new ballpark.

Garry Herrmann and Reds directors now knew that to get the workhouse land tract, they would have to cough up a lot of dollars. On July 22, they sent a letter to Mayor Seasongood offering to valuate the workhouse and refuge property for free. Seasongood replied that the Park Board declined their offer because the city already had a fixed value on the property, not from a real estate point of view, but as to its value to the department for park and athletic field purposes. Therefore, the city did not care for any other valuation to be made on the property. The fact of the matter was that the Park Board had already put a price tag on the land and if they were going to surrender it to Herrmann and the Reds, they wanted $500,000.

Murray Seasongood, mayor of Cincinnati, 1926–1929. Cincinnati Museum Center–Cincinnati Historical Society Library.

On September 1, Herrmann requested a meeting with Mayor Seasongood. Following the meeting, Seasongood performed a fundamental exercise at the request of Herrmann and wrote the Park Board, asking them to state their intentions in the land deal. On November 20, the Board of Park Commissioners, in a letter responding to Mayor Seasongood, wrote in part,

> From the letter of the Base Ball Company it seems to us apparent that it considers as 'fair and impartial" the valuation of $150,000 upon the residue of the Work House property, encumbered as it is with buildings which will have to be razed at a cost of not less than $50,000. This is the valuation of the Cincinnati Real Estate Board upon 7,557 acres. The portion of the House of Refuge property for which the Board was willing to consider a proposition of $500,000 comprises 20.295 acres, is practically unencumbered by buildings, and borders upon the Rapid Transit right-of-way and the new Parkway Boulevard. We are satisfied that our valuation of $500,000 is "fair and impartial." It would seem, therefore, from the statements of the Cincinnati Baseball Company that the situation has reached a deadlock, and that there is really nothing further for this Board to consider, that we have come definitely to the end of the discussion and that the whole matter, as the Base Ball Company suggests, "should be dropped, and at once.[4]

The Reds stood firm. They would not pay $500,000 for the part of the land owned by the Park Board, and the proposal and plans for the ballpark were dead. On December 19, 1926, just a little over a year since Garry Herrmann had first publicly stated his intentions to build a new ballpark on workhouse property, the Board of Park Commissioners officially closed the matter.

In 1948, a Charter Party-dominated Cincinnati City Council would adopt a new master plan for the city that included a stadium on the Riverfront. However, there still wouldn't be any construction plans for a new stadium until the late 1960s, when an American Football League expansion team, the Cincinnati Bengals, headed by Paul Brown, started play. A serious threat also was made by the Bill DeWitt group that had gained control the Reds in the mid–1960s to move the franchise to San Diego. In the end it took Republican mayor Eugene P. Ruehlmann to head the drive for a new stadium, and in June 1970, Garry Herrmann's old ballpark, Redland Field, later renamed Crosley Field, was closed when the Reds moved into the 52,000-seat Riverfront Stadium.

The Rapid Transit system under construction was about to come to an end, too. While Murray Seasongood viewed the rapid transit system as a lasting legacy to the Cox-Hynicka-Herrmann era in Cincinnati municipal government, he also opposed continuing its construction because he felt that it would require the development of satellite communities such as Norwood at the expense of the Cincinnati taxpayers. In early 1927, Seasongood hired the Beeler Corporation to study the mass transportation needs of Cincinnati. When the report was released in late 1927, it stated that it would require $10–$12 million to complete. At present, $6 million had already been spent. Also, Beeler privately told Seasongood that the rapid system being built in the city could not make a profit without a city population of one million to support it, and the only city that had was Boston, which had been aided by Cambridge, which borne part of the costs.

Seasongood had been at odds with the Rapid Transit Board. He was worried about having the Rapid Transit System negotiate a lease for the system with the Cincinnati Street Railway Company, a holdover from the Cox era. Seasongood even appointed grocery store king B. H. "Barney" Kroger to the board to keep tabs on the other members. Now Seasongood was alleging that the board had drawn their salaries out of a bond issue and that the Ohio Supreme Court had held the opinion that was illegal. However, the Common Pleas Court in Cincinnati had handed down a different decision, stating that board members were entitled to salaries as city officials. Regardless, the project was doomed when the Charterites came to power. Seasongood pointed out the new city charter stated that as of January 1, 1929, the Transit Board would cease to exist. On December 22, 1927, Seasongood remarked, "I believe we will have a better study made of this thing if we wait until the present 'bunch' is out." When Transit Board member Richard Greninger was told of Seasongood's remark, he replied, "He can check on the experts and we can check on the Mayor's checking. In that way we can all keep checking and checking forever."[5]

In the end Greninger's remarks became prophetic. Although millions of dollars had been spent constructing miles of underground tunnels, above-ground stations and right of ways, the rapid transit system construction came to a stop. It stopped for one reason and one reason only: Murray Seasongood and the Charter Party wanted it stopped. Consequently, the rapid transit project became a white elephant and today the subway portion of the system still sits crumbling beneath Central Parkway. Over the past 80 years since construction stopped on the system, the subway tubes have been used from time to time as storage areas by the Cincinnati Public Works Department and during both World War II and the Cold War as designated civil defense shelters.

On May 20, 1926, the tenth anniversary of the death of George B. Cox, Rud Hynicka retired as chairman of the Hamilton County Republican Executive and Central Committee.

Hynicka had been ill for more than a year and on February 22, 1927, he died in St. Petersburg, Florida. The rise of Hynicka from a clerk in the Davis Book Store on 4th Street to the City Hall reporter for the *Cincinnati News Journal* to head of the Republican Party in Cincinnati had been a remarkable success story. With the demise of Hynicka, it left Garry Herrmann as the sole survivor of the once powerhouse political triumvirate of Cox, Hynicka and himself that would dominate Cincinnati politics for nearly forty years. But now Herrmann's health was rapidly declining as well.

The National League moguls still needed Herrmann, and at the annual league meeting in December 1926, they elected him to the Board of Directors along with William F. Baker of Philadelphia, Sam Breadon of St. Louis and Wilbert Robinson of Brooklyn. After losing four of their first five games, the Reds finished 5th in the 1927 National League pennant race. The press was aware of the decline in Herrmann's health and covered for him. Often during the day, Herrmann would doze off and then find it hard to sleep at night. Also, his legs were bothering him badly. In September when Herrmann had to leave the team in Pittsburgh and return to Cincinnati, the press stated in their articles that Herrmann had to return to Cincinnati for several important matters. As the Reds prepared to leave Pittsburgh for New York, Herrmann was nearly at a loss for words as he addressed the players. Stammering and just about weeping, Herrmann said, "Don't come back home until you've clinched the pennant, boys."[6] Although the Reds won the season series from the Pirates 13 games to nine, Pittsburgh won its second pennant in the past three years before losing to the powerful New York Yankees in the World Series, four games to none.

Garry Herrmann attended the World Series, but there was only a minimal entourage with him. In Pittsburgh, Herrmann checked into a suite at the William Penn Hotel, then kept to himself, spending most of his time making travel arrangements for the Reds in New York. On October 10, 1927, after spending 25 years as president of the Cincinnati Reds, Garry Herrmann at the age of 68 resigned due to the decline in his health. He also resigned as a member of the board and sold his stock in the club to C. J. McDiarmid. Herrmann was diabetic and had been slowly going deaf. The board named McDiarmid to succeed Herrmann as president and James P. Orr to succeed McDiarmid as secretary. The Reds' Board of Directors realized that for many years while the franchise struggled to stay afloat financially, Herrmann had performed his duties as president for a pittance of a salary. Therefore, in recognition of Herrmann's service and loyalty, they voted him a $25,000 bonus and $10,000 annuity for the remainder of his life. With McDiarmid, a practicing attorney, now president of the Reds, the press was quick to point out that things would change dramatically in their relationship with the club. Where Herrmann had preferred the Laughery Club for socialization, McDiarmid preferred the Hyde Park Country Club.

In July 1927, Ban Johnson had been forced to resign as president of the American League. Ever since the arrival of Judge Kenesaw Mountain Landis on the major league scene, Johnson's influence in the game had been minimized. That bothered Johnson, and the confrontational relationship that resulted between he and Landis was embarrassing and unsettling to the American League owners. Even some of Johnson's closest allies, such as Frank Navin of Detroit and Connie Mack of Philadelphia, became increasingly aloof. The crowning blow to the demise of Johnson's leadership occurred in 1926 when he received letters from pitcher Dutch Leonard accusing Ty Cobb and Tris Speaker of fixing games. Johnson sent the letters to Landis, who in turn held a hearing on the matter. When the story was leaked to the press, Johnson accused Landis of publicity-seeking and went on the attack, even stating that neither Cobb nor Speaker would ever play in the American League again while he was president. When Landis exonerated both players in early 1927, and then both Cobb (Philadelphia Athletics) and Speaker (Washington Nationals) signed contracts, Johnson was mortified, and he intensified his attacks on Landis. Johnson had painted himself in a corner politically, and in July 1927, yielded to the pressure of the American League moguls and resigned. There has always been speculation that the time for Herrmann's retirement was just as much a factor of the retirement of Ban Johnson as were the health issues confronting him.

With Herrmann's retirement from baseball, Republican leaders in Cincinnati held out hope that perhaps he would become active in party affairs once more as both friends and the Republican Party leaders attempted to recruit him to run for city council. But they soon became aware of how serious Herrmann's condition was. Shortly after his retirement, Herrmann was hospitalized for several weeks. However, he rallied and by November 29 was discharged and resting at home on Hollister Street. Meanwhile, the major league moguls began to reflect on what Herrmann had truly meant to the administration of the game. When the war between the National and American leagues had been in full swing in the early 1900s, both sides were convinced that there was no room for two major leagues and were hellbent on the destruction of one another. It was Herrmann who entered the picture and became a calming influence and one that brought reason rather than anger into the process. Modern major league baseball owed a huge debt to August Garry Herrmann. In a cursory jester of appreciation, at its annual meeting in New York on December 13, 1927, the National League moguls passed a resolution making August Garry Herrmann an honorary member for life.

Garry Herrmann spent his final years in retirement in seclusion and as a fan. With Herrmann's leadership void, the Reds' franchise went into decline and attendance quickly fell off. In 1928, the Reds finished in 5th place. It would not be until 1936 that the club would finish that high in the standings again. The Reds' ownership group became nervous about their investment and local businessman Sidney Weil saw an opportunity and began a massive stock-buying campaign to gain majority ownership of the team. The Cincinnati newspapers began to refer to Weil as "Mr. Money Bags." By the spring of 1929, Weil had become titular owner of the ballclub, which was now in a free-fall in the standings, finishing 7th, and in attendance, drawing only 295,040. Then the Great Depression descended upon America and the very existence of major league baseball was threatened. Sidney Weil would spend over a million dollars trying to rebuild the Reds before going bankrupt and selling the club to local industrialist Powell Crosley, Jr.

By 1930, Garry Herrmann's diabetes was becoming very serious. Dr. J. Stewart Hagen operated on him and removed part of his foot in an attempt to stop the spread of arterial sclerosis. On election day in November 1930, Herrmann felt well enough that his son-in-law took him to the polls to vote. However, that night he suffered a stroke. While Herrmann once again rallied, he never fully recovered. As he convalesced, the health of his old friend Ban Johnson went into serious decline. In October 1930, Johnson was hospitalized in St. Louis with complications associated with diabetes. Following his discharge from the hospital in January 1931, Johnson went for a brief respite to Hot Springs, Arkansas. However, in February it was necessary for Johnson to have surgery and a toe and bone in his foot were removed. While Johnson's doctors insisted on amputating his leg to stop the spread of infection, he refused. Consequently, the infection spread and at 8:10 A.M. on March 28, 1931, Ban Johnson died at the age of 67. Charles Comiskey and Ban Johnson had never fully reconciled their differences and, consequently, Comiskey did not attend Johnson's funeral. However, in a ceremonial gesture, Comiskey gave approval for his son, Louis, to attend.

The day before Ban Johnson died, Ernest S. Barnard, the man that had succeeded him as president of the American League, passed away. Only a few weeks later, the end would come for Garry Herrmann, too. At the breakfast hour on Saturday, April 25, 1931, at his home at 47 Hollister Street in the neighborhood of Mt. Auburn in Cincinnati, Herrmann was suffering no pain, although the arterial sclerosis had spread terribly in his leg. There with him at his bedside was his daughter, Lena, and her husband, Karl S. Finke. Suddenly Herrmann fell into a coma. Then shortly before 9:00 A.M., he died. August Garry Herrmann was 71 years old and only a week shy of his 72nd birthday on May 3. In one account of his death, a reporter wrote that the Rhineland had lost one of its most important sons. The following Tuesday, April 28, 1931, at 10:00 A.M., Herrmann's funeral was held at Charles E. Meyer and Son mortuary. The Reds were scheduled to play in Chicago and Sidney Weil asked John Heydler for permission to cancel the game in respect to the memory of Herrmann. The Reverend Hugo Eisenlohr, who had also officiated at the funeral of George B. Cox, conducted a private service at the funeral home. Herrmann's body was then moved to the Elks Temple at Ninth and Elm Streets where it was to lie in state from 11:00 A.M. until 1:00 P.M. Then his remains were taken for burial in the family plot at the Vine Street Cemetery.

After transferring ownership of his property to his daughter, Herrmann, who had made and spent millions in his lifetime, left an estate of $120. In 1937, Garry Herrmann's home on Hollister Street, built in 1898, was razed. Herrmann's son-in-law, Karl B. Finke, who served the Reds as club auditor for many years under Herrmann's tenure, stated that he could not find a buyer or renter for the 165' × 165' property. Finke stated that he had intended to build a 32-unit apartment building on the site. But today there is no building on the site of the Herrmann home.

While major league baseball was still mourning the deaths of Ernest Barnard, Ban Johnson and Garry Herrmann, on October 26, 1931, another icon of the game was to meet his demise. Charles A. Comiskey had also been ailing for months and died at Eagle River, Wisconsin. Comiskey was 72 years old. In January 1931, major league baseball had voted Herrmann a $500 a month pension for life, but it was too little, too late. Unlike Ban Johnson and Charles Comiskey, all traces of Garry Herrmann's contributions to major league baseball slowly and steadily faded into history, and it seems that his legacy as a sportsman, civic leader and politician were buried along with his remains.

Chapter Notes

Chapter I

1. Homer Croy, "The King of Diamonds: Garry Herrmann of Cincinnati — The Fan and Financier of Baseball," *Human Life — The Magazine About People,* Volume XI (May 1910).
2. Ibid.
3. Source noted as "Brill 12–15–27" in document from the archives of the National Baseball Hall of Fame and Museum, Cooperstown, N.Y.
4. Croy, "The King of Diamonds."
5. Zane L. Miller, *Boss Cox's Cincinnati — Urban Politics in the Progressive Era* (New York, London, Toronto: Oxford University Press, 1971).
6. Alfred Henderson, "Herrmann Was City Manager Here," *Cincinnati Times-Star* (April 25, 1931): 11.
7. Croy, "The King of Diamonds."
8. Henderson, "Herrmann Was City Manager Here," 11.
9. Alfred Segal, "Political Playboy Famed as Good Host," *Cincinnati Post* (April 25, 1931): 1.
10. Ted Sullivan, "The Baseball Career of Charles A. Comiskey," *Sporting News* (February 15, 1912): 7.
11. Lee Allen, *The American League Story* (New York: Hill & Wang, 1962).
12. Ibid.
13. Ibid.
14. *Cincinnati Commercial Gazette* (March 26, 1893): 3.
15. August Herrmann, "Address to the Young Men's Business Club of Cincinnati, Ohio at the Zoological Garden, June 24, 1895" (Cincinnati: *Commercial Gazette* Job Print, 1895): 17–19.
16. Lee Allen, *100 Years of Baseball* (New York: Bartholomew House, 1950).
17. Miller, *Boss Cox's Cincinnati.*
18. *Cincinnati Enquirer* (April 26, 1931): 20.
19. August Herrmann, "Rates of Taxation in the Larger Cities of the United States," submitted to the American Society of Municipal Improvements (October 26, 1898), archives of the Cincinnati Historical Society Library.

Chapter II

1. Allen, *The American League Story.*
2. Philip Seib, *The Player, Christy Mathewson, Baseball and the American Century* (New York, London: Four Walls Eight Windows, 2003).
3. *Cincinnati Commercial Tribune* (April 18, 1902): 8.
4. *Cincinnati Commercial Tribune* (May 19, 1902): 8.

Chapter III

1. *Cincinnati Times-Star* (July 29, 1902): 1.
2. Ibid.
3. Charles W. Murphy, *Cincinnati Times-Star* (July 29, 1902): 1.
4. J. Ed Grillo, *Cincinnati Commercial Tribune* (August 10, 1902): 1.
5. *Cincinnati Commercial Tribune* (May 20, 1902): 1.

Chapter IV

1. Dan Daniel, "Old Time Boss Wined, Dined, Scribes" (December 22, 1962).
2. Allen, *The American League Story.*
3. Croy, "The King of Diamonds."
4. "Now Say Committee Has Power to Act," *Philadelphia Inquirer* (January 5, 1903): 10.
5. "The National League Trying to Avoid the Issue," *Philadelphia Inquirer* (January 5, 1903): 10.
6. "Indications Are That Leagues Will Get Together," *Cincinnati Commercial Tribune* (January 10, 1903): 10.
7. Ibid.
8. "Peace Talk Picked Up in the Lobby," *Cincinnati Commercial Tribune* (January 10, 1903): 10.
9. J. Ed Grillo, "Committees of the Rival Leagues Sign Agreement," *Cincinnati Commercial Tribune* (January 11, 1903): 12.
10. *Sporting Life* (March 3, 1908): 1.
11. "Here Is the Peace Agreement," *Philadelphia Inquirer* (January 11, 1903): 13.
12. "Brush Talks," *Cincinnati Commercial Tribune* (January 11, 1903): 12.

Chapter V

1. *Cincinnati Enquirer* (April 7, 1903): 3.
2. Ibid.
3. From the Grand Portfolio, B.P.O.E. Convention held in Cincinnati, July 17–23, 1904, Cincinnati Historical Society Archives (366.5 qE 43).
4. *Cincinnati: The Queen City, 1788–1912, Illustrated,* Volume III (Chicago, Cincinnati: S. J. Clarke Publishing, 1912): 493–494.
5. Allen, *The American League Story.*
6. "Said by the Magnates," *Sporting News* (December 25, 1908): 2.
7. From an untitled and undated document in the

August Herrmann files in archives of the National Baseball Hall of Fame and Museum.

8. Daniel Okrent and Steve Wulf, *Baseball Anecdotes* (New York: Harper & Row, 1989).

9. Damon Runyon, "Garry Herrmann Rejoiced in Pleasure of His Guests," *Cincinnati Enquirer* (April 27, 1931).

10. "Laughery Club Orgy Ends in Blows," *Cincinnati Post* (October 9, 1905): 3.

Chapter VI

1. "Cox Glum; Keeps Mum," *Cincinnati Post* (October 23, 1905): 2.

2. "LaFollette Flays Graft," *Cincinnati Post* (October 23, 1905): 2.

3. "Crusader for Good Water for Common People's Little Ones Is 'Foolish' Says City's Executive," *Cincinnati Post* (October 16, 1905): 1.

4. Segal, "Political Playboy Famed As Good Host."

5. "Boost Values to Deceive Taxpayers," *Cincinnati Post* (October 10, 1905): 7.

6. *Cincinnati Post* (October 21, 1905): 8.

7. "Cox Doesn't Take Chance," *Cincinnati Post* (October 22, 1905): 3.

8. Ibid.

9. "AGAIN, Mr. Cox Has Retired," *Cincinnati Enquirer* (November 8, 1905): 5.

10. Ibid.

Chapter VII

1. "Not Without Friends," *Sporting Life* (August 4, 1906).

Chapter VIII

1. Franklin P. Adams, "Baseball's Sad Lexicon," *100 Years of Baseball* (New York: Bartholomew House, 1950).

2. Cincinnati Board of Trustees, "Commissioners of Water Works," Cincinnati Historical Society archives (February 16, 1907): 7.

3. Ibid.

Chapter IX

1. *Sporting Life* (March 14, 1908).

2. Ibid.

3. "New York Muddle — Should Have Been Decided At Once," *Sporting News* (October 6, 1908): 2.

4. Ibid.

5. "Giants Still in Fight," *New York Tribune* (October 5, 1908): 5.

6. Seib, *The Player: Christy Mathewson*.

7. "New York Muddle," *Sporting News*.

8. Ibid.

9. Seib, *The Player: Christy Mathewson*.

10. Allen, *100 Years of Baseball*.

Chapter X

1. *Sporting News* (November 26, 1908): 1.

2. *Sporting News* (December 17, 1908): 4.

3. "Said by the Magnates," *Sporting News* (February 4, 1909): 1.

4. "Notice to Base Ball Players," *Sporting News* (September 11, 1908): 8.

5. "Life to Herrmann — Has No Thought of Quitting Base Ball," *Sporting News* (February 11, 1909): 5.

6. "Bribery Committee Is Inactive," *Sporting News* (February 11, 1909): 1.

7. Harry C. Pulliam, *Sporting Life* (March 14, 1908).

8. "Pulliam Has Love of Press And Public," *Sporting News* (February 25, 1909): 2.

9. *New York Tribune* (March 4, 1909): 1.

10. "Late News," *Sporting News* (April 22, 1909): 1.

11. Letter from W. H. Taft to widow of Leopold Markbreit, July 28, 1909, *Cincinnati Times-Star* (July 28, 1909): 1.

12. "A Masterly Tribute," *Cincinnati Times-Star,* (July 30, 1909): 3.

13. "Heydler Likely to Be Chosen President," *Philadelphia Inquirer* (July 30, 1909): 10.

14. *Sporting News* (August 3, 1909): 1.

15. "Pulliam Worried," *Philadelphia Inquirer* (July 30, 1909): 10.

16. "Capable Leader," *Sporting News* (August 19, 1909): 1.

17. Ibid.

18. "Redvillie Is Quiet," *Sporting News* (October 20, 1909): 6.

19. *Sporting News* (November 25, 1909): 4.

20. "Herrmann Steers Clear of Muss," *Sporting News* (December 2, 1909): 1.

21. "Ward's Version of Davis Case," *Sporting News* (December 2, 1909): 1.

22. *Sporting News* (December 2, 1909): 4.

23. "Theatrical Syndicate Must Not Get a Hold," *Sporting News* (December 16, 1909): 1.

24. *Sporting News* (December 2, 1909): 4.

25. Note of December 8 from Robert W. Brown to Garry Herrmann, from the archives of the National Baseball Hall of Fame and Museum.

26. "President Fogel on the Scene," *Philadelphia Inquirer* (December 15, 1909): 10.

27. "President Johnson's Telegram," *Philadelphia Inquirer* (December 18, 1909): 1.

28. Ibid.

29. "If Ward Elected, Trouble Is Brewing," *Philadelphia Inquirer* (December 18, 1909): 10.

30. "Nothing But Square Deal," *Philadelphia Inquirer* (December 19, 1909): 9.

31. *Sporting News* (December 23, 1909): 4.

32. "Herrmann and Others Displayed Fine Broad Mindness," *Sporting News* (December 23, 1909): 1.

33. "Ward Volunteers a Statement," *Sporting News* (December 23, 1909): 1.

34. *Sporting News* (January 27, 1909): 4.

Chapter XI

1. "Emblems Limited," *Sporting News* (March 7, 1910): 7.

2. "Commission Announces Gift of Automobile," *Sporting News* (March 31, 1910): 6.

3. Geoffrey C. Ward and Ken Burns, *Baseball: An Illustrated History* (New York: Alfred A. Knopf, 1994).

4. "Cobb Is Tickled," *Sporting News* (October 20, 1910): 5.

5. *Sporting News* (October 20, 1910): 5.
6. "Herrmann-Finke Wedding," *Cincinnati Enquirer* (November 17, 1910): 14.
7. "New Move in Baseball Flury," *New York Tribune* (November 1, 1910): 8.
8. *Sporting News* (November 3, 1910): 1.
9. *Sporting News* (December 1, 1910).
10. "Murphy Adds to Complications," *Sporting News* (November 17, 1910): 6.
11. *Sporting News* (November 17, 1910): 4.
12. *Sporting News* (November 17, 1910): 6.
13. Letter to Garry Herrmann from Robert W. Brown, November 16, 1910, from archives of the National Baseball Hall of Fame and Museum, Cooperstown, N.Y.
14. Letter to Garry Herrmann from Robert W. Brown, November 22, 1910, from archives of the National Baseball Hall of Fame and Museum, Cooperstown, N.Y.

Chapter XII

1. *Sporting News* (January 5, 1911): 4.
2. "Baseball Men Appear in Slander Suit Roles," *New York World* (May 10, 1911): 10.
3. Ibid.
4. "Signature a Forgery," *New York World* (May 12, 1911): 9.
5. George B. Cox, "How Did I Make My Millions," *New York World* (May 14, 1911): 6–7.
6. Ibid.
7. "No Difference in Balls," *New York Tribune* (October 1911).
8. Letter from Robert Brown to August Herrmann, September 21, 1911, from archives of the National Baseball Hall of Fame and Museum, Cooperstown, N.Y.

Chapter XIII

1. "Navin with His Players," *Sporting News* (May 23, 1912): 2.
2. "Reds Players All for Cobb," *Sporting News* (May 23, 1912): 2.
3. "Cobb Is Held to Blame," *Sporting News* (May 30, 1912): 1.
4. Correspondence from Charles P. Taft to William Howard Taft, June 5, 1912, the William Howard Taft Papers, from archives of the Library of Congress, Washington, D.C.
5. "Now Taft Plans Bolt If T.R. Wins," *Cincinnati Post* (May 25, 1912): 1.
6. "Mike Pleads, But Taft Is Denied Vote," *Cincinnati Post* (May 25, 1912): 1.
7. Charles L. Mee, Jr., *The Ohio Gang: The World of Warren G. Harding; An Historical Entertainment* (New York: M. Evans, 1981).
8. Francis Russell, *The Shadow of Blooming Grove: Warren G. Harding in His Times* (New York and Toronto: McGraw-Hill, 1968).
9. *Sporting News* (August 22, 1912): 1.
10. Ibid.
11. "Fogel and His Charges," *Sporting News* (October 10, 1912): 4.
12. Ernest J. Lanigan, "Two Heavenly Ingrates," *Sporting News* (October 10, 1912): 4.
13. Letter to Garry Herrmann from Robert W. Brown, September 16, 1912, from archives of the National Baseball Hall of Fame and Museum, Cooperstown, N.Y.
14. Letter to Garry Herrmann from Robert W. Brown, September 23, 1912, from archives of the National Baseball Hall of Fame and Museum, Cooperstown, N.Y.
15. *New York Tribune* (October 15, 1912): 2.
16. Ibid.
17. *Cincinnati Times-Star* (October 15, 1912): 1.
18. Ibid.
19. *New York Tribune* (October 15, 1912): 1.
20. "Roosevelt's Wound More Serious Than It Seemed; Bullet Not Yet Extracted," National News Service, *New Brunswick Times* (October 15, 1912).
21. *New York Tribune* (October 15, 1912): 1.
22. National News Service, "Roosevelt's Wound More Serious."
23. Ibid.
24. Miller, *Boss Cox's Cincinnati*.
25. "President at Home to Cast His Ballot," *New York Tribune* (November 5, 1912): 1.

Chapter XIV

1. "Red Boss, for His Part, Near Killed with Kindness but Steels Heart to Refuse Generous Offer," *Sporting News* (November 14, 1912): 3.
2. "The National League Is Beginning to 'Crawl,'" *New York Tribune* (November 7, 1912): 11.
3. "Fogel Only the 'Goat,'" *New York Tribune* (November 27, 1912): 10.
4. "Horace Fogel No Longer President of the Phillies," *New York Tribune* (November 27, 1912): 10.
5. Ibid.
6. Ibid.
7. "Fogel Guilty of Defaming Baseball" *New York Tribune* (November 28, 1912): 10.
8. *New York Tribune* (November 26, 1912): 10.
9. Letter from Robert W. Brown to Garry Herrmann, December 5, 1912, from archives of the National Baseball Hall of Fame and Museum.
10. W.A. Phelon, "Joe Is Handsome, Intelligent and an Alert Athlete," *Cincinnati Times-Star* (December 13, 1912): 18.

Chapter XV

1. "Jury Chosen to Try Boss in Bank Case," *Cincinnati Post* (June 2, 1913): 1.
2. "Bars Testimony About Tax Note," *Cincinnati Post* (June 3, 1913): 2.
3. Ibid.
4. Ibid.

Chapter XVI

1. Cynthia Grey, *Cincinnati Post* (January 1, 1913): 2.
2. Unknown source archive article dated August 14, 1913, in the August Herrmann file of archives of the National Baseball Hall of Fame, Cooperstown, N.Y.
3. "What Lynch And Tener Had to Say," *Sporting News* (December 18, 1913): 3.

4. Thomas Rice, *Sporting News* (December 18, 1913): 5.

5. "President Herrmann Admits Manager Talked With Mordecai Brown," *Cincinnati Commercial Tribune* (December 12, 1913): 6.

6. "Tinker's Views," *Cincinnati Commercial Tribune* (December 13, 1913): 1.

7. "Brooklyn Dodgers Purchase Tinker For Round Figure," *Cincinnati Commercial Tribune* (December 13, 1913): 6.

8. Ibid.

9. Ibid.

10. Ibid.

11. Ibid.

12. Ibid.

13. Ibid.

14. "Brooklyn's President Confident," *Cincinnati Commercial Tribune* (December 15, 1913): 6.

15. "Two Yarns About Sale Different," *Cincinnati Commercial Tribune* (December 14, 1913): 12.

16. "'We Will Stand Pat,'" Says Brooklyn Head," *Cincinnati Commercial Tribune* (December 16, 1913); 6.

17. Ibid.

18. "Jocund Joseph Is Relenting," *Cincinnati Commercial Tribune* (December 17, 1913): 6.

19. "Brooklyn Purchase Ratified," *Cincinnati Commercial Tribune* (December 18, 1913): 6.

Chapter XVII

1. Allen, *The American League Story*.

2. Microsoft Complete Baseball, 1994 Edition, Microsoft Corporation, 1994.

3. Russell, *The Shadow of Blooming Grove*.

4. Warren W. Brown, source unknown, published April 1, 1914, from archives of the National Baseball Hall of Fame and Museum, Cooperstown, N.Y.

5. *Sporting News* (June 1, 1960), from the archives of the National Baseball Hall of Fame and Museum, Cooperstown, N.Y.

6. Frank Graham, *McGraw of the Giants: An Informal Biography* (New York: G. P. Putnam's, 1944).

7. George L. Flynn, *Great Moments in Baseball* (New York: Gallery Books, 1987).

Chapter XVIII

1. Clarence E. Eldridge, "Wreck of National Game," *Sporting News* (January 14, 1915): 3.

2. *Sporting News* (January 14, 1915): 7.

3. Microsoft Complete Baseball 1994 Edition.

4. *Sporting News* (January 28, 1915): 3.

5. J. G. Taylor Spink, *Judge Landis and Twenty-Five Years of Baseball* (New York: Thomas Y. Crowell, 1947).

6. *Sporting Life* (February 13, 1915), from archives of the National Baseball Hall of Fame and Museum, Cooperstown, N.Y.

7. "Reveals Things in Eleventh Annual Report," unknown source (March 3, 1915), from the archives of the National Baseball Hall of Fame and Museum, Cooperstown, N.Y.

8. "Cincinnati Club May Be Sold," unknown source (August 21, 1915), from the archives of the National Baseball Hall of Fame and Museum, Cooperstown, New York.

9. *Cincinnati Post* (October 22, 1915): 12.

Chapter XIX

1. "From the Unsold Reds." *Sporting News* (January 6, 1916): 6.

2. George S. Robbins, "Outlaw Anti-Trust Suit Is Dismissed by Judge Landis," *Sporting News* (February 10, 1916): 1.

3. "Never So Many Notables at a Baseball Event," *Sporting News* (February 17, 1916): 1.

4. Frank Graham, *McGraw of the Giants: An Informal Biography* (New York: G. P. Putnam's, 1944).

5. Ibid.

6. *Sporting News* (March 2, 1916): 1.

7. *Sporting News* (April 13, 1916): 2.

8. "Death Calls Geo. B. Cox As He Sleeps," *Cincinnati Post* (May 20, 1916): 1.

9. Graham, *McGraw of the Giants*.

10. Ibid.

11. *New York Tribune* (July 21, 1916): 14.

12. "Reds, with Matty Leading, Lose Game to Phillies," *New York Tribune* (July 22, 1916): 14.

13. W. O. M'Geehan, "McGraw Says His Team Quit as Robins Win," *New York Tribune* (October 4, 1916): 1.

14. "Taft and T.R. Shake Hands," *New York Tribune* (October 4, 1916): 6.

15. Sid C. Keener, *Sporting News* (December 14, 1916): 5.

Chapter XX

1. *Washington Post* (January 17, 1917): 8.

2. Ibid.

3. Ibid.

4. *Sporting News* (February 22, 1917): 1.

5. *New York Tribune* (April 7, 1917): 1.

6. Graham, *McGraw of the Giants*.

7. Spink, *Judge Landis and Twenty-Five Years of Baseball*.

8. *Sporting News* (August 29, 1918): 3.

9. "Red Sox and Cubs on Strike, While Crowd Yells, 'Play Ball,'" *Boston Globe* (September 10, 1918): 4.

10. Ibid.

11. Spink, *Judge Landis and Twenty-Five Years of Baseball*.

Chapter XXI

1. *Sporting News* (January 16, 1919): 1.

2. "Hal Chase Is Declared 'Not Guilty' By Heydler," *Cincinnati Commercial-Tribune* (February 6, 1919): 6.

3. "Redlegs Defeat Cardinals 6–2 Before a Big Crowd at Redland," *Cincinnati Commercial-Tribune* (April 24, 1919): 3.

4. Ibid.

5. John I.B. "Toney" Marsh, "How the Series Looks to Me," *Boston Herald* (September 25, 1919): 14.

6. Joe Villa, "Are Offering 8 To 5 That Sox Will Win," *Philadelphia Inquirer* (October 1, 1919): 14.

7. Hugh Fullerton, "I Recall," *Sporting News* (October 17, 1935): 5.

8. Ibid.

9. Christy Mathewson, "Pitching Is Most Important Factor," *New York Times* (October 1, 1919).

10. Allen, *The American League Story*.

11. Lawrence S. Ritter, *The Complete Armchair Book of Baseball* (New York: Galahad Books, 1997).

12. "Cicotte Bares Pitching Secrets—as Far as He Says He Has Any," *Sporting News* (October 2, 1919): 2.

13. Hugh Fullerton, *Atlanta Constitution* (October 21, 1919): 20.

14. "No Inquiry by Commission," *Sporting News* (December 25, 1919): 1.

15. "Make What You Can of Moran's Denial," *Sporting News* (January 1, 1920): 1.

Chapter XXII

1. "Herrmann Resigns," *Cincinnati Commercial-Tribune* (January 9, 1920): 9.

2. "John Heydler Tells of Sort Man National Game Needs," *Sporting News* (January 15, 1920): 1.

3. "Baseball Men Drop Fight and Get Busy," *Cincinnati Commercial-Tribune* (February 12, 1920): 9.

4. Randolph C. Downes, *The Rise Of Warren Gamaliel Harding 1865–1920* (Columbus: Ohio State University Press, 1970).

5. "Harding Scores," *Cincinnati Post* (September 2, 1920): 12.

6. "Grand Jury Testimony of Rube Benton," *Philadelphia Inquirer* (September 25, 1920).

7. "Jury Convinced Crooked Work Was Done by Players in League with Gamblers," *Philadelphia Inquirer* (September 25, 1920): 14.

8. "Harry Redmon Testified," *Sporting News* (November 4, 1920): 3.

9. "Herrmann Will Gladly Take Witness Stand," *Philadelphia Inquirer* (September 28, 1920): 14.

10. Letter from August Herrmann to Ban Johnson, September 25, 1920, on letterhead stationary of The Cincinnati BaseBall Club Company.

11. "John Heydler Puts Blame on Gleason," *Philadelphia Inquirer* (September 28, 1920): 14.

12. "Attell Says He Will 'Shoot Lid Sky High'," *Cincinnati Commercial-Tribune* (September 29, 1920): 1.

13. "Tears in Eyes, Star Confesses Crooked Play," *Cincinnati Commercial-Tribune* (September 29, 1920): 1.

14. "Cicotte Says Bribe Paid for His Farm," *Philadelphia Inquirer* (September 30, 1920): 4.

15. "I'm Here to Tell Whole Truth," *Cincinnati Commercial-Tribune* (September 29, 1920): 1.

16. "Action Taken Against Fixers Who Paid Bribe," *Cincinnati Commercial-Tribune* (September 30, 1920): 1.

17. "Three More Players and Two Gamblers to Be Indicted," *Philadelphia Inquirer* (October 2, 1920): 16.

18. "Nothing Doing at Pittsburgh on Account of Downpour—Double Bill Saturday—Players Discuss Scandal," *Cincinnati Commercial-Tribune* (October 1, 1920): 8.

19. "Baseball Probers Ordered to Dig to Bottom of Scandal," *Philadelphia Inquirer* (October 1, 1920): 18.

20. "Judge Dixon Says Essential Parts of World Series Fraud Were Carried On in Cincinnati—No Suspicion Against Reds," *Cincinnati Post* (October 8, 1920): 1.

21. "Sift Rumors of Fixing Games for 1920 Series," *Cincinnati Commercial-Tribune* (September 30, 1920): 1.

22. Tom Swope, "Garry Loses Overcoat in Deal," *Cincinnati Post* (October 12, 1920): 14.

Chapter XXIII

1. Spink, *Judge Landis and Twenty-Five Years of Baseball.*

2. Associated Press, "Jury Acquits White Sox After 2 Hrs.; Lifts Them on Shoulders," *New York Tribune* (August 3, 1921): 1.

3. Ibid.

4. Ibid.

5. *Sporting News* (August 11, 1921): 2.

6. "I Recall by Hugh Fullerton," *Sporting News* (October 17, 1935): 5.

7. Ibid.

Chapter XXIV

1. W.A. Phelon, "Red Club Will Fight to the Last Ditch for Benton," *Cincinnati Times-Star* (February 7, 1923): 20.

2. *Cincinnati Enquirer* (August 4, 1923): 9.

3. "In Triumph of City Manager Plan Cincinnatians Emphasized Desire For Change of Municipal Affairs," *Cincinnati Commercial-Tribune* (November 5, 1924): 6.

4. Letter from the Board of Park Commissioners to the Honorable Murray Seasongood, November 20, 1926, contained in the archives of the Cincinnati Park Board, Bettman Natural Resources Center, Cincinnati, Ohio.

5. "Transit Board Again Is Target of Seasongood," *Cincinnati Commercial-Tribune* (December 22, 1927): 1.

6. *Sporting News* (September 16, 1926): 1.

Bibliography

Books and Periodicals

Allen, Lee. *The American League Story*. New York: Hill & Wang, 1962.

_____. *100 Years of Baseball*. New York: Bartholomew House, 1950.

Brands, H.W. *T.R.: The Last Romantic*. New York: Basic Books, 1997.

Chadwick, Bruce, and David M. Spindel. *The Giants: Memories and Memorabilia from a Century of Baseball*. New York: Abbeville Press, 1993.

Creamer, Robert W. *Babe: The Legend Comes to Life*. New York: Fireside, 1992.

Croy, Homer. "The King of Diamonds: 'Garry' Herrmann of Cincinnati—The Fan and Financier of Baseball." *Human Life*, May 1910.

Downes, Randolph C. *The Rise of Warren Gamaliel Harding 1865–1920*. Columbus: Ohio State University Press, 1970.

Feck, Luke. *Yesterday's Cincinnati*. Miami: E.A. Seemann Publishing, 1975.

Graham, Frank. *McGraw of the Giants: An Informal Biography*. New York: G.P. Putnam's, 1944.

Herrmann, August. Address delivered before the Young Men's Business Club of Cincinnati, Ohio, at the Zoological Garden. Cincinnati: The Commercial Gazette Job Print, June 24, 1895.

Hugo, William F. "The 1876 Cincinnati Red Stockings: Charter Members of the New National League." In *Baseball in Cincinnati: From Wooden Fences to Astroturf*. Cincinnati: Cincinnati Historical Society, 1988.

Mee, Charles L., Jr. *The Ohio Gang: The World of Warren G. Harding*. New York: M. Evans, 1981.

Miller, Zane L. *Boss Cox's Cincinnati: Urban Politics in the Progressive Era*. New York: Oxford University Press, 1971.

Pringle, Henry F. *The Life and Times of William Howard Taft: A Biography*. Norwalk, Conn.: Easton Press, 1967.

Rhodes, Greg, and John Erardi. *Cincinnati's Crosley Field: The Illustrated History of a Classic Ballpark*. Cincinnati: Road West Publishing, 1995.

Riechler, Joseph L. *The Baseball Encyclopedia*, 7th edition. New York: Macmillan, 1988.

Russell, Francis. *The Shadow of Blooming Grove: Warren G. Harding in His Times*. New York: McGraw-Hill, 1968.

Seib, Philip. *The Player: Christy Mathewson, Baseball and the American Century*. New York: Four Walls Eight Windows, 2003.

Singer, Allen J. *The Cincinnati Subway: History of Rapid Transit*. Charleston, S.C.: Arcadia, 2003.

Spink, J.G. Taylor. *Judge Landis and Twenty-Five Years of Baseball*. New York: Thomas Y. Crowell, 1947.

Ward, Geoffrey C., and Ken Burns. *Baseball: An Illustrated History* (New York: Alfred A. Knopf, 1994).

Archives

Albert G. Spalding Collection, New York Public Library, New York, New York.

August "Garry" Herrmann Collection, National Baseball Hall of Fame Library, Cooperstown, New York.

Cincinnati Museum Center–Cincinnati Historical Society, Cincinnati, Ohio.

Cincinnati Park Board, Bettman Natural Resources Center, Cincinnati, Ohio.

Library of Congress, Manuscript Division, Washington, D.C.

National Baseball Hall of Fame & Museum, Cooperstown, New York.

William Howard Taft Papers, Library of Congress, Manuscript Division, Washington, D.C.

Newspapers

Atlanta Constitution
Boston Daily Globe
Cincinnati Commercial-Tribune
Cincinnati Enquirer
Cincinnati Post
Cincinnati Times-Star
Daily Home News
New Brunswick Times

New York Tribune
New York World
Philadelphia Inquirer
Sporting News
Washington Post

Reference Works

Cincinnati: The Queen City 1788–1912, Illustrated, volume III. Chicago: S.J. Clarke Publishing, 1912.

Complete Baseball: The Ultimate Multimedia Reference for Every Baseball Fan. Seattle: Microsoft Corporation, 1994.

The WPA Guide to Cincinnati. Cincinnati: The Cincinnati Historical Society, 1987.

Web Sites

Baseball Library. http://baseballlibrary.com.

Chicago Public Library. "CPL Chicago Conventions: An Unconventional Chronology." http://www.chipublib.org.

Ohio Historical Society. http:// www.ohiohistory. org.

Sinclair, Harry. http://www.spartacus.schoolnet. co.uk/USAsinclairHF.htm.

The New Nationalism. http://history.osu.edu/projects/1912.

Index